New York Review Comics

Trots and Bonnie

Shary Flenniken
is a cartoonist, writer, and editor. Her work has
appeared in a variety of books and magazines including
The American Bystander, *Graphic Classics*, and *Drunk
Stoned Brilliant Dead: The Writers and Artists Who
Made the National Lampoon Insanely Great*. After living
and working in San Francisco, Los Angeles, the Florida
Keys, and New York, she now resides where she grew up,
in the Magnolia neighborhood of Seattle, Washington.
Shary holds degrees in commercial art, computer
technology, web design, and professional technical
education and instructional design. She loves post-
apocalyptic science fiction, the artist Charles M. Russell,
and walking her dogs.

Emily Flake
is a cartoonist and illustrator. Her work has appeared
in *The New Yorker*, *The New York Times*, *Time*, and
many other publications. Her weekly comic strip,
Lulu Eightball, has appeared in numerous alternative
newsweeklies since 2002. She lives in Brooklyn.

Norman Hathaway
is a designer, editor, and curator. He is the editor and
author of several books, including *Electrical Banana:
Masters of Psychedelia* and *Dorothy and Otis: Designing
the American Dream*, and has lead creative initiatives
for the Outsider Art Fair, London's Design Museum
and Royal Academy of Arts, and artists, including Paul
McCartney. He has taught widely on the history of
design and typography. He lives in Brooklyn.

THIS IS A NEW YORK REVIEW COMIC
PUBLISHED BY THE NEW YORK REVIEW OF BOOKS

435 Hudson Street, New York, NY 10014
www.nyrb.com

Cover and interior designed by Norman Hathaway.

Library of Congress Cataloging-in-Publication Data
Names: Flenniken, Shary, author, artist. | Hathaway,
Norman, editor.
Title: Trots and Bonnie / by Shary Flenniken ; edited by
Norman Hathaway.
Other titles: Trots and Bonnie. Selections
Description: New York : New York Review Comics, 2020.
Identifiers: LCCN 2020002114 | ISBN 9781681374857
(hardcover)
Subjects: LCSH: Comic books, strips, etc.
Classification: LCC PN6728.T8 F57 2020 | DDC
741.5/973—dc23
LC record available at https://lccn.loc.gov/2020002114

ISBN 978-1-68137-485-7

Printed in South Korea
0 9 8 7 6 5 4 3 2 1

Trots and Bonnie

By Shary Flenniken

Introduction by Emily Flake
Edited by Norman Hathaway

New York Review Comics · New York

Contents

Introduction

Emily Flake

I don't know how old I was when I first read *Trots and Bonnie*, but I definitely wasn't old enough. I was a precocious reader and pretty sex-obsessed for a child, and my parents would buy *National Lampoon* every now and again and leave it where it could fall into my unsupervised little hands (parenting was a different animal entirely in 1984, kids). I couldn't have been more than seven, but the experience is as clear and vital as if it happened yesterday: here was something that looked friendly and kidlike, but it was dangerous. It was confusing, it was weird, and it was very, very hot.

By the time I came of age, I had put *National Lampoon* on my mental backburner. I wouldn't say I forgot about *Trots and Bonnie*, but I'd stored it away deep in my subconscious, where it formed a bedrock of my sensibility I wouldn't recognize until years later. When I reacquainted myself with the strip in my twenties, it was like seeing a long-lost and deeply beloved friend. I also realized I'd been ripping Shary off for years. Those blank Little Orphan Annie eyes, the cheerful willingness to be absolutely disgusting, the heady mix of raunch and innocence— all things that had percolated through my own mind and heart and spilled out into my own work, a dim echo of the masterful original.

How to explain *Trots and Bonnie* to the uninitiated? It's a bit like *Little Nemo*, if *Little Nemo* had been drawn for and by pervs. The titular characters are a girl in early adolescence, Bonnie, and her wry, horny dog, Trots. Bonnie stands as a kind of wise-fool character, observing the often hypocritical, sometimes hedonistic world around her with the candor and freshness of a child and the lust of a dirty old man (if parenting was different in the 80s, cartooning was different in the 70s: a strip featuring a young teen rubbing one out to literary porn penned by her dog might raise more lawsuits than eyebrows in today's cultural climate). Bonnie's floppy trousers and slouching posture paired with Trots's smart-cracking wise-acre role have antecedents in Bud Fisher's *Mutt and Jeff*. The drawing is lyrical and lovely—all swooping lines and flat textures, like an Erté drawn in the girls' bathroom at a particularly ill-run reformatory. Flenniken draws like an angel, but, like Caravaggio, prefers the company of sinners.

Bonnie's adventures are more quotidian than Nemo's, but no less wild. The lands between girlhood and womanhood are weirder and more unsettling than anything Winsor McCay ever dreamed up. The monsters traversing her landscape are real: neighborhood drunks, uncaring parents, and that biggest bogeyman of all, puberty. Yet she moves through the world with amiable good cheer, in danger yet never a victim. Her hair is a semi-androgynous shag; her high-waisted, baggy pants conceal the randy monster that throbs beneath. Her more worldly best friend, Pepsi, dresses in an incongruously childlike pinafore paired with fishnets, a perfect metaphor for the terrifying underage sex fiend she is. When Pepsi rhapsodizes about condoms or proclaims proudly that her perfect gentleman boyfriend has "the smallest cock in all eighth grade," it's both hilarious and deeply unnerving. Supporting character Elrod, a younger neighborhood boy, gets the worst of their impulses: shot, mutilated, and drowned like an X-rated Wile E. Coyote. Their world is brutal and lecherous and gross, yet suffused with heart and a fierce solidarity with the point of view of its main inhabitants.

Trots and Bonnie (detail)
From *National Lampoon*
1975

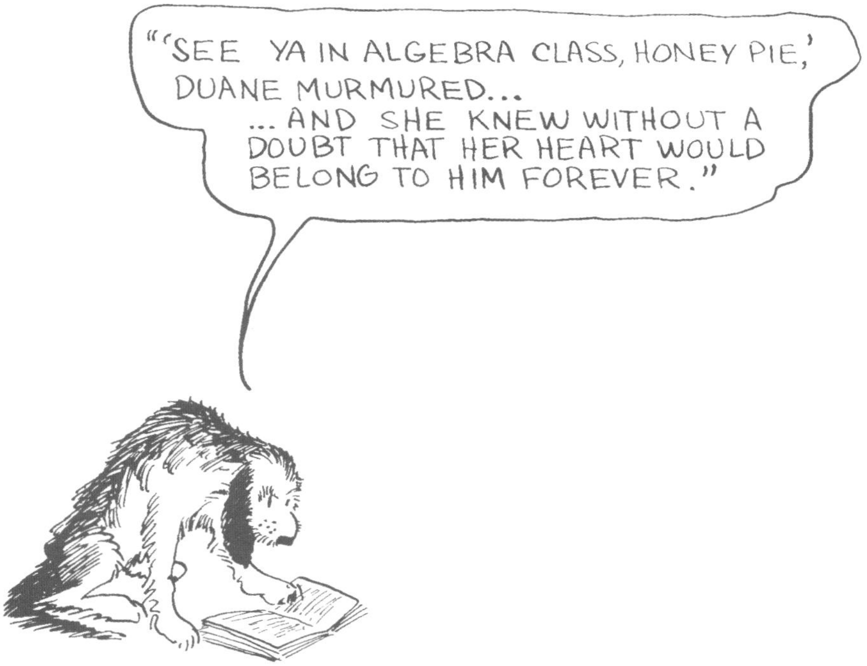
"'SEE YA IN ALGEBRA CLASS, HONEY PIE,' DUANE MURMURED...
...AND SHE KNEW WITHOUT A DOUBT THAT HER HEART WOULD BELONG TO HIM FOREVER."

What Flenniken understands and brings gleefully to the page is that adolescent girlhood is positively feral and that teenage girls are both threatened and threats themselves. J. M. Barrie tells us in *Peter Pan* that children are "gay and innocent and heartless," and that little weirdo had it right—that's the terrible power of children, the monstrous innocence that makes them capable of anything, a state of being we fatuously describe as "pure." You dump a bunch of hormones into a child's body and all of a sudden you have this awful hybrid creature: a changeling with the self-centeredness and nonexistent impulse control of a child but the body and urges of a breeding-age adult. It's a dangerous time in a young woman's life, but as with most dangers, it has a messy, chaotic, super-hot fun side as well. To speak frankly of this fun side is tricky for adults, to say the least. We remember it, if at all, as a fever dream, a sticky, humid jungle of lust and stink. Grown-ups have to blind themselves to the sexual power of eighth-graders, for reasons I sincerely hope are obvious. But the kids can see each other head-on, and they wield their sexuality with all the grace and care of a toddler toting an AK-47. Flenniken dares to write and draw from that swamp with a complete lack of adult-world moralizing or editorial restraint. Arguably, "moralizing" and "restraint" weren't really anyone's bag when she was creating these strips, but there's still an audacity in her work that I imagine felt as electrifying then as it does now.

Bonnie and Pepsi are obsessed with sex, but they're not here for the male gaze. Their desire is frank and straightforward and more than a little demented, and it's depicted with a bracing honesty that feels less like a political statement and more like Flenniken is reporting from the front lines with no filter, no safety net, and no intention of telling anything but the truth. *Trots and Bonnie* ran into the late 80s, but it was born from a 70s worldview, a decadent, anything-goes carnival where thirteen wouldn't get you twenty. The hangover from this era was vicious and the societal course-correction necessary, but the importance of hearing from girls of the era rather than from the guys who liked to ball girls of the era cannot be emphasized enough. Bonnie isn't masturbating on the toilet because she wants you to watch. She's doing it because her body belongs to her and she's horny as fuck.

As a child I was mystified and entranced by these strips. As a twenty-year-old, I was delighted anew by their bawdy, anarchic swagger and their pie-eyed charm. As a forty-two-year-old, I am so far from the lawless, deeply screwed-up Eden that *Trots and Bonnie* inhabit that it may as well be documenting life among the Stone Age clans. Part of me wants to call protective services—have I become a scold, or just a mother? Barrie tells us that those who are no longer gay and innocent and heartless can no longer fly. Being earthbound is the price we pay for our experience in this world, perhaps, and maybe to understand danger and value safety is to run the risk of identifying with the wing-clippers of this world. But looking at these strips I feel an echo of that old and savage glee, a distant memory from when I lived in those lands. Would I move back there if I could? Probably not, but we are so lucky to have in Shary Flenniken a cartographer of our most treacherous and rewarding landscapes. Would that we all had such balls.

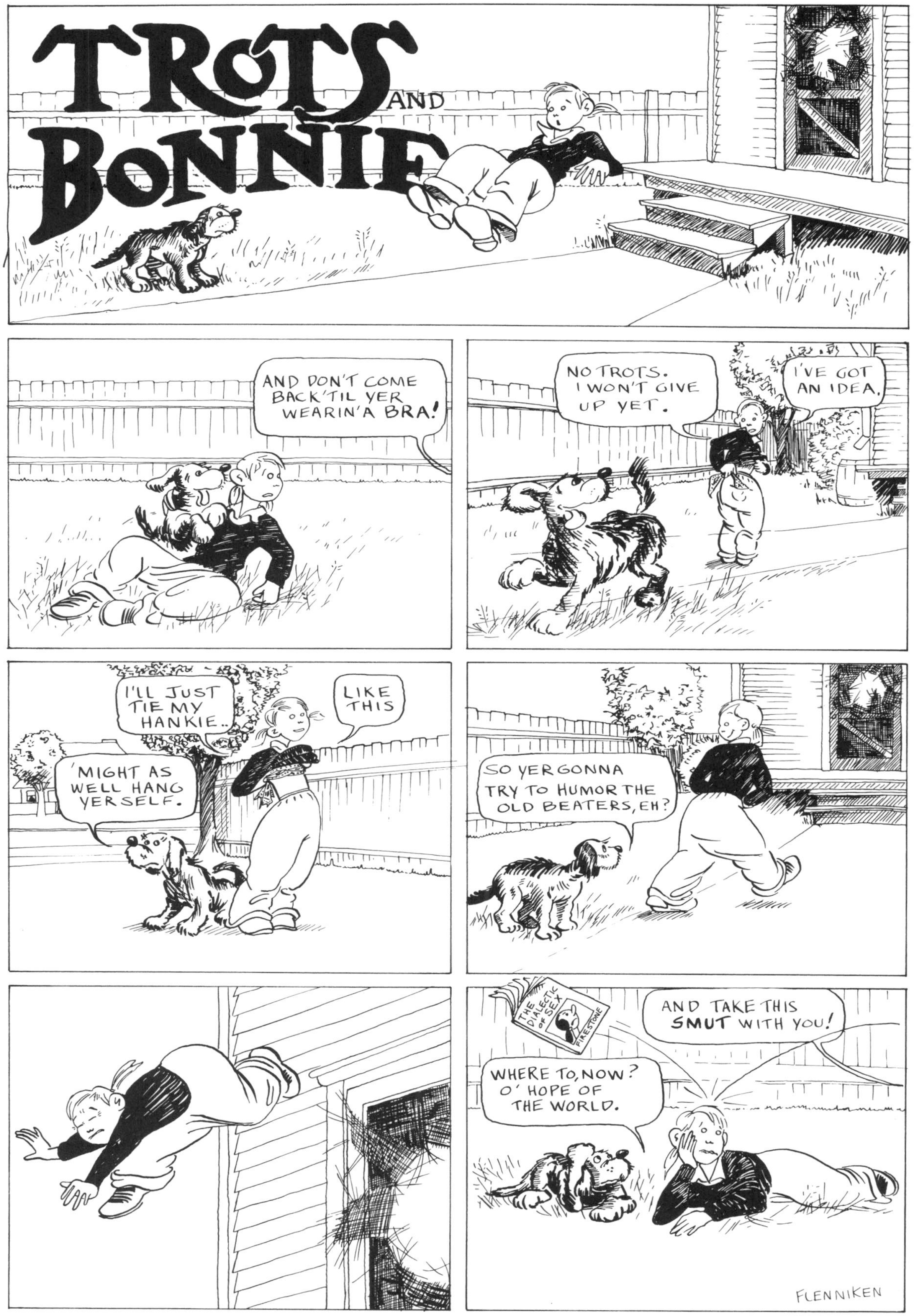
TROTS AND BONNIE
AND DON'T COME BACK 'TIL YER WEARIN' A BRA!
NO TROTS. I WON'T GIVE UP YET.
I'VE GOT AN IDEA.
I'LL JUST TIE MY HANKIE..
LIKE THIS
'MIGHT AS WELL HANG YERSELF.
SO YER GONNA TRY TO HUMOR THE OLD BEATERS, EH?
THE DIALECTIC of SEX
FIRESTONE
AND TAKE THIS SMUT WITH YOU!
WHERE TO, NOW? O' HOPE OF THE WORLD.
FLENNIKEN

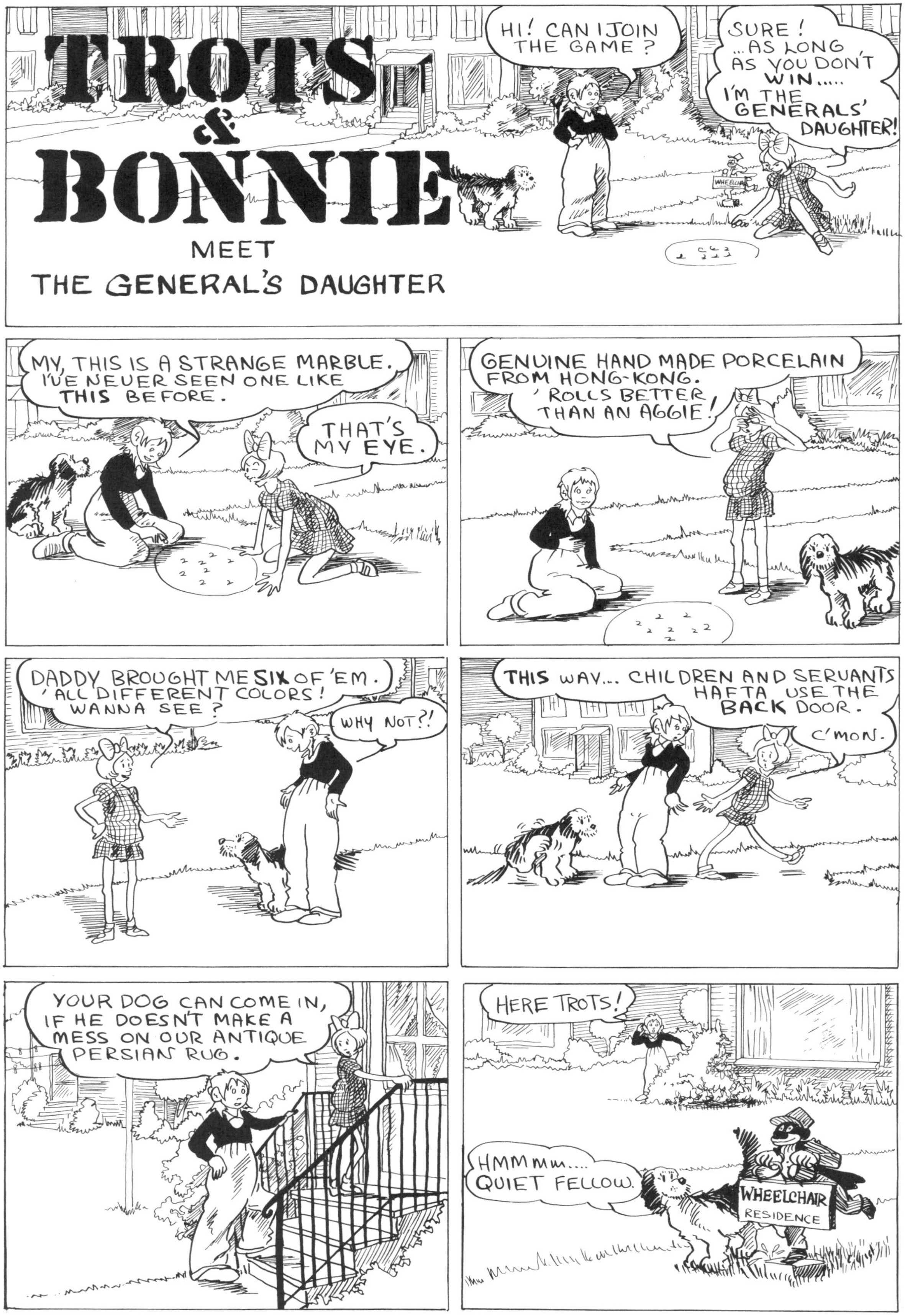
TROTS & BONNIE
MEET
THE GENERAL'S DAUGHTER
HI! CAN I JOIN THE GAME?
SURE! ...AS LONG AS YOU DON'T WIN..... I'M THE GENERALS' DAUGHTER!
WHEELCHAIR
MY, THIS IS A STRANGE MARBLE. I'VE NEVER SEEN ONE LIKE THIS BEFORE.
THAT'S MY EYE.
GENUINE HAND MADE PORCELAIN FROM HONG-KONG. 'ROLLS BETTER THAN AN AGGIE!
DADDY BROUGHT ME SIX OF 'EM. 'ALL DIFFERENT COLORS! WANNA SEE?
WHY NOT?!
THIS WAY... CHILDREN AND SERVANTS HAFTA USE THE BACK DOOR.
C'MON.
YOUR DOG CAN COME IN, IF HE DOESN'T MAKE A MESS ON OUR ANTIQUE PERSIAN RUG.
HERE TROTS!
HMMMM.... QUIET FELLOW.
WHEELCHAIR RESIDENCE

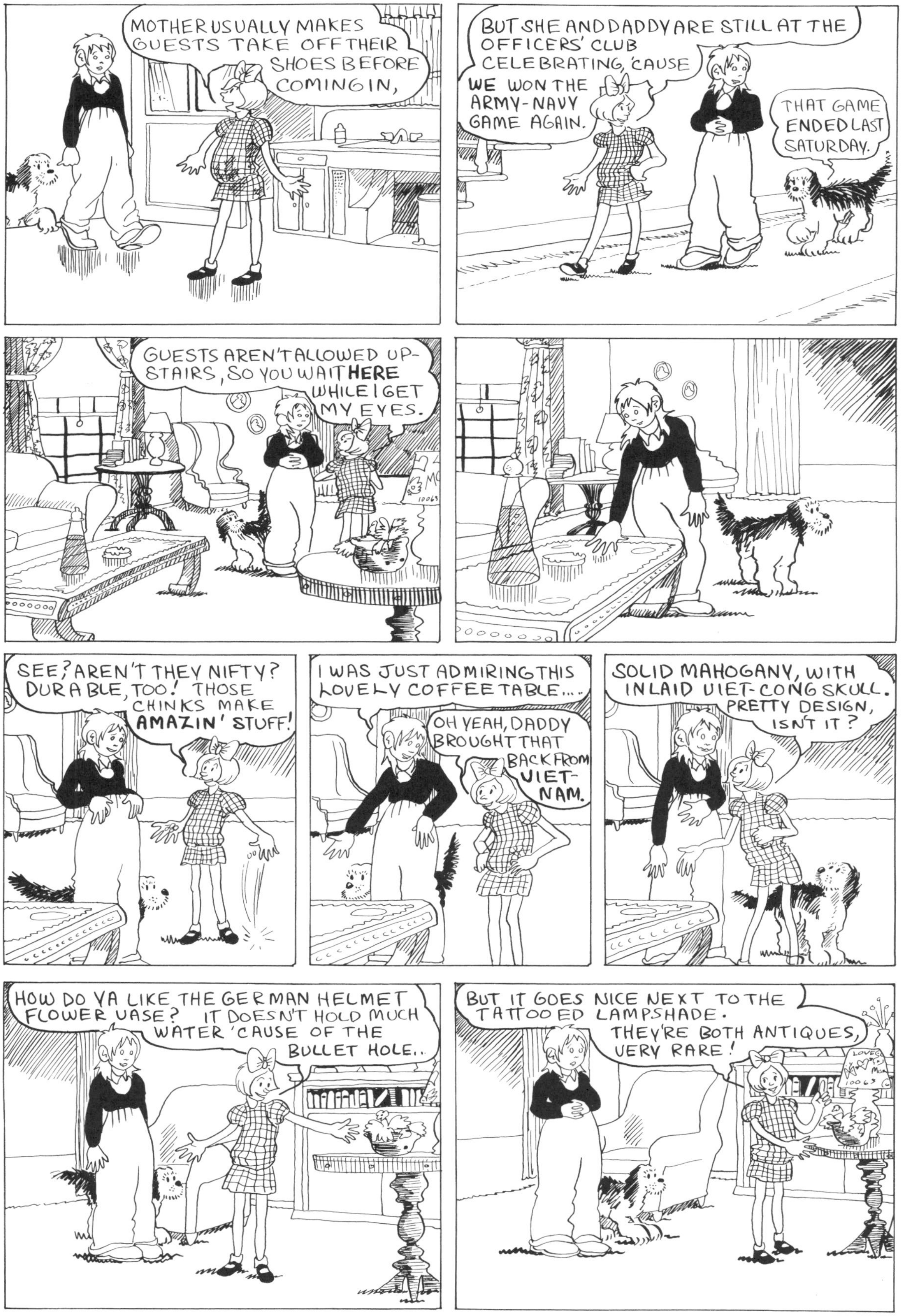
MOTHER USUALLY MAKES GUESTS TAKE OFF THEIR SHOES BEFORE COMING IN,
BUT SHE AND DADDY ARE STILL AT THE OFFICERS' CLUB CELEBRATING, 'CAUSE **WE** WON THE ARMY-NAVY GAME AGAIN.
THAT GAME **ENDED** LAST SATURDAY.
GUESTS AREN'T ALLOWED UP-STAIRS, SO YOU WAIT **HERE** WHILE I GET MY EYES.
SEE? AREN'T THEY NIFTY? DURABLE, TOO! THOSE CHINKS MAKE **AMAZIN'** STUFF!
I WAS JUST ADMIRING THIS LOVELY COFFEE TABLE....
OH YEAH, DADDY BROUGHT THAT BACK FROM **VIET-NAM.**
SOLID MAHOGANY, WITH INLAID VIET-CONG SKULL. PRETTY DESIGN, ISN'T IT?
HOW DO YA LIKE THE GERMAN HELMET FLOWER VASE? IT DOESN'T HOLD MUCH WATER 'CAUSE OF THE BULLET HOLE..
BUT IT GOES NICE NEXT TO THE TATTOOED LAMPSHADE. THEY'RE BOTH ANTIQUES, VERY RARE!

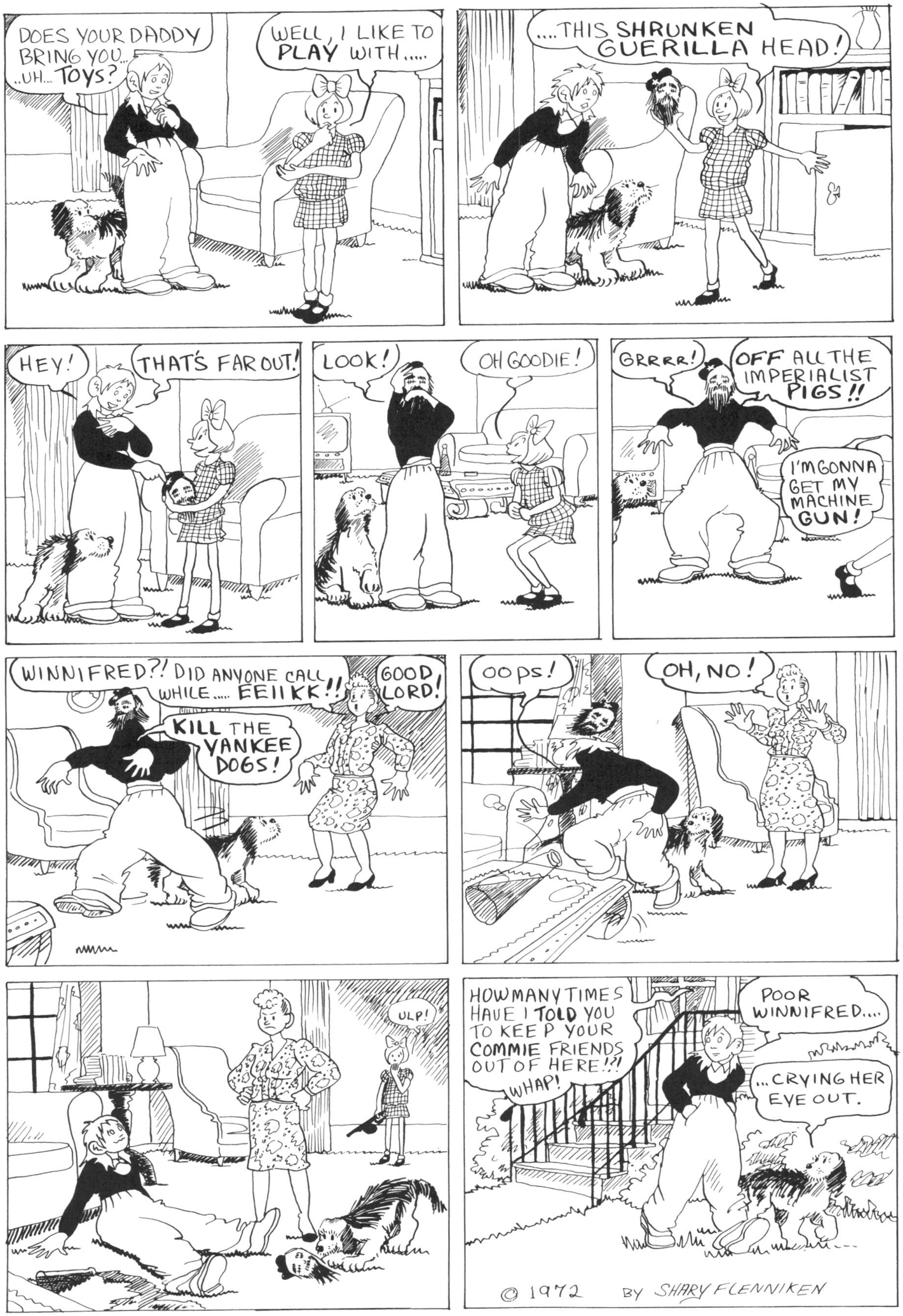
DOES YOUR DADDY BRING YOU... ..UH... TOYS?
WELL, I LIKE TO PLAY WITH.....
....THIS SHRUNKEN GUERILLA HEAD!
HEY!
THAT'S FAR OUT!
LOOK!
OH GOODIE!
GRRRR!
OFF ALL THE IMPERIALIST PIGS!!
I'M GONNA GET MY MACHINE GUN!
WINNIFRED?! DID ANYONE CALL WHILE..... EEIIKK!!
GOOD LORD!
KILL THE YANKEE DOGS!
OOPS!
OH, NO!
ULP!
HOW MANY TIMES HAVE I TOLD YOU TO KEEP YOUR COMMIE FRIENDS OUT OF HERE!?!
WHAP!
POOR WINNIFRED....
...CRYING HER EYE OUT.
© 1972 BY SHARY FLENNIKEN

AAAH! SUCH OLFACTORY PLEASURES THE SUMMER BREEZES BRING!
TROTS AND BONNIE
I SMELL OL' SOCKS.
HI YA, PEPSIE.
WHERE'R YA GOIN'?
RIFLE PRACTICE!
I'M GONNA BE PREPARED,
JUST IN CASE...
I SHOULD BE WALKIN' DOWN THE STREET SOMEDAY,
AN' SEE.
HUGH HEFNER!
THE ONLY LEAD POISONING HE'LL EVER GET COMES FROM CHEWING PENCILS.
HE LIKES THE ATHLETIC TYPE, EH?
I DON'T THINK HE'D BE IMPRESSED.
FLENNIKEN

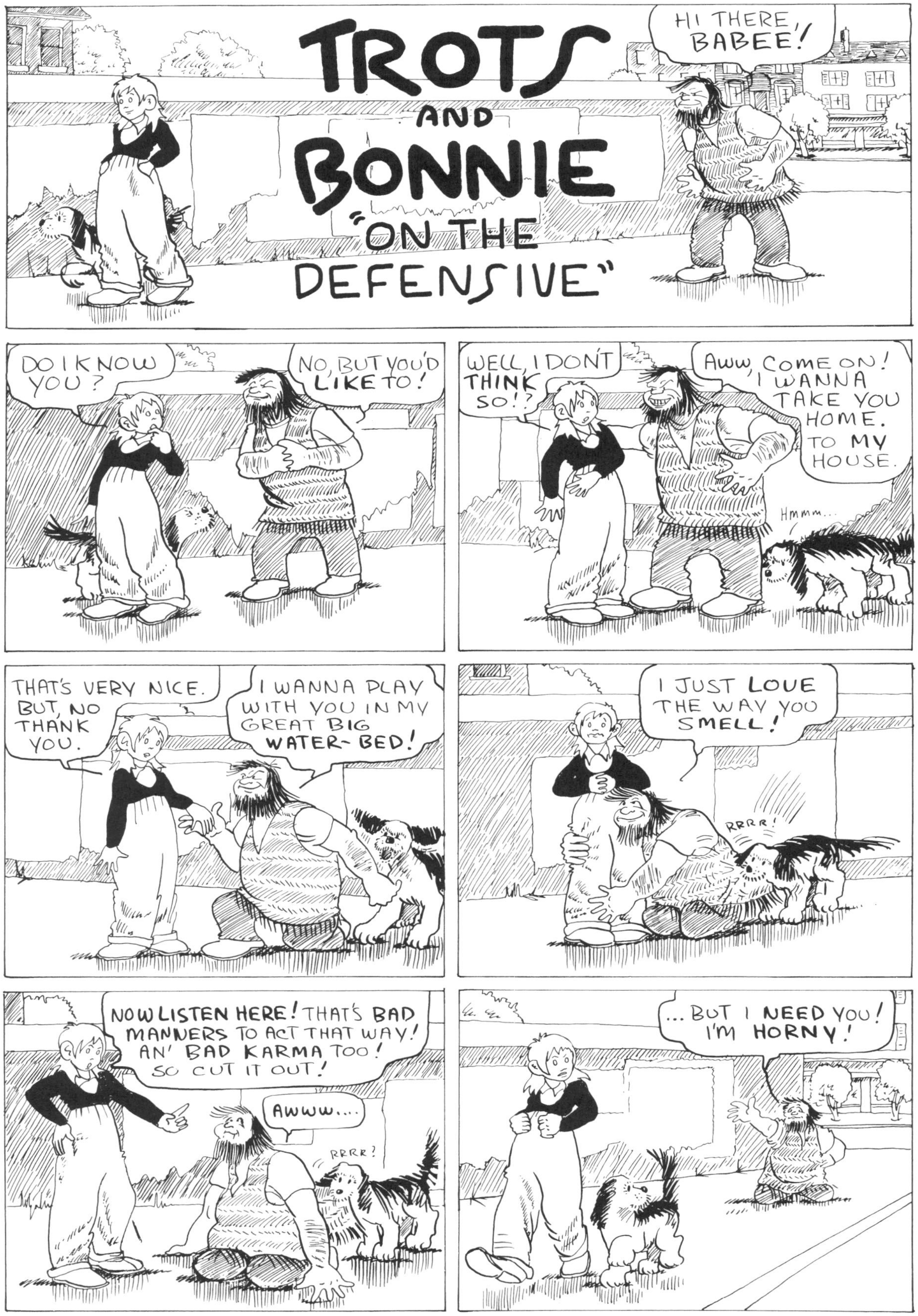
TROTS AND BONNIE
"ON THE DEFENSIVE"
HI THERE, BABEE!
DO I KNOW YOU?
NO, BUT YOU'D LIKE TO!
WELL, I DON'T THINK SO!?
AWW, COME ON! I WANNA TAKE YOU HOME. TO MY HOUSE.
HMMM...
THAT'S VERY NICE. BUT, NO THANK YOU.
I WANNA PLAY WITH YOU IN MY GREAT BIG WATER-BED!
I JUST LOVE THE WAY YOU SMELL!
RRRR!
NOW LISTEN HERE! THAT'S BAD MANNERS TO ACT THAT WAY! AN' BAD KARMA TOO! SO CUT IT OUT!
AWWW....
RRRR?
...BUT I NEED YOU! I'M HORNY!

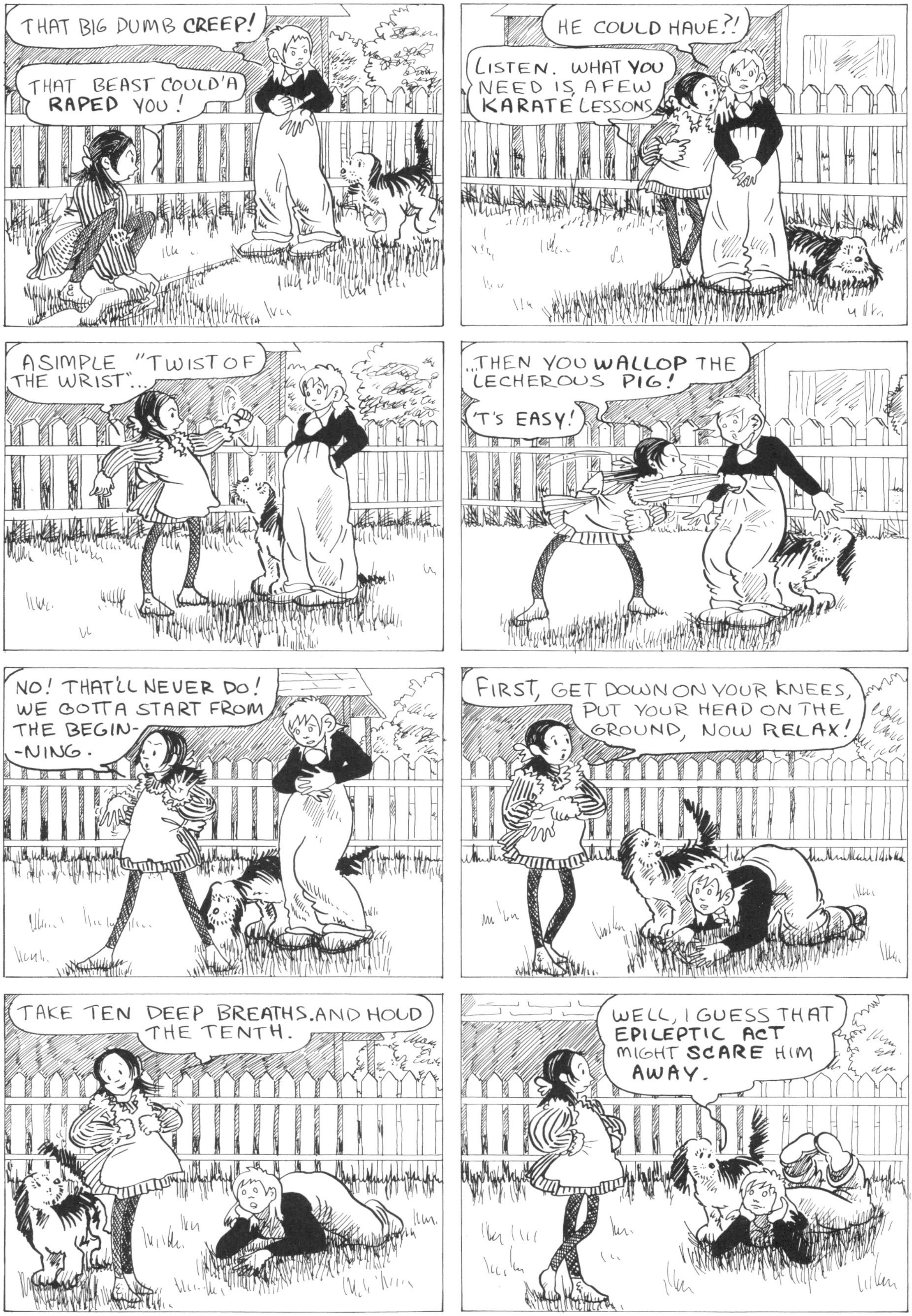
THAT BIG DUMB CREEP!
THAT BEAST COULD'A RAPED YOU!
HE COULD HAVE?!
LISTEN. WHAT YOU NEED IS A FEW KARATE LESSONS.
A SIMPLE "TWIST OF THE WRIST"...
...THEN YOU WALLOP THE LECHEROUS PIG!
'T'S EASY!
NO! THAT'LL NEVER DO! WE GOTTA START FROM THE BEGIN--NING.
FIRST, GET DOWN ON YOUR KNEES, PUT YOUR HEAD ON THE GROUND, NOW RELAX!
TAKE TEN DEEP BREATHS. AND HOLD THE TENTH.
WELL, I GUESS THAT EPILEPTIC ACT MIGHT SCARE HIM AWAY.

IT'S EASY TO SEE THAT YOU'RE READY FOR ADVANCED TRAINING.
I THINK WE SHOULD PRACTICE HITTING A DUMMY.
OH NO YOU DON'T! NOT AGAIN!
WAIT A MINUTE!
A DUMMY! LIKE THIS!
SEE?!
HOW'S THIS!?
GREAT FORM!
OOPS!
OH NO!
MAYBE WE SHOULD WORK ON OUR PRIMAL SCREAM.

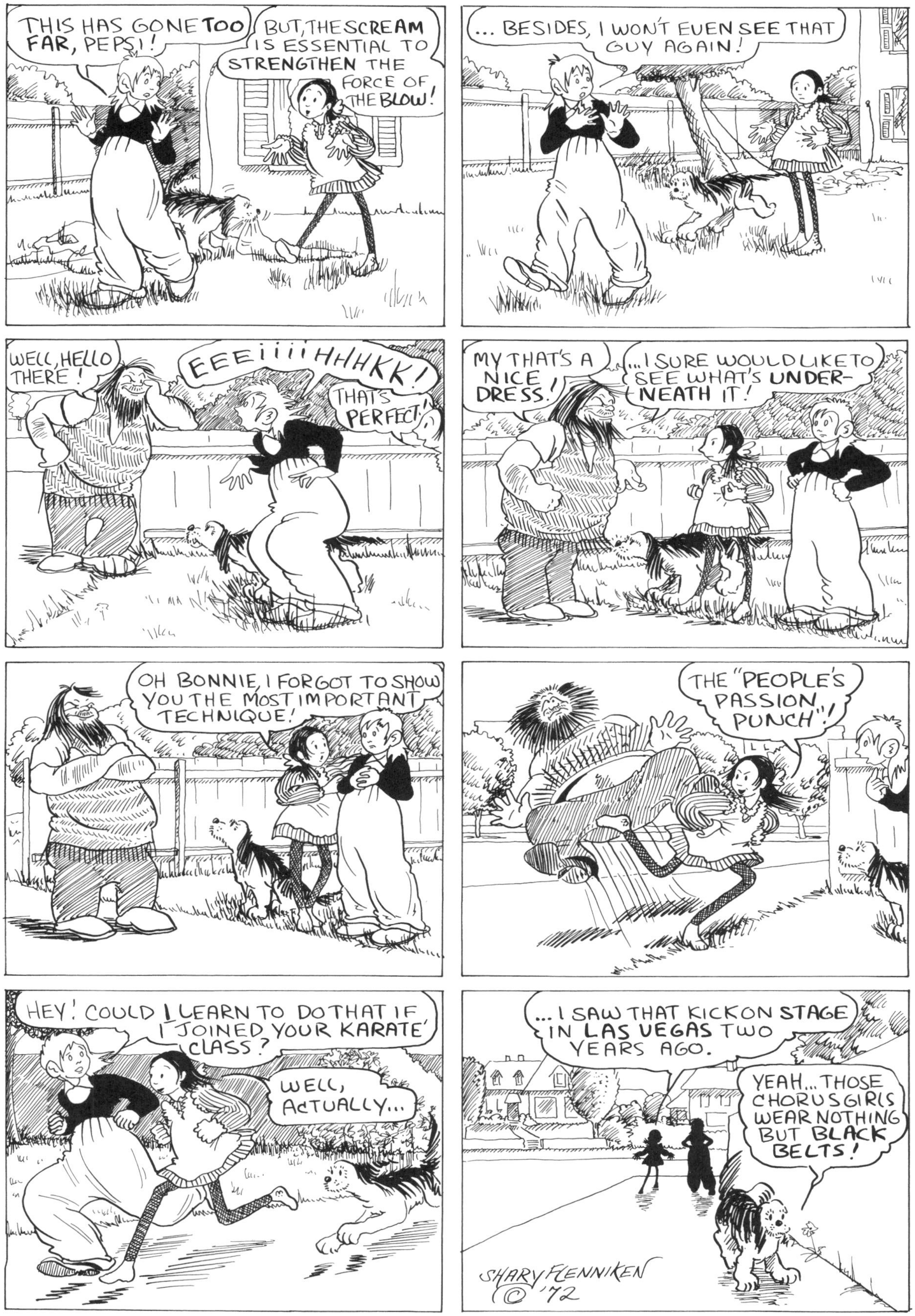
THIS HAS GONE TOO FAR, PEPSI!
BUT, THE SCREAM IS ESSENTIAL TO STRENGTHEN THE FORCE OF THE BLOW!
... BESIDES, I WON'T EVEN SEE THAT GUY AGAIN!
WELL, HELLO THERE!
EEEiiiiHHHKK!
THAT'S PERFECT!
MY THAT'S A NICE DRESS!
...I SURE WOULD LIKE TO SEE WHAT'S UNDERNEATH IT!
OH BONNIE, I FORGOT TO SHOW YOU THE MOST IMPORTANT TECHNIQUE!
THE "PEOPLE'S PASSION PUNCH"!
HEY! COULD I LEARN TO DO THAT IF I JOINED YOUR KARATE CLASS?
WELL, ACTUALLY...
...I SAW THAT KICK ON STAGE IN LAS VEGAS TWO YEARS AGO.
YEAH... THOSE CHORUS GIRLS WEAR NOTHING BUT BLACK BELTS!
SHARY FLENNIKEN © '72

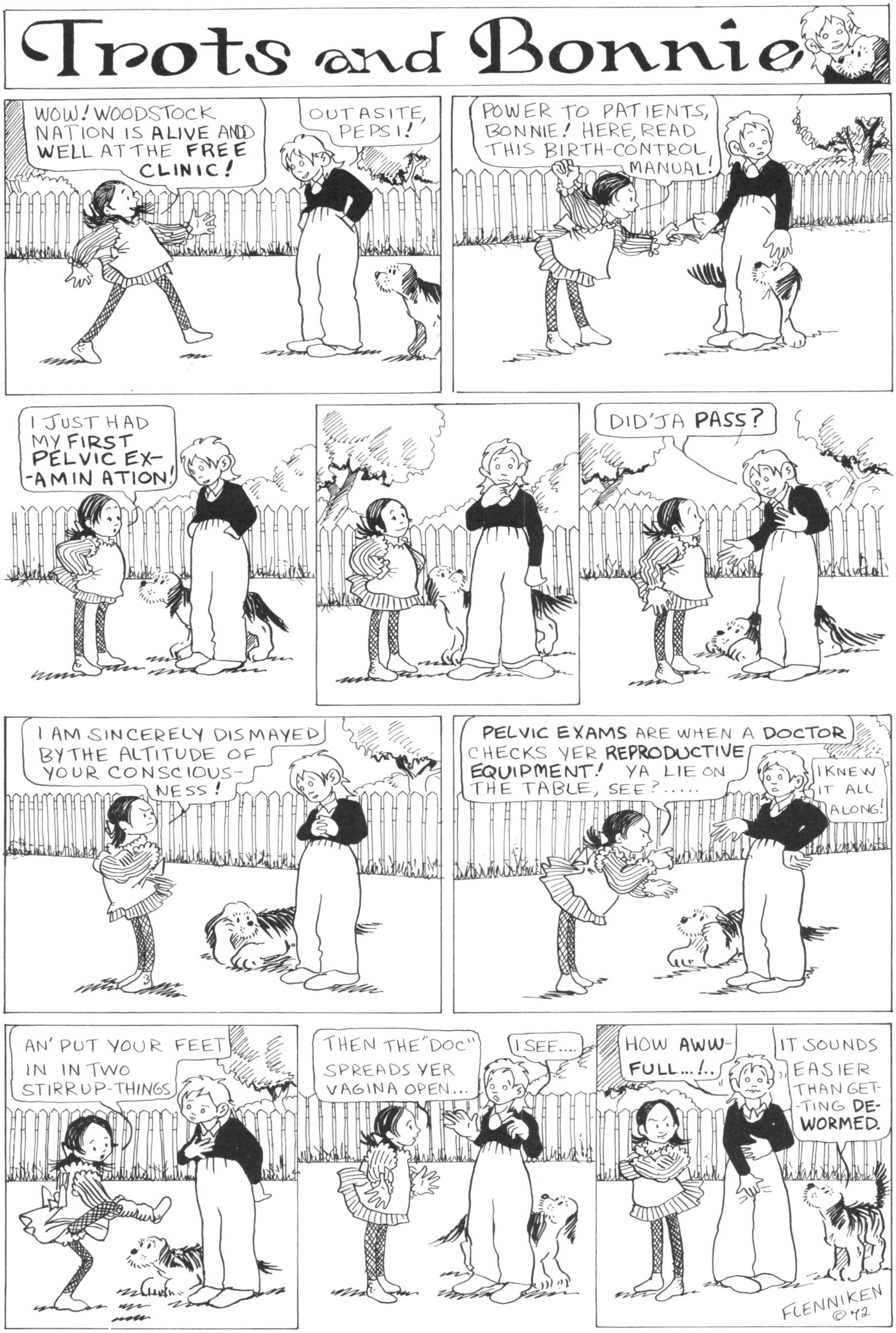
Trots and Bonnie
WOW! WOODSTOCK NATION IS ALIVE AND WELL AT THE FREE CLINIC!
OUTASITE, PEPSI!
POWER TO PATIENTS, BONNIE! HERE, READ THIS BIRTH-CONTROL MANUAL!
I JUST HAD MY FIRST PELVIC EX-AMIN ATION!
DID'JA PASS?
I AM SINCERELY DISMAYED BY THE ALTITUDE OF YOUR CONSCIOUS-NESS!
PELVIC EXAMS ARE WHEN A DOCTOR CHECKS YER REPRODUCTIVE EQUIPMENT! YA LIE ON THE TABLE, SEE?.....
I KNEW IT ALL ALONG!
AN' PUT YOUR FEET IN IN TWO STIRRUP-THINGS
THEN THE "DOC" SPREADS YER VAGINA OPEN...
I SEE....
HOW AWW-FULL...!..
IT SOUNDS EASIER THAN GET-TING DE-WORMED.
FLENNIKEN ©'72

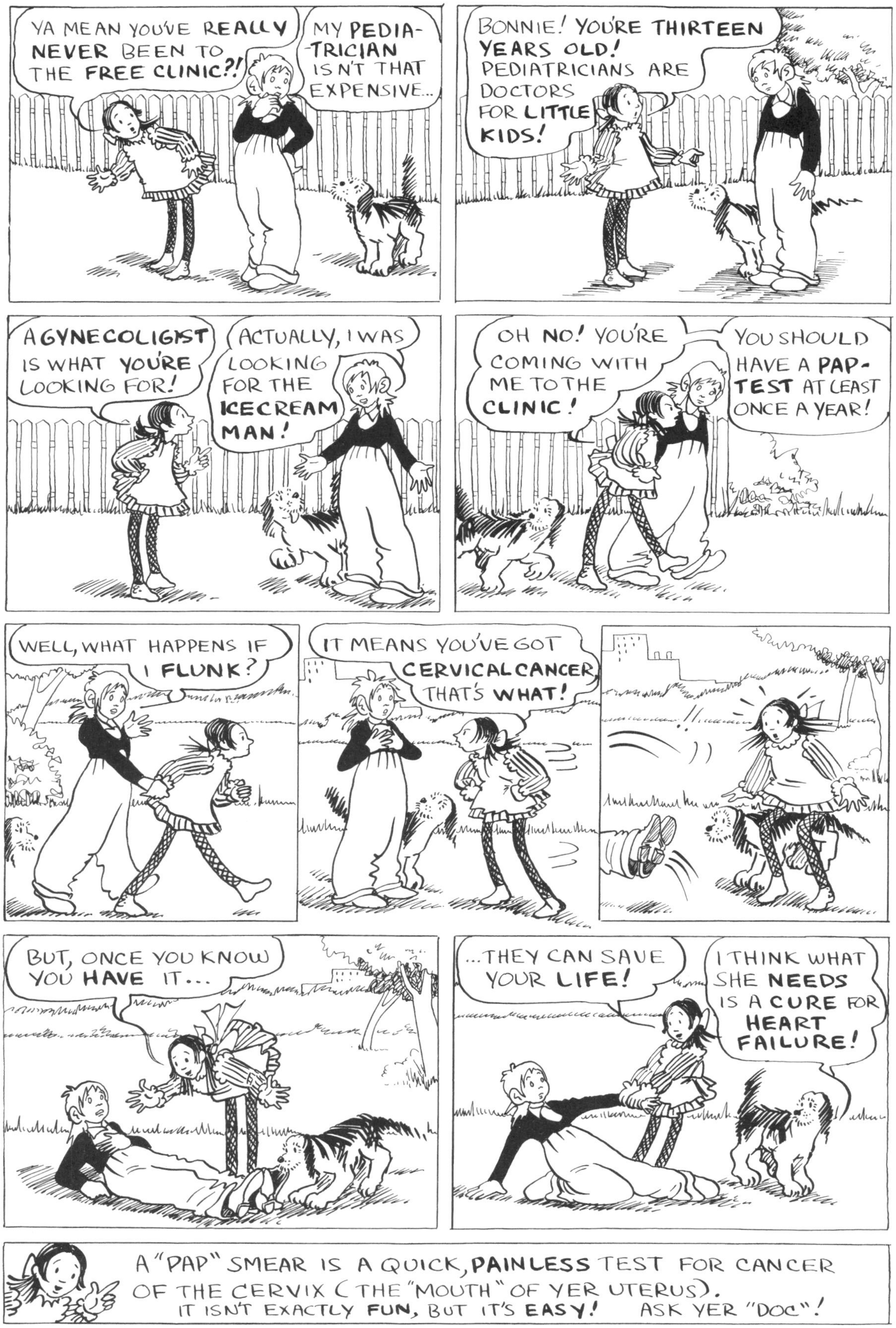
YA MEAN YOU'VE REALLY NEVER BEEN TO THE FREE CLINIC?!
MY PEDIA-TRICIAN ISN'T THAT EXPENSIVE...
BONNIE! YOU'RE THIRTEEN YEARS OLD! PEDIATRICIANS ARE DOCTORS FOR LITTLE KIDS!
A GYNECOLIGIST IS WHAT YOU'RE LOOKING FOR!
ACTUALLY, I WAS LOOKING FOR THE ICECREAM MAN!
OH NO! YOU'RE COMING WITH ME TO THE CLINIC!
YOU SHOULD HAVE A PAP-TEST AT LEAST ONCE A YEAR!
WELL, WHAT HAPPENS IF I FLUNK?
IT MEANS YOU'VE GOT CERVICAL CANCER, THAT'S WHAT!
BUT, ONCE YOU KNOW YOU HAVE IT...
...THEY CAN SAVE YOUR LIFE!
I THINK WHAT SHE NEEDS IS A CURE FOR HEART FAILURE!
A "PAP" SMEAR IS A QUICK, PAINLESS TEST FOR CANCER OF THE CERVIX (THE "MOUTH" OF YER UTERUS).
IT ISN'T EXACTLY FUN, BUT IT'S EASY! ASK YER "DOC"!

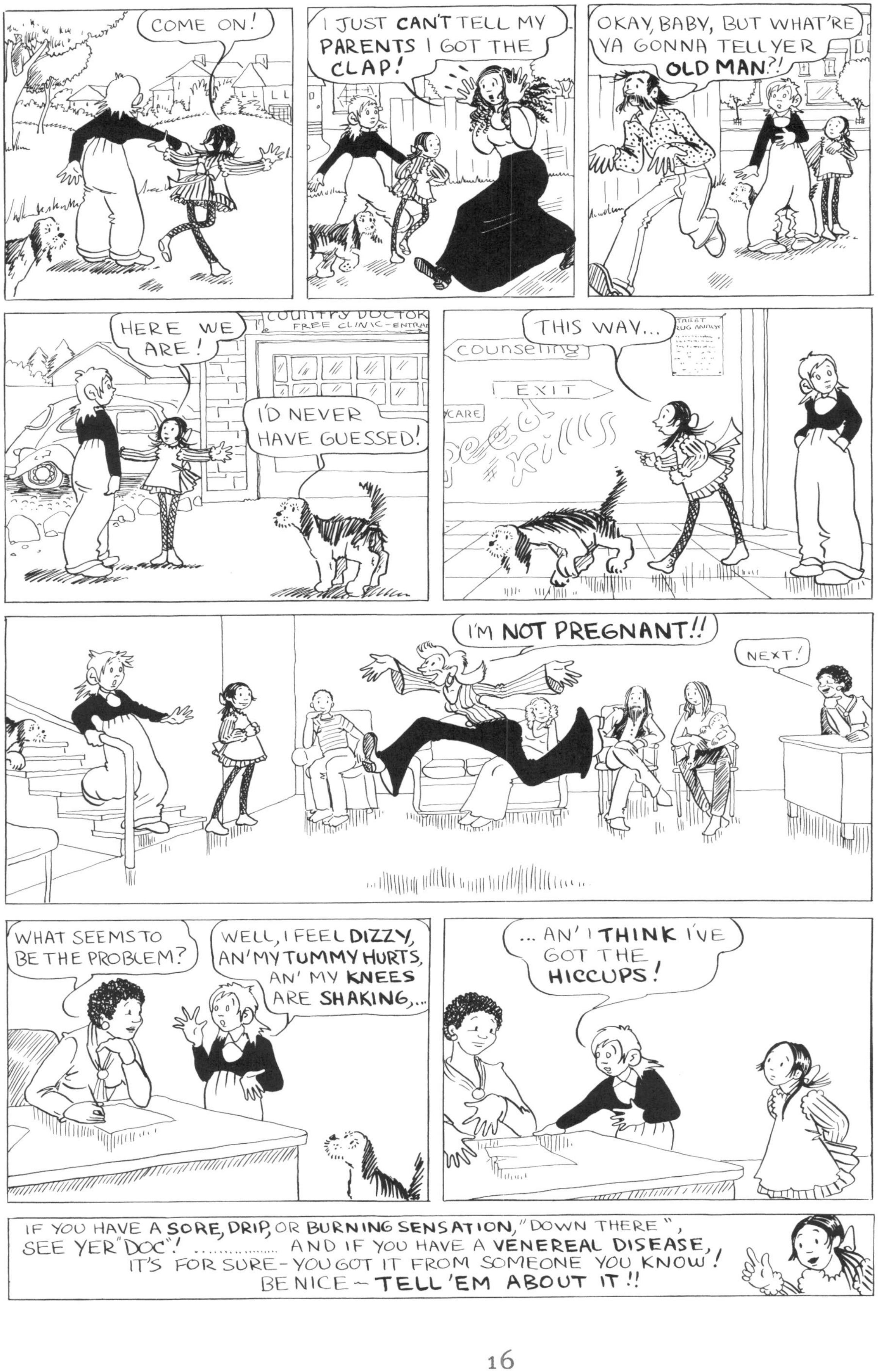
COME ON!
I JUST CAN'T TELL MY PARENTS I GOT THE CLAP!
OKAY, BABY, BUT WHAT'RE YA GONNA TELL YER OLD MAN?!
HERE WE ARE!
I'D NEVER HAVE GUESSED!
THIS WAY...
counseling
EXIT
I'M NOT PREGNANT!!
NEXT!
WHAT SEEMS TO BE THE PROBLEM?
WELL, I FEEL DIZZY, AN' MY TUMMY HURTS, AN' MY KNEES ARE SHAKING,...
... AN' I THINK I'VE GOT THE HICCUPS!
IF YOU HAVE A SORE, DRIP, OR BURNING SENSATION, "DOWN THERE", SEE YER "DOC"! .... AND IF YOU HAVE A VENEREAL DISEASE, IT'S FOR SURE - YOU GOT IT FROM SOMEONE YOU KNOW! BE NICE - TELL 'EM ABOUT IT!!

JUST WAIT OVER THERE.
HEY MAN, LIKE, I'M ON A BUMMER. WILL YOU HOLD MY FOOT?
YES, YOU CAN GO IN NOW.
Later...
WELL? DID YA GET AN EXAM? A BLOODTEST? A VASECTOMY?
THE DOCTOR SAID TO DRINK A GLASS OF WARM MILK...
TO CALM MY NERVES.
NOT EVEN BIRTH-CONTROL PILLS?
HE SAID I SHOULD COME BACK WHEN I START HAVING PERIODS.
USED CORRECTLY, THE "PILL" IS A 99% EFFECTIVE METHOD OF BIRTH-CONTROL. "I.U.D.'s ARE 97% SAFE. A DIAPHRAGM IS 95% SAFE, CONDOMS ARE 95% SAFE, FOAM-60%, ABSTINENCE-100% SAFE. I USE ALL SIX, AN' I'M 546% SAFE FROM PREGNANCY!
©'72 SHARY FLENNIKEN

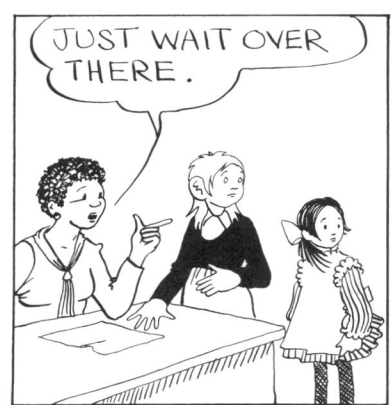

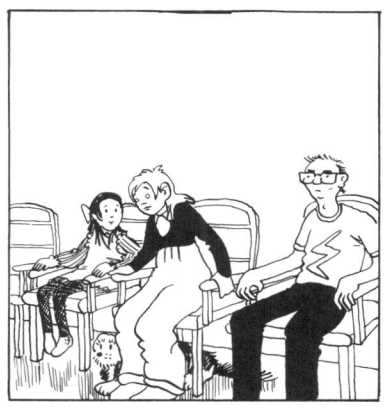

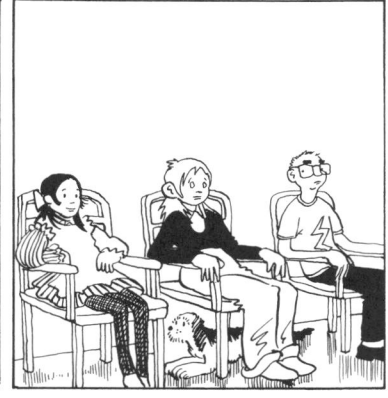

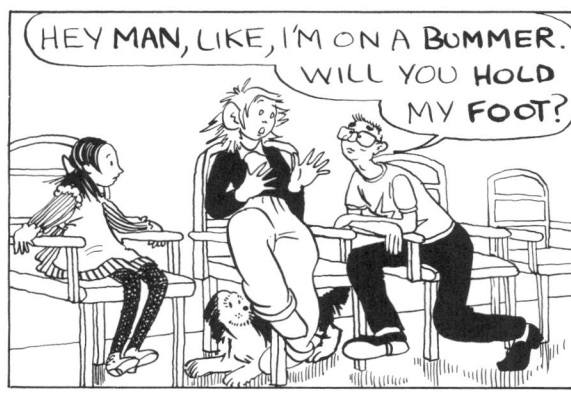

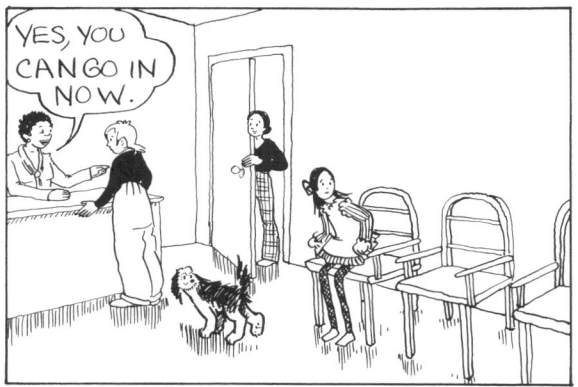

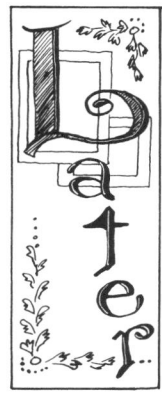

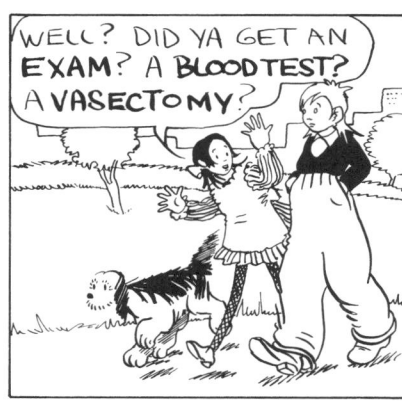

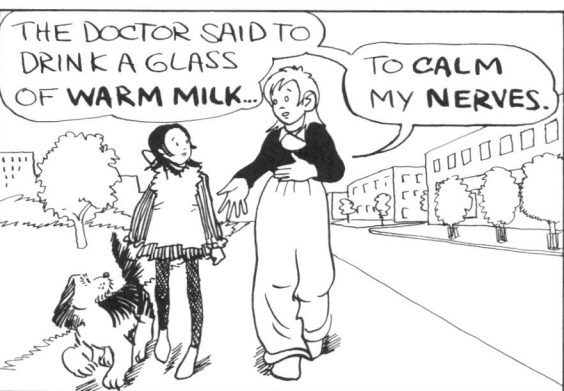

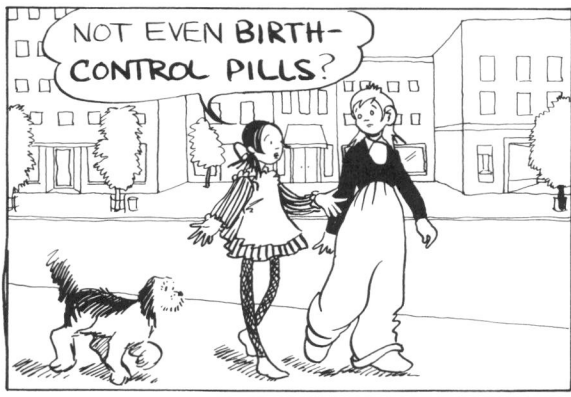

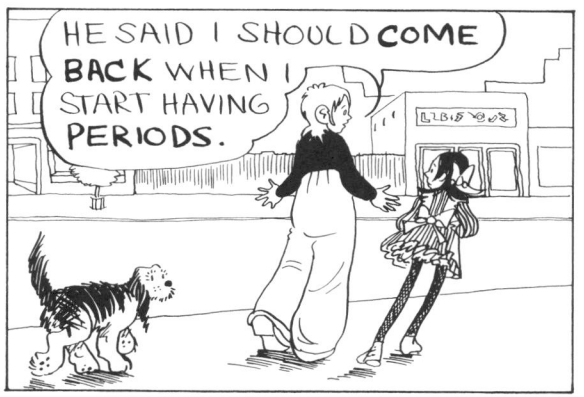

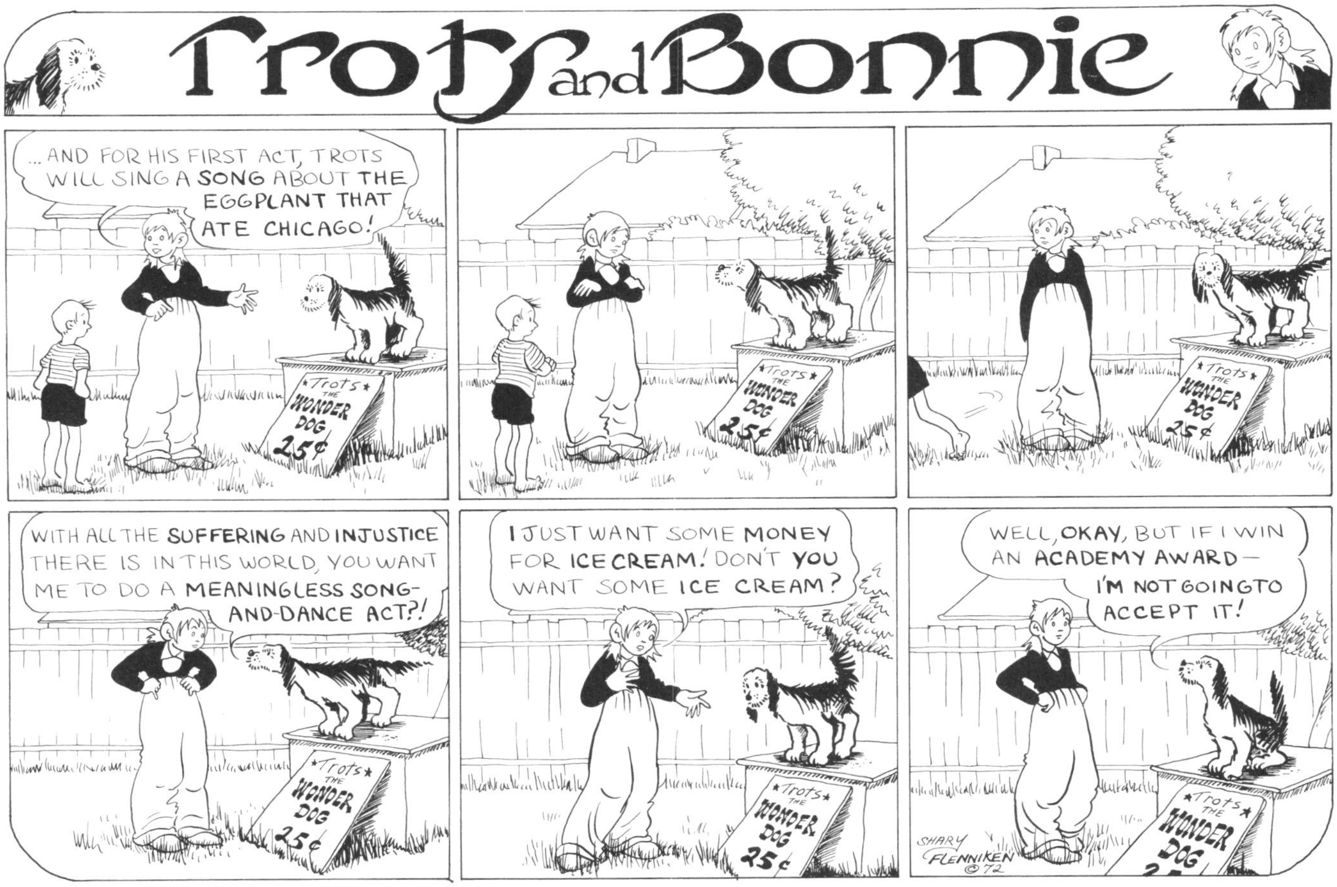
Trots and Bonnie
...AND FOR HIS FIRST ACT, TROTS WILL SING A SONG ABOUT THE EGGPLANT THAT ATE CHICAGO!
★Trots★ THE WONDER DOG 25¢
WITH ALL THE SUFFERING AND INJUSTICE THERE IS IN THIS WORLD, YOU WANT ME TO DO A MEANINGLESS SONG-AND-DANCE ACT?!
I JUST WANT SOME MONEY FOR ICE CREAM! DON'T YOU WANT SOME ICE CREAM?
WELL, OKAY, BUT IF I WIN AN ACADEMY AWARD— I'M NOT GOING TO ACCEPT IT!
SHARY FLENNIKEN ©72

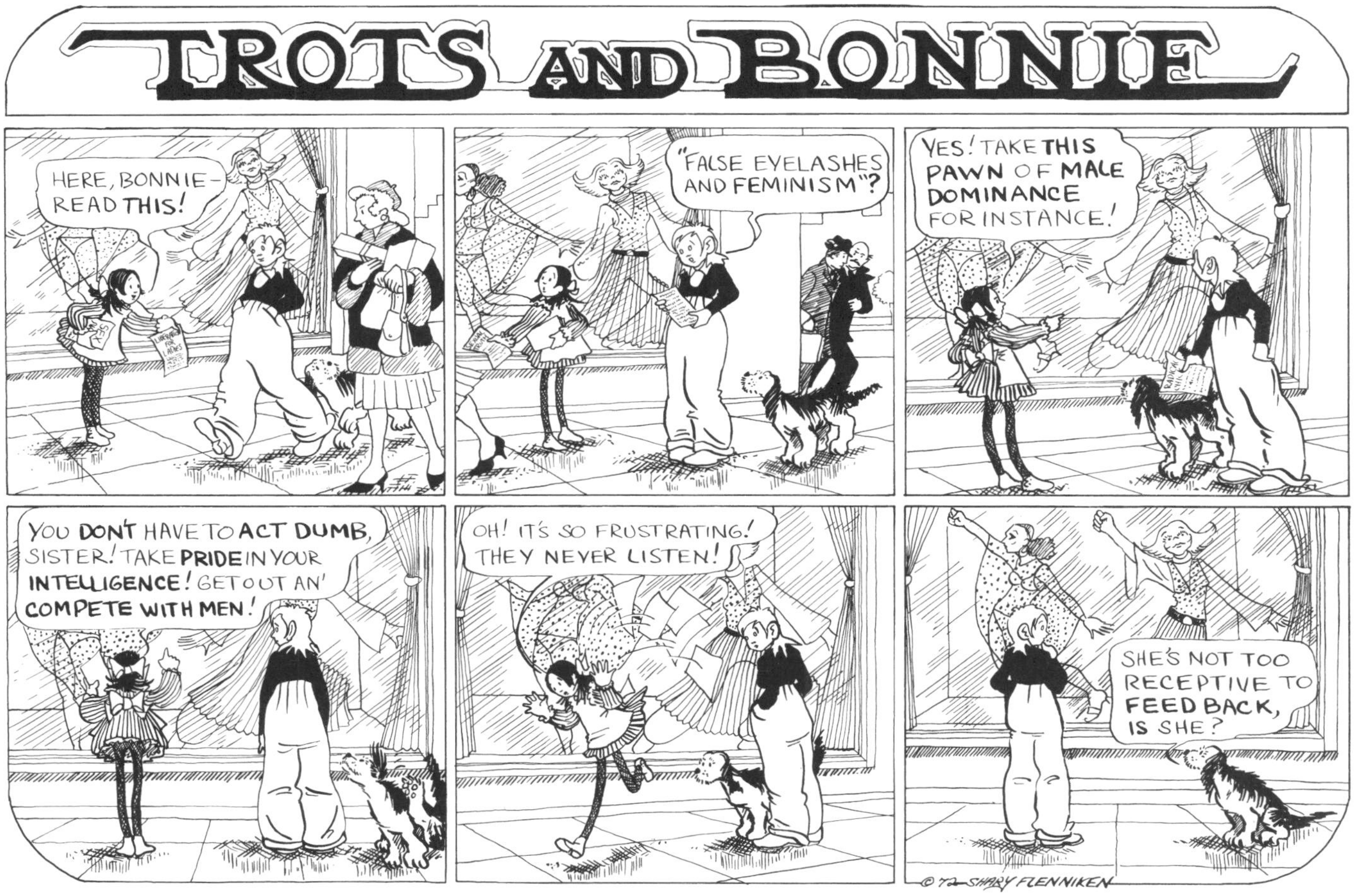
TROTS AND BONNIE
HERE, BONNIE-READ THIS!
"FALSE EYELASHES AND FEMINISM"?
YES! TAKE THIS PAWN OF MALE DOMINANCE FOR INSTANCE!
YOU DON'T HAVE TO ACT DUMB, SISTER! TAKE PRIDE IN YOUR INTELLIGENCE! GET OUT AN' COMPETE WITH MEN!
OH! IT'S SO FRUSTRATING! THEY NEVER LISTEN!
SHE'S NOT TOO RECEPTIVE TO FEED BACK, IS SHE?
© 72 SHARY FLENNIKEN

Trots and Bonnie
UM... THIS BOOK IS ABOUT A YOUNG GIRL WHO FALLS IN LOVE ON HER SUMMER VACATION.
IT WAS WELL WRITTEN, AND... UM... I DON'T WANT TO GIVE AWAY THE ENDING, BUT I ESPECIALLY LIKED THE PART WHERE...
...SHE WRAPPED HER HUNGRY THIGHS PAS-SIONATELY AROUND HIS HOT, THRUSTING LOINS AND ....
WELL, HOW'D THEY LIKE IT?
TROTS, I DON'T THINK I SHOULD'VE LET YOU WRITE THIS BOOK REPORT FOR ME...
WHY NOT? I WROTE THE BOOK!
©73 SHARY FLENNIKEN

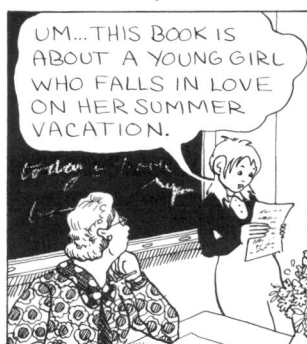

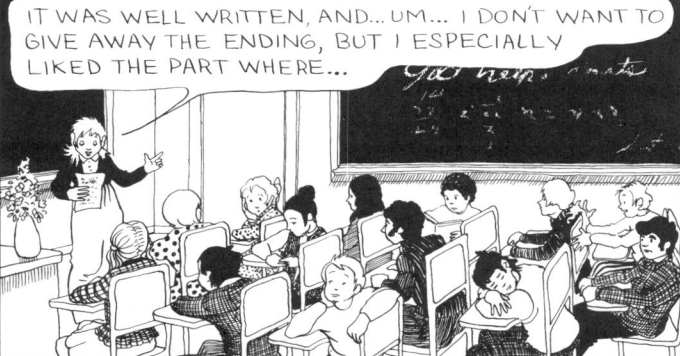

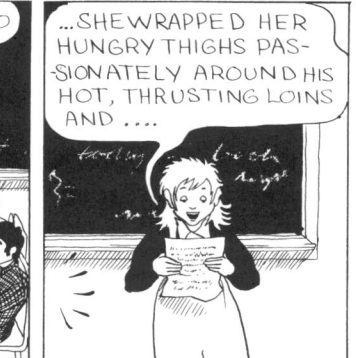

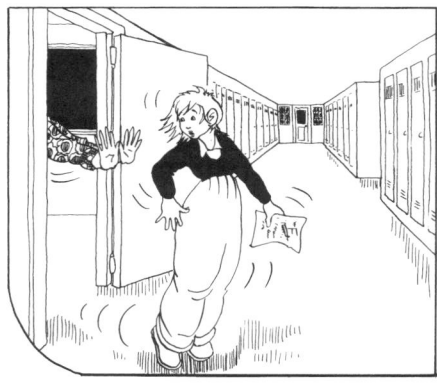

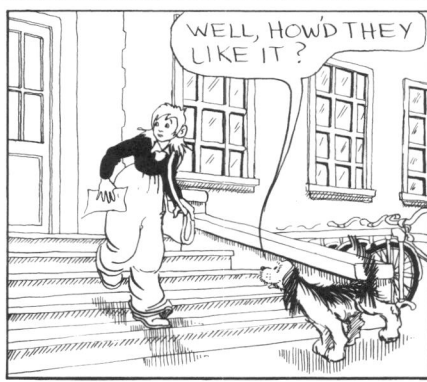

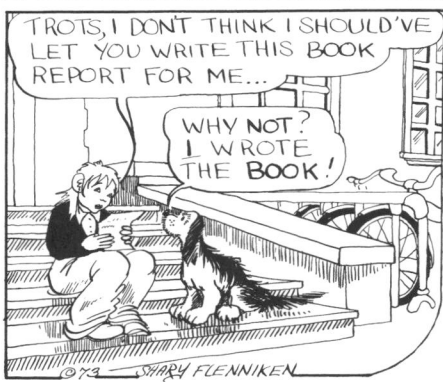

Trots and Bonnie
Alice! Oh, to steal the stars from the skies... A collar for your throat to fashion...
'Twould be but a shadow of your eyes,
and but a glimmer of my Passion!
I need not fear the dark of night. Your Love glows constantly. You've given me a Guiding Light....
What can I give to Thee?
BAD DOGS!!
©73 SHARY FLENNIKEN

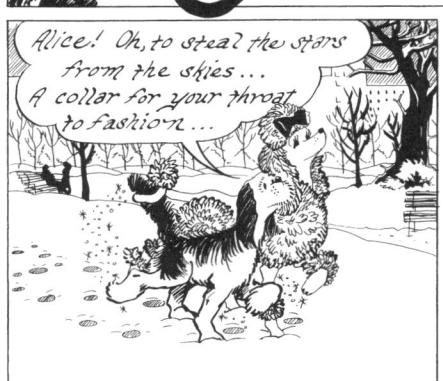

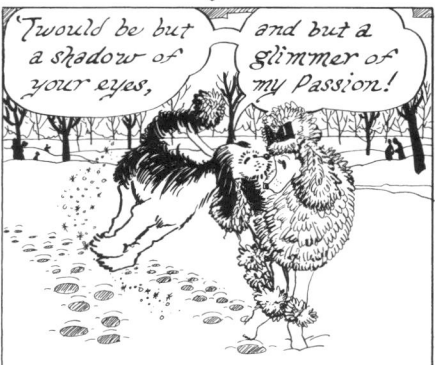

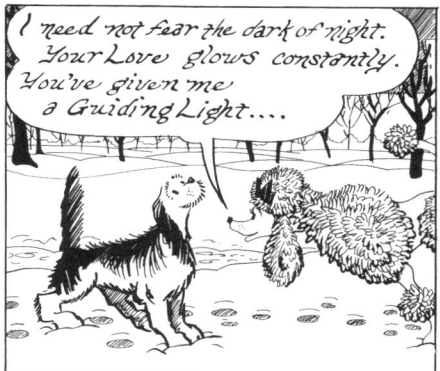

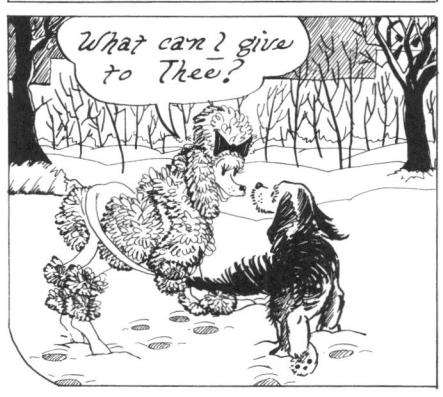

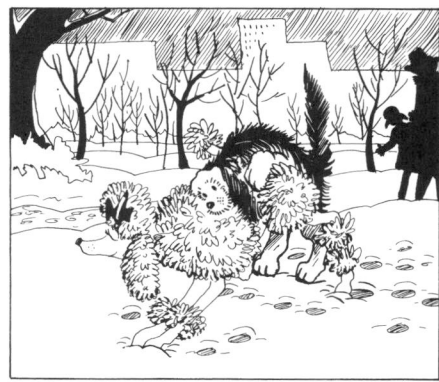

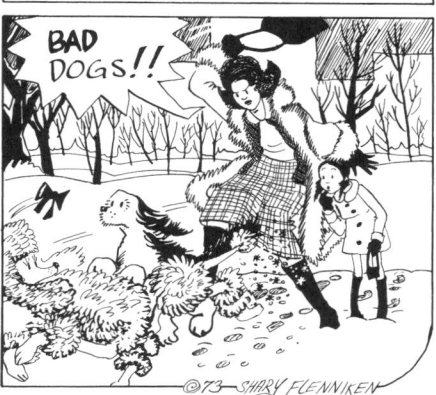

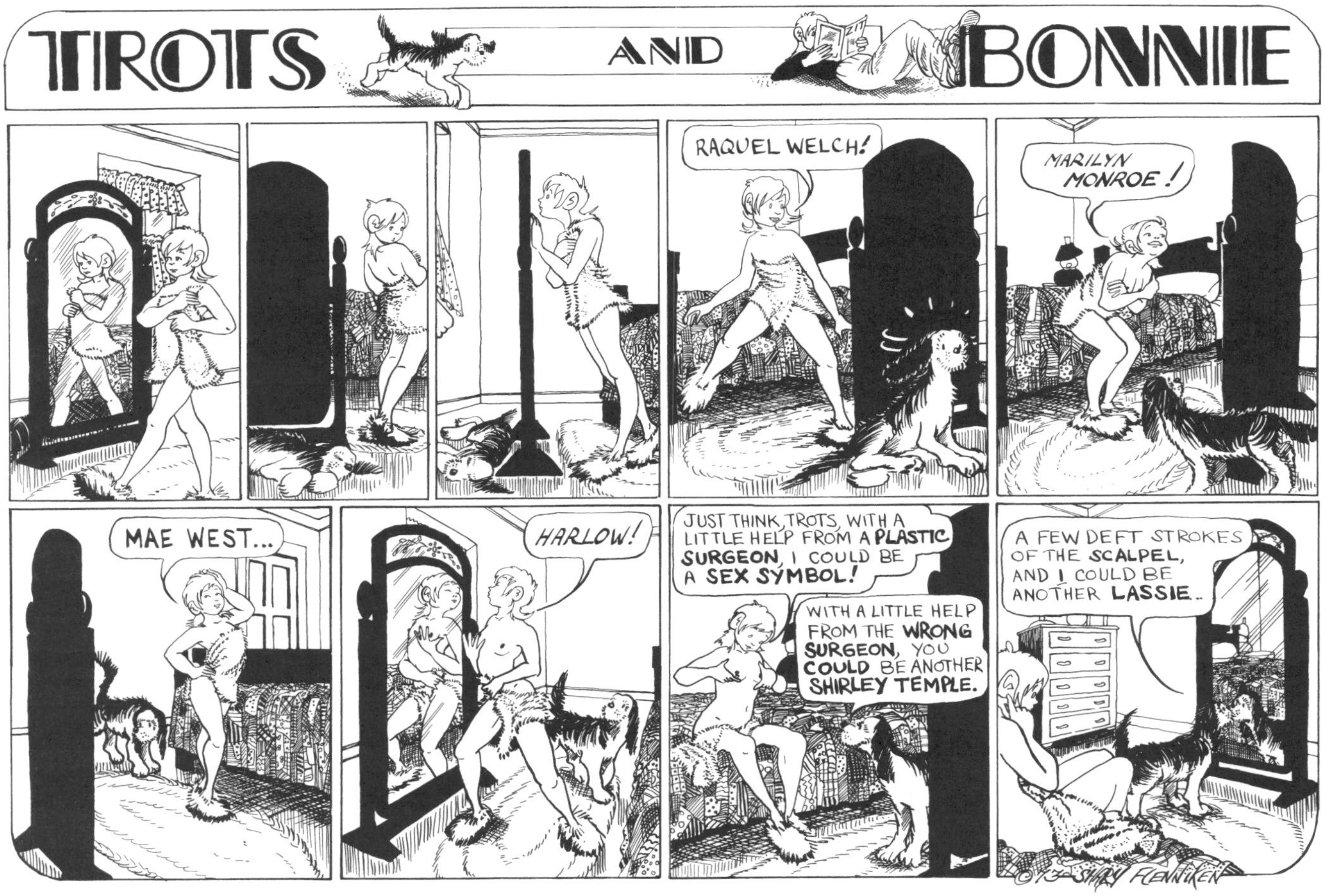
TROTS AND BONNIE
RAQUEL WELCH!
MARILYN MONROE!
MAE WEST...
HARLOW!
JUST THINK, TROTS, WITH A LITTLE HELP FROM A PLASTIC SURGEON, I COULD BE A SEX SYMBOL!
WITH A LITTLE HELP FROM THE WRONG SURGEON, YOU COULD BE ANOTHER SHIRLEY TEMPLE.
A FEW DEFT STROKES OF THE SCALPEL, AND I COULD BE ANOTHER LASSIE..
©'73-SHARY FLENNIKEN

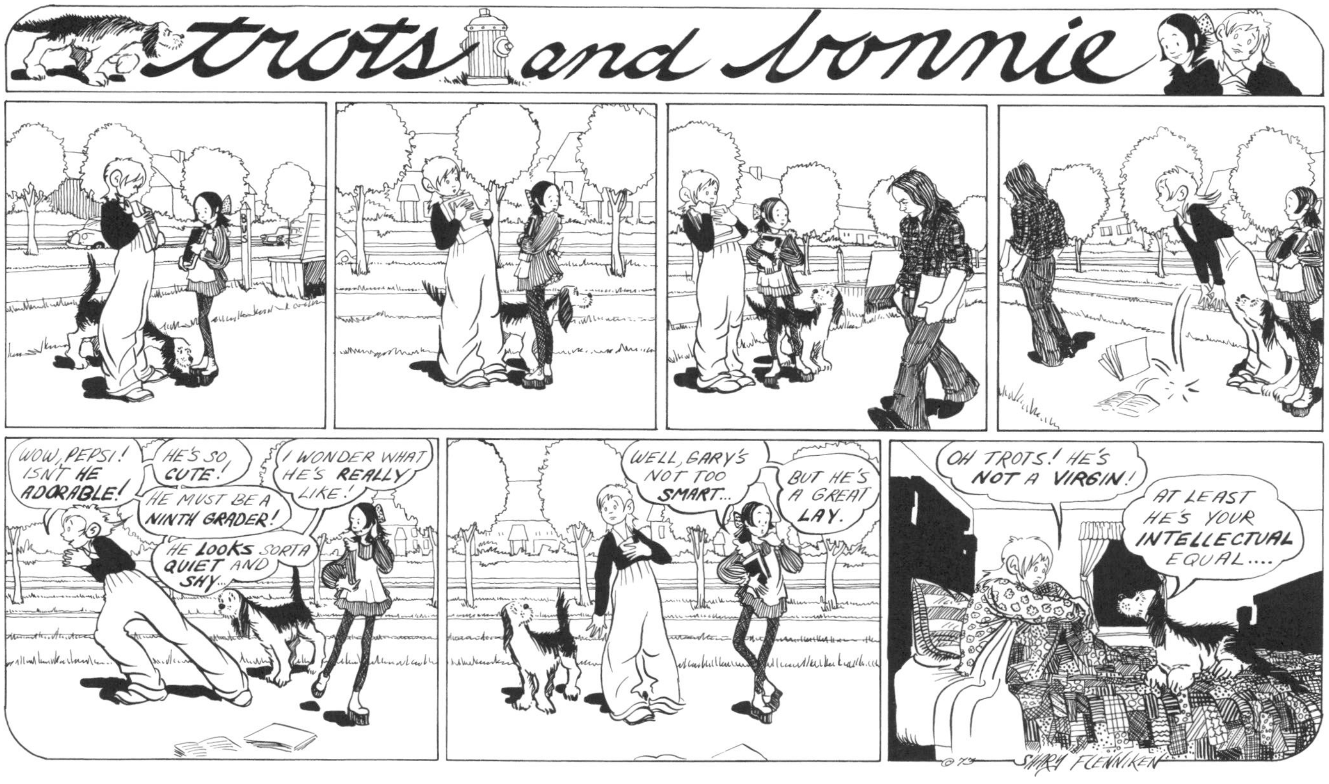
trots and bonnie
WOW, PEPSI! ISN'T HE ADORABLE!
HE'S SO CUTE!
HE MUST BE A NINTH GRADER!
HE LOOKS SORTA QUIET AND SHY...
I WONDER WHAT HE'S REALLY LIKE!
WELL, GARY'S NOT TOO SMART...
BUT HE'S A GREAT LAY.
OH TROTS! HE'S NOT A VIRGIN!
AT LEAST HE'S YOUR INTELLECTUAL EQUAL....
©73 SHARY FLENNIKEN

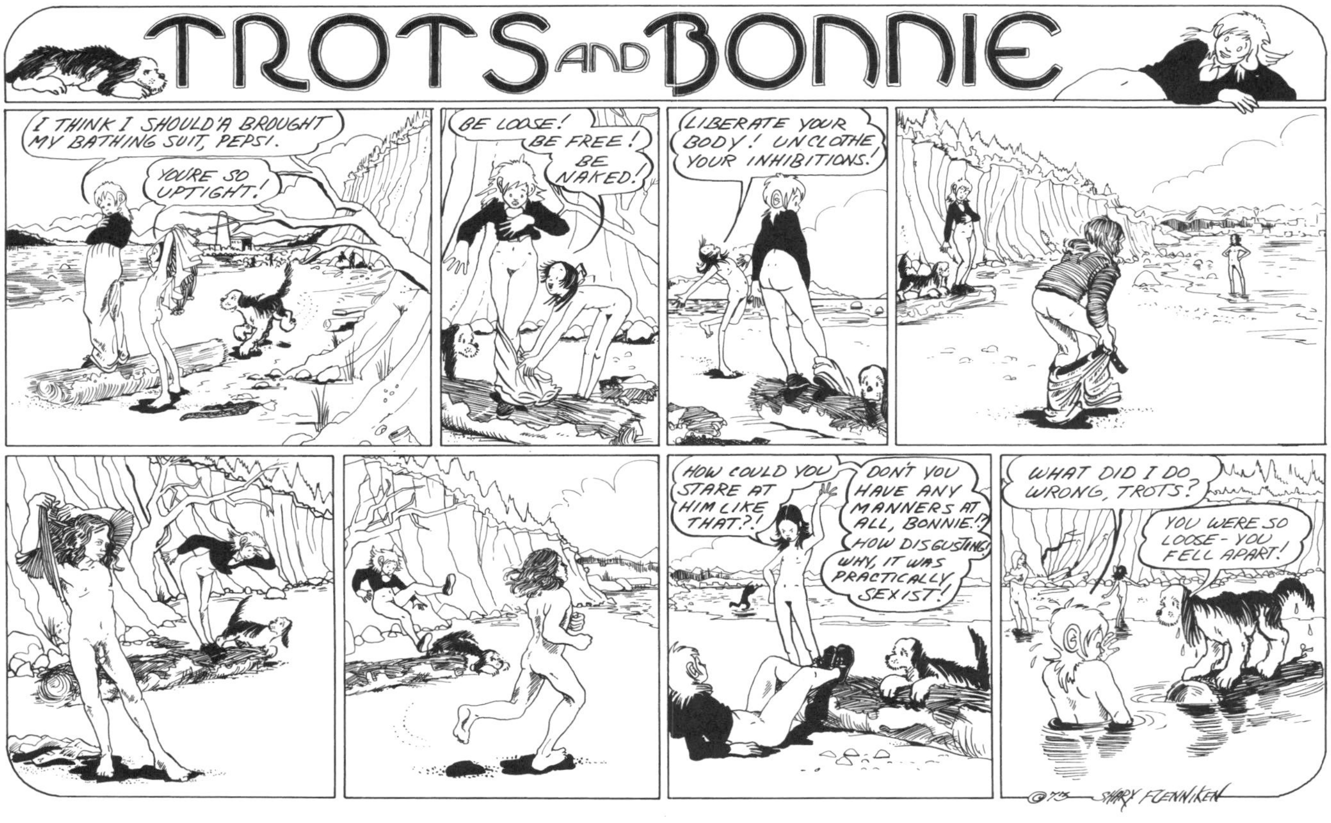
TROTS AND BONNIE
I THINK I SHOULD'A BROUGHT MY BATHING SUIT, PEPSI.
YOU'RE SO UPTIGHT!
BE LOOSE!
BE FREE!
BE NAKED!
LIBERATE YOUR BODY! UNCLOTHE YOUR INHIBITIONS!
HOW COULD YOU STARE AT HIM LIKE THAT?!
DON'T YOU HAVE ANY MANNERS AT ALL, BONNIE!? HOW DISGUSTING! WHY, IT WAS PRACTICALLY SEXIST!
WHAT DID I DO WRONG, TROTS?
YOU WERE SO LOOSE - YOU FELL APART!
©'75 SHARY FLENNIKEN

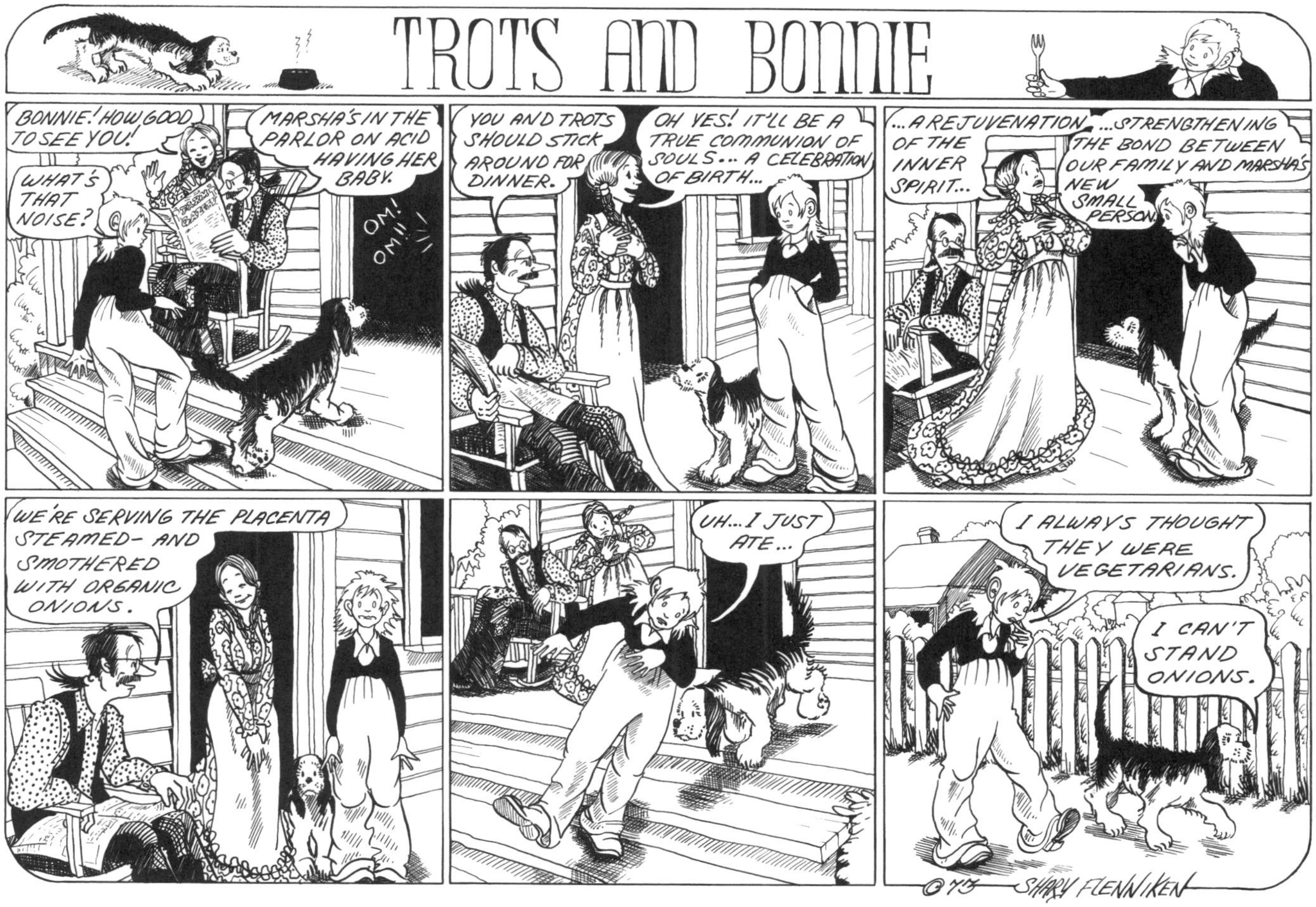
TROTS AND BONNIE
BONNIE! HOW GOOD TO SEE YOU!
WHAT'S THAT NOISE?
MARSHA'S IN THE PARLOR ON ACID HAVING HER BABY.
OM! OM!
YOU AND TROTS SHOULD STICK AROUND FOR DINNER.
OH YES! IT'LL BE A TRUE COMMUNION OF SOULS... A CELEBRATION OF BIRTH...
...A REJUVENATION OF THE INNER SPIRIT...
...STRENGTHENING THE BOND BETWEEN OUR FAMILY AND MARSHA'S NEW SMALL PERSON.
WE'RE SERVING THE PLACENTA STEAMED- AND SMOTHERED WITH ORGANIC ONIONS.
UH...I JUST ATE...
I ALWAYS THOUGHT THEY WERE VEGETARIANS.
I CAN'T STAND ONIONS.
©'73 SHARY FLENNIKEN

TROTS and BONNIE
THIS IS A FINE TIME FOR YOU TO HAVE TO GO FOR A WALK, TROTS!
MOM SAYS THIS PARK IS FULL OF MUGGERS AT NIGHT...
AND DADDY SAYS THERE ARE PERVERTS LURKING IN THE BUSHES!
TROTS? WERE THOSE PERVERTS?
OR MUGGERS?
WELL, IF THEY WERE PERVERTS, THEY WOULD'VE ASKED US TO JOIN THEM...
'MUST BE MUGGERS THEN.
I'M GLAD I WASN'T WEARING MY RHINESTONE COLLAR!
© '73 SHARY FLENNIKEN

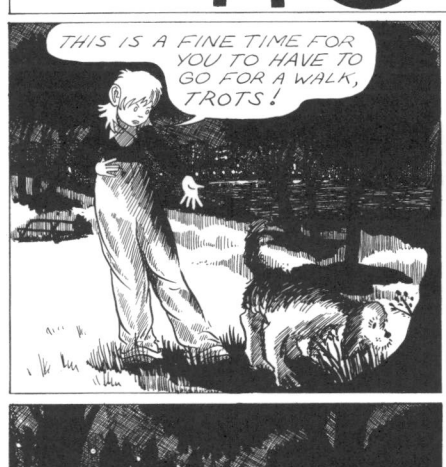

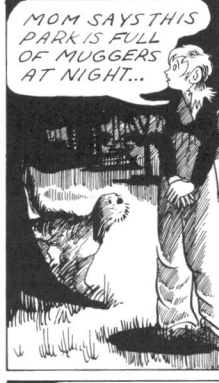

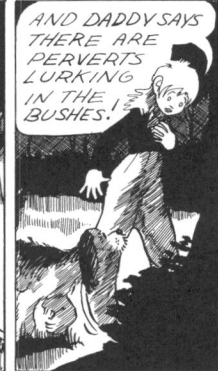

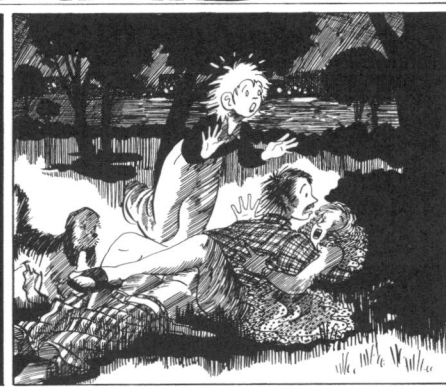

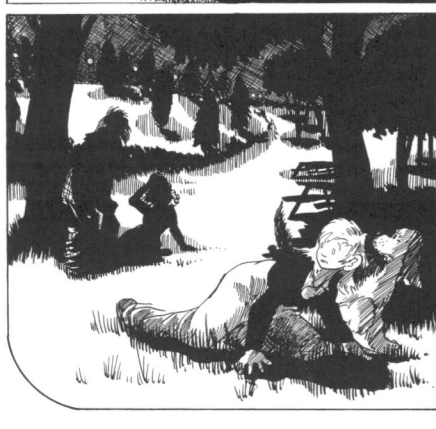

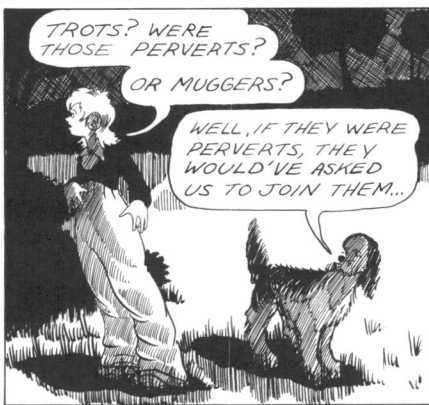

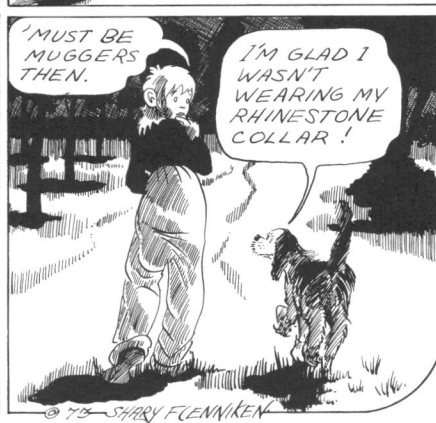

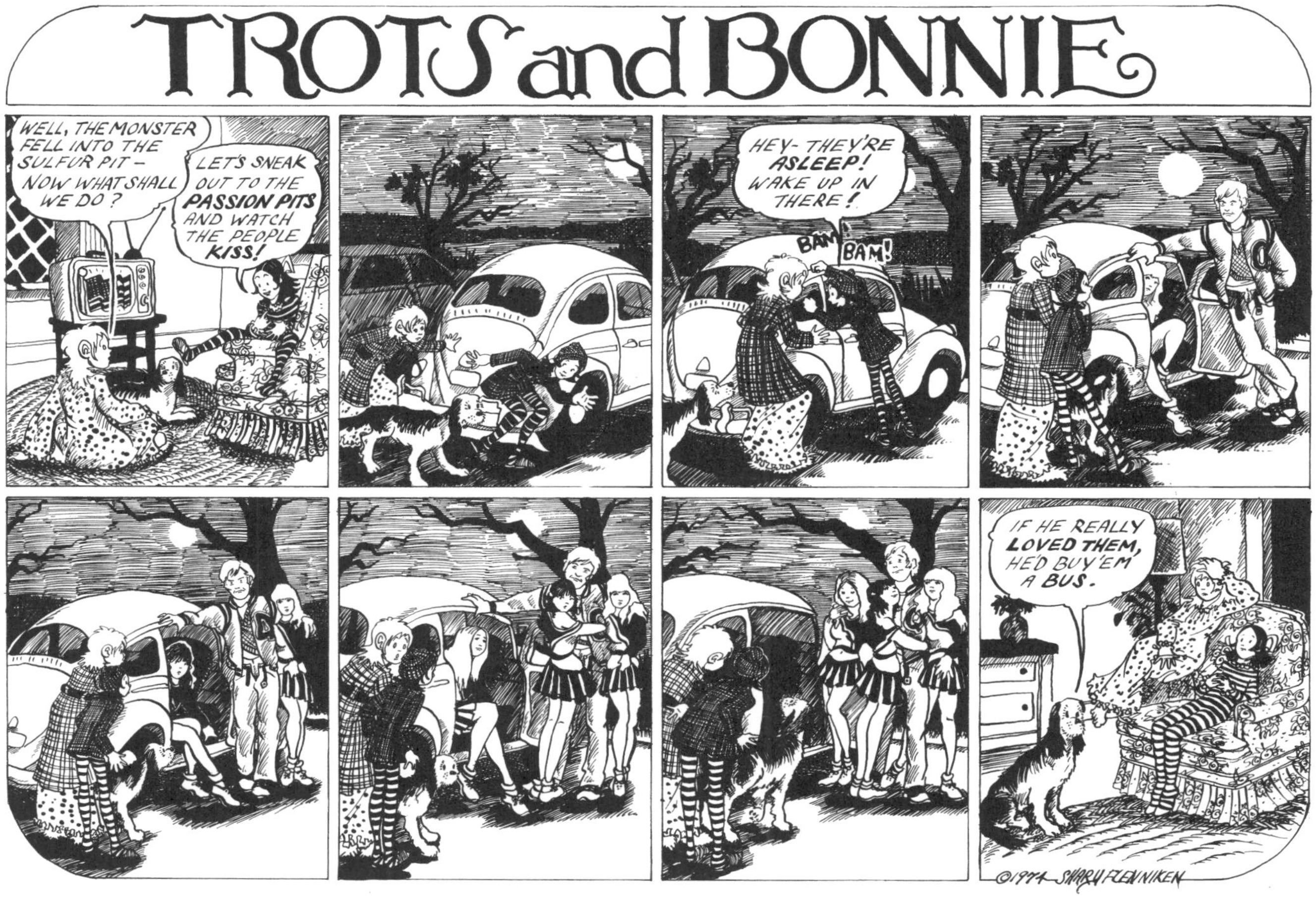
TROTS and BONNIE
WELL, THE MONSTER FELL INTO THE SULFUR PIT – NOW WHAT SHALL WE DO?
LET'S SNEAK OUT TO THE PASSION PITS AND WATCH THE PEOPLE KISS!
HEY- THEY'RE ASLEEP! WAKE UP IN THERE!
BAM! BAM!
IF HE REALLY LOVED THEM, HE'D BUY 'EM A BUS.
©1974 SHARY FLENNIKEN

Trots and Bonnie
ARE WE GONNA TAKE OUT HIS TONSILS OR HIS PREFRONTAL LOBE, DOCTOR?
SHEARS!
NO, NURSE~ WRONG END... THIS IS A VASECTOMY!
AS USUAL, PEPSI'S NOT INTERESTED IN HIS MIND.
I TOLD ELROD HE COULD "DO IT" TO ME IF HE LET ME STERILIZE HIM FIRST.
ELROD'S GOING TO WISH SHE'D STERILIZED THOSE GARDEN SHEARS FIRST.
HOLD STILL, ELROD, THIS WON'T HURT A BIT.
GEE, IF WE DID IT TO TROTS, MAYBE HE'D HAVE MORE GIRLFRIENDS...
NO, WAIT!
AAIIEEE!!
DOCTOR
DR. PEPSI BIRTH CONTROL CLINIC
VASECTOMY 50¢
SEXCHANGE
©74 SHARY FLENNIKEN

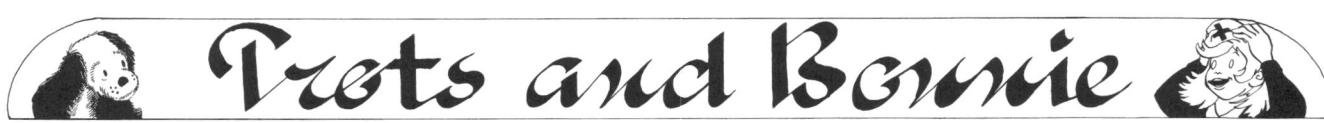

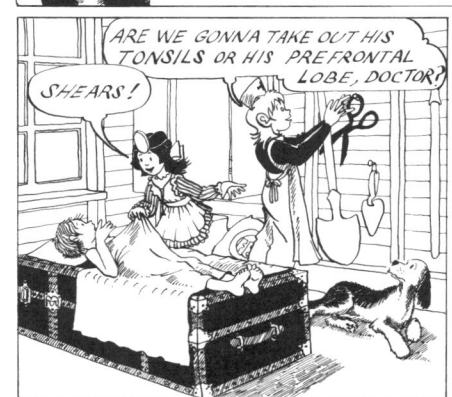

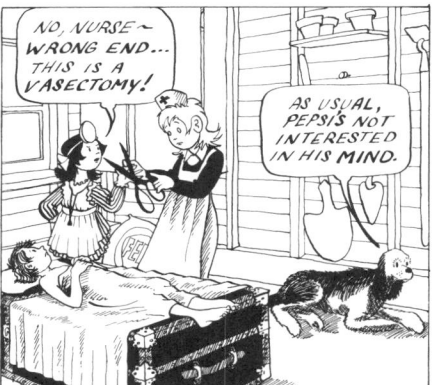

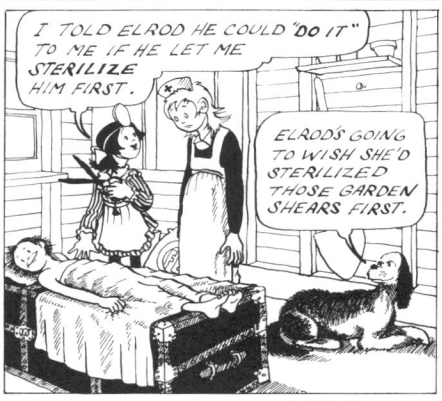

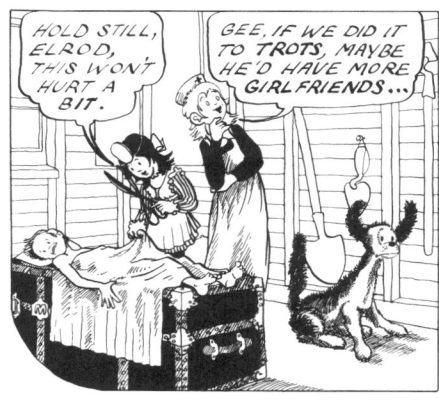

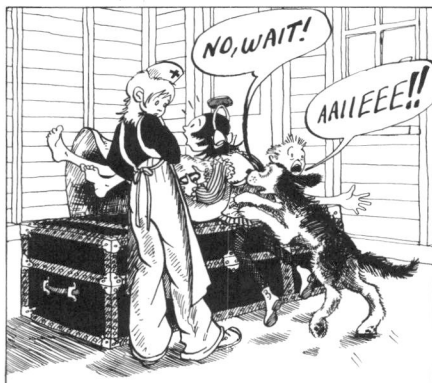

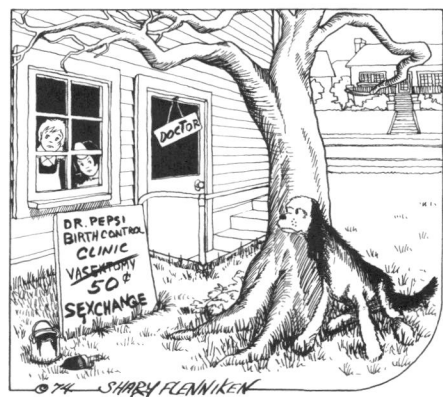

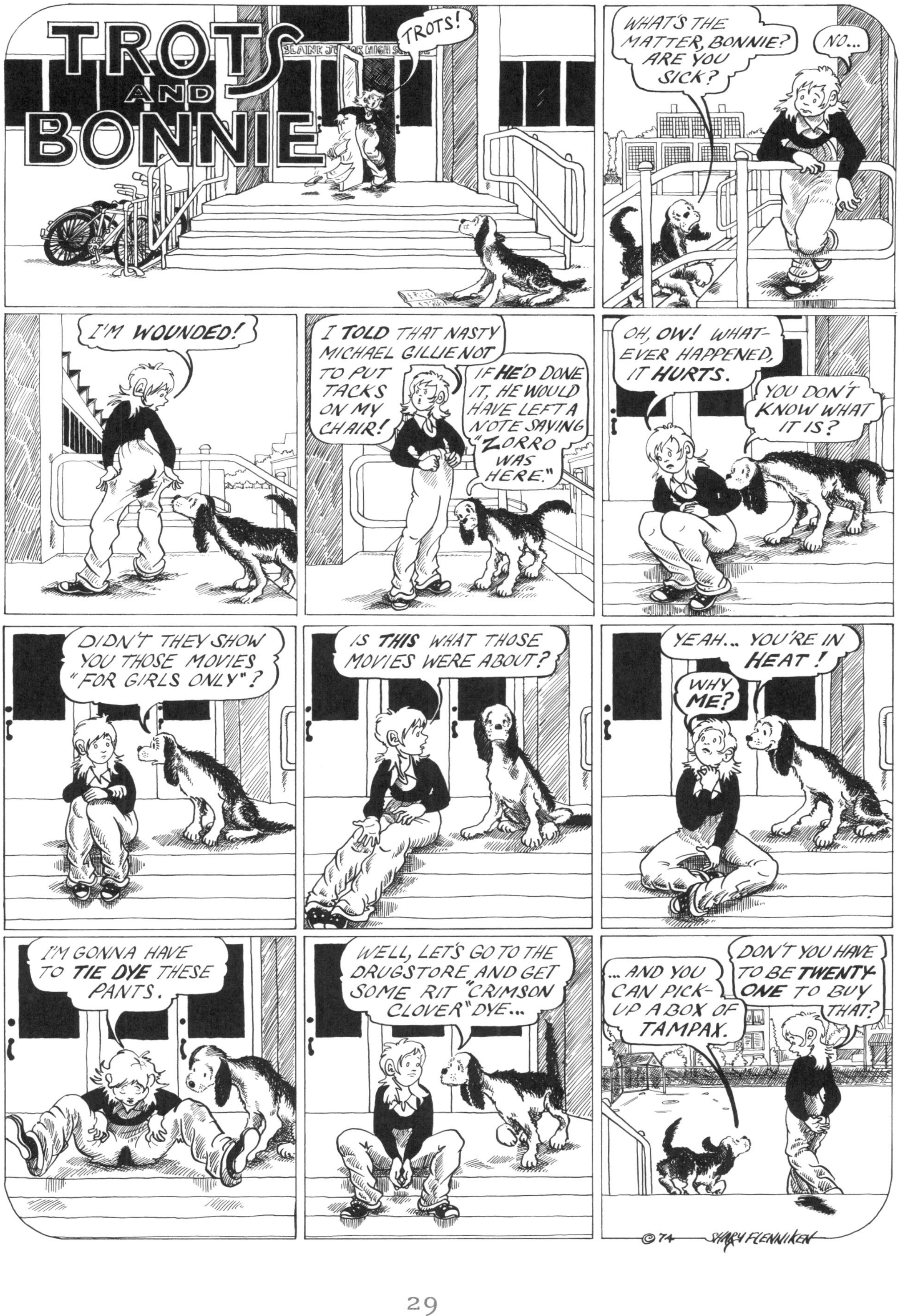
TROTS AND BONNIE
BLAINE JU... HIGH SC...
TROTS!
WHAT'S THE MATTER, BONNIE? ARE YOU SICK?
NO...
I'M WOUNDED!
I TOLD THAT NASTY MICHAEL GILLIE NOT TO PUT TACKS ON MY CHAIR!
IF HE'D DONE IT, HE WOULD HAVE LEFT A NOTE SAYING "ZORRO WAS HERE."
OH, OW! WHAT-EVER HAPPENED, IT HURTS.
YOU DON'T KNOW WHAT IT IS?
DIDN'T THEY SHOW YOU THOSE MOVIES "FOR GIRLS ONLY"?
IS THIS WHAT THOSE MOVIES WERE ABOUT?
YEAH... YOU'RE IN HEAT!
WHY ME?
I'M GONNA HAVE TO TIE DYE THESE PANTS.
WELL, LET'S GO TO THE DRUGSTORE AND GET SOME RIT "CRIMSON CLOVER" DYE...
...AND YOU CAN PICK-UP A BOX OF TAMPAX.
DON'T YOU HAVE TO BE TWENTY-ONE TO BUY THAT?
©74 SHARY FLENNIKEN

TROTS and BONNIE
HOW DOES THIS SOUND, BONNIE? "DEAR MR. AND MS. STELMACK: WE, THE LITTLE LADIES' LIBERATION FRONT, ARE HOLDING ELROD HOSTAGE. WE DEMAND THAT...
... YOU DISTRIBUTE FREE PEANUT BUTTER MOUNTAIN BARS TO THE UNDERPRIVILEGED RESIDENTS OF MAGNOLIA."
I JUST DON'T THINK WE SHOULD GO AROUND KIDNAPPING PEOPLE'S CHILDREN, PEPSI!
WHY NOT? I HATE CHILDREN!
... AND I LOVE PEANUT BUTTER MOUNTAIN BARS. DON'T YOU?
YEAH!
BAM!
WHAT DO YOU THINK MR. AND MS. STELMACK WILL GIVE US FOR HALF OF ELROD?
I'M GOING TO TURN MYSELF IN TO THE DOG POUND.
©74 SHARY FLENNIKEN

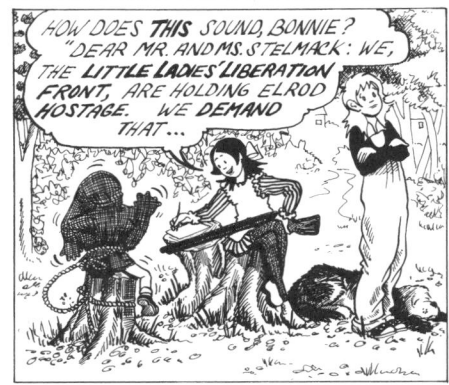

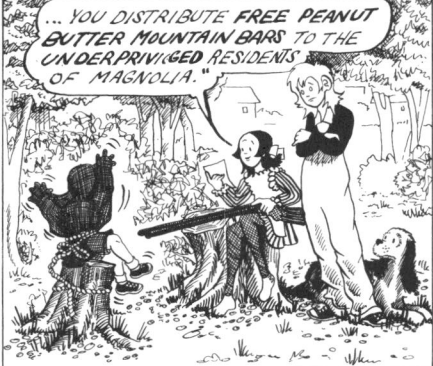

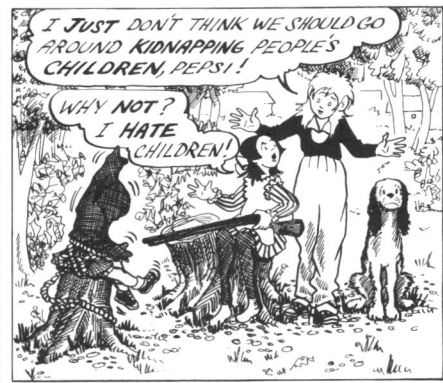

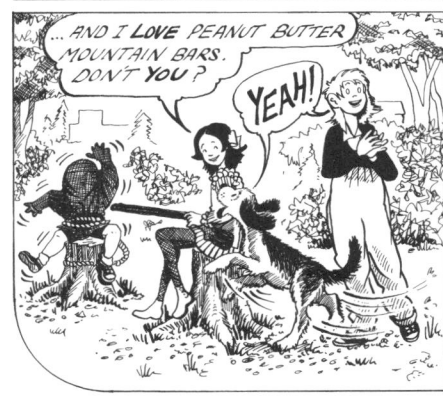

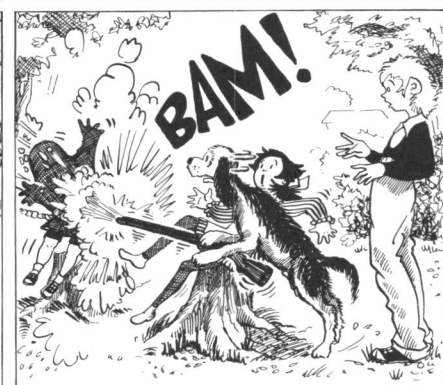

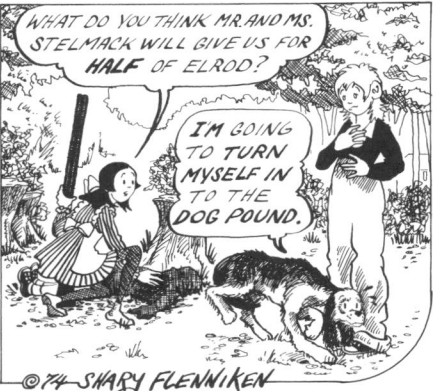

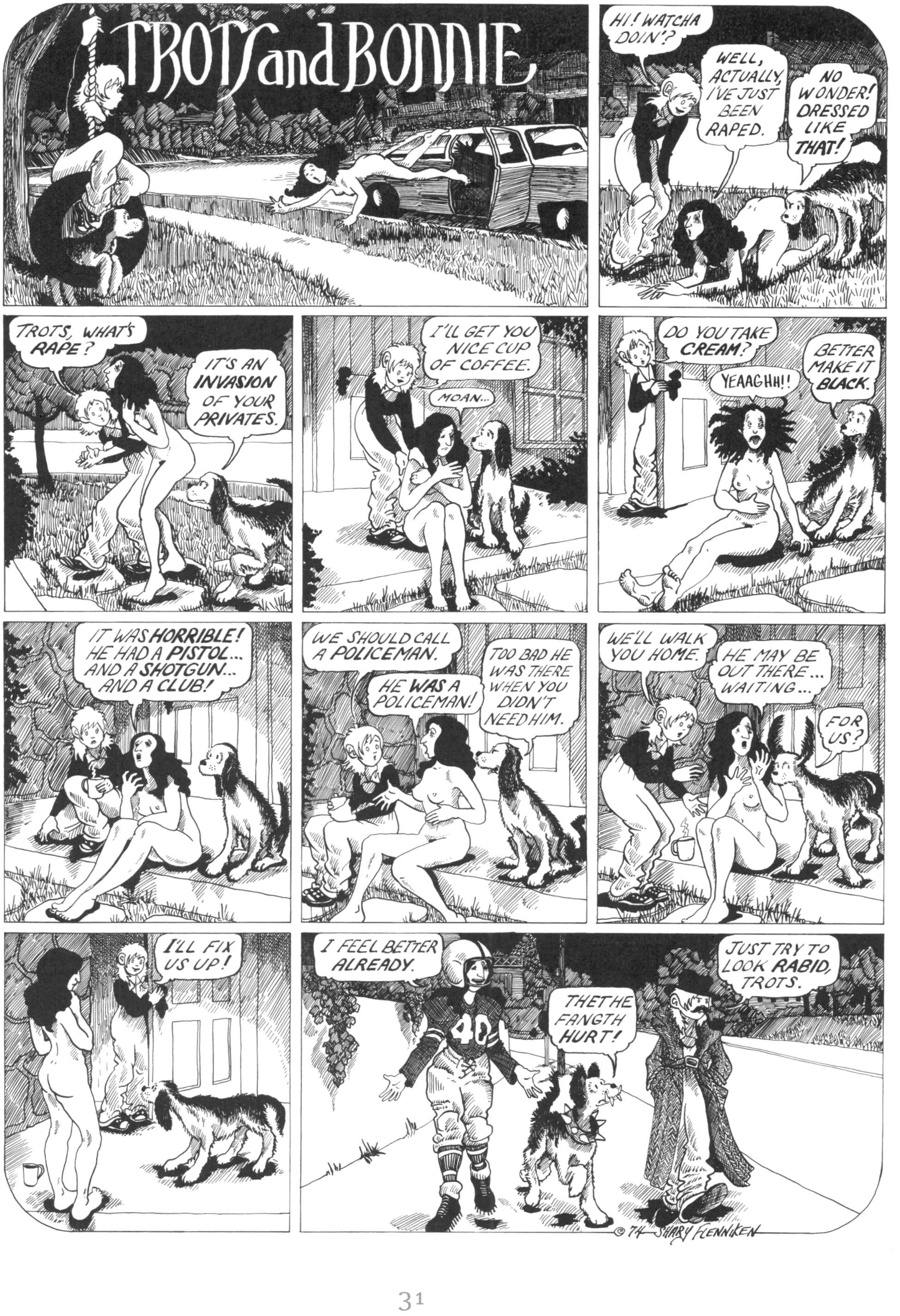
TROTS and BONNIE
HI! WATCHA DOIN'?
WELL, ACTUALLY, I'VE JUST BEEN RAPED.
NO WONDER! DRESSED LIKE THAT!
TROTS, WHAT'S RAPE?
IT'S AN INVASION OF YOUR PRIVATES.
I'LL GET YOU NICE CUP OF COFFEE.
MOAN...
DO YOU TAKE CREAM?
YEAAGHH!!
BETTER MAKE IT BLACK.
IT WAS HORRIBLE! HE HAD A PISTOL... AND A SHOTGUN... AND A CLUB!
WE SHOULD CALL A POLICEMAN.
HE WAS A POLICEMAN!
TOO BAD HE WAS THERE WHEN YOU DIDN'T NEED HIM.
WE'LL WALK YOU HOME.
HE MAY BE OUT THERE ... WAITING ...
FOR US?
I'LL FIX US UP!
I FEEL BETTER ALREADY.
THETHE FANGTH HURT!
JUST TRY TO LOOK RABID, TROTS.
© 74 SHARY FLENNIKEN

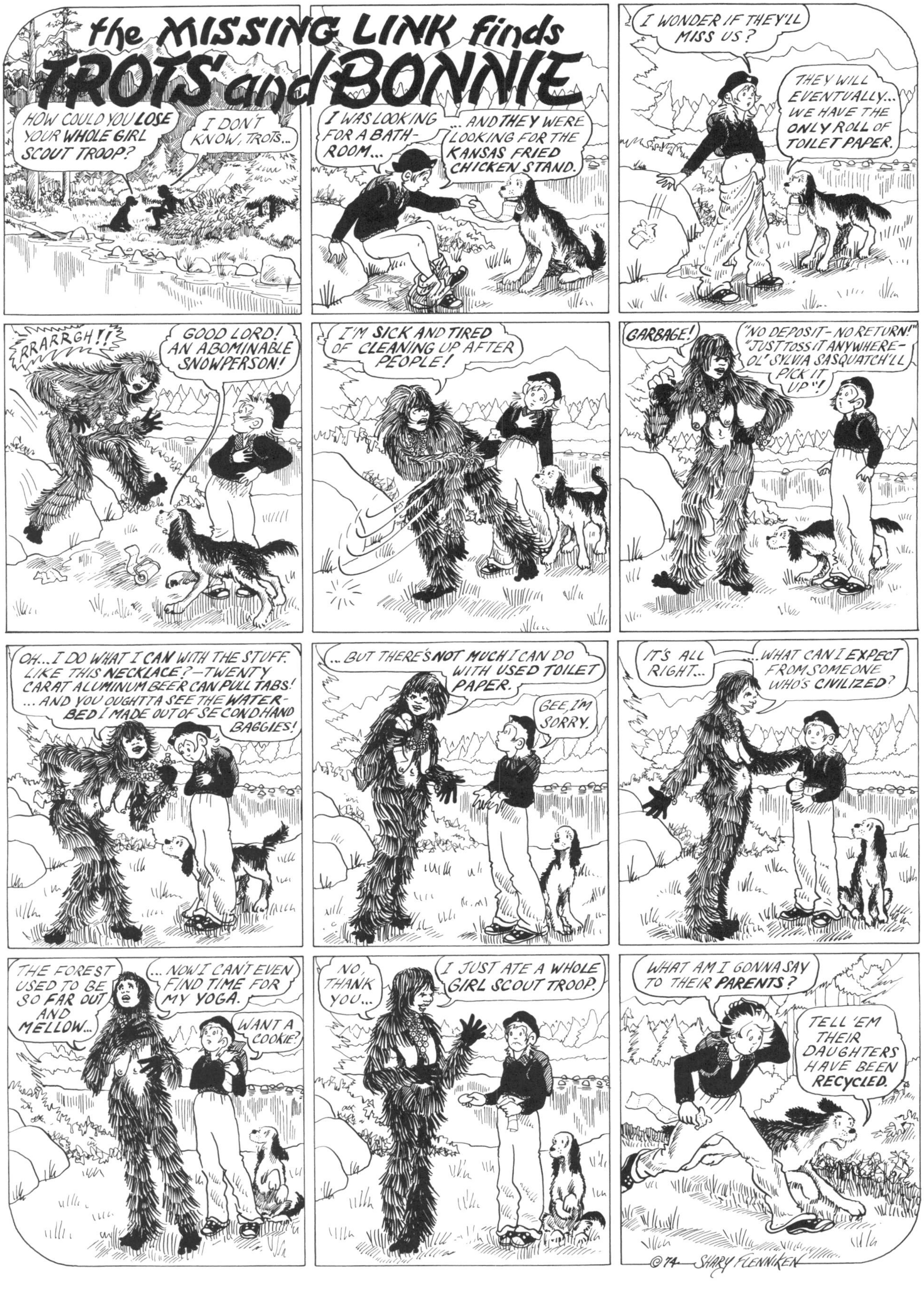

the MISSING LINK finds TROTS and BONNIE
HOW COULD YOU LOSE YOUR WHOLE GIRL SCOUT TROOP?
I DON'T KNOW, TROTS...
I WAS LOOKING FOR A BATH-ROOM...
...AND THEY WERE LOOKING FOR THE KANSAS FRIED CHICKEN STAND.
I WONDER IF THEY'LL MISS US?
THEY WILL EVENTUALLY... WE HAVE THE ONLY ROLL OF TOILET PAPER.
RRARRGH!!
GOOD LORD! AN ABOMINABLE SNOWPERSON!
I'M SICK AND TIRED OF CLEANING UP AFTER PEOPLE!
GARBAGE!
"NO DEPOSIT-NO RETURN!" "JUST TOSS IT ANYWHERE- OL' SYLVIA SASQUATCH'LL PICK IT UP"!
OH... I DO WHAT I CAN WITH THE STUFF. LIKE THIS NECKLACE?—TWENTY CARAT ALUMINUM BEER CAN PULL TABS! ...AND YOU OUGHTTA SEE THE WATER-BED I MADE OUT OF SECONDHAND BAGGIES!
...BUT THERE'S NOT MUCH I CAN DO WITH USED TOILET PAPER.
GEE, I'M SORRY.
IT'S ALL RIGHT...
...WHAT CAN I EXPECT FROM SOMEONE WHO'S CIVILIZED?
THE FOREST USED TO BE SO FAR OUT AND MELLOW...
...NOW I CAN'T EVEN FIND TIME FOR MY YOGA.
WANT A COOKIE?
NO, THANK YOU...
I JUST ATE A WHOLE GIRL SCOUT TROOP.
WHAT AM I GONNA SAY TO THEIR PARENTS?
TELL 'EM THEIR DAUGHTERS HAVE BEEN RECYCLED.
©'74 SHARY FLENNIKEN

Trots and Bonnie
HO HO HO
MERRY CHRISTMAS!
glory is hallelujah
Season's Greetings
HOW DO YOU LIKE IT, PEPSI?
IT'S ALL RIGHT, I GUESS...
...IF YOU'RE INTO CHRISTMAS.
PERSONALLY, I PREFER A SIMPLE MENORAH.
HO HO HO
BUT WHAT CAN SHE DO WITH A STOCKING FULL OF MATZOH BALLS?
©74 SHARY FLENNIKEN

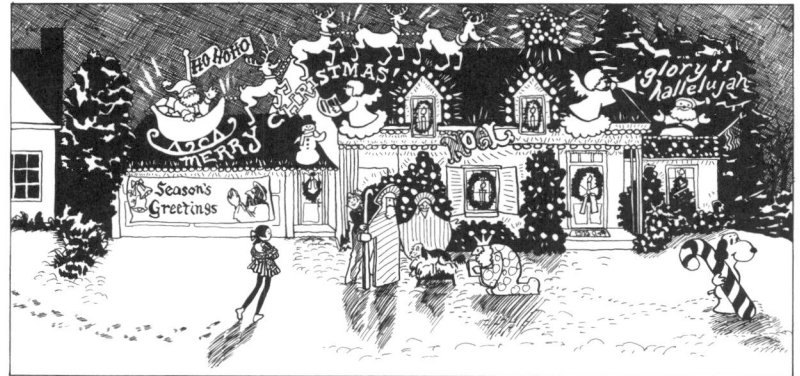

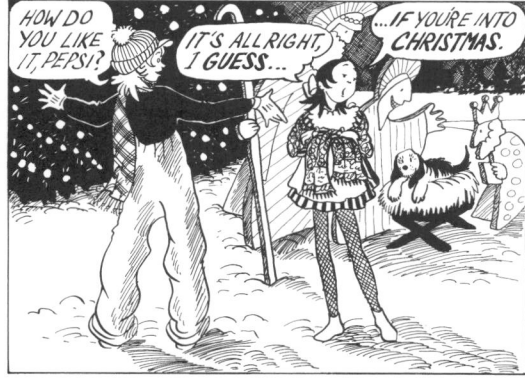

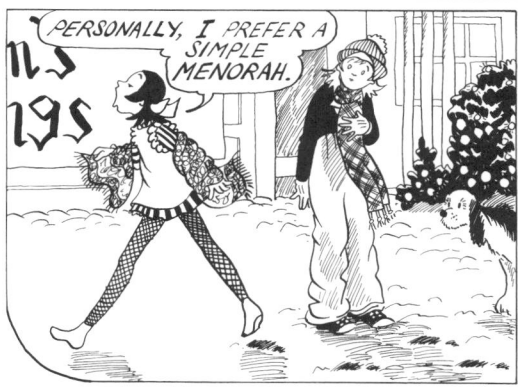

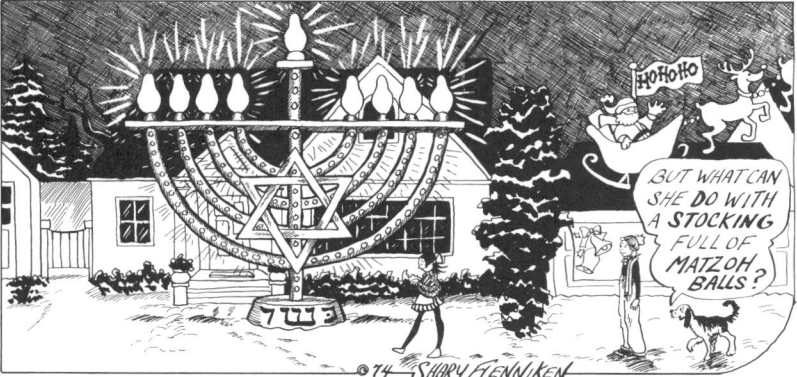

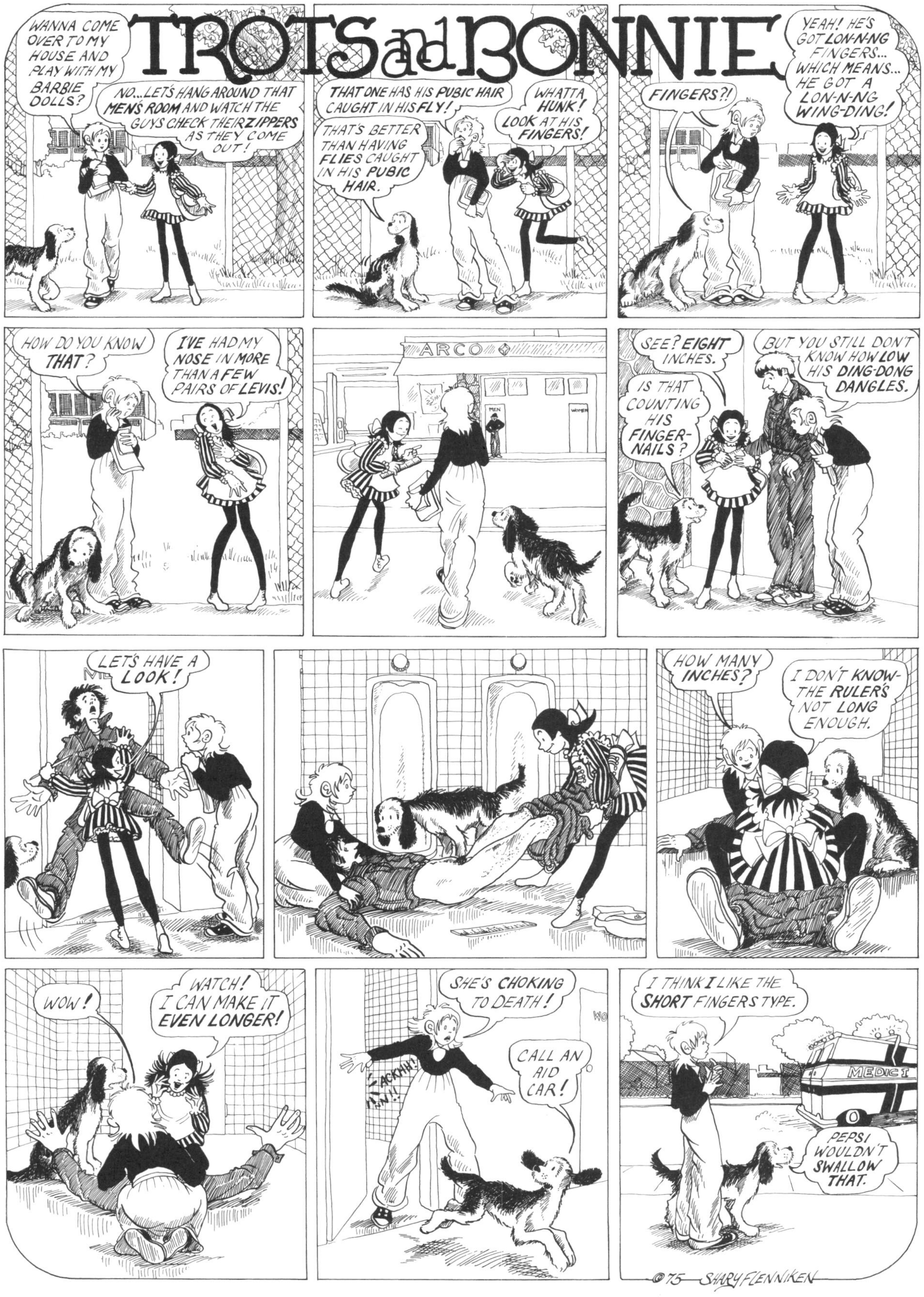
TROTS and BONNIE
WANNA COME OVER TO MY HOUSE AND PLAY WITH MY BARBIE DOLLS?
NO...LET'S HANG AROUND THAT MEN'S ROOM AND WATCH THE GUYS CHECK THEIR ZIPPERS AS THEY COME OUT!
THAT ONE HAS HIS PUBIC HAIR CAUGHT IN HIS FLY!
WHATTA HUNK! LOOK AT HIS FINGERS!
THAT'S BETTER THAN HAVING FLIES CAUGHT IN HIS PUBIC HAIR.
FINGERS?!
YEAH! HE'S GOT LON-N-NG FINGERS... WHICH MEANS... HE GOT A LON-N-NG WING-DING!
HOW DO YOU KNOW THAT?
I'VE HAD MY NOSE IN MORE THAN A FEW PAIRS OF LEVIS!
ARCO
MEN
WOMEN
SEE? EIGHT INCHES.
IS THAT COUNTING HIS FINGER-NAILS?
BUT YOU STILL DON'T KNOW HOW LOW HIS DING-DONG DANGLES.
LET'S HAVE A LOOK!
HOW MANY INCHES?
I DON'T KNOW- THE RULER'S NOT LONG ENOUGH.
WOW!
WATCH! I CAN MAKE IT EVEN LONGER!
SHE'S CHOKING TO DEATH!
CALL AN AID CAR!
I THINK I LIKE THE SHORT FINGERS TYPE.
MEDIC I
PEPSI WOULDN'T SWALLOW THAT.
©75 SHARY FLENNIKEN

TROTS AND BONNIE
BARK! BARK! I'M DOUG DOG!... THE IDEAL CANINE ALTERNATIVE! I'M THE PERFECT PET FOR CITY DWELLERS! THROW AWAY THAT MESSY POOPER SCOOPER!...
...I'M CLEAN AND ECONOMICAL! YOU WON'T FIND FLEAS OR OTHER NASTY PARASITES ON ME! NO DISGUSTING DROOL! NO DOGGIE ODOR!
I DO TRICKS! WATCH ME SIT UP AND BEG!
I CAN ROLL OVER AND PLAY DEAD!
HOW CUTE!
ZZZZIT!
I HATE HUMANS!
©75 SHARY FLENNIKEN

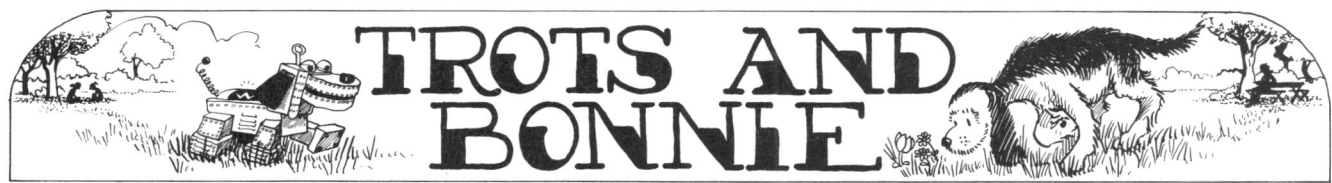

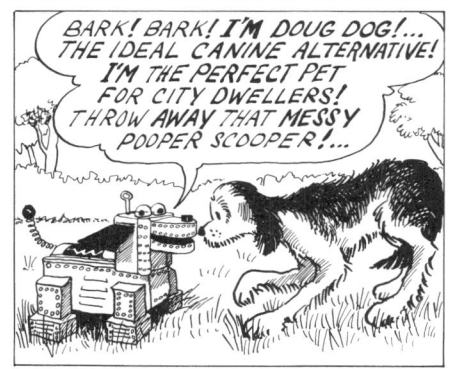

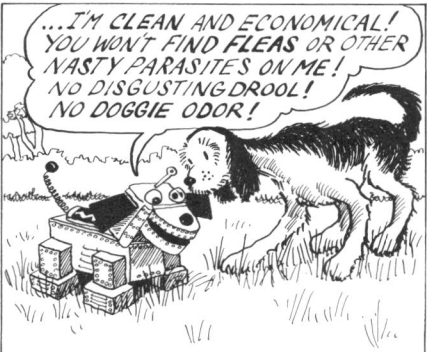

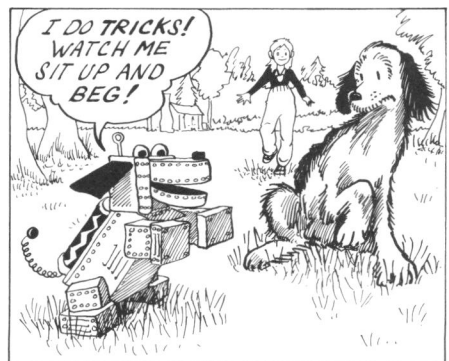

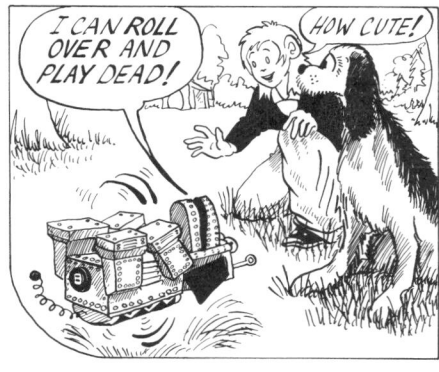

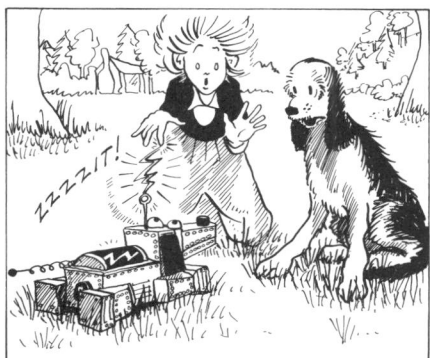

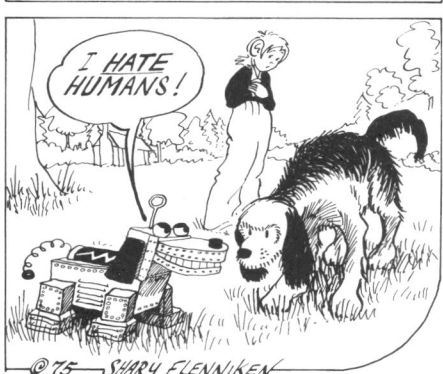

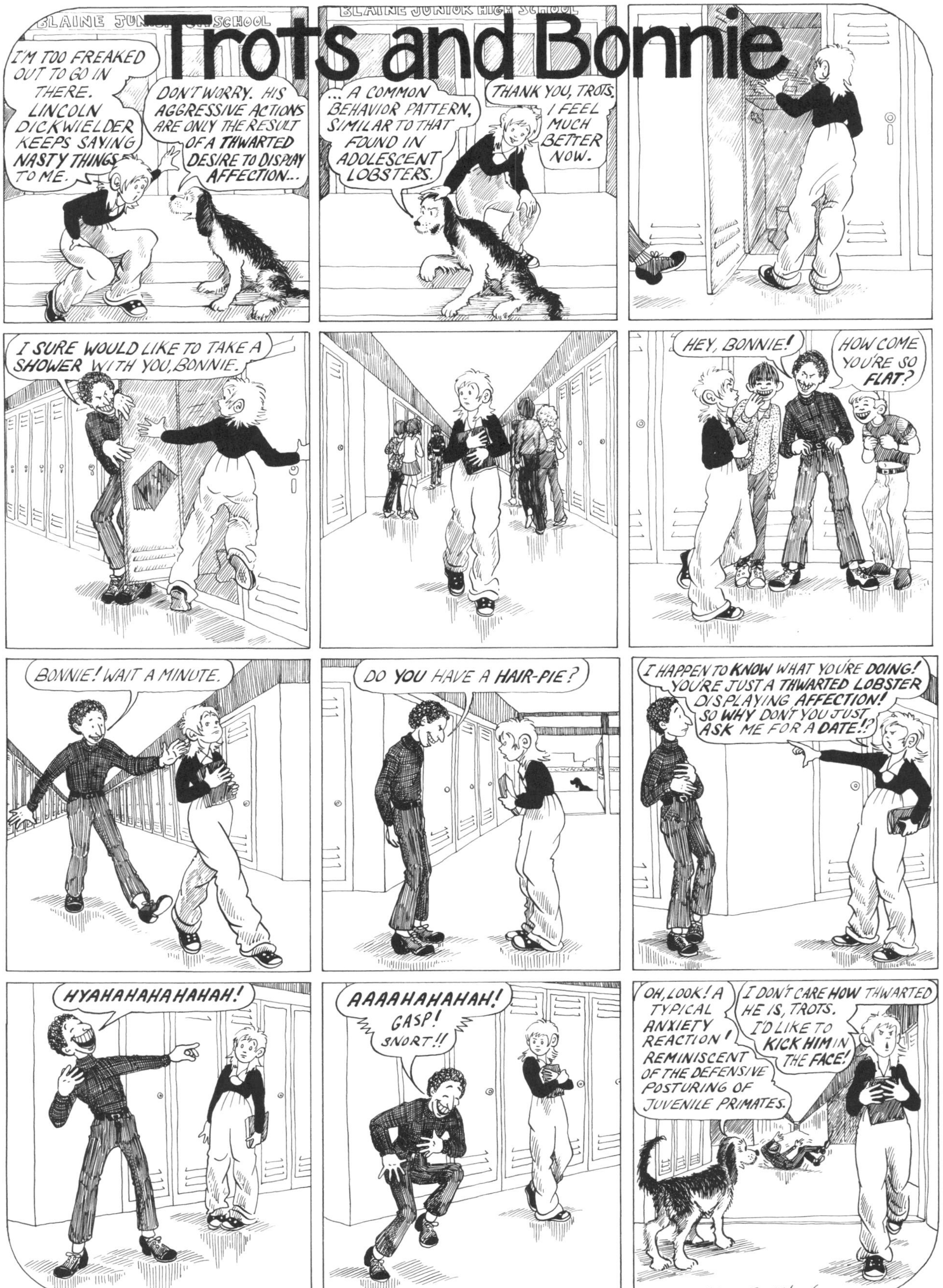
Trots and Bonnie
BLAINE JUNIOR HIGH SCHOOL
I'M TOO FREAKED OUT TO GO IN THERE. LINCOLN DICKWIELDER KEEPS SAYING NASTY THINGS TO ME.
DON'T WORRY. HIS AGGRESSIVE ACTIONS ARE ONLY THE RESULT OF A THWARTED DESIRE TO DISPLAY AFFECTION...
... A COMMON BEHAVIOR PATTERN, SIMILAR TO THAT FOUND IN ADOLESCENT LOBSTERS.
THANK YOU, TROTS. I FEEL MUCH BETTER NOW.
I SURE WOULD LIKE TO TAKE A SHOWER WITH YOU, BONNIE.
HEY, BONNIE!
HOW COME YOU'RE SO FLAT?
BONNIE! WAIT A MINUTE.
DO YOU HAVE A HAIR-PIE?
I HAPPEN TO KNOW WHAT YOU'RE DOING! YOU'RE JUST A THWARTED LOBSTER DISPLAYING AFFECTION! SO WHY DON'T YOU JUST ASK ME FOR A DATE!?
HYAHAHAHAHAHAH!
AAAAHAHAHAH! GASP! SNORT!!
OH, LOOK! A TYPICAL ANXIETY REACTION! REMINISCENT OF THE DEFENSIVE POSTURING OF JUVENILE PRIMATES.
I DON'T CARE HOW THWARTED HE IS, TROTS. I'D LIKE TO KICK HIM IN THE FACE!
©75 SHARY FLENNIKEN

TROTS AND BONNIE
IT'S A NICE YACHT, BUT IT STILL NEEDS SOMETHING.
FORWARD FULL RUDDER!
OIL SLICK OFF THE PORT BOW!
DING DING! WHOOP! WHOOP!
HEY! OUR TIMBERS ARE SHIVERING!
WE'RE EN-GULFED IN THE OILSLICK AND SINKING FAST!
ABANDON YACHT!
WOMEN AND DOGS FIRST!
AHOY! ELROD! WHERE ARE YOU?
YOU'RE STANDING ON HIS HEAD.
©1975—SHARY FLENNIKEN

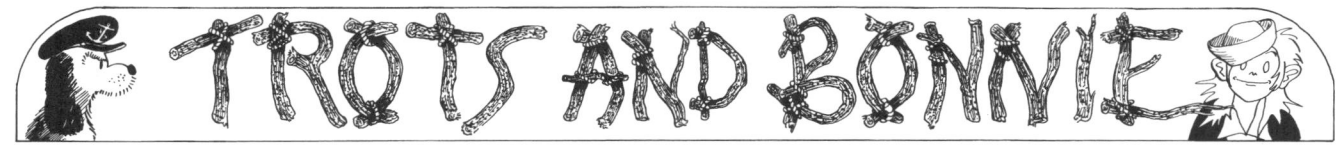

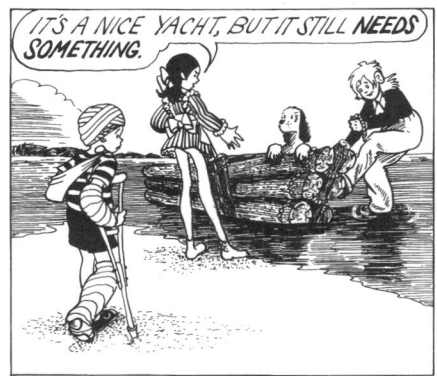

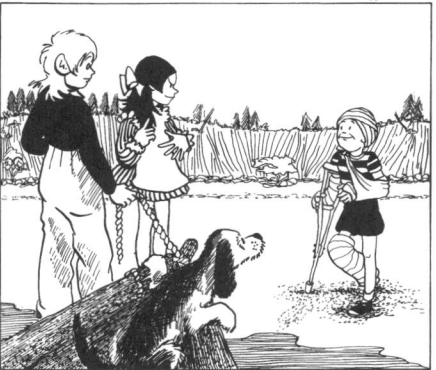

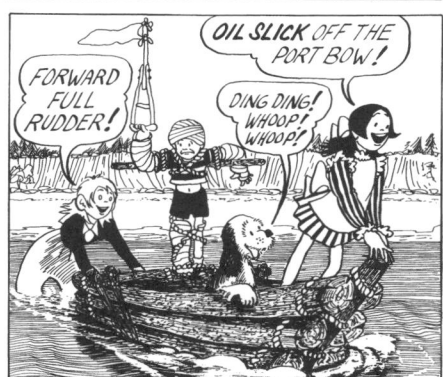

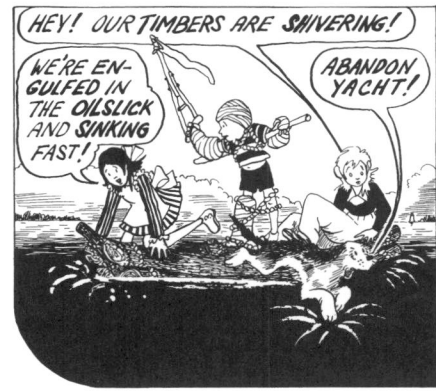

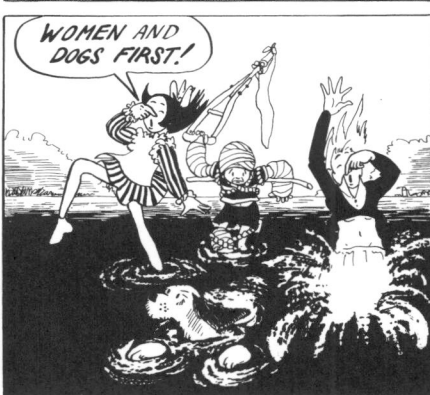

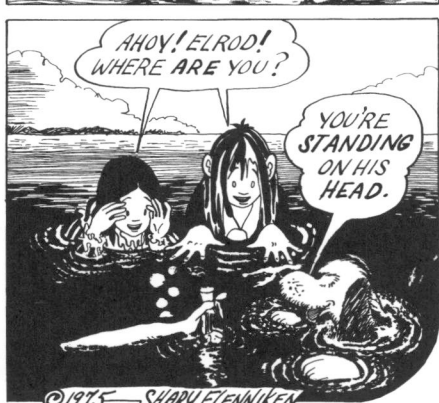

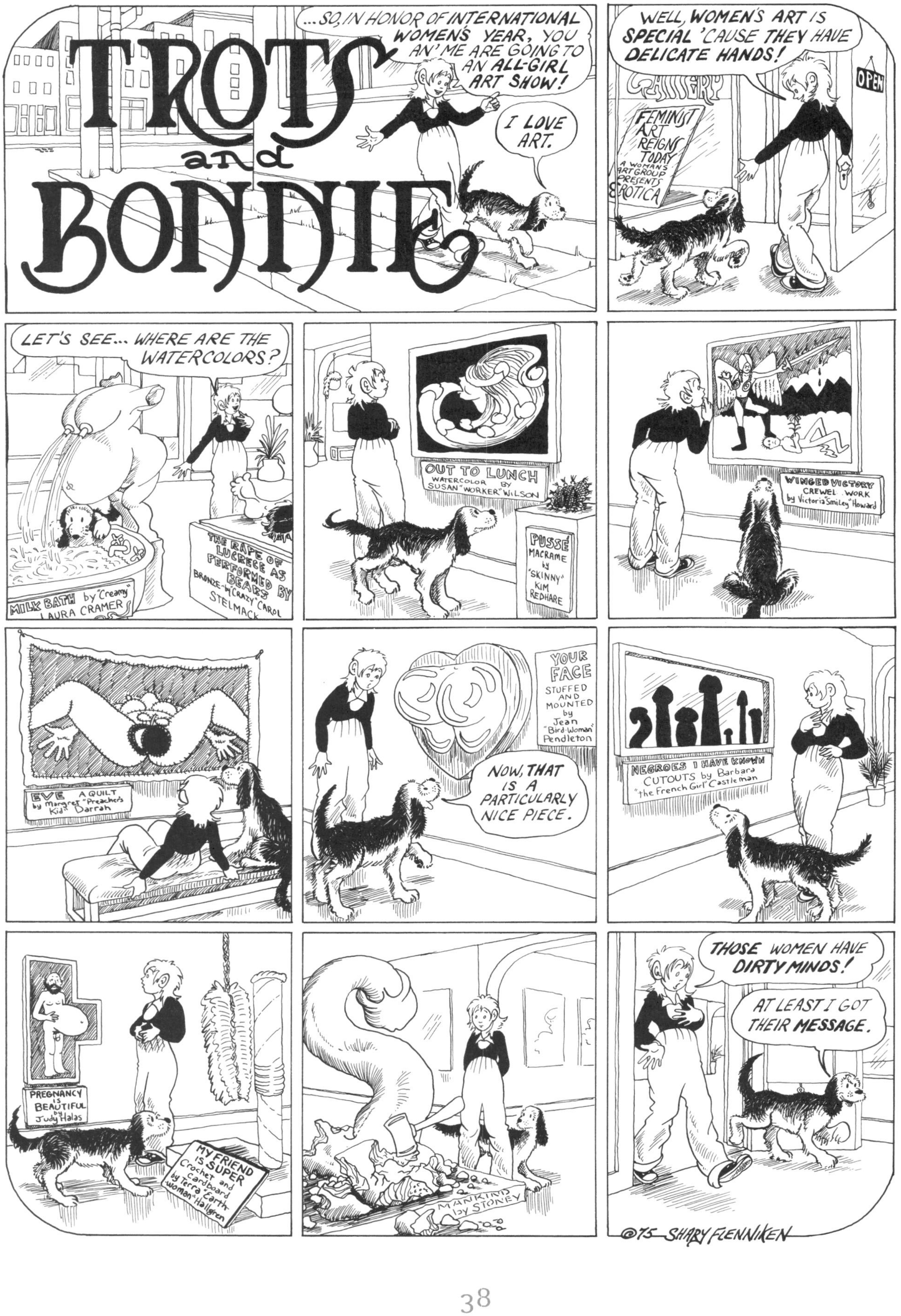
TROTS and BONNIE
...SO, IN HONOR OF INTERNATIONAL WOMEN'S YEAR, YOU AN' ME ARE GOING TO AN ALL-GIRL ART SHOW!
I LOVE ART.
WELL, WOMEN'S ART IS SPECIAL 'CAUSE THEY HAVE DELICATE HANDS!
GALLERY
OPEN
FEMINIST ART REIGNS TODAY A WOMAN'S ART GROUP PRESENTS EROTICA
LET'S SEE... WHERE ARE THE WATERCOLORS?
MILK BATH by "Creamy" LAURA CRAMER
THE RAPE OF LUCRECE AS PERFORMED BY BEARS BRONZE-by "CRAZY" CAROL STELMACK
OUT TO LUNCH WATERCOLOR BY SUSAN "WORKER" WILSON
PUSSÉ MACRAME by "SKINNY" KIM REDHARE
WINGED VICTORY CREWEL WORK by Victoria "Smiley" Howard
EVE A QUILT by Margret "Preacher's Kid" Darrah
YOUR FACE STUFFED AND MOUNTED by Jean "Bird-Woman" Pendleton
NOW, THAT IS A PARTICULARLY NICE PIECE.
NEGROES I HAVE KNOWN CUTOUTS by Barbara "the French Girl" Castleman
PREGNANCY IS BEAUTIFUL by Judy Halas
MY FRIEND IS SUPER Crochet and cardboard by Terra "Earth-woman" Hallgren
MANKIND by STONEY
THOSE WOMEN HAVE DIRTY MINDS!
AT LEAST I GOT THEIR MESSAGE.
©75 SHARY FLENNIKEN

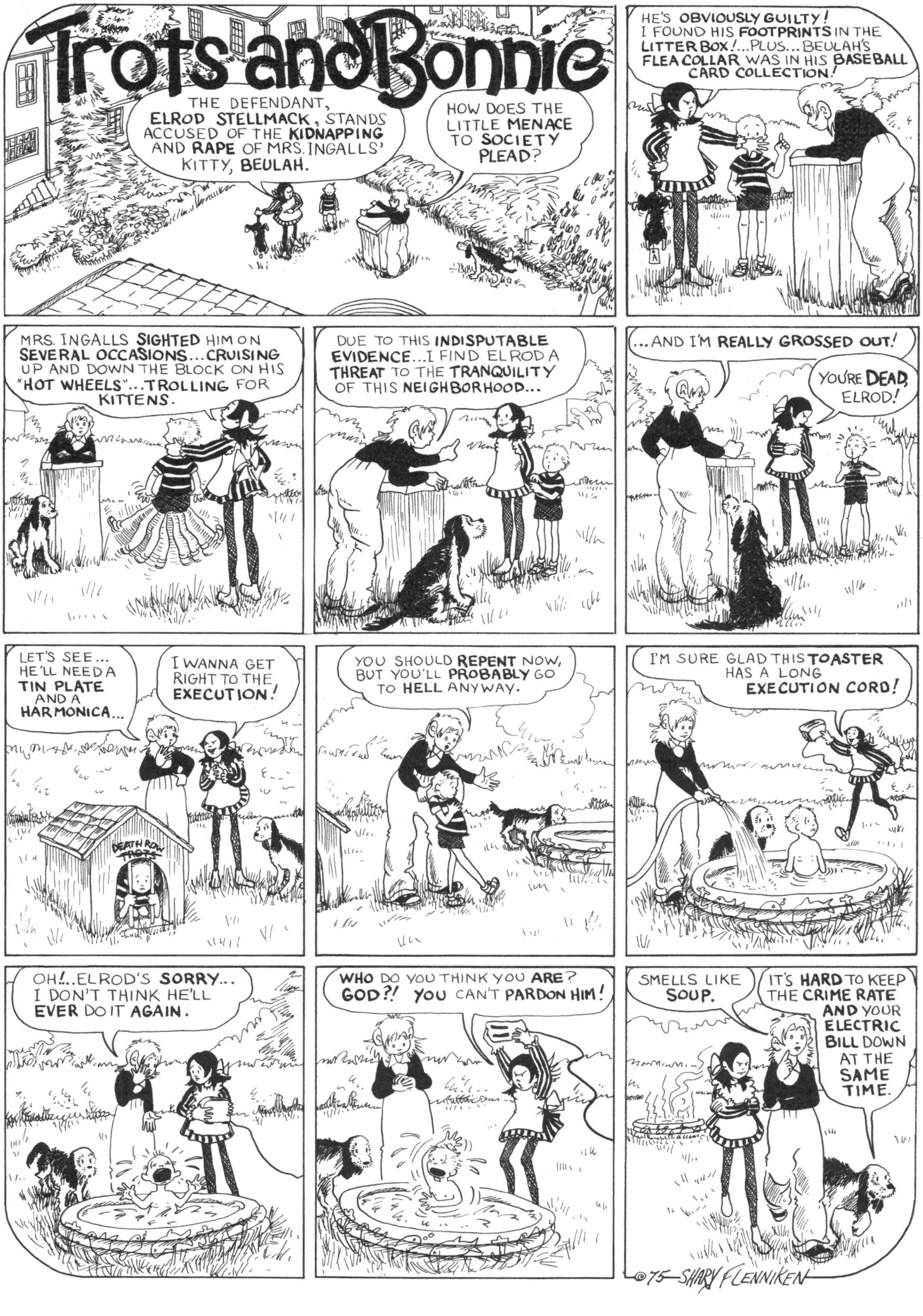
Trots and Bonnie
THE DEFENDANT, ELROD STELLMACK, STANDS ACCUSED OF THE KIDNAPPING AND RAPE OF MRS. INGALLS' KITTY, BEULAH.
HOW DOES THE LITTLE MENACE TO SOCIETY PLEAD?
HE'S OBVIOUSLY GUILTY! I FOUND HIS FOOTPRINTS IN THE LITTER BOX!...PLUS... BEULAH'S FLEA COLLAR WAS IN HIS BASEBALL CARD COLLECTION!
MRS. INGALLS SIGHTED HIM ON SEVERAL OCCASIONS...CRUISING UP AND DOWN THE BLOCK ON HIS "HOT WHEELS"...TROLLING FOR KITTENS.
DUE TO THIS INDISPUTABLE EVIDENCE...I FIND ELROD A THREAT TO THE TRANQUILITY OF THIS NEIGHBORHOOD...
...AND I'M REALLY GROSSED OUT!
YOU'RE DEAD, ELROD!
LET'S SEE... HE'LL NEED A TIN PLATE AND A HARMONICA...
I WANNA GET RIGHT TO THE EXECUTION!
DEATH ROW TROTS
YOU SHOULD REPENT NOW, BUT YOU'LL PROBABLY GO TO HELL ANYWAY.
I'M SURE GLAD THIS TOASTER HAS A LONG EXECUTION CORD!
OH!...ELROD'S SORRY... I DON'T THINK HE'LL EVER DO IT AGAIN.
WHO DO YOU THINK YOU ARE? GOD?! YOU CAN'T PARDON HIM!
SMELLS LIKE SOUP.
IT'S HARD TO KEEP THE CRIME RATE AND YOUR ELECTRIC BILL DOWN AT THE SAME TIME.
©75—SHARY FLENNIKEN

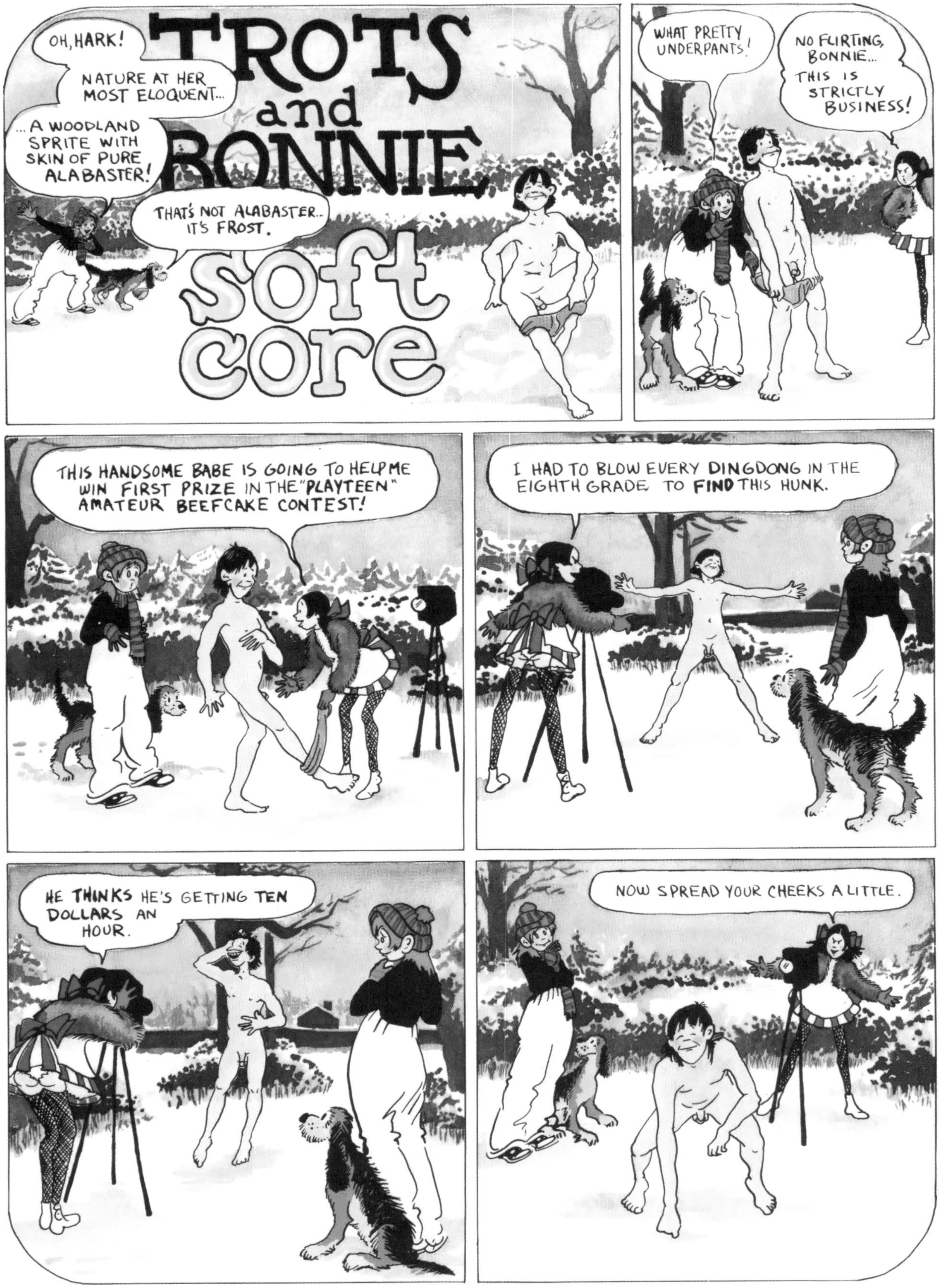
OH, HARK!
NATURE AT HER MOST ELOQUENT...
...A WOODLAND SPRITE WITH SKIN OF PURE ALABASTER!
TROTS and BONNIE
soft core
THAT'S NOT ALABASTER... IT'S FROST.
WHAT PRETTY UNDERPANTS!
NO FLIRTING, BONNIE... THIS IS STRICTLY BUSINESS!
THIS HANDSOME BABE IS GOING TO HELP ME WIN FIRST PRIZE IN THE "PLAYTEEN" AMATEUR BEEFCAKE CONTEST!
I HAD TO BLOW EVERY DINGDONG IN THE EIGHTH GRADE TO FIND THIS HUNK.
HE THINKS HE'S GETTING TEN DOLLARS AN HOUR.
NOW SPREAD YOUR CHEEKS A LITTLE.

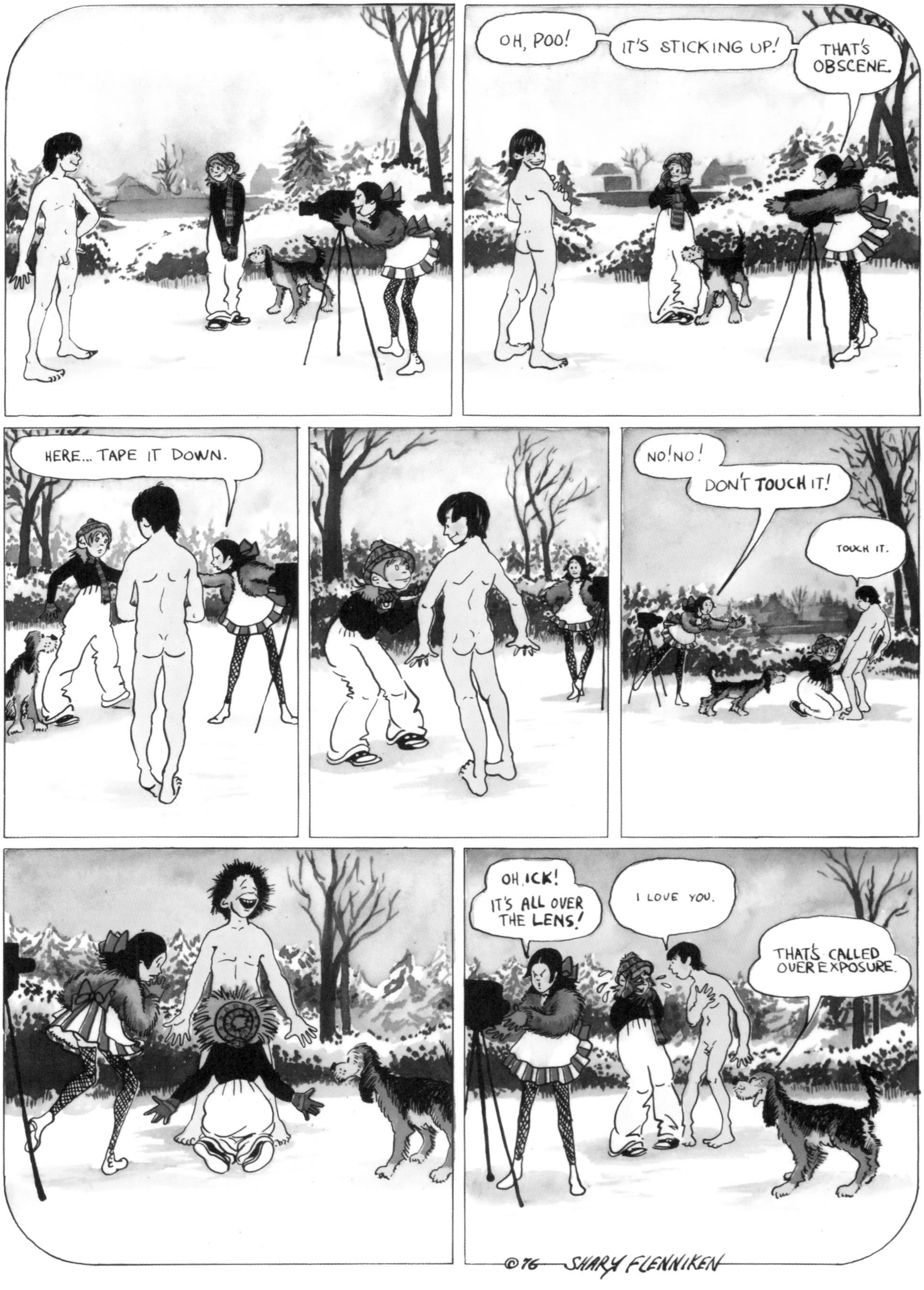
OH, POO!
IT'S STICKING UP!
THAT'S OBSCENE.
HERE... TAPE IT DOWN.
NO! NO!
DON'T TOUCH IT!
TOUCH IT.
OH, ICK! IT'S ALL OVER THE LENS!
I LOVE YOU.
THAT'S CALLED OVEREXPOSURE.
©76 SHARY FLENNIKEN

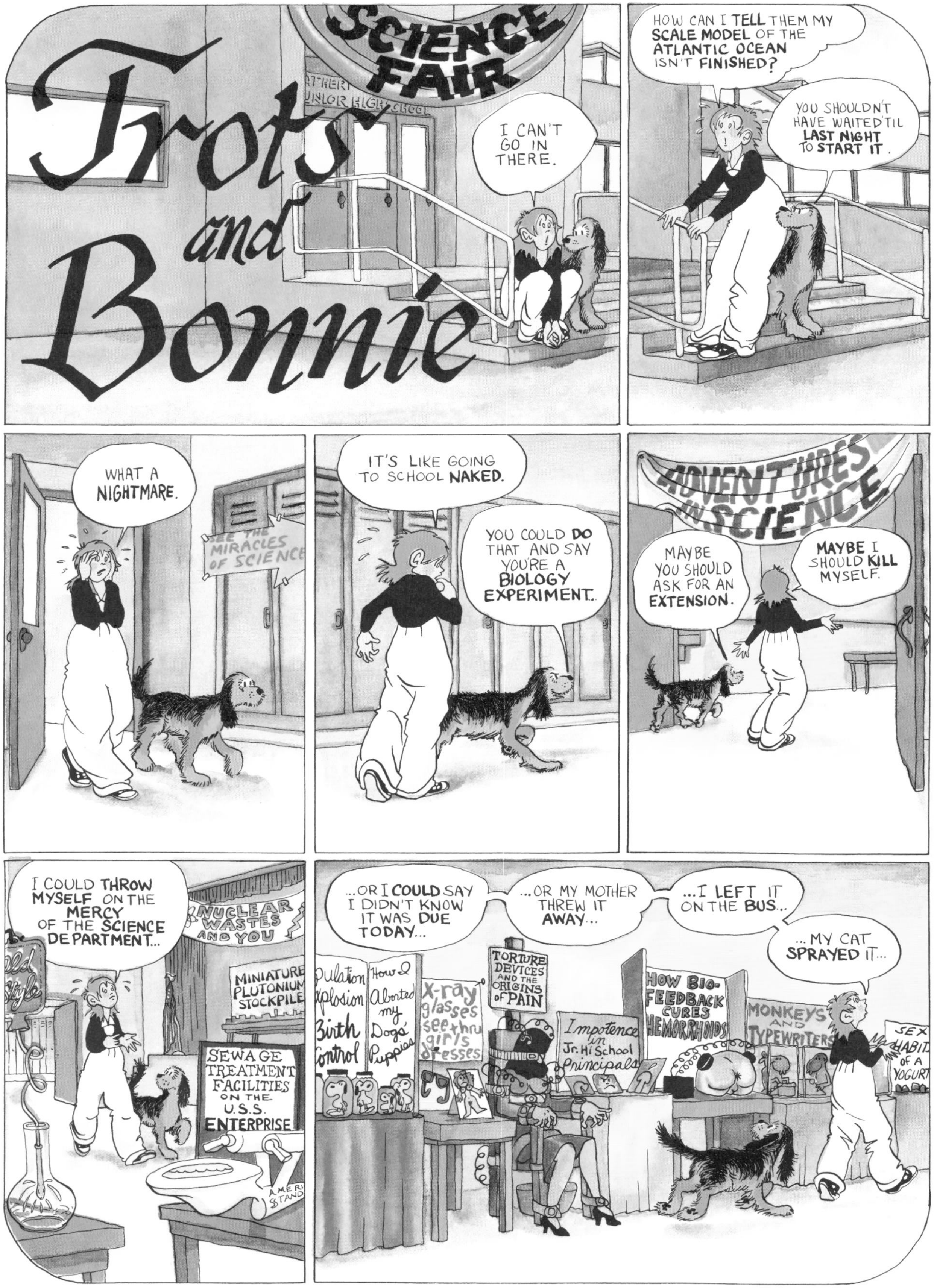

Trots and Bonnie
SCIENCE FAIR
I CAN'T GO IN THERE.
HOW CAN I TELL THEM MY SCALE MODEL OF THE ATLANTIC OCEAN ISN'T FINISHED?
YOU SHOULDN'T HAVE WAITED 'TIL LAST NIGHT TO START IT.
WHAT A NIGHTMARE.
SEE THE MIRACLES OF SCIENCE
IT'S LIKE GOING TO SCHOOL NAKED.
YOU COULD DO THAT AND SAY YOU'RE A BIOLOGY EXPERIMENT...
ADVENTURES IN SCIENCE
MAYBE YOU SHOULD ASK FOR AN EXTENSION.
MAYBE I SHOULD KILL MYSELF.
I COULD THROW MYSELF ON THE MERCY OF THE SCIENCE DEPARTMENT...
NUCLEAR WASTES AND YOU
MINIATURE PLUTONIUM STOCKPILE
SEWAGE TREATMENT FACILITIES ON THE U.S.S. ENTERPRISE
...OR I COULD SAY I DIDN'T KNOW IT WAS DUE TODAY...
...OR MY MOTHER THREW IT AWAY...
...I LEFT IT ON THE BUS...
...MY CAT SPRAYED IT...
Birth Control
How I Aborted my Dog's Puppies
X-ray glasses see-thru girls dresses
TORTURE DEVICES AND THE ORIGINS OF PAIN
Impotence in Jr. Hi School Principals
HOW BIO-FEEDBACK CURES HEMORRHOIDS
MONKEYS AND TYPEWRITERS

BONNIE!
WHY SO GLUM?
DON'T YOU LIKE FAIRS?
my Big Sister's Diary
MINERAL SALTS OF THE BODY AS TRIGGERS OF DEVASTATING EARTHQUAKES
WHITE SUGAR FRIEND? OR FIEND?
Coca Cola AND Tooth
I DIDN'T FINISH MY PROJECT.
results of frustration of the LIBIDO of GUINEA PIGS
THALIDOMIDE KITTENS
OH!
EVERYBODY KNOWS THAT!
THEY ANNOUNCED IT OVER THE LOUDSPEAKER THIS MORNING!
recycling nitrous oxide
DOCTOR SPOCK? OR DOCTOR MALTHUS?
PROSTATE CANCER IN SPERM WHALES
I'VE GOT TO FIND MR. BUNSEN AND BEG HIM NOT TO FLUNK ME.
DOPE PARAPHENALIA
TERRORISM AND HERBAL TEAS
common Bacteria in your water SUPPLY
BLINDNESS CAN BE FUN!
GLASSES
DOG
CANE
CUP
HE'S WITH THE REST OF THE SCIENCE TEACHERS...
... AT MY EXHIBIT!
BRYCE ANDERSON a fetus at 14 years
POLLUTION and how we Deal with our DEVIATES
my Scabs
SEE YOURSELF CLOSED CIRCUIT T.V.
MEN
WOMEN
PEPSI'S ALCOHOL TOLERANCE TESTING CENTER
MR. BUNSEN'S THE ONE WITH THE WHITE SOCKS.
FIRST, YOU DRINK THIS... THEN SEE IF YOU CAN MAKE IT TO THE DOOR.
I DIDN'T DO MY SCIENCE FAIR PROJECT 'CAUSE I HATE SCIENCE!
THASS WHY!
BECAUSH SCIENCE ISH CA-CA.
© 76 SHARY FLENNIKEN

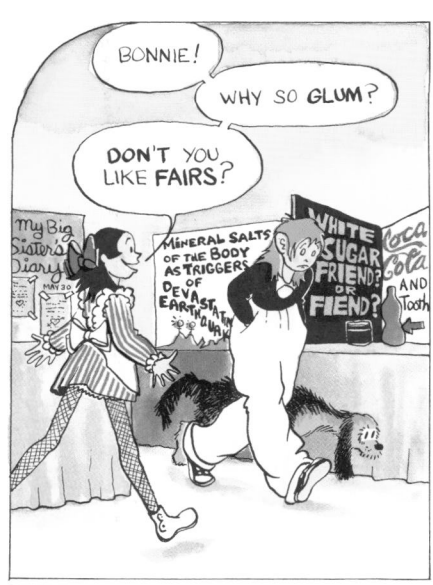

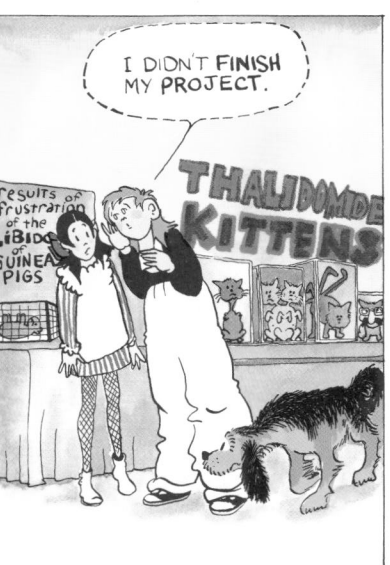

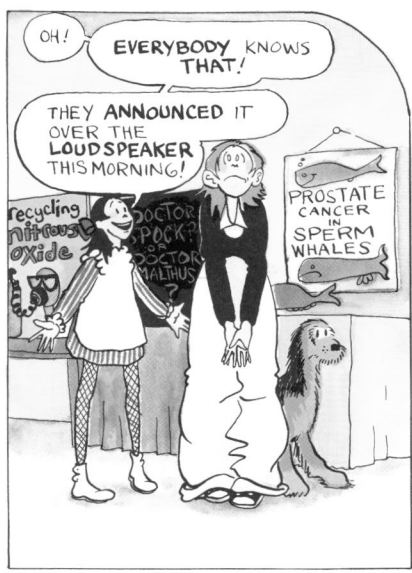

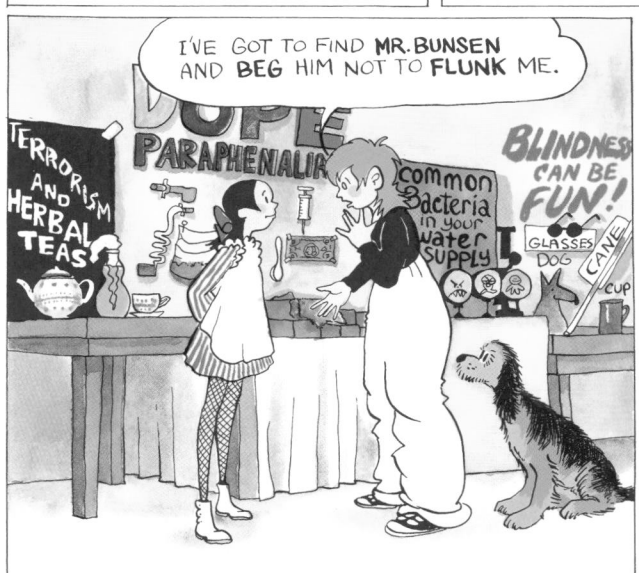

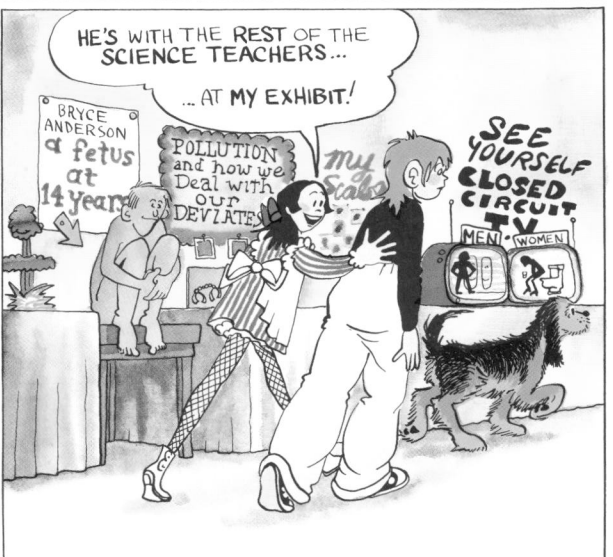

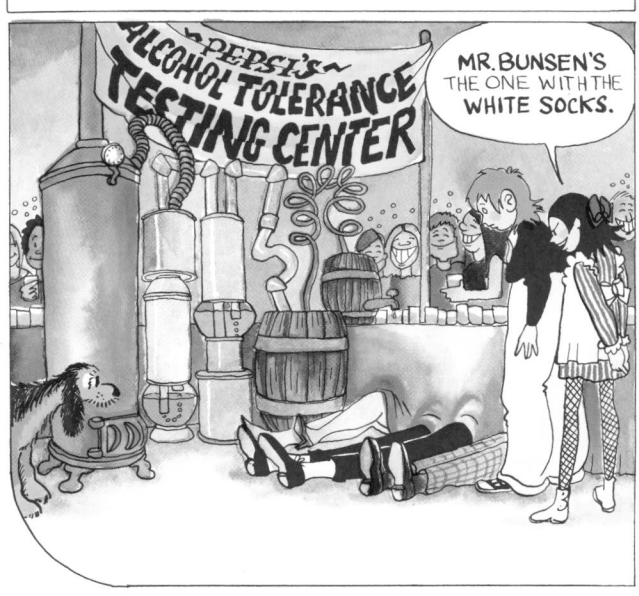

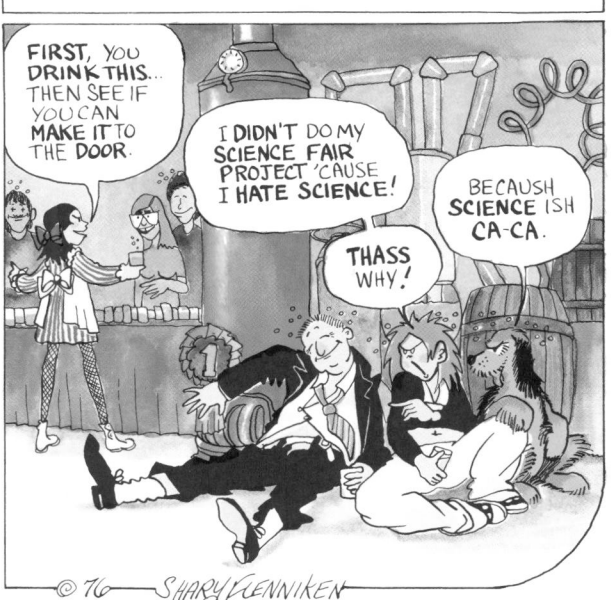

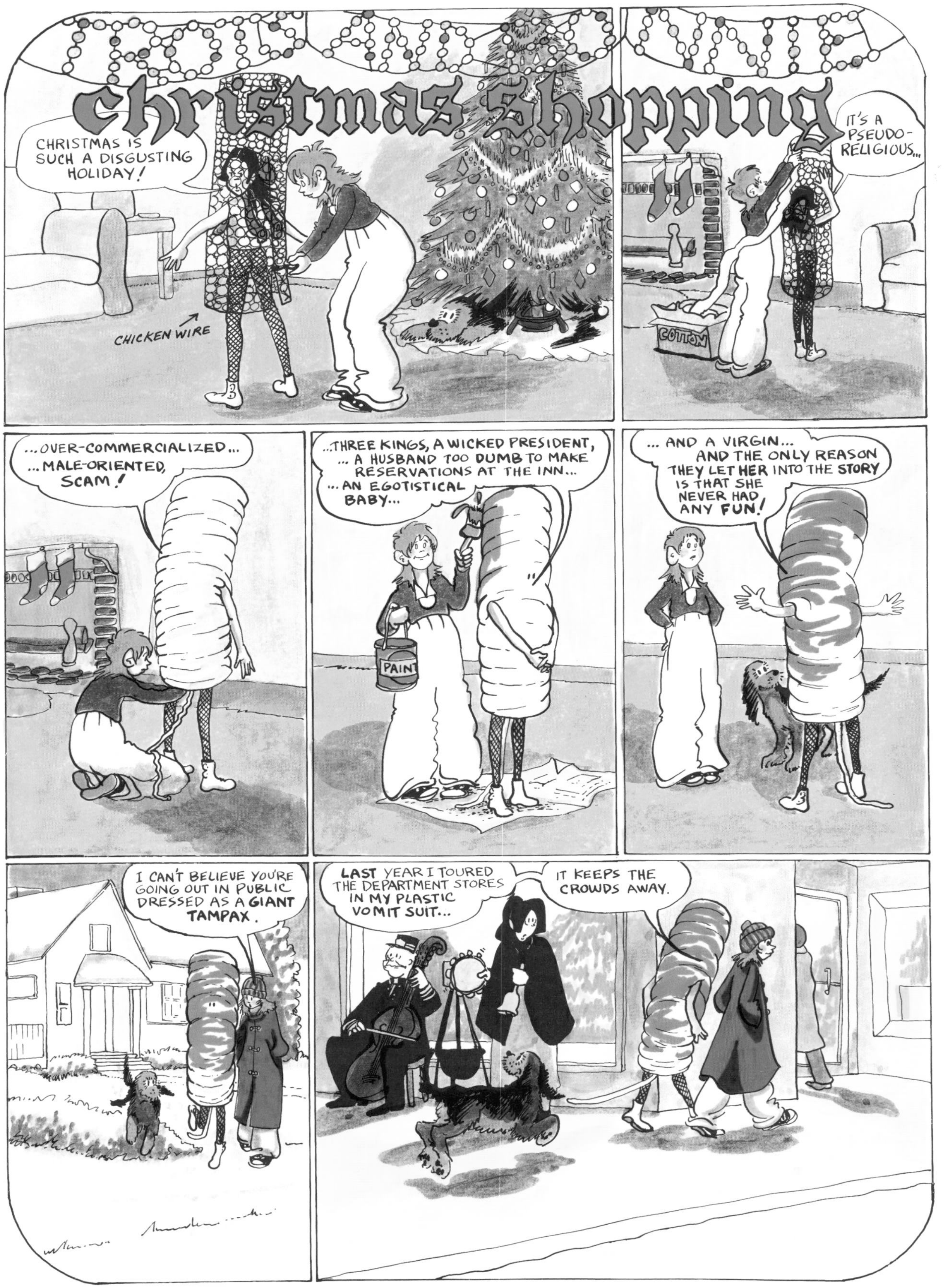
TROTS AND BONNIE
Christmas Shopping
CHRISTMAS IS SUCH A DISGUSTING HOLIDAY!
CHICKEN WIRE
IT'S A PSEUDO-RELIGIOUS...
COTTON
...OVER-COMMERCIALIZED...
...MALE-ORIENTED, SCAM!
...THREE KINGS, A WICKED PRESIDENT,
... A HUSBAND TOO DUMB TO MAKE RESERVATIONS AT THE INN...
...AN EGOTISTICAL BABY...
PAINT
... AND A VIRGIN...
AND THE ONLY REASON THEY LET HER INTO THE STORY IS THAT SHE NEVER HAD ANY FUN!
I CAN'T BELIEVE YOU'RE GOING OUT IN PUBLIC DRESSED AS A GIANT TAMPAX.
LAST YEAR I TOURED THE DEPARTMENT STORES IN MY PLASTIC VOMIT SUIT...
IT KEEPS THE CROWDS AWAY.

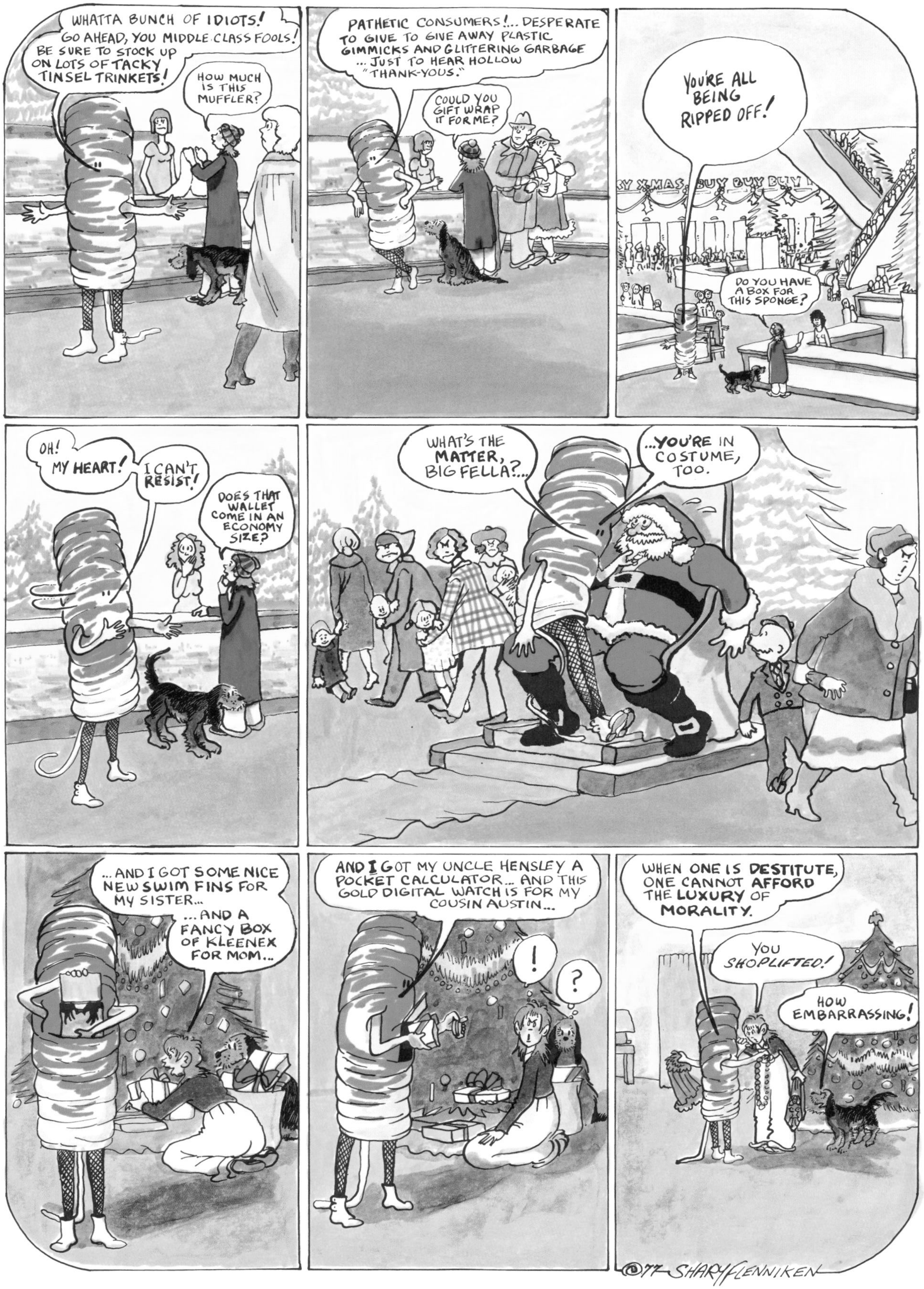
WHATTA BUNCH OF IDIOTS! GO AHEAD, YOU MIDDLE CLASS FOOLS! BE SURE TO STOCK UP ON LOTS OF TACKY TINSEL TRINKETS!
HOW MUCH IS THIS MUFFLER?
PATHETIC CONSUMERS!... DESPERATE TO GIVE TO GIVE AWAY PLASTIC GIMMICKS AND GLITTERING GARBAGE ... JUST TO HEAR HOLLOW "THANK-YOUS."
COULD YOU GIFT WRAP IT FOR ME?
YOU'RE ALL BEING RIPPED OFF!
XMAS BUY BUY BUY
DO YOU HAVE A BOX FOR THIS SPONGE?
OH! MY HEART!
I CAN'T RESIST!
DOES THAT WALLET COME IN AN ECONOMY SIZE?
WHAT'S THE MATTER, BIG FELLA?...
...YOU'RE IN COSTUME, TOO.
...AND I GOT SOME NICE NEW SWIM FINS FOR MY SISTER...
...AND A FANCY BOX OF KLEENEX FOR MOM...
AND I GOT MY UNCLE HENSLEY A POCKET CALCULATOR... AND THIS GOLD DIGITAL WATCH IS FOR MY COUSIN AUSTIN...
!
?
WHEN ONE IS DESTITUTE, ONE CANNOT AFFORD THE LUXURY OF MORALITY.
YOU SHOPLIFTED!
HOW EMBARRASSING!
©'77 SHARY FLENNIKEN

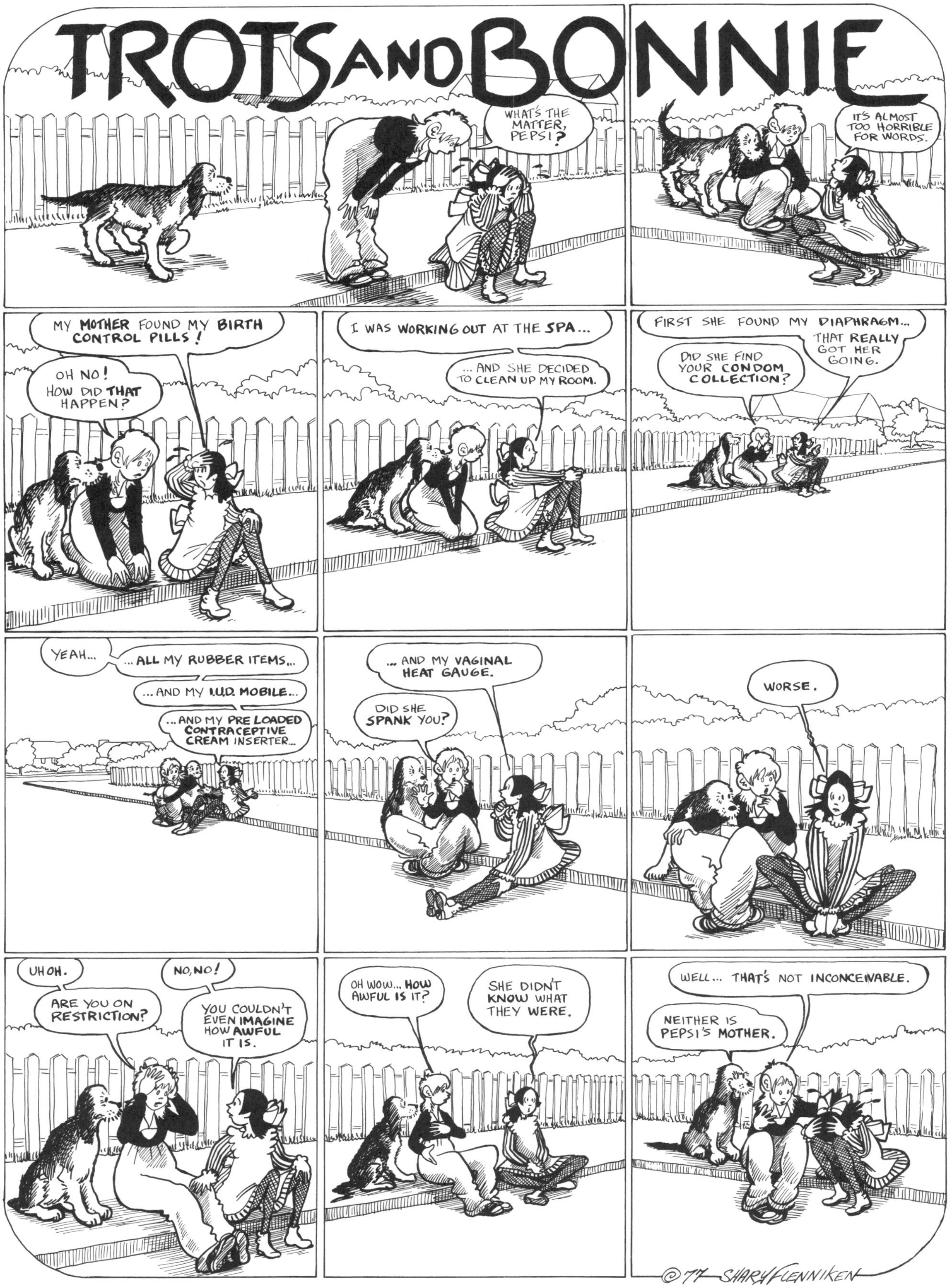
TROTS AND BONNIE
WHAT'S THE MATTER, PEPSI?
IT'S ALMOST TOO HORRIBLE FOR WORDS.
MY MOTHER FOUND MY BIRTH CONTROL PILLS!
OH NO! HOW DID THAT HAPPEN?
I WAS WORKING OUT AT THE SPA...
...AND SHE DECIDED TO CLEAN UP MY ROOM.
FIRST SHE FOUND MY DIAPHRAGM...
THAT REALLY GOT HER GOING.
DID SHE FIND YOUR CONDOM COLLECTION?
YEAH...
...ALL MY RUBBER ITEMS...
...AND MY I.U.D. MOBILE...
...AND MY PRE LOADED CONTRACEPTIVE CREAM INSERTER...
...AND MY VAGINAL HEAT GAUGE.
DID SHE SPANK YOU?
WORSE.
UH OH.
ARE YOU ON RESTRICTION?
NO, NO!
YOU COULDN'T EVEN IMAGINE HOW AWFUL IT IS.
OH WOW... HOW AWFUL IS IT?
SHE DIDN'T KNOW WHAT THEY WERE.
WELL... THAT'S NOT INCONCEIVABLE.
NEITHER IS PEPSI'S MOTHER.
©77 SHARY FLENNIKEN

Trots and Bonnie
Growling fiercely Shep bared his teeth at the intruder
He lunged and felt his
razor sharp teeth rip through flesh and muscle
Hot, tangy blood spurted down his throat
screaming in agony the stranger fled out of the yard
Shep was proudly recording his conquest on his diary rock when an unmistakably pungent scent made him turn
Shep stood stiffly staring
Her haunches were covered with fine soft fur. She boldly raised her tail and invited him in.
continued next wee
FRESH CAT LUNGS
!! UNITE !! OVERTHROW THE BIPEDS
LUCKY HAS EAR MITES
MIMI IS IN HEAT GET IT WHILE YOU CAN
EAT POOCH NUGGETS
ick sounds like something I leave on lawns
HEY, TROTS... HOW COME GIRL DOGS DON'T WRITE?
BARNEY LONGEST TAIL IN TOWN
THEY NEVER WROTE ANYTHING IMPORTANT, SO GOD TOOK THEIR ABILITY AWAY.
Trots was here
©77 SHARY FLENNIKEN

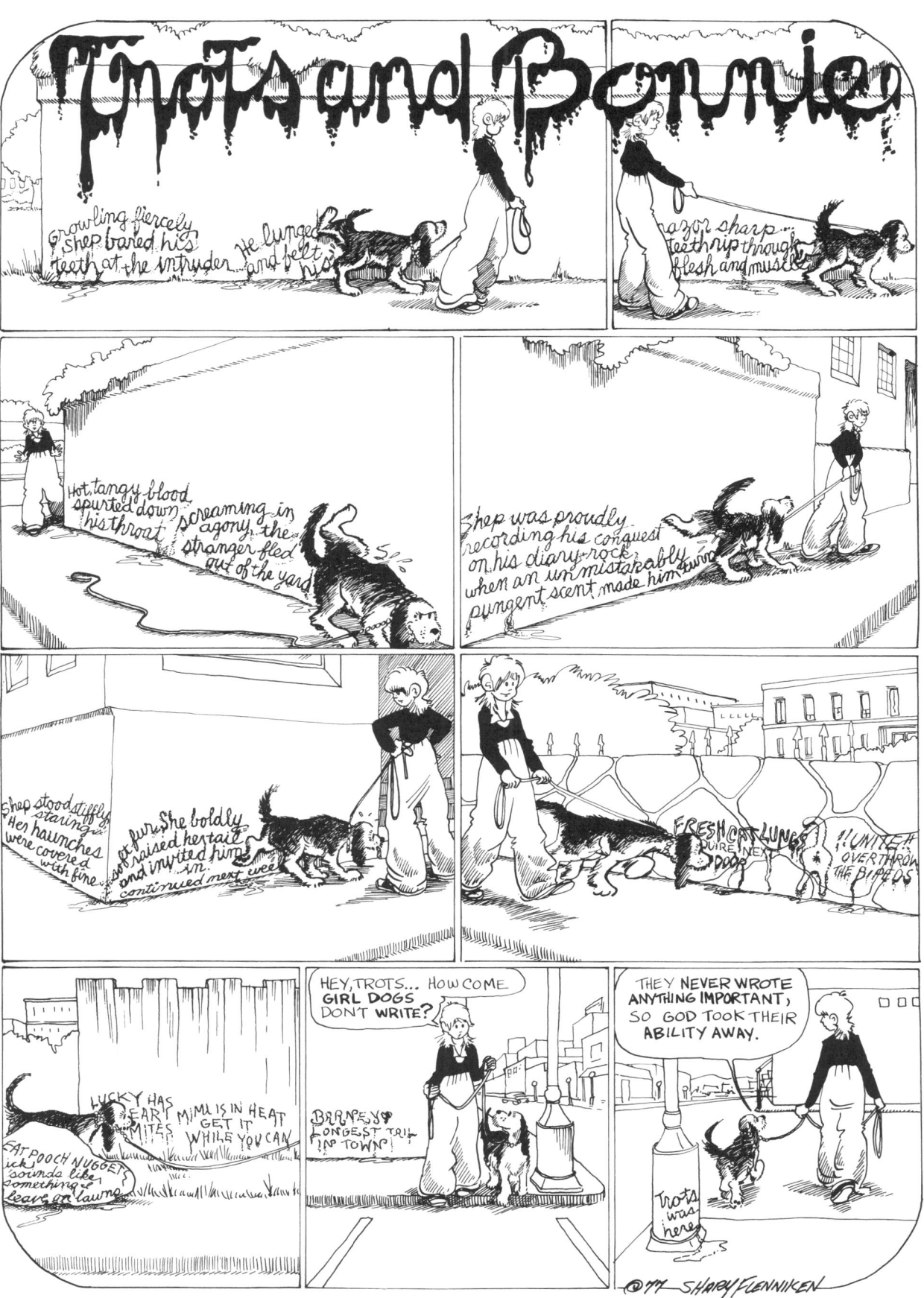

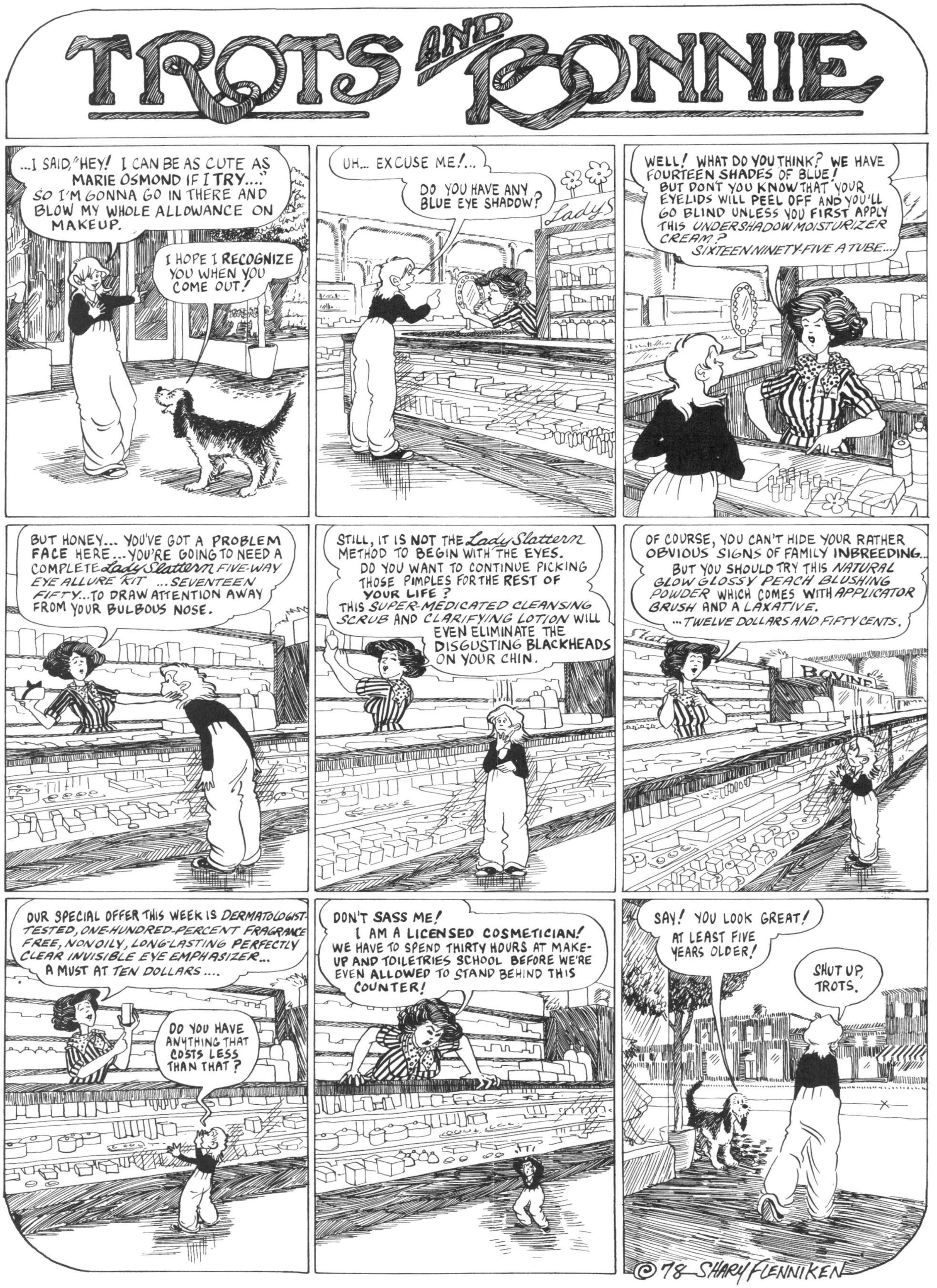
TROTS AND BONNIE
...I SAID, "HEY! I CAN BE AS CUTE AS MARIE OSMOND IF I TRY...." SO I'M GONNA GO IN THERE AND BLOW MY WHOLE ALLOWANCE ON MAKEUP.
I HOPE I RECOGNIZE YOU WHEN YOU COME OUT!
UH... EXCUSE ME!...
DO YOU HAVE ANY BLUE EYE SHADOW?
WELL! WHAT DO YOU THINK? WE HAVE FOURTEEN SHADES OF BLUE! BUT DON'T YOU KNOW THAT YOUR EYELIDS WILL PEEL OFF AND YOU'LL GO BLIND UNLESS YOU FIRST APPLY THIS UNDERSHADOW MOISTURIZER CREAM? SIXTEEN NINETY-FIVE A TUBE....
BUT HONEY... YOU'VE GOT A PROBLEM FACE HERE... YOU'RE GOING TO NEED A COMPLETE Lady Slattern FIVE-WAY EYE ALLURE KIT ...SEVENTEEN FIFTY... TO DRAW ATTENTION AWAY FROM YOUR BULBOUS NOSE.
STILL, IT IS NOT THE Lady Slattern METHOD TO BEGIN WITH THE EYES. DO YOU WANT TO CONTINUE PICKING THOSE PIMPLES FOR THE REST OF YOUR LIFE? THIS SUPER-MEDICATED CLEANSING SCRUB AND CLARIFYING LOTION WILL EVEN ELIMINATE THE DISGUSTING BLACKHEADS ON YOUR CHIN.
OF COURSE, YOU CAN'T HIDE YOUR RATHER OBVIOUS SIGNS OF FAMILY INBREEDING... BUT YOU SHOULD TRY THIS NATURAL GLOW GLOSSY PEACH BLUSHING POWDER WHICH COMES WITH APPLICATOR BRUSH AND A LAXATIVE. ...TWELVE DOLLARS AND FIFTY CENTS.
BOVINE
OUR SPECIAL OFFER THIS WEEK IS DERMATOLOGIST-TESTED, ONE-HUNDRED-PERCENT FRAGRANCE FREE, NONOILY, LONG-LASTING PERFECTLY CLEAR INVISIBLE EYE EMPHASIZER... A MUST AT TEN DOLLARS....
DO YOU HAVE ANYTHING THAT COSTS LESS THAN THAT?
DON'T SASS ME! I AM A LICENSED COSMETICIAN! WE HAVE TO SPEND THIRTY HOURS AT MAKE-UP AND TOILETRIES SCHOOL BEFORE WE'RE EVEN ALLOWED TO STAND BEHIND THIS COUNTER!
SAY! YOU LOOK GREAT! AT LEAST FIVE YEARS OLDER!
SHUT UP, TROTS.
© 78 SHARY FLENNIKEN

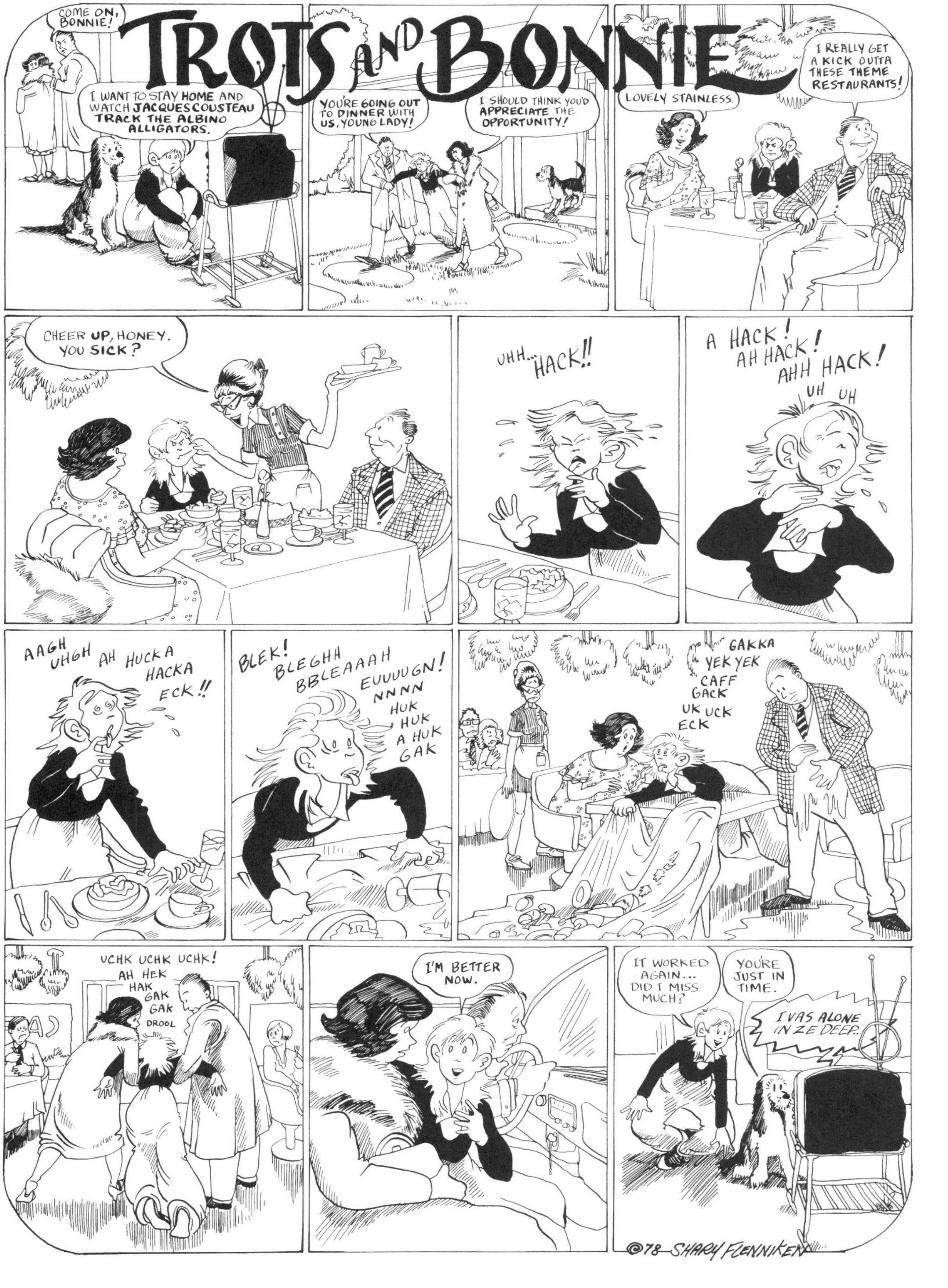
TROTS AND BONNIE
COME ON, BONNIE!
I WANT TO STAY HOME AND WATCH JACQUES COUSTEAU TRACK THE ALBINO ALLIGATORS.
YOU'RE GOING OUT TO DINNER WITH US, YOUNG LADY!
I SHOULD THINK YOU'D APPRECIATE THE OPPORTUNITY!
LOVELY STAINLESS.
I REALLY GET A KICK OUTTA THESE THEME RESTAURANTS!
CHEER UP, HONEY. YOU SICK?
UHH... HACK!!
A HACK! AH HACK! AHH HACK!
UH UH
AAGH UHGH AH HUCKA HACKA ECK!!
BLEK! BLEGHA BBLEAAAAH EUUUUGN! NNNN HUK HUK A HUK GAK
GAKKA YEK YEK CAFF GACK UK UCK ECK
UCHK UCHK UCHK! AH HEK HAK GAK GAK DROOL
I'M BETTER NOW.
IT WORKED AGAIN... DID I MISS MUCH?
YOU'RE JUST IN TIME.
I VAS ALONE IN ZE DEEP..
©78 SHARY FLENNIKEN

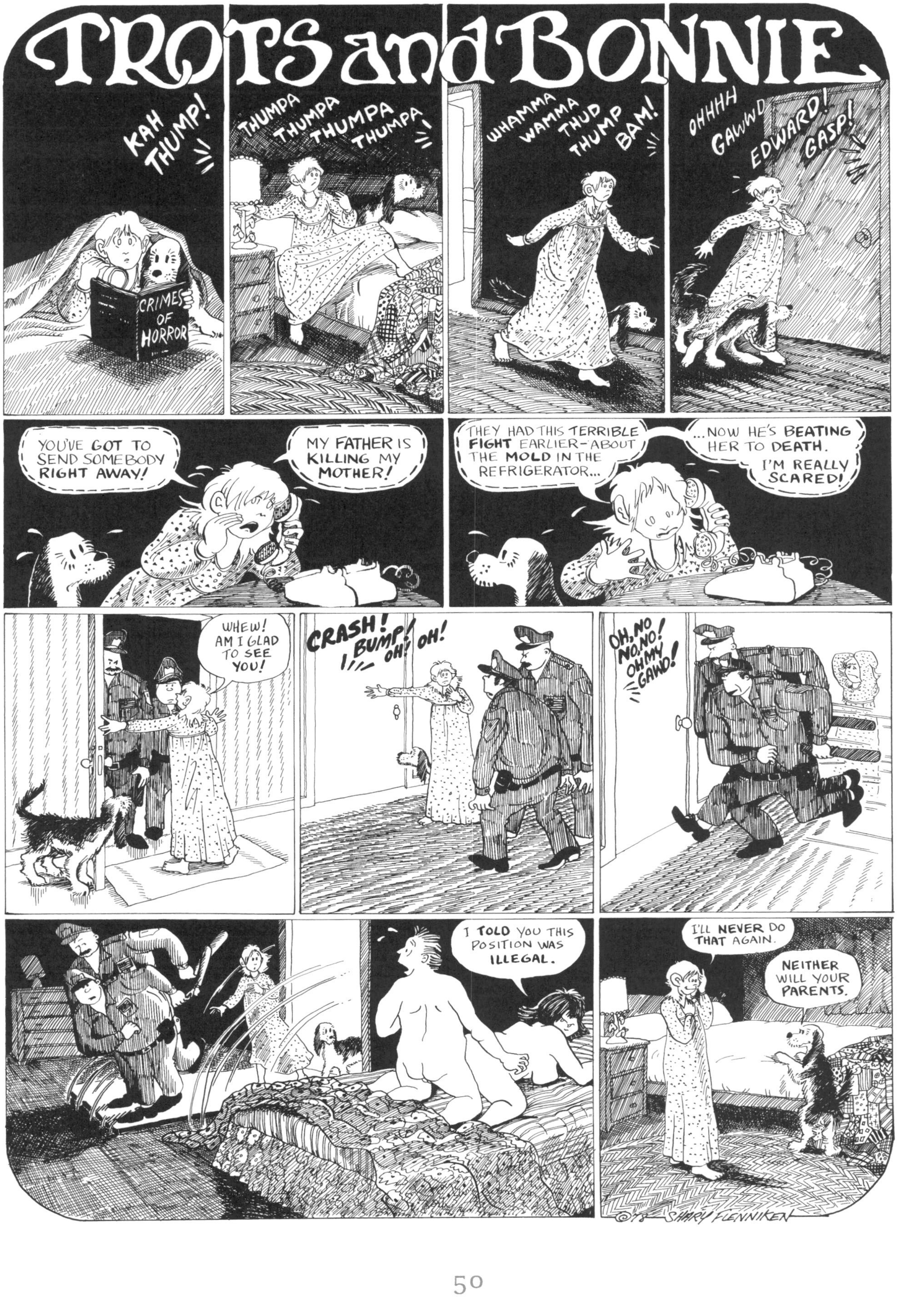
TROTS and BONNIE
KAH THUMP!
CRIMES OF HORROR
THUMPA THUMPA THUMPA THUMPA
WHAMMA WAMMA THUD THUMP BAM!
OHHHH GAWWD EDWARD! GASP!
YOU'VE GOT TO SEND SOMEBODY RIGHT AWAY!
MY FATHER IS KILLING MY MOTHER!
THEY HAD THIS TERRIBLE FIGHT EARLIER–ABOUT THE MOLD IN THE REFRIGERATOR...
...NOW HE'S BEATING HER TO DEATH.
I'M REALLY SCARED!
WHEW! AM I GLAD TO SEE YOU!
CRASH! BUMP! OH! OH!
OH, NO NO, NO! OH MY GAWD!
I TOLD YOU THIS POSITION WAS ILLEGAL.
I'LL NEVER DO THAT AGAIN.
NEITHER WILL YOUR PARENTS.
©78 SHARY FLENNIKEN

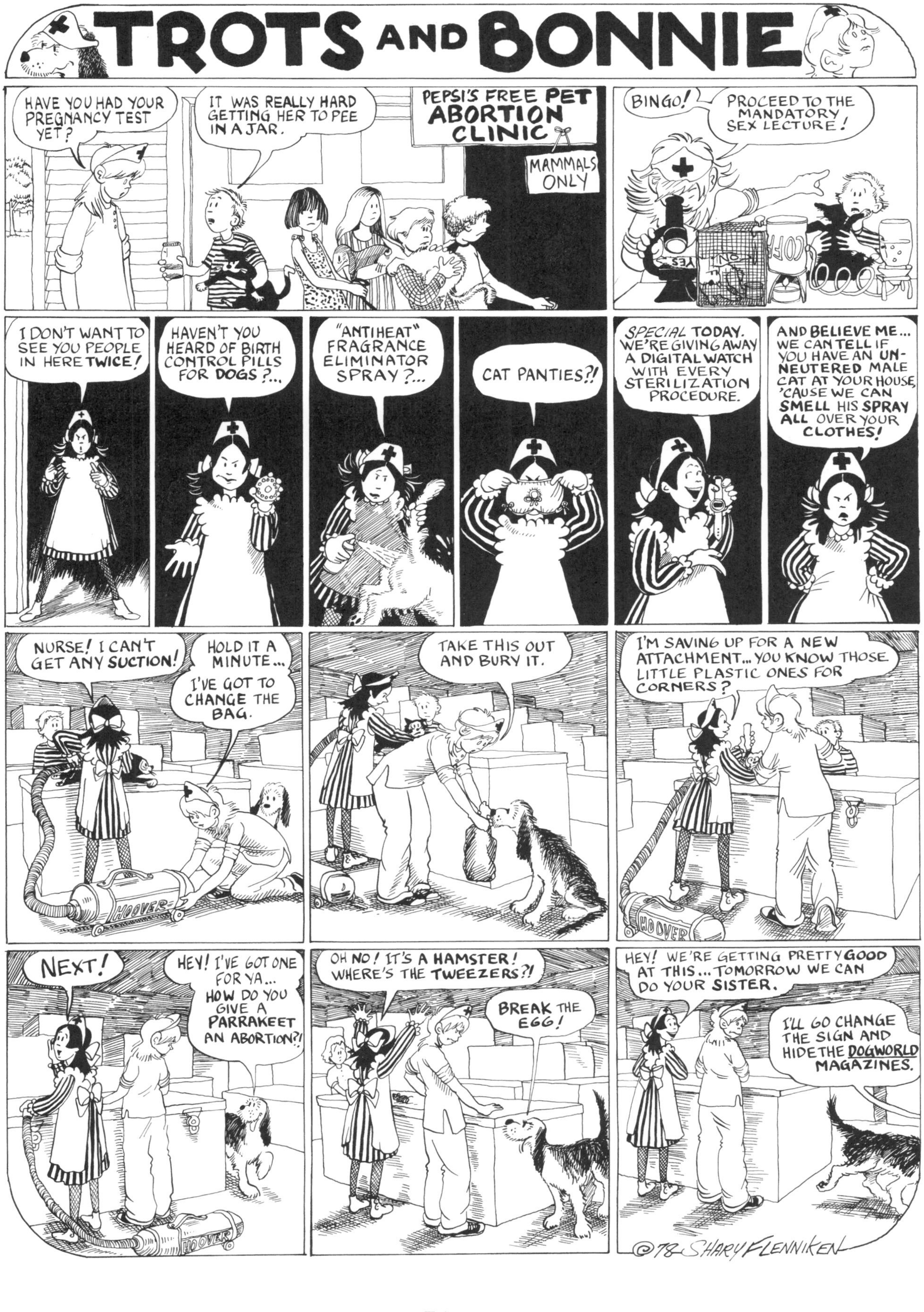

TROTS AND BONNIE
HAVE YOU HAD YOUR PREGNANCY TEST YET?
IT WAS REALLY HARD GETTING HER TO PEE IN A JAR.
PEPSI'S FREE PET ABORTION CLINIC
MAMMALS ONLY
BINGO!
PROCEED TO THE MANDATORY SEX LECTURE!
I DON'T WANT TO SEE YOU PEOPLE IN HERE TWICE!
HAVEN'T YOU HEARD OF BIRTH CONTROL PILLS FOR DOGS?...
"ANTIHEAT" FRAGRANCE ELIMINATOR SPRAY?...
CAT PANTIES?!
SPECIAL TODAY. WE'RE GIVING AWAY A DIGITAL WATCH WITH EVERY STERILIZATION PROCEDURE.
AND BELIEVE ME... WE CAN TELL IF YOU HAVE AN UN-NEUTERED MALE CAT AT YOUR HOUSE, 'CAUSE WE CAN SMELL HIS SPRAY ALL OVER YOUR CLOTHES!
NURSE! I CAN'T GET ANY SUCTION!
HOLD IT A MINUTE... I'VE GOT TO CHANGE THE BAG.
HOOVER
TAKE THIS OUT AND BURY IT.
I'M SAVING UP FOR A NEW ATTACHMENT... YOU KNOW THOSE LITTLE PLASTIC ONES FOR CORNERS?
HOOVER
NEXT!
HEY! I'VE GOT ONE FOR YA... HOW DO YOU GIVE A PARRAKEET AN ABORTION?!
HOOVER
OH NO! IT'S A HAMSTER! WHERE'S THE TWEEZERS?!
BREAK THE EGG!
HEY! WE'RE GETTING PRETTY GOOD AT THIS... TOMORROW WE CAN DO YOUR SISTER.
I'LL GO CHANGE THE SIGN AND HIDE THE DOGWORLD MAGAZINES.
©78 SHARY FLENNIKEN

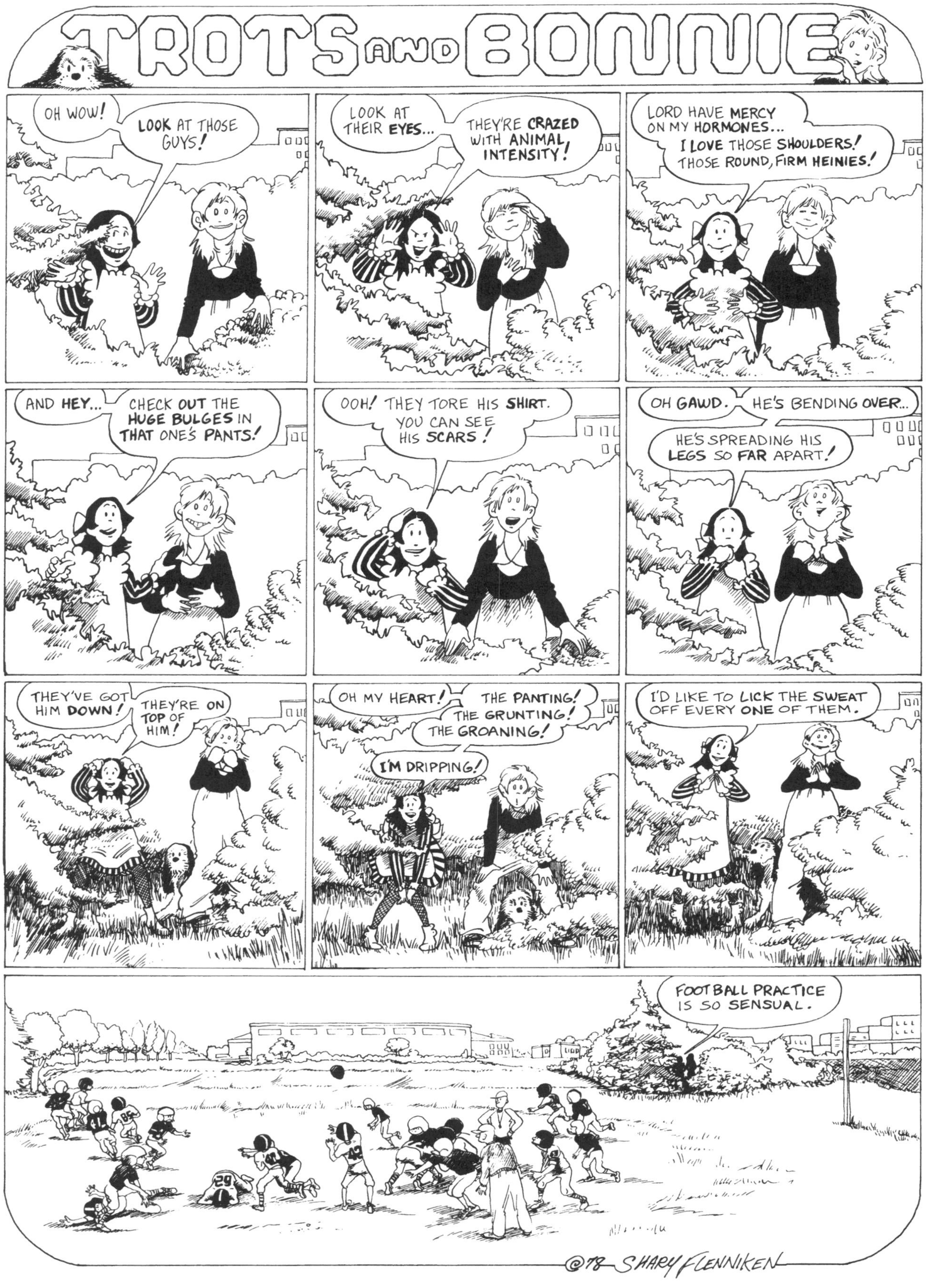
TROTS AND BONNIE
OH WOW!
LOOK AT THOSE GUYS!
LOOK AT THEIR EYES...
THEY'RE CRAZED WITH ANIMAL INTENSITY!
LORD HAVE MERCY ON MY HORMONES...
I LOVE THOSE SHOULDERS! THOSE ROUND, FIRM HEINIES!
AND HEY...
CHECK OUT THE HUGE BULGES IN THAT ONE'S PANTS!
OOH! THEY TORE HIS SHIRT. YOU CAN SEE HIS SCARS!
OH GAWD.
HE'S BENDING OVER...
HE'S SPREADING HIS LEGS SO FAR APART!
THEY'VE GOT HIM DOWN!
THEY'RE ON TOP OF HIM!
OH MY HEART!
THE PANTING! THE GRUNTING! THE GROANING!
I'M DRIPPING!
I'D LIKE TO LICK THE SWEAT OFF EVERY ONE OF THEM.
FOOTBALL PRACTICE IS SO SENSUAL.
©78 SHARY FLENNIKEN

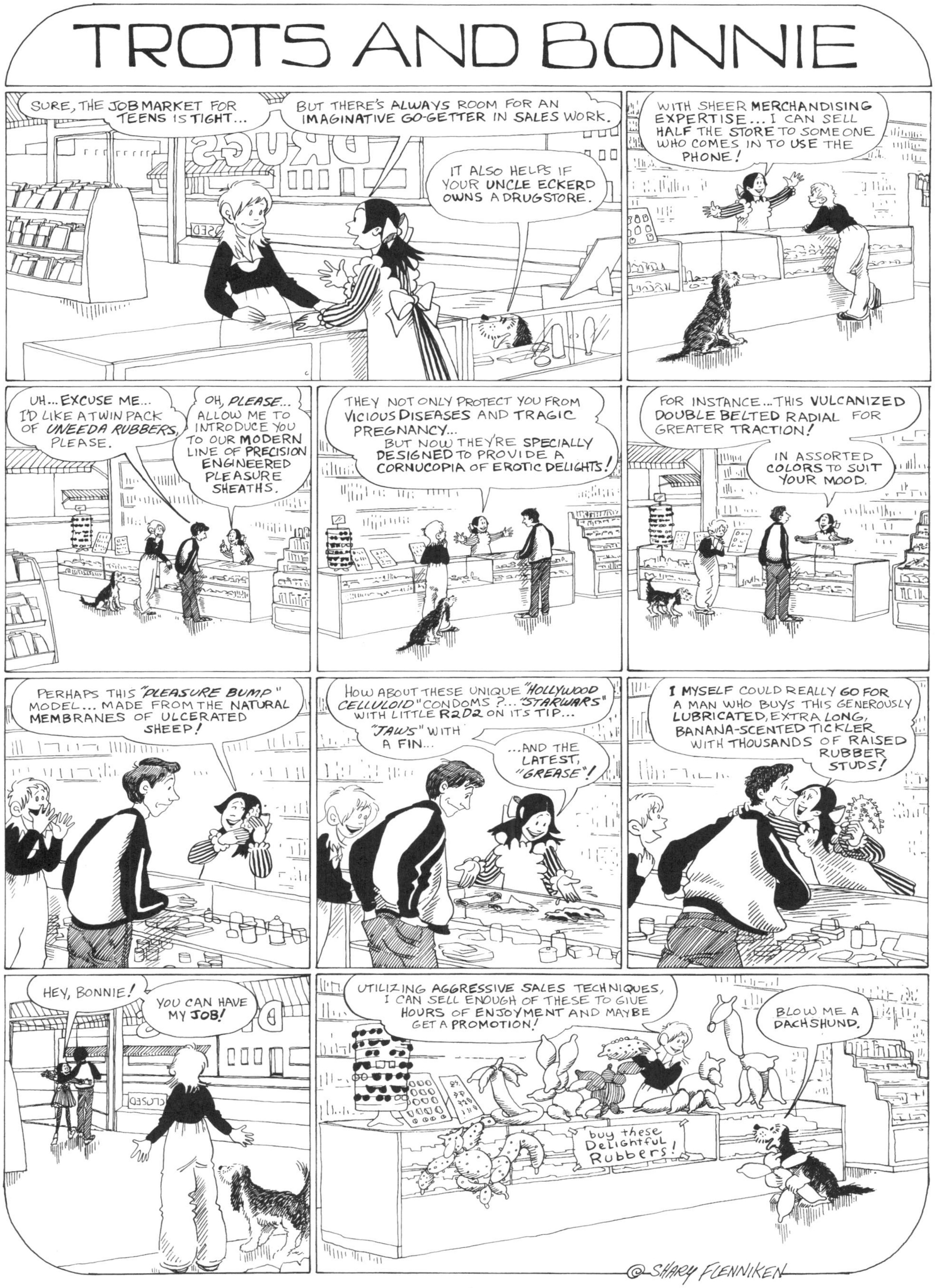
TROTS AND BONNIE
SURE, THE JOB MARKET FOR TEENS IS TIGHT...
BUT THERE'S ALWAYS ROOM FOR AN IMAGINATIVE GO-GETTER IN SALES WORK.
DRUGS
IT ALSO HELPS IF YOUR UNCLE ECKERD OWNS A DRUGSTORE.
WITH SHEER MERCHANDISING EXPERTISE... I CAN SELL HALF THE STORE TO SOME ONE WHO COMES IN TO USE THE PHONE!
UH... EXCUSE ME... I'D LIKE A TWIN PACK OF UNEEDA RUBBERS, PLEASE.
OH, PLEASE... ALLOW ME TO INTRODUCE YOU TO OUR MODERN LINE OF PRECISION ENGINEERED PLEASURE SHEATHS.
THEY NOT ONLY PROTECT YOU FROM VICIOUS DISEASES AND TRAGIC PREGNANCY... BUT NOW THEY'RE SPECIALLY DESIGNED TO PROVIDE A CORNUCOPIA OF EROTIC DELIGHTS!
FOR INSTANCE... THIS VULCANIZED DOUBLE BELTED RADIAL FOR GREATER TRACTION!
IN ASSORTED COLORS TO SUIT YOUR MOOD.
PERHAPS THIS "PLEASURE BUMP" MODEL... MADE FROM THE NATURAL MEMBRANES OF ULCERATED SHEEP!
HOW ABOUT THESE UNIQUE "HOLLYWOOD CELLULOID" CONDOMS?... "STARWARS" WITH LITTLE R2D2 ON ITS TIP... "JAWS" WITH A FIN...
...AND THE LATEST, "GREASE"!
I MYSELF COULD REALLY GO FOR A MAN WHO BUYS THIS GENEROUSLY LUBRICATED, EXTRA LONG, BANANA-SCENTED TICKLER WITH THOUSANDS OF RAISED RUBBER STUDS!
HEY, BONNIE!
YOU CAN HAVE MY JOB!
CLOSED
UTILIZING AGGRESSIVE SALES TECHNIQUES, I CAN SELL ENOUGH OF THESE TO GIVE HOURS OF ENJOYMENT AND MAYBE GET A PROMOTION!
BLOW ME A DACHSHUND.
buy these Delightful Rubbers!
© SHARY FLENNIKEN

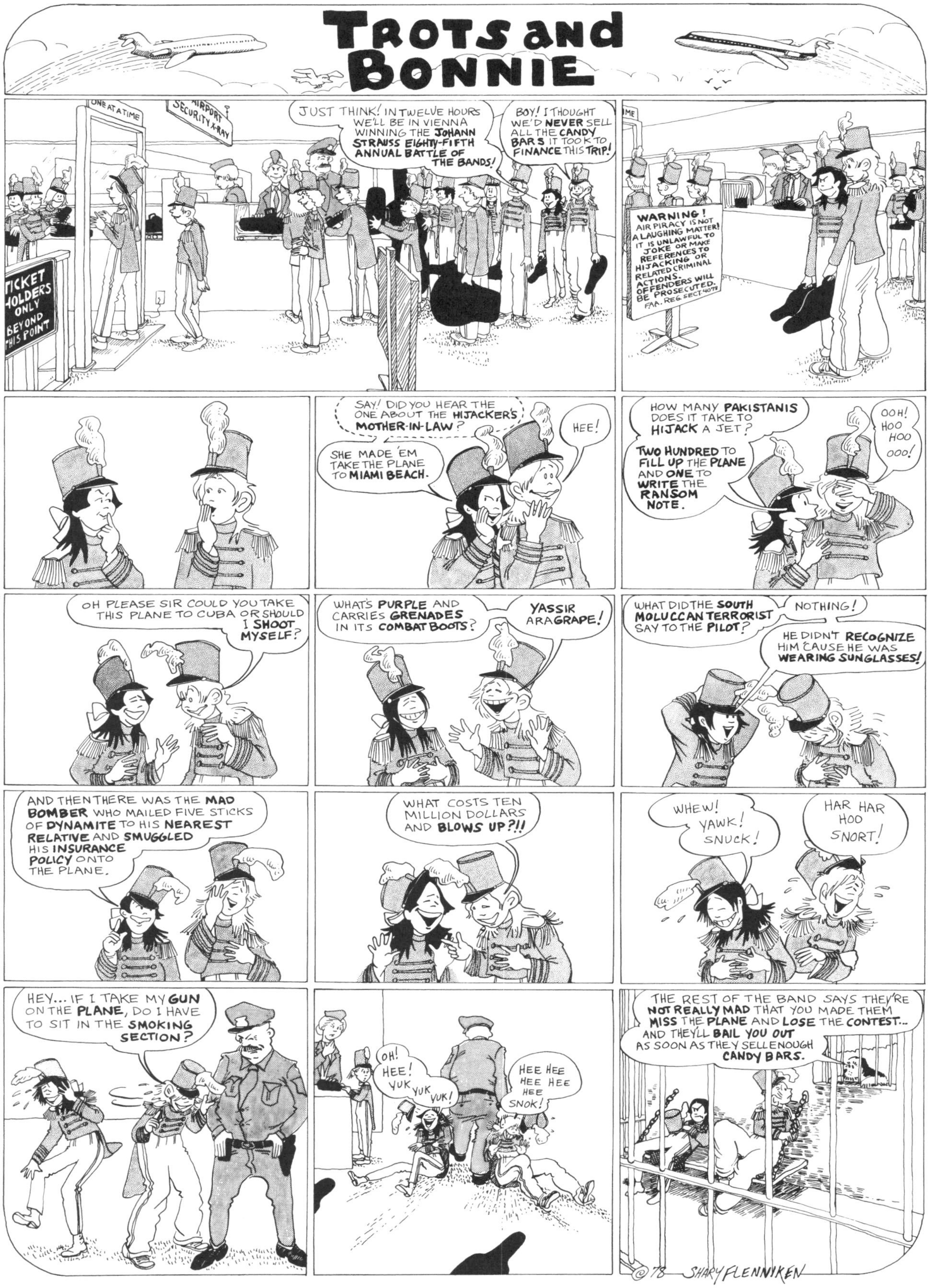
TROTS AND BONNIE
ONE AT A TIME
AIRPORT SECURITY X-RAY
TICKET HOLDERS ONLY BEYOND THIS POINT
JUST THINK! IN TWELVE HOURS WE'LL BE IN VIENNA WINNING THE JOHANN STRAUSS EIGHTY-FIFTH ANNUAL BATTLE OF THE BANDS!
BOY! I THOUGHT WE'D NEVER SELL ALL THE CANDY BARS IT TOOK TO FINANCE THIS TRIP!
WARNING! AIR PIRACY IS NOT A LAUGHING MATTER! IT IS UNLAWFUL TO JOKE OR MAKE REFERENCES TO HIJACKING OR RELATED CRIMINAL ACTIONS. OFFENDERS WILL BE PROSECUTED. FAA. REG. SECT. 4078
SAY! DID YOU HEAR THE ONE ABOUT THE HIJACKER'S MOTHER-IN-LAW?
SHE MADE 'EM TAKE THE PLANE TO MIAMI BEACH.
HEE!
HOW MANY PAKISTANIS DOES IT TAKE TO HIJACK A JET?
TWO HUNDRED TO FILL UP THE PLANE AND ONE TO WRITE THE RANSOM NOTE.
OOH! HOO HOO OOO!
OH PLEASE SIR COULD YOU TAKE THIS PLANE TO CUBA OR SHOULD I SHOOT MYSELF?
WHAT'S PURPLE AND CARRIES GRENADES IN ITS COMBAT BOOTS?
YASSIR ARAGRAPE!
WHAT DID THE SOUTH MOLUCCAN TERRORIST SAY TO THE PILOT?
NOTHING!
HE DIDN'T RECOGNIZE HIM 'CAUSE HE WAS WEARING SUNGLASSES!
AND THEN THERE WAS THE MAD BOMBER WHO MAILED FIVE STICKS OF DYNAMITE TO HIS NEAREST RELATIVE AND SMUGGLED HIS INSURANCE POLICY ONTO THE PLANE.
WHAT COSTS TEN MILLION DOLLARS AND BLOWS UP?!!
WHEW! YAWK! SNUCK!
HAR HAR HOO SNORT!
HEY... IF I TAKE MY GUN ON THE PLANE, DO I HAVE TO SIT IN THE SMOKING SECTION?
OH! HEE! YUK YUK YUK!
HEE HEE HEE HEE HEE SNOK!
THE REST OF THE BAND SAYS THEY'RE NOT REALLY MAD THAT YOU MADE THEM MISS THE PLANE AND LOSE THE CONTEST... AND THEY'LL BAIL YOU OUT AS SOON AS THEY SELL ENOUGH CANDY BARS.
©'78 SHARY FLENNIKEN

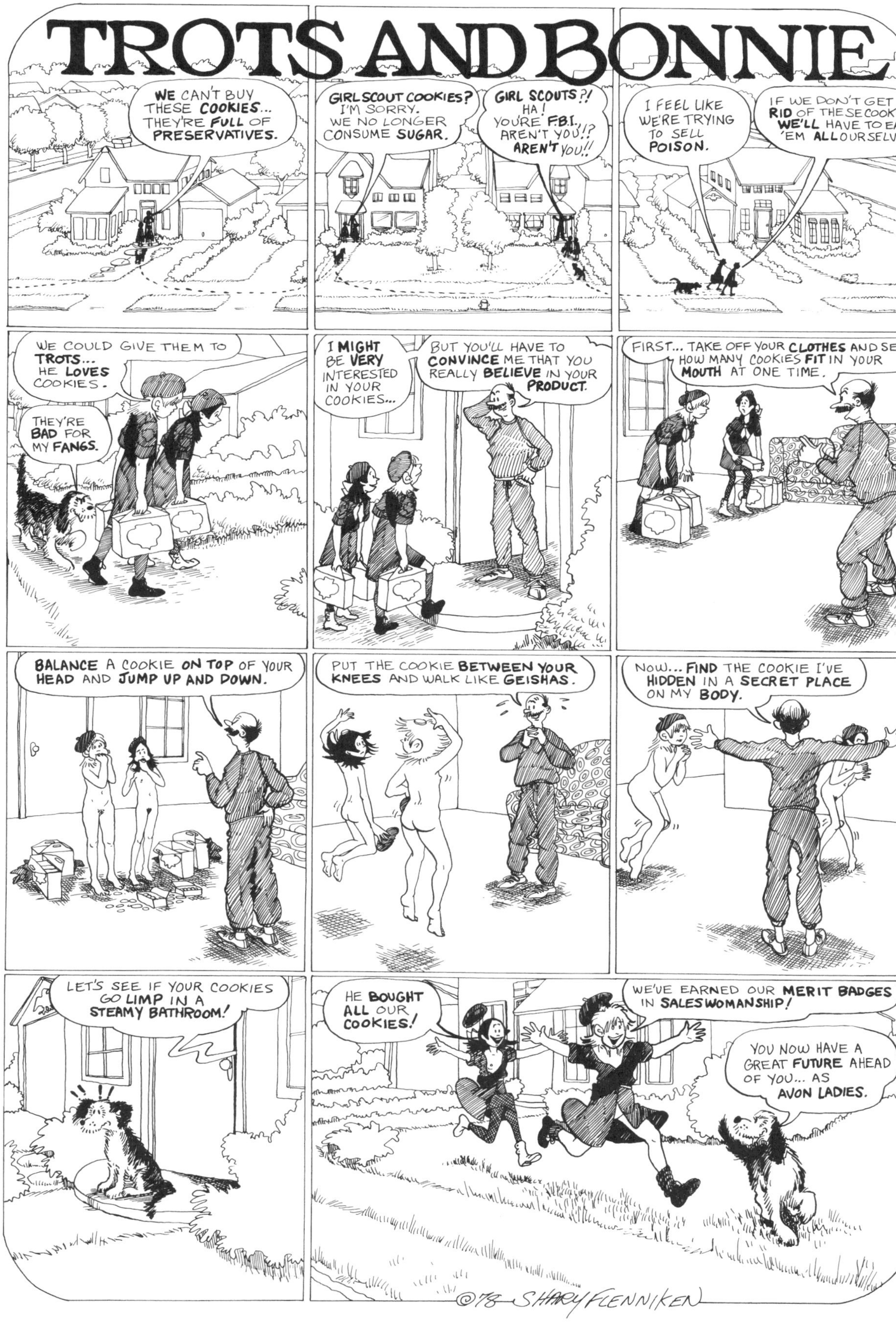
TROTS AND BONNIE
WE CAN'T BUY THESE COOKIES... THEY'RE FULL OF PRESERVATIVES.
GIRL SCOUT COOKIES? I'M SORRY. WE NO LONGER CONSUME SUGAR.
GIRL SCOUTS?! HA! YOU'RE F.B.I., AREN'T YOU!? AREN'T YOU!!
I FEEL LIKE WE'RE TRYING TO SELL POISON.
IF WE DON'T GET RID OF THESE COOKIES, WE'LL HAVE TO EAT 'EM ALL OURSELVES.
WE COULD GIVE THEM TO TROTS... HE LOVES COOKIES.
THEY'RE BAD FOR MY FANGS.
I MIGHT BE VERY INTERESTED IN YOUR COOKIES...
BUT YOU'LL HAVE TO CONVINCE ME THAT YOU REALLY BELIEVE IN YOUR PRODUCT.
FIRST... TAKE OFF YOUR CLOTHES AND SEE HOW MANY COOKIES FIT IN YOUR MOUTH AT ONE TIME.
BALANCE A COOKIE ON TOP OF YOUR HEAD AND JUMP UP AND DOWN.
PUT THE COOKIE BETWEEN YOUR KNEES AND WALK LIKE GEISHAS.
NOW... FIND THE COOKIE I'VE HIDDEN IN A SECRET PLACE ON MY BODY.
LET'S SEE IF YOUR COOKIES GO LIMP IN A STEAMY BATHROOM!
HE BOUGHT ALL OUR COOKIES!
WE'VE EARNED OUR MERIT BADGES IN SALESWOMANSHIP!
YOU NOW HAVE A GREAT FUTURE AHEAD OF YOU... AS AVON LADIES.
©'78 SHARY FLENNIKEN

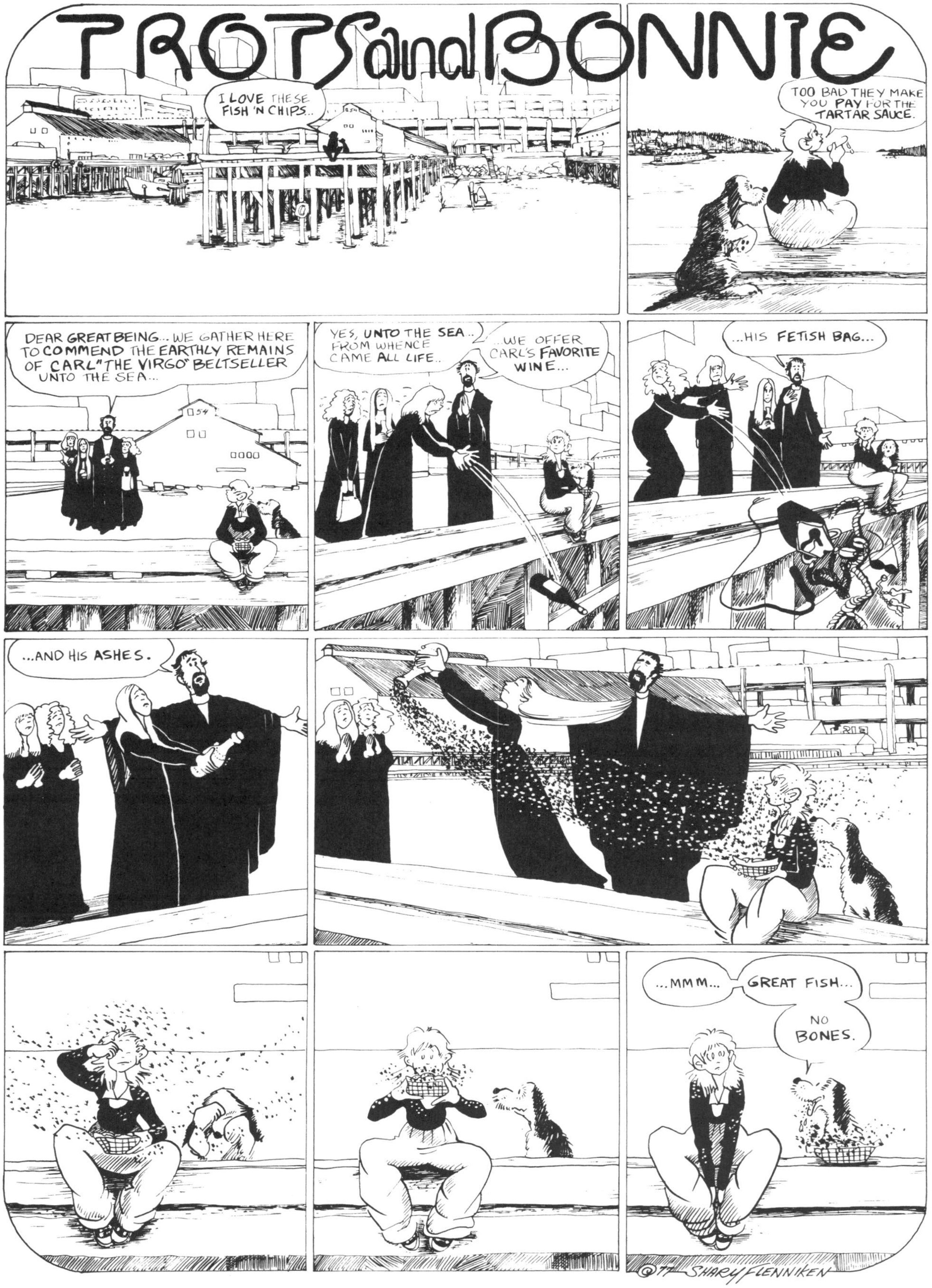
TROTS and BONNIE
I LOVE THESE FISH 'N CHIPS...
TOO BAD THEY MAKE YOU PAY FOR THE TARTAR SAUCE.
DEAR GREAT BEING... WE GATHER HERE TO COMMEND THE EARTHLY REMAINS OF CARL "THE VIRGO" BELTSELLER UNTO THE SEA...
YES, UNTO THE SEA.. FROM WHENCE CAME ALL LIFE..
...WE OFFER CARL'S FAVORITE WINE...
...HIS FETISH BAG...
...AND HIS ASHES.
...MMM...
GREAT FISH...
NO BONES.
©77 SHARY FLENNIKEN

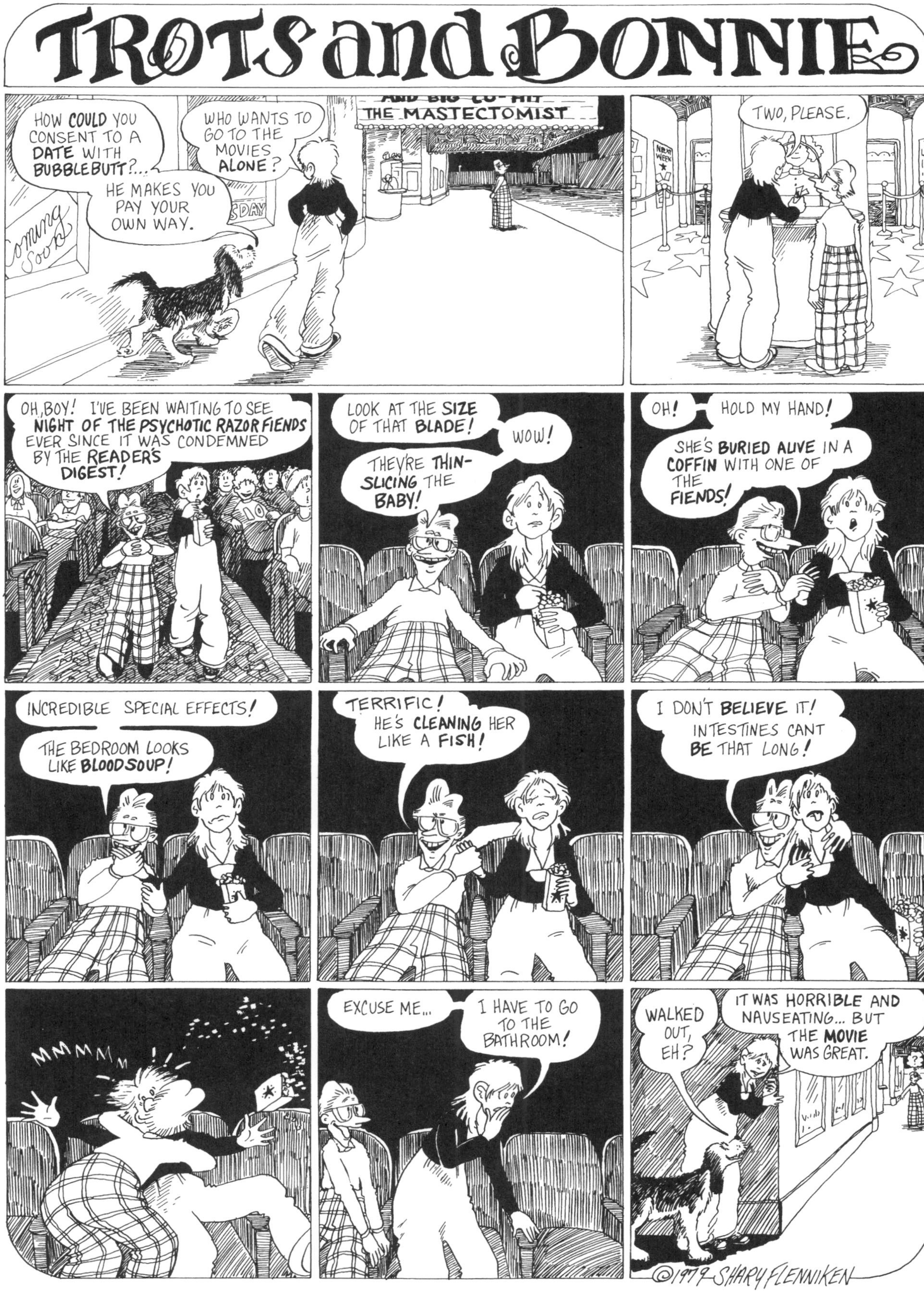
TROTS and BONNIE
AND BIG CO-HIT
THE MASTECTOMIST
HOW COULD YOU CONSENT TO A DATE WITH BUBBLEBUTT?...
WHO WANTS TO GO TO THE MOVIES ALONE?
HE MAKES YOU PAY YOUR OWN WAY.
Coming Soon
TWO, PLEASE.
NEXT WEEK
OH, BOY! I'VE BEEN WAITING TO SEE NIGHT OF THE PSYCHOTIC RAZOR FIENDS EVER SINCE IT WAS CONDEMNED BY THE READER'S DIGEST!
LOOK AT THE SIZE OF THAT BLADE!
WOW!
THEY'RE THIN-SLICING THE BABY!
OH!
HOLD MY HAND!
SHE'S BURIED ALIVE IN A COFFIN WITH ONE OF THE FIENDS!
INCREDIBLE SPECIAL EFFECTS!
THE BEDROOM LOOKS LIKE BLOODSOUP!
TERRIFIC! HE'S CLEANING HER LIKE A FISH!
I DON'T BELIEVE IT! INTESTINES CANT BE THAT LONG!
MMMMM
EXCUSE ME...
I HAVE TO GO TO THE BATHROOM!
WALKED OUT, EH?
IT WAS HORRIBLE AND NAUSEATING... BUT THE MOVIE WAS GREAT.
©1979 SHARY FLENNIKEN

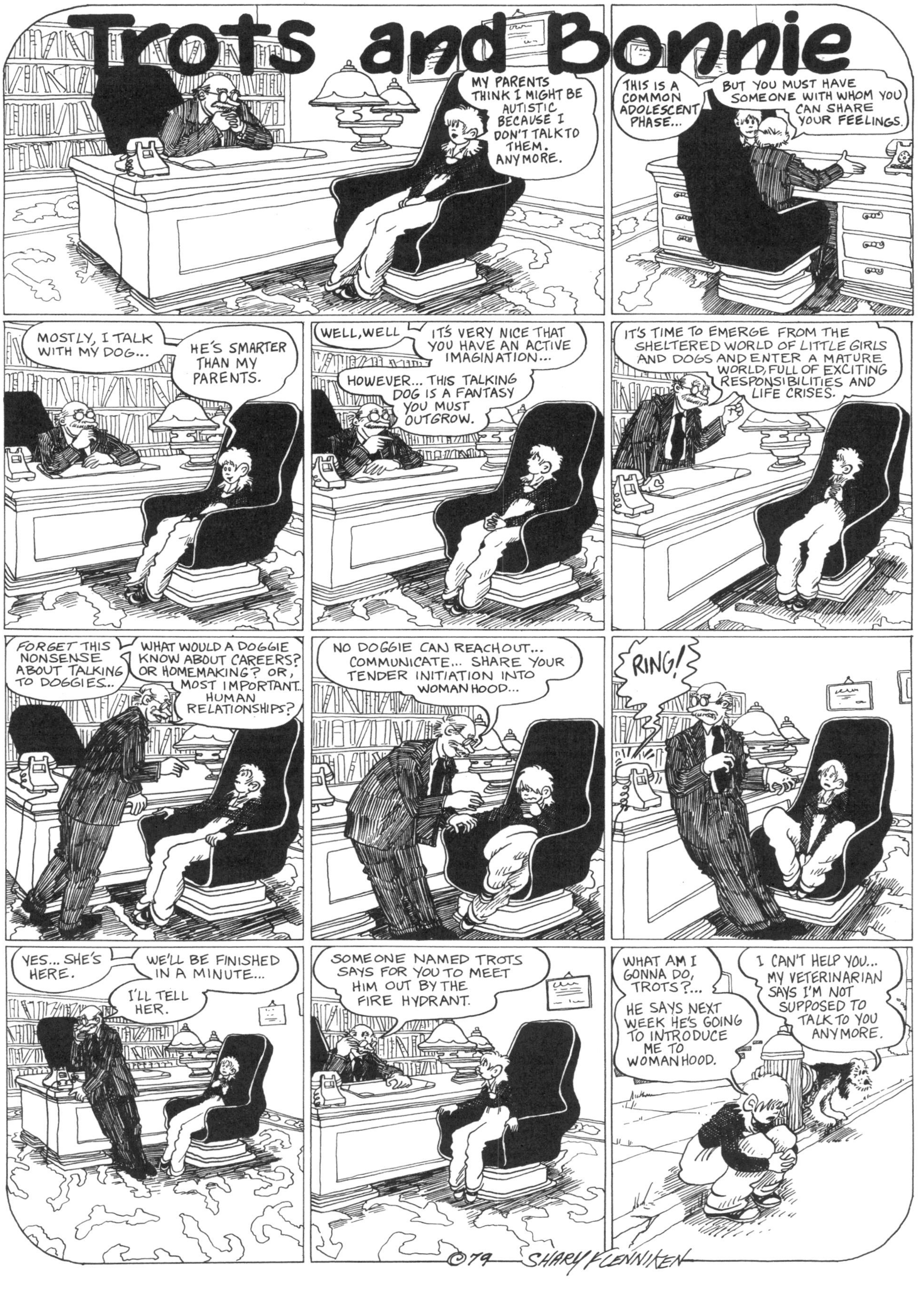
Trots and Bonnie
MY PARENTS THINK I MIGHT BE AUTISTIC BECAUSE I DON'T TALK TO THEM. ANYMORE.
THIS IS A COMMON ADOLESCENT PHASE...
BUT YOU MUST HAVE SOMEONE WITH WHOM YOU CAN SHARE YOUR FEELINGS.
MOSTLY, I TALK WITH MY DOG...
HE'S SMARTER THAN MY PARENTS.
WELL, WELL
IT'S VERY NICE THAT YOU HAVE AN ACTIVE IMAGINATION...
HOWEVER... THIS TALKING DOG IS A FANTASY YOU MUST OUTGROW.
IT'S TIME TO EMERGE FROM THE SHELTERED WORLD OF LITTLE GIRLS AND DOGS AND ENTER A MATURE WORLD, FULL OF EXCITING RESPONSIBILITIES AND LIFE CRISES.
FORGET THIS NONSENSE ABOUT TALKING TO DOGGIES...
WHAT WOULD A DOGGIE KNOW ABOUT CAREERS? OR HOMEMAKING? OR, MOST IMPORTANT... HUMAN RELATIONSHIPS?
NO DOGGIE CAN REACH OUT... COMMUNICATE... SHARE YOUR TENDER INITIATION INTO WOMANHOOD...
RING!
YES... SHE'S HERE.
WE'LL BE FINISHED IN A MINUTE...
I'LL TELL HER.
SOMEONE NAMED TROTS SAYS FOR YOU TO MEET HIM OUT BY THE FIRE HYDRANT.
WHAT AM I GONNA DO, TROTS?...
HE SAYS NEXT WEEK HE'S GOING TO INTRODUCE ME TO WOMANHOOD.
I CAN'T HELP YOU... MY VETERINARIAN SAYS I'M NOT SUPPOSED TO TALK TO YOU ANYMORE.
©79 SHARY FLENNIKEN

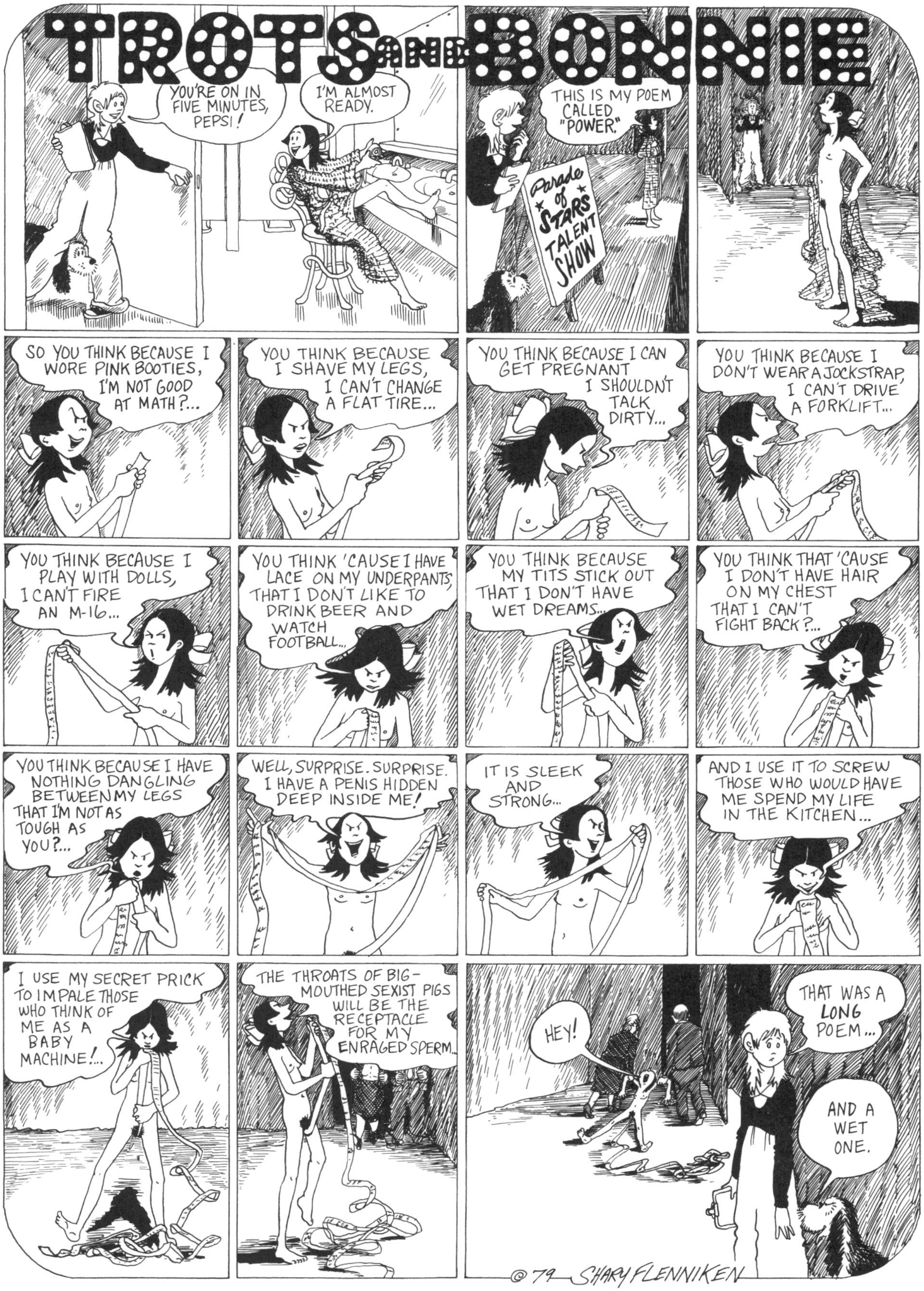

TROTS AND BONNIE
YOU'RE ON IN FIVE MINUTES, PEPSI!
I'M ALMOST READY.
THIS IS MY POEM CALLED "POWER."
Parade of STARS TALENT SHOW
SO YOU THINK BECAUSE I WORE PINK BOOTIES, I'M NOT GOOD AT MATH?...
YOU THINK BECAUSE I SHAVE MY LEGS, I CAN'T CHANGE A FLAT TIRE...
YOU THINK BECAUSE I CAN GET PREGNANT I SHOULDN'T TALK DIRTY...
YOU THINK BECAUSE I DON'T WEAR A JOCKSTRAP, I CAN'T DRIVE A FORKLIFT...
YOU THINK BECAUSE I PLAY WITH DOLLS, I CAN'T FIRE AN M-16...
YOU THINK 'CAUSE I HAVE LACE ON MY UNDERPANTS, THAT I DON'T LIKE TO DRINK BEER AND WATCH FOOTBALL...
YOU THINK BECAUSE MY TITS STICK OUT THAT I DON'T HAVE WET DREAMS...
YOU THINK THAT 'CAUSE I DON'T HAVE HAIR ON MY CHEST THAT I CAN'T FIGHT BACK?...
YOU THINK BECAUSE I HAVE NOTHING DANGLING BETWEEN MY LEGS THAT I'M NOT AS TOUGH AS YOU?...
WELL, SURPRISE. SURPRISE. I HAVE A PENIS HIDDEN DEEP INSIDE ME!
IT IS SLEEK AND STRONG...
AND I USE IT TO SCREW THOSE WHO WOULD HAVE ME SPEND MY LIFE IN THE KITCHEN...
I USE MY SECRET PRICK TO IMPALE THOSE WHO THINK OF ME AS A BABY MACHINE!...
THE THROATS OF BIG-MOUTHED SEXIST PIGS WILL BE THE RECEPTACLE FOR MY ENRAGED SPERM...
HEY!
THAT WAS A LONG POEM...
AND A WET ONE.
© 79 SHARY FLENNIKEN

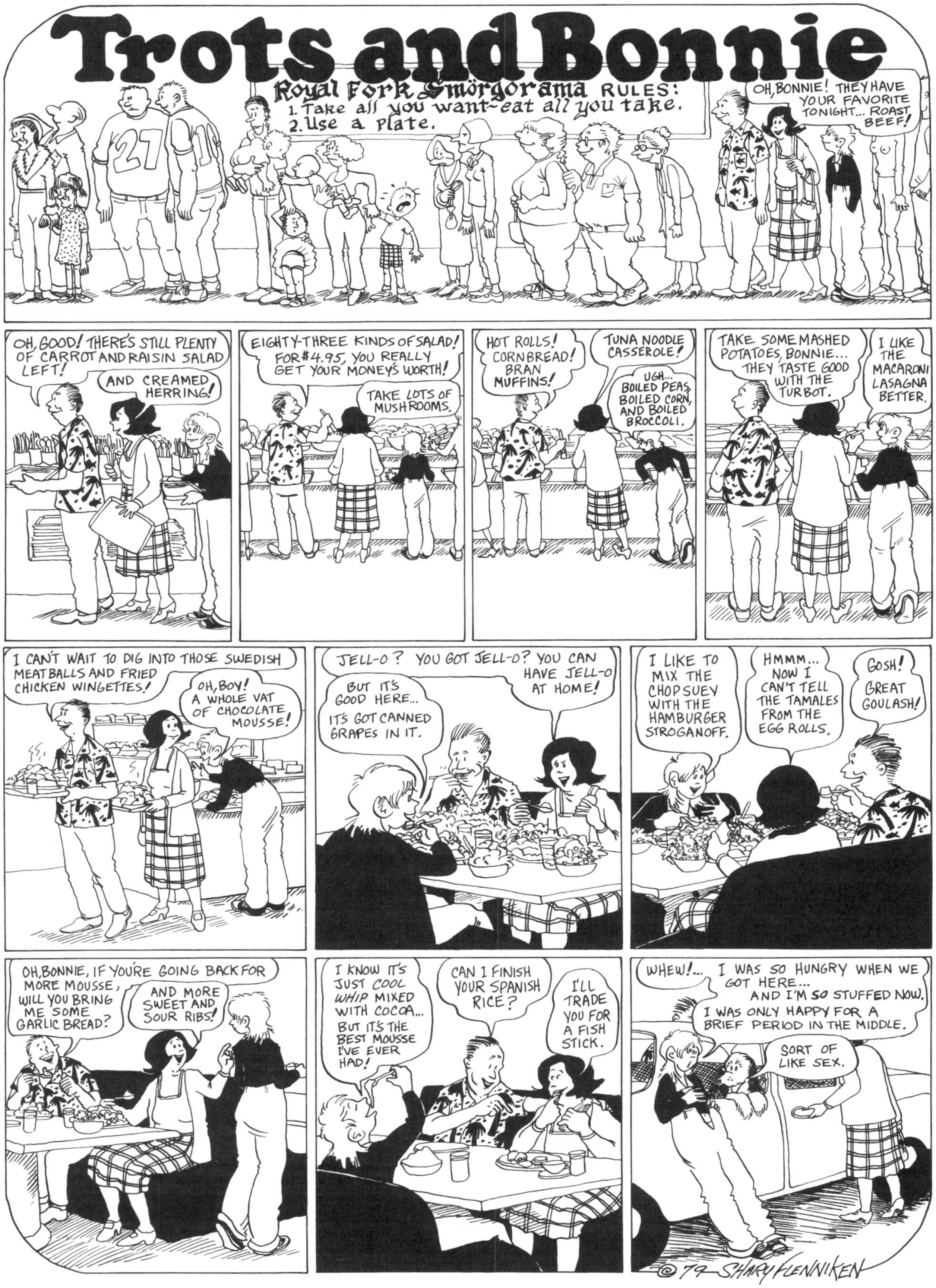
Trots and Bonnie
Royal Fork Smörgorama RULES:
1. Take all you want~eat all you take.
2. Use a plate.
OH, BONNIE! THEY HAVE YOUR FAVORITE TONIGHT... ROAST BEEF!
OH, GOOD! THERE'S STILL PLENTY OF CARROT AND RAISIN SALAD LEFT!
AND CREAMED HERRING!
EIGHTY-THREE KINDS OF SALAD! FOR $4.95, YOU REALLY GET YOUR MONEY'S WORTH!
TAKE LOTS OF MUSHROOMS.
HOT ROLLS! CORNBREAD! BRAN MUFFINS!
TUNA NOODLE CASSEROLE!
UGH... BOILED PEAS, BOILED CORN, AND BOILED BROCCOLI.
TAKE SOME MASHED POTATOES, BONNIE... THEY TASTE GOOD WITH THE TURBOT.
I LIKE THE MACARONI LASAGNA BETTER.
I CAN'T WAIT TO DIG INTO THOSE SWEDISH MEATBALLS AND FRIED CHICKEN WINGETTES!
OH, BOY! A WHOLE VAT OF CHOCOLATE MOUSSE!
JELL-O? YOU GOT JELL-O? YOU CAN HAVE JELL-O AT HOME!
BUT IT'S GOOD HERE... IT'S GOT CANNED GRAPES IN IT.
I LIKE TO MIX THE CHOP SUEY WITH THE HAMBURGER STROGANOFF.
HMMM... NOW I CAN'T TELL THE TAMALES FROM THE EGG ROLLS.
GOSH! GREAT GOULASH!
OH, BONNIE, IF YOU'RE GOING BACK FOR MORE MOUSSE, WILL YOU BRING ME SOME GARLIC BREAD?
AND MORE SWEET AND SOUR RIBS!
I KNOW IT'S JUST COOL WHIP MIXED WITH COCOA... BUT IT'S THE BEST MOUSSE I'VE EVER HAD!
CAN I FINISH YOUR SPANISH RICE?
I'LL TRADE YOU FOR A FISH STICK.
WHEW!... I WAS SO HUNGRY WHEN WE GOT HERE... AND I'M SO STUFFED NOW. I WAS ONLY HAPPY FOR A BRIEF PERIOD IN THE MIDDLE.
SORT OF LIKE SEX.
©79 SHARY FLENNIKEN

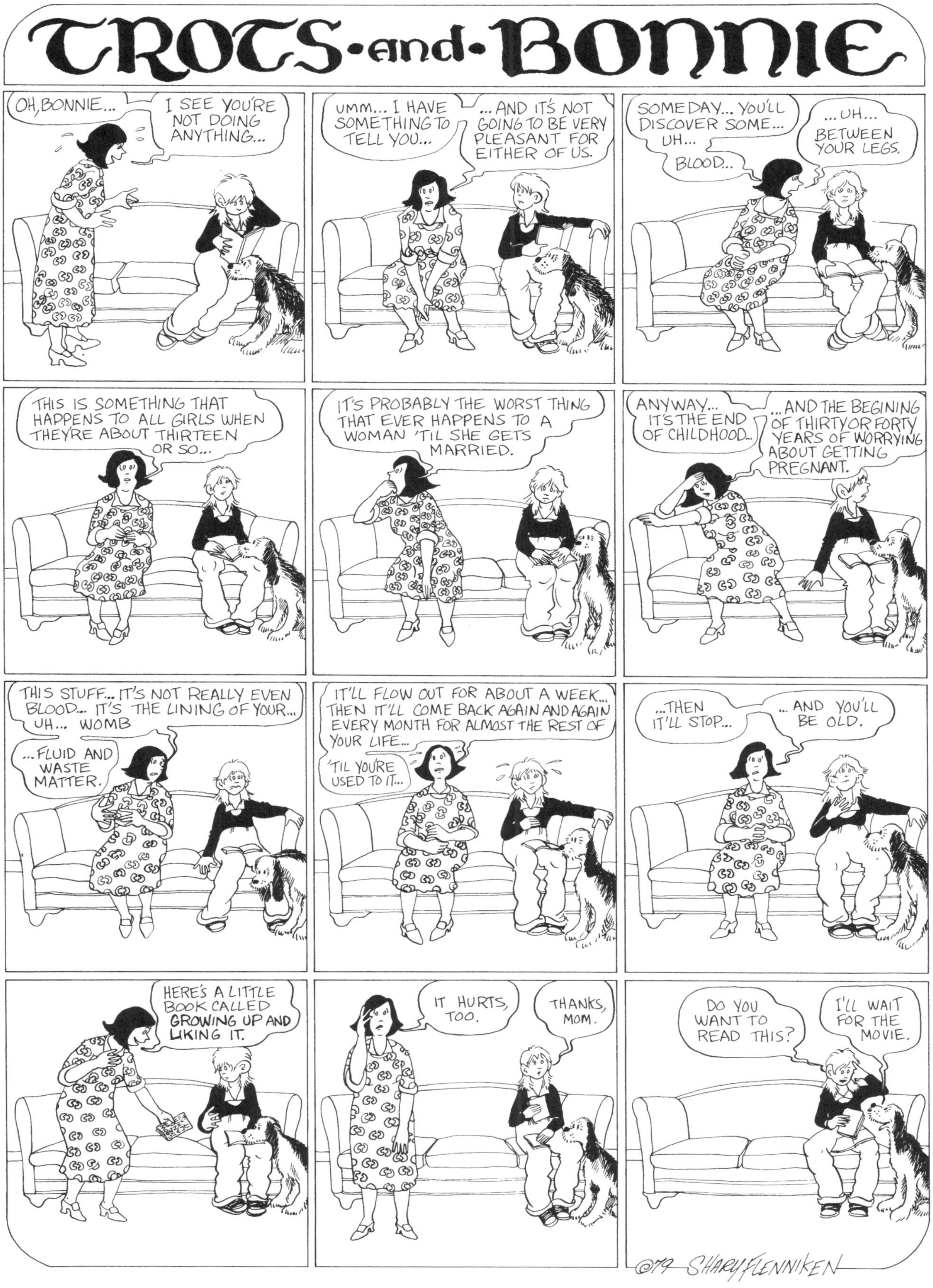
TROTS and BONNIE
OH, BONNIE...
I SEE YOU'RE NOT DOING ANYTHING...
UMM... I HAVE SOMETHING TO TELL YOU...
...AND IT'S NOT GOING TO BE VERY PLEASANT FOR EITHER OF US.
SOMEDAY... YOU'LL DISCOVER SOME... UH...
BLOOD...
...UH... BETWEEN YOUR LEGS.
THIS IS SOMETHING THAT HAPPENS TO ALL GIRLS WHEN THEY'RE ABOUT THIRTEEN OR SO...
IT'S PROBABLY THE WORST THING THAT EVER HAPPENS TO A WOMAN 'TIL SHE GETS MARRIED.
ANYWAY... IT'S THE END OF CHILDHOOD...
...AND THE BEGINING OF THIRTY OR FORTY YEARS OF WORRYING ABOUT GETTING PREGNANT.
THIS STUFF... IT'S NOT REALLY EVEN BLOOD... IT'S THE LINING OF YOUR... UH... WOMB
...FLUID AND WASTE MATTER.
IT'LL FLOW OUT FOR ABOUT A WEEK... THEN IT'LL COME BACK AGAIN AND AGAIN EVERY MONTH FOR ALMOST THE REST OF YOUR LIFE...
'TIL YOU'RE USED TO IT...
...THEN IT'LL STOP...
...AND YOU'LL BE OLD.
HERE'S A LITTLE BOOK CALLED GROWING UP AND LIKING IT.
IT HURTS, TOO.
THANKS, MOM.
DO YOU WANT TO READ THIS?
I'LL WAIT FOR THE MOVIE.
©79 SHARY FLENNIKEN

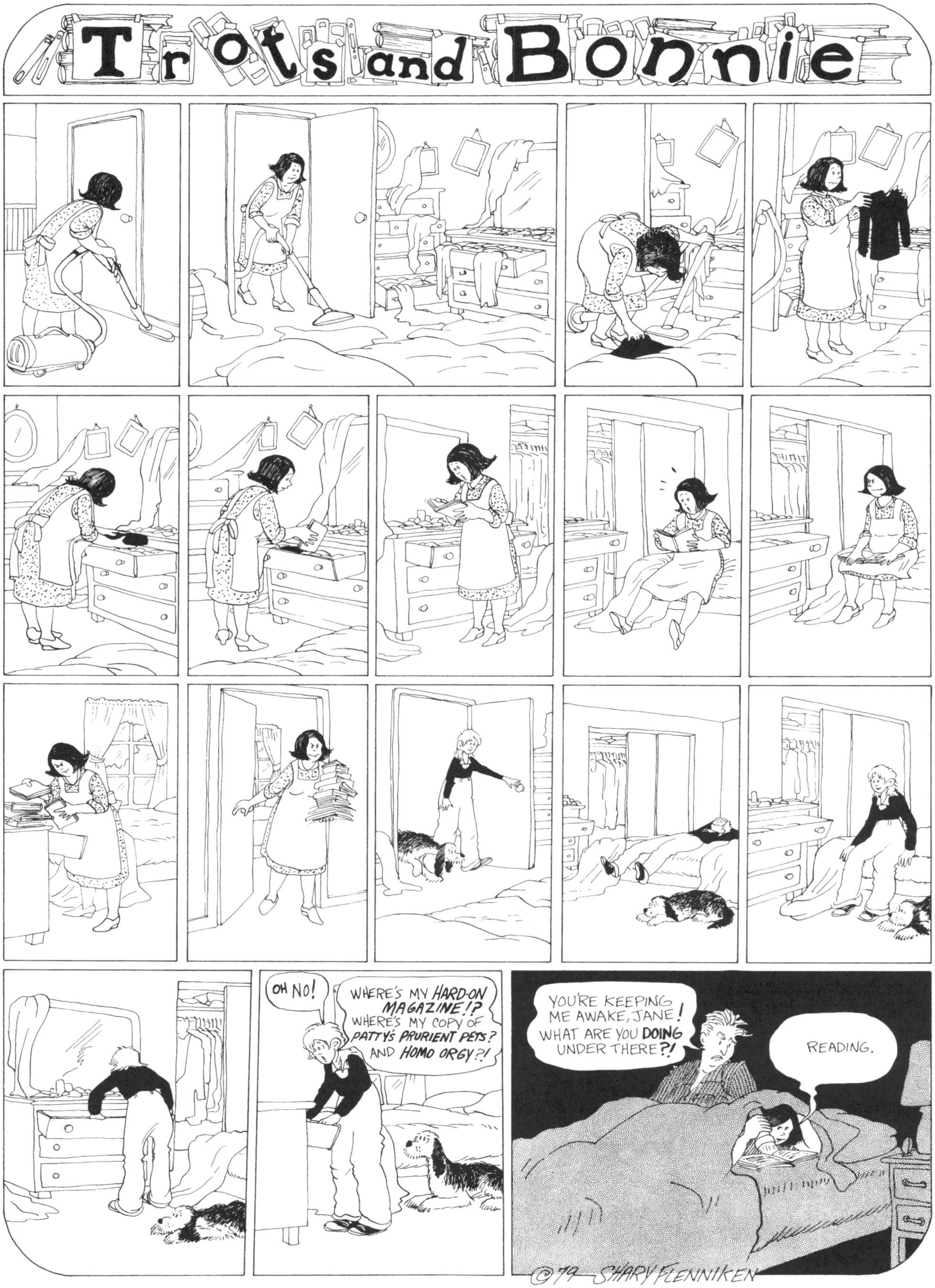
Trots and Bonnie
OH NO!
WHERE'S MY HARD-ON MAGAZINE!? WHERE'S MY COPY OF PATTY'S PRURIENT PETS? AND HOMO ORGY?!
YOU'RE KEEPING ME AWAKE, JANE! WHAT ARE YOU DOING UNDER THERE?!
READING.
©79 SHARY FLENNIKEN

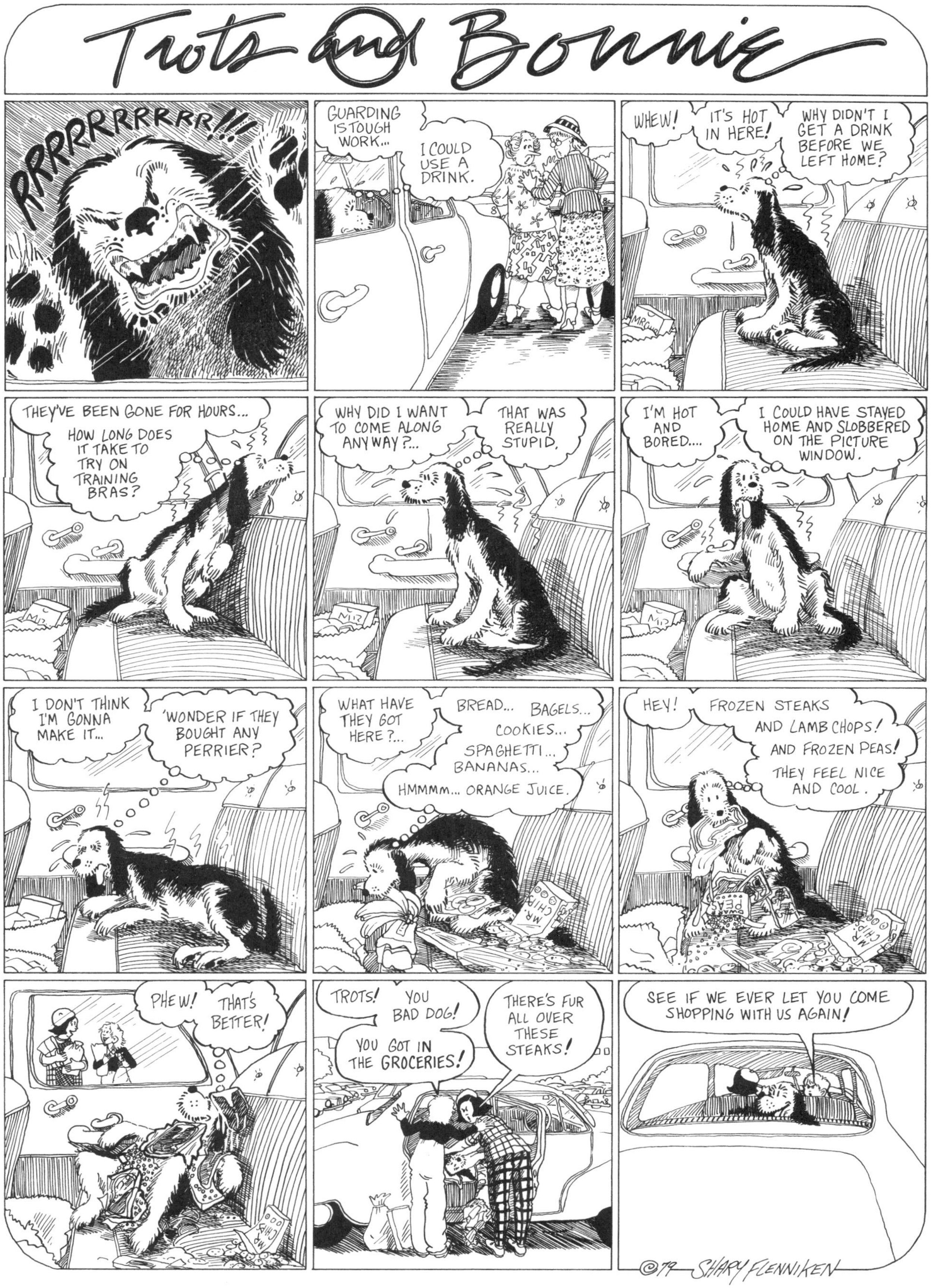
Trots and Bonnie
RRRRRRRRRRR!!!
GUARDING IS TOUGH WORK...
I COULD USE A DRINK.
WHEW!
IT'S HOT IN HERE!
WHY DIDN'T I GET A DRINK BEFORE WE LEFT HOME?
THEY'VE BEEN GONE FOR HOURS...
HOW LONG DOES IT TAKE TO TRY ON TRAINING BRAS?
WHY DID I WANT TO COME ALONG ANYWAY?...
THAT WAS REALLY STUPID.
I'M HOT AND BORED....
I COULD HAVE STAYED HOME AND SLOBBERED ON THE PICTURE WINDOW.
I DON'T THINK I'M GONNA MAKE IT...
'WONDER IF THEY BOUGHT ANY PERRIER?
WHAT HAVE THEY GOT HERE?...
BREAD... BAGELS... COOKIES... SPAGHETTI... BANANAS...
HMMMM... ORANGE JUICE.
HEY!
FROZEN STEAKS AND LAMB CHOPS! AND FROZEN PEAS! THEY FEEL NICE AND COOL.
PHEW! THAT'S BETTER!
TROTS! YOU BAD DOG!
YOU GOT IN THE GROCERIES!
THERE'S FUR ALL OVER THESE STEAKS!
SEE IF WE EVER LET YOU COME SHOPPING WITH US AGAIN!
©79 SHARY FLENNIKEN

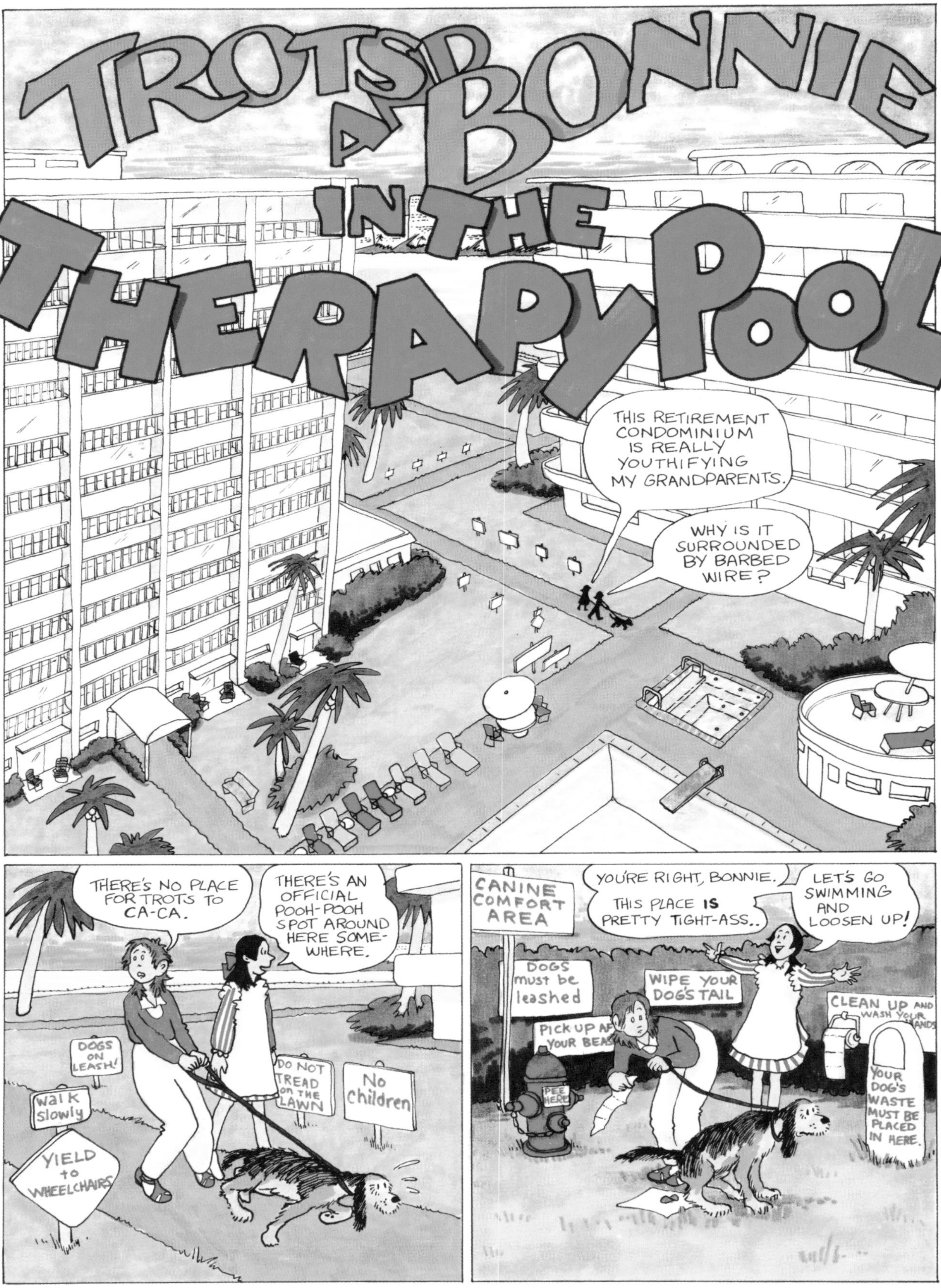
TROTS AND BONNIE IN THE THERAPY POOL
THIS RETIREMENT CONDOMINIUM IS REALLY YOUTHIFYING MY GRANDPARENTS.
WHY IS IT SURROUNDED BY BARBED WIRE?
THERE'S NO PLACE FOR TROTS TO CA-CA.
THERE'S AN OFFICIAL POOH-POOH SPOT AROUND HERE SOME-WHERE.
DOGS ON LEASH!
walk slowly
YIELD to WHEELCHAIRS
DO NOT TREAD on THE LAWN
No Children
CANINE COMFORT AREA
YOU'RE RIGHT, BONNIE.
THIS PLACE IS PRETTY TIGHT-ASS..
LET'S GO SWIMMING AND LOOSEN UP!
DOGS must be leashed
WIPE YOUR DOG'S TAIL
CLEAN UP AND WASH YOUR HANDS
PEE HERE
YOUR DOG'S WASTE MUST BE PLACED IN HERE.

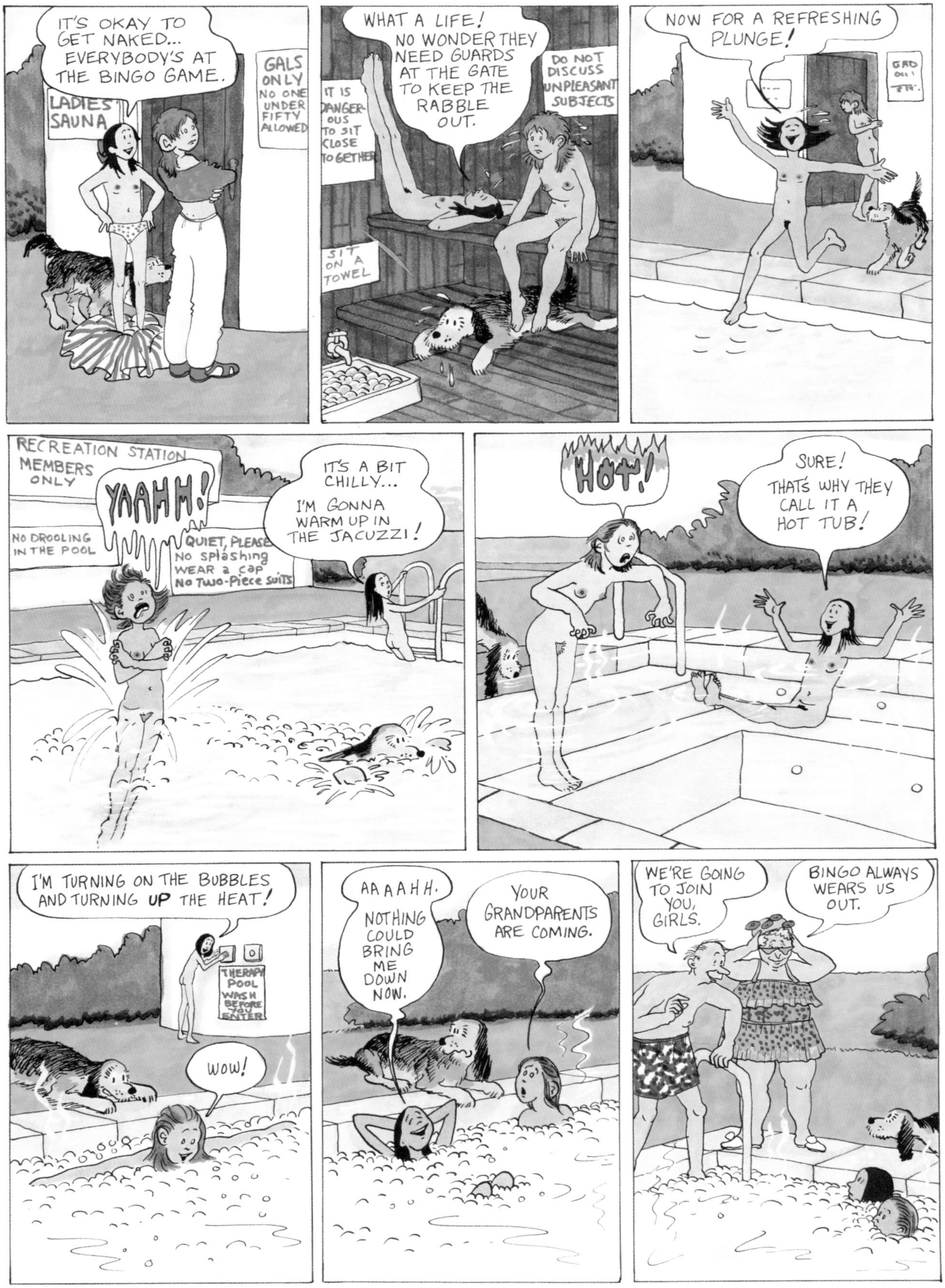
IT'S OKAY TO GET NAKED... EVERYBODY'S AT THE BINGO GAME.
LADIES' SAUNA
GALS ONLY NO ONE UNDER FIFTY ALLOWED
WHAT A LIFE! NO WONDER THEY NEED GUARDS AT THE GATE TO KEEP THE RABBLE OUT.
IT IS DANGEROUS TO SIT CLOSE TOGETHER
DO NOT DISCUSS UNPLEASANT SUBJECTS
SIT ON A TOWEL
NOW FOR A REFRESHING PLUNGE!
RECREATION STATION MEMBERS ONLY
YAAHH!
NO DROOLING IN THE POOL
QUIET, PLEASE No splashing WEAR a cap No Two-Piece SUITS
IT'S A BIT CHILLY... I'M GONNA WARM UP IN THE JACUZZI!
HOT!
SURE! THAT'S WHY THEY CALL IT A HOT TUB!
I'M TURNING ON THE BUBBLES AND TURNING UP THE HEAT!
THERAPY POOL WASH BEFORE YOU ENTER
WOW!
AAAAHH. NOTHING COULD BRING ME DOWN NOW.
YOUR GRANDPARENTS ARE COMING.
WE'RE GOING TO JOIN YOU, GIRLS.
BINGO ALWAYS WEARS US OUT.

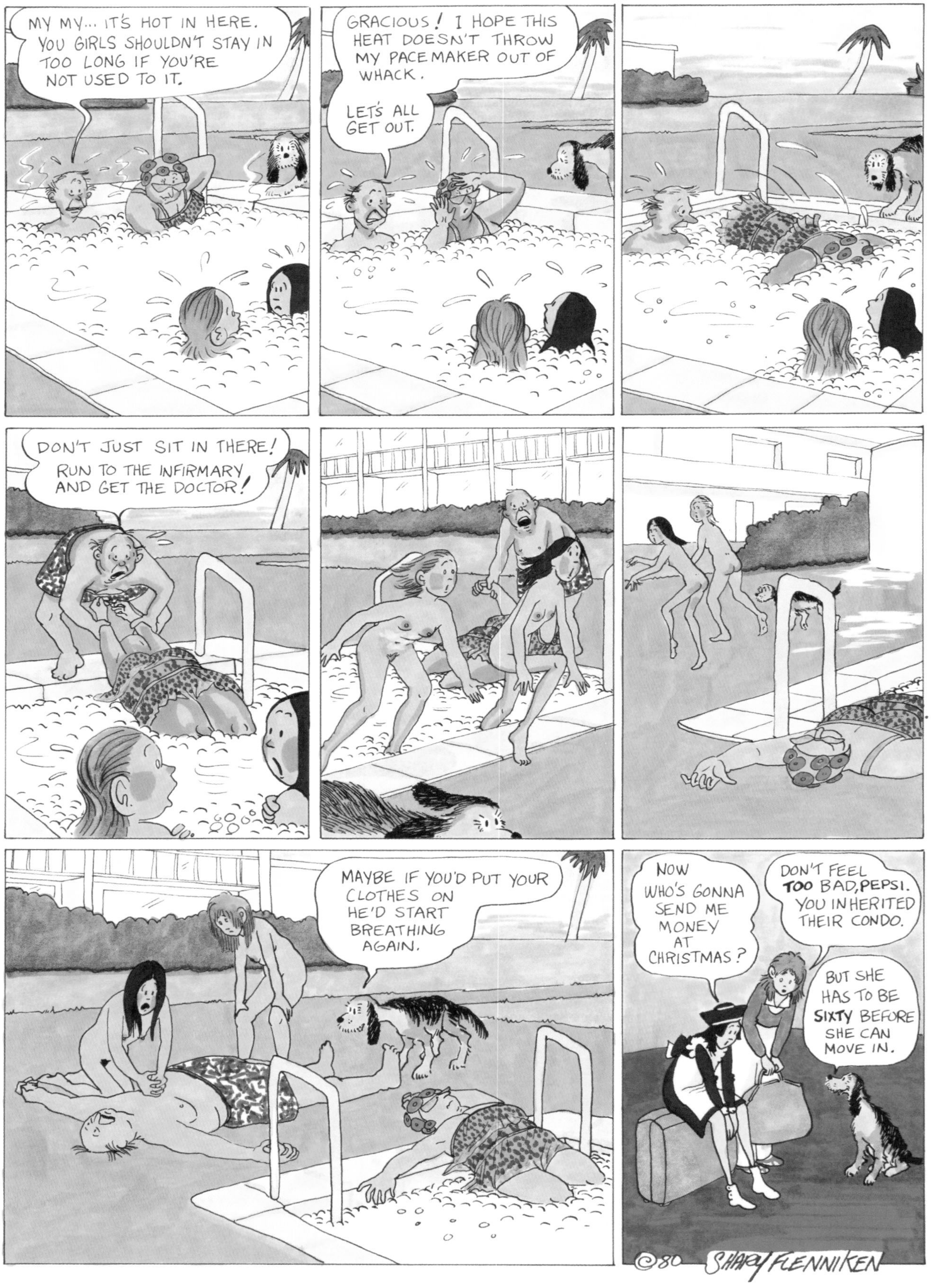

MY MY... IT'S HOT IN HERE. YOU GIRLS SHOULDN'T STAY IN TOO LONG IF YOU'RE NOT USED TO IT.
GRACIOUS! I HOPE THIS HEAT DOESN'T THROW MY PACEMAKER OUT OF WHACK.
LET'S ALL GET OUT.
DON'T JUST SIT IN THERE! RUN TO THE INFIRMARY AND GET THE DOCTOR!
MAYBE IF YOU'D PUT YOUR CLOTHES ON HE'D START BREATHING AGAIN.
NOW WHO'S GONNA SEND ME MONEY AT CHRISTMAS?
DON'T FEEL TOO BAD, PEPSI. YOU INHERITED THEIR CONDO.
BUT SHE HAS TO BE SIXTY BEFORE SHE CAN MOVE IN.
©80 SHARY FLENNIKEN

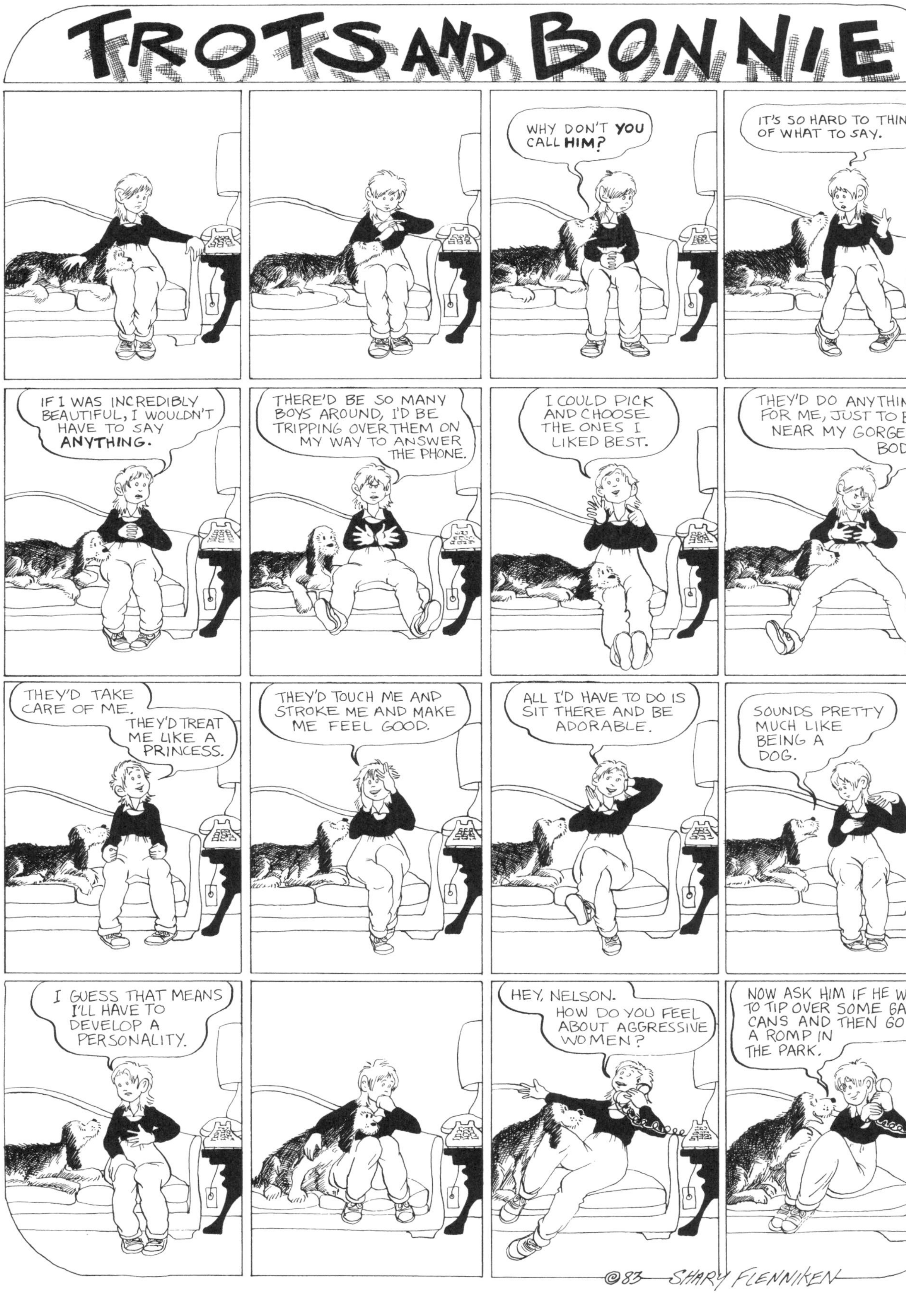
TROTS AND BONNIE
WHY DON'T YOU CALL HIM?
IT'S SO HARD TO THINK OF WHAT TO SAY.
IF I WAS INCREDIBLY BEAUTIFUL, I WOULDN'T HAVE TO SAY ANYTHING.
THERE'D BE SO MANY BOYS AROUND, I'D BE TRIPPING OVER THEM ON MY WAY TO ANSWER THE PHONE.
I COULD PICK AND CHOOSE THE ONES I LIKED BEST.
THEY'D DO ANYTHING FOR ME, JUST TO BE NEAR MY GORGEOUS BODY.
THEY'D TAKE CARE OF ME.
THEY'D TREAT ME LIKE A PRINCESS.
THEY'D TOUCH ME AND STROKE ME AND MAKE ME FEEL GOOD.
ALL I'D HAVE TO DO IS SIT THERE AND BE ADORABLE.
SOUNDS PRETTY MUCH LIKE BEING A DOG.
I GUESS THAT MEANS I'LL HAVE TO DEVELOP A PERSONALITY.
HEY, NELSON.
HOW DO YOU FEEL ABOUT AGGRESSIVE WOMEN?
NOW ASK HIM IF HE WANTS TO TIP OVER SOME GARBAGE CANS AND THEN GO FOR A ROMP IN THE PARK.
©83 SHARY FLENNIKEN

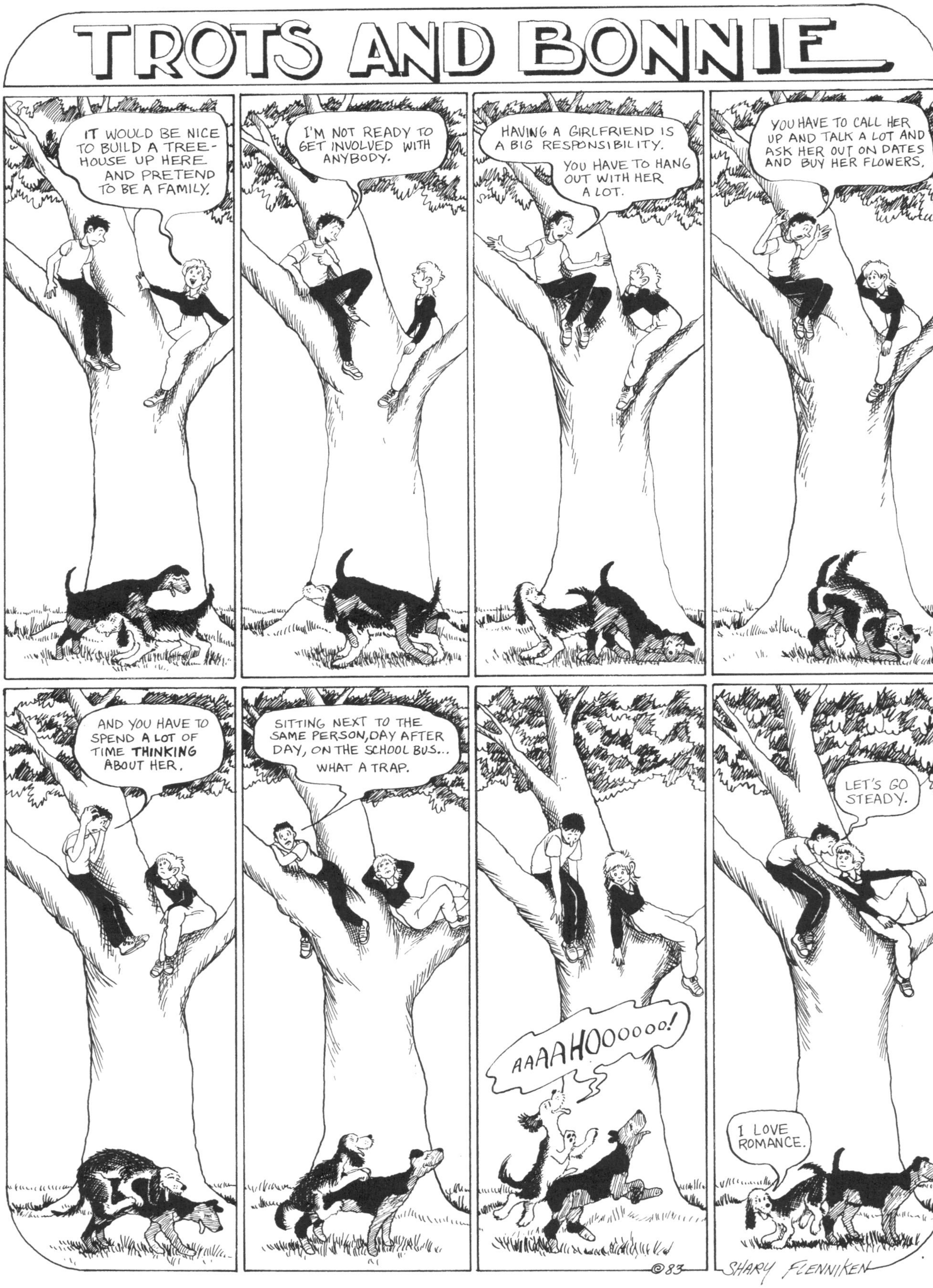
TROTS AND BONNIE
IT WOULD BE NICE TO BUILD A TREE-HOUSE UP HERE AND PRETEND TO BE A FAMILY.
I'M NOT READY TO GET INVOLVED WITH ANYBODY.
HAVING A GIRLFRIEND IS A BIG RESPONSIBILITY.
YOU HAVE TO HANG OUT WITH HER A LOT.
YOU HAVE TO CALL HER UP AND TALK A LOT AND ASK HER OUT ON DATES AND BUY HER FLOWERS.
AND YOU HAVE TO SPEND A LOT OF TIME THINKING ABOUT HER.
SITTING NEXT TO THE SAME PERSON, DAY AFTER DAY, ON THE SCHOOL BUS...
WHAT A TRAP.
AAAAHOOooooo!
LET'S GO STEADY.
I LOVE ROMANCE.
©83
SHARY FLENNIKEN

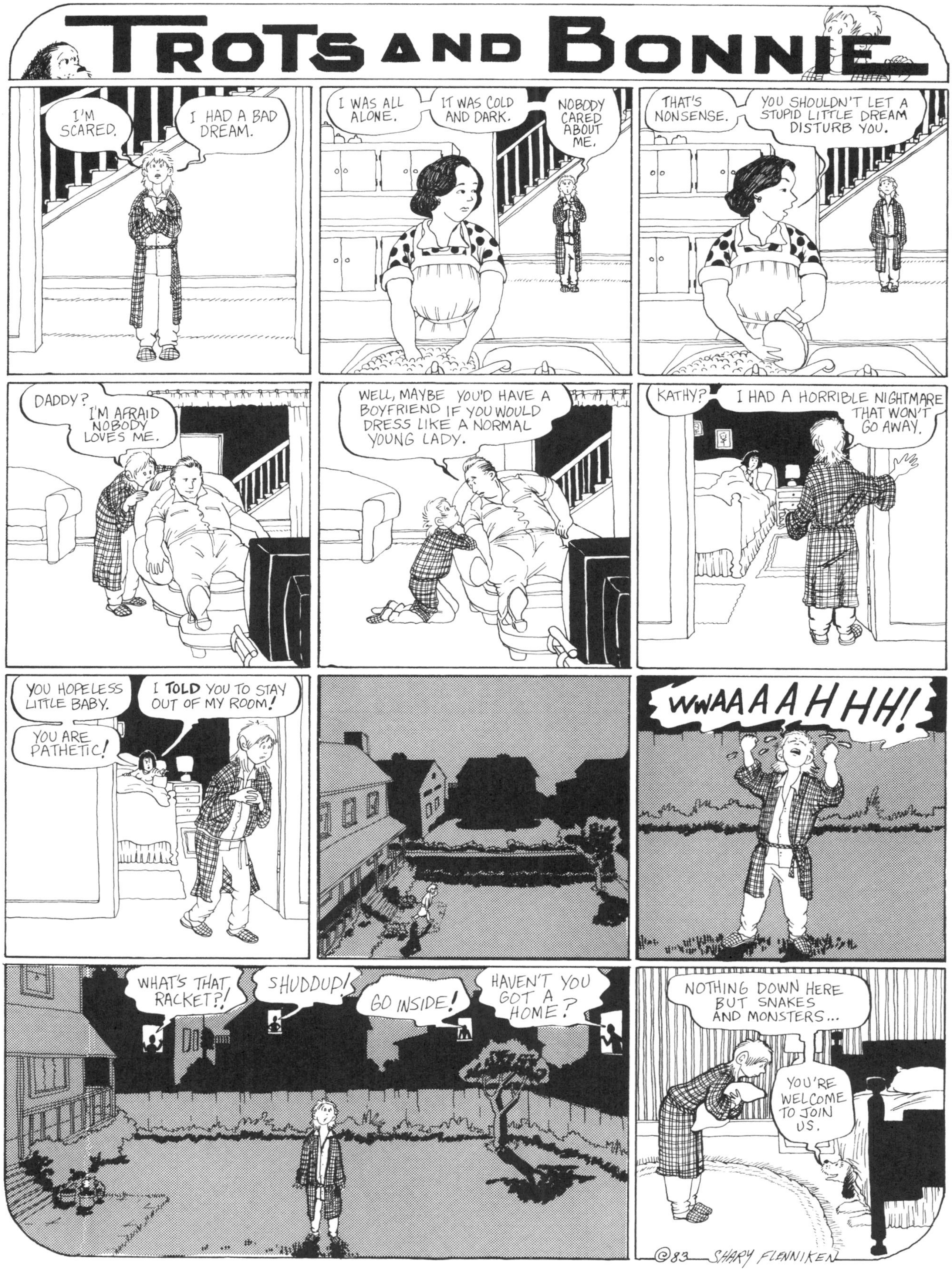
TROTS AND BONNIE
I'M SCARED.
I HAD A BAD DREAM.
I WAS ALL ALONE.
IT WAS COLD AND DARK.
NOBODY CARED ABOUT ME.
THAT'S NONSENSE.
YOU SHOULDN'T LET A STUPID LITTLE DREAM DISTURB YOU.
DADDY?
I'M AFRAID NOBODY LOVES ME.
WELL, MAYBE YOU'D HAVE A BOYFRIEND IF YOU WOULD DRESS LIKE A NORMAL YOUNG LADY.
KATHY?
I HAD A HORRIBLE NIGHTMARE THAT WON'T GO AWAY.
YOU HOPELESS LITTLE BABY.
YOU ARE PATHETIC!
I TOLD YOU TO STAY OUT OF MY ROOM!
WWAAAAHHHH!
WHAT'S THAT RACKET?!
SHUDDUP!
GO INSIDE!
HAVEN'T YOU GOT A HOME?
NOTHING DOWN HERE BUT SNAKES AND MONSTERS...
YOU'RE WELCOME TO JOIN US.
©83 SHARY FLENNIKEN

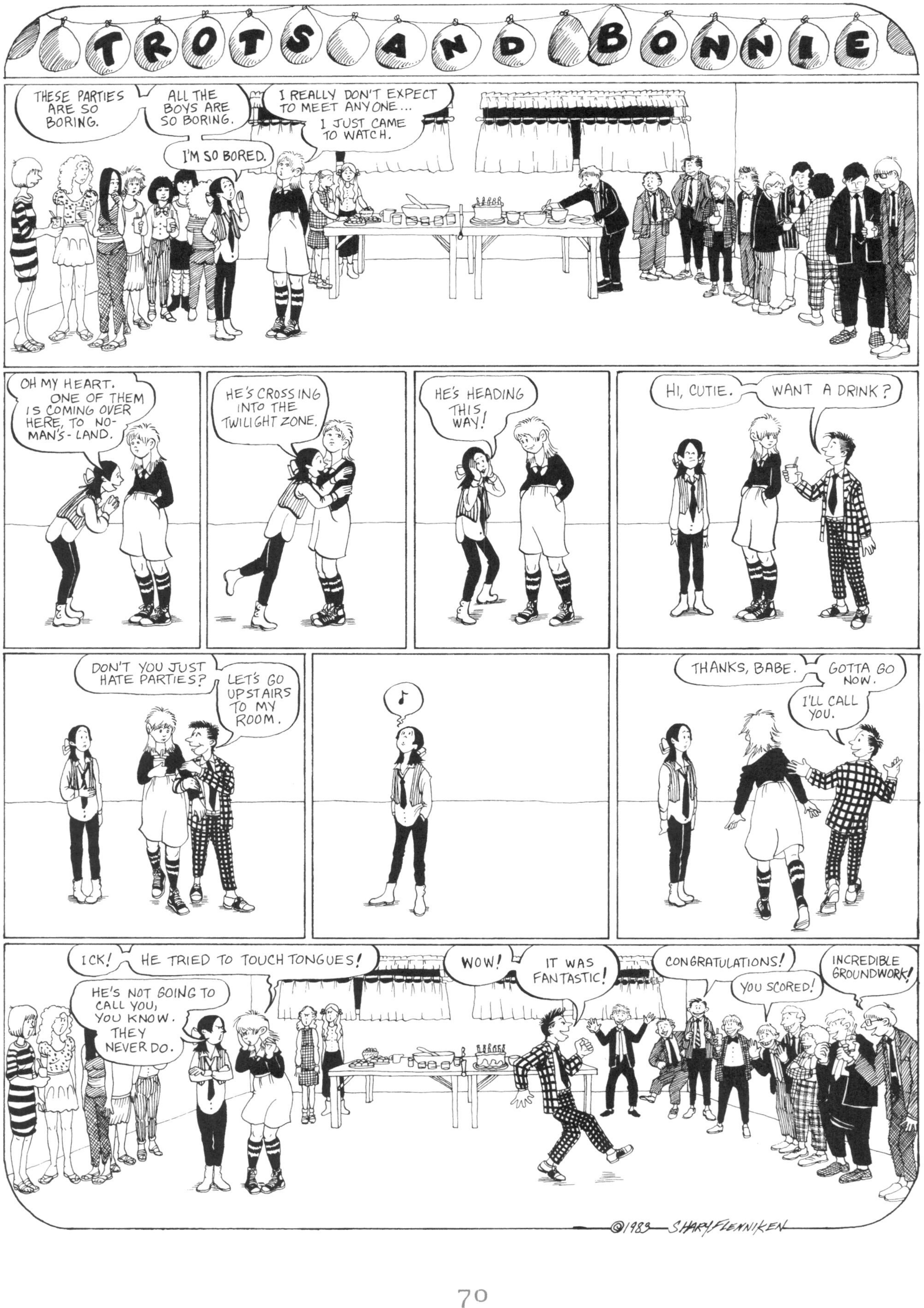
TROTS AND BONNIE
THESE PARTIES ARE SO BORING.
ALL THE BOYS ARE SO BORING.
I'M SO BORED.
I REALLY DON'T EXPECT TO MEET ANYONE... I JUST CAME TO WATCH.
OH MY HEART. ONE OF THEM IS COMING OVER HERE, TO NO-MAN'S-LAND.
HE'S CROSSING INTO THE TWILIGHT ZONE.
HE'S HEADING THIS WAY!
HI, CUTIE.
WANT A DRINK?
DON'T YOU JUST HATE PARTIES?
LET'S GO UPSTAIRS TO MY ROOM.
♪
THANKS, BABE.
GOTTA GO NOW.
I'LL CALL YOU.
ICK!
HE TRIED TO TOUCH TONGUES!
HE'S NOT GOING TO CALL YOU, YOU KNOW. THEY NEVER DO.
WOW!
IT WAS FANTASTIC!
CONGRATULATIONS!
YOU SCORED!
INCREDIBLE GROUNDWORK!
©1983 SHARY FLENNIKEN

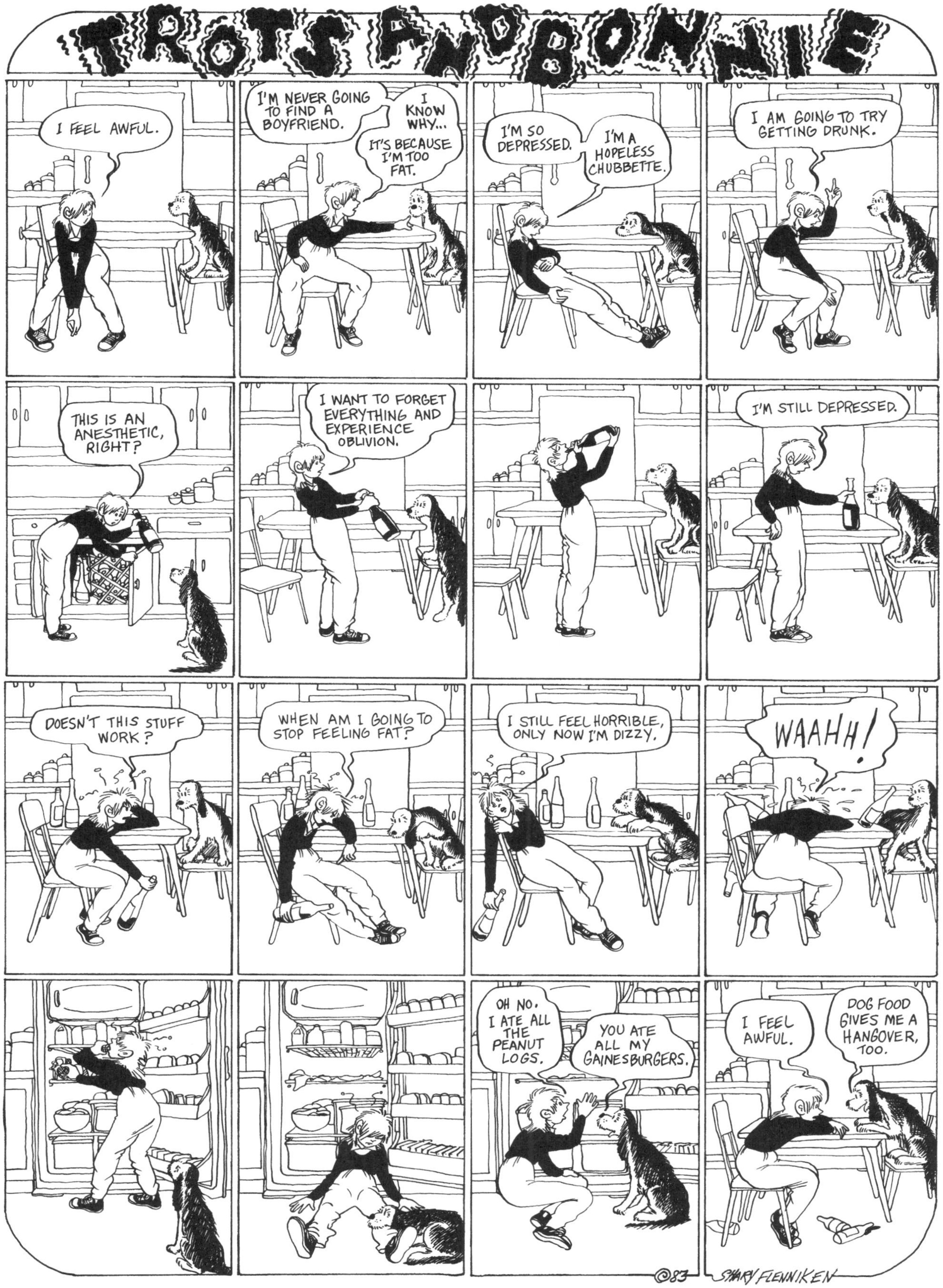
TROTS AND BONNIE
I FEEL AWFUL.
I'M NEVER GOING TO FIND A BOYFRIEND.
I KNOW WHY...
IT'S BECAUSE I'M TOO FAT.
I'M SO DEPRESSED.
I'M A HOPELESS CHUBBETTE.
I AM GOING TO TRY GETTING DRUNK.
THIS IS AN ANESTHETIC, RIGHT?
I WANT TO FORGET EVERYTHING AND EXPERIENCE OBLIVION.
I'M STILL DEPRESSED.
DOESN'T THIS STUFF WORK?
WHEN AM I GOING TO STOP FEELING FAT?
I STILL FEEL HORRIBLE, ONLY NOW I'M DIZZY.
WAAHH!
OH NO. I ATE ALL THE PEANUT LOGS.
YOU ATE ALL MY GAINESBURGERS.
I FEEL AWFUL.
DOG FOOD GIVES ME A HANGOVER, TOO.
©83 SHARY FLENNIKEN

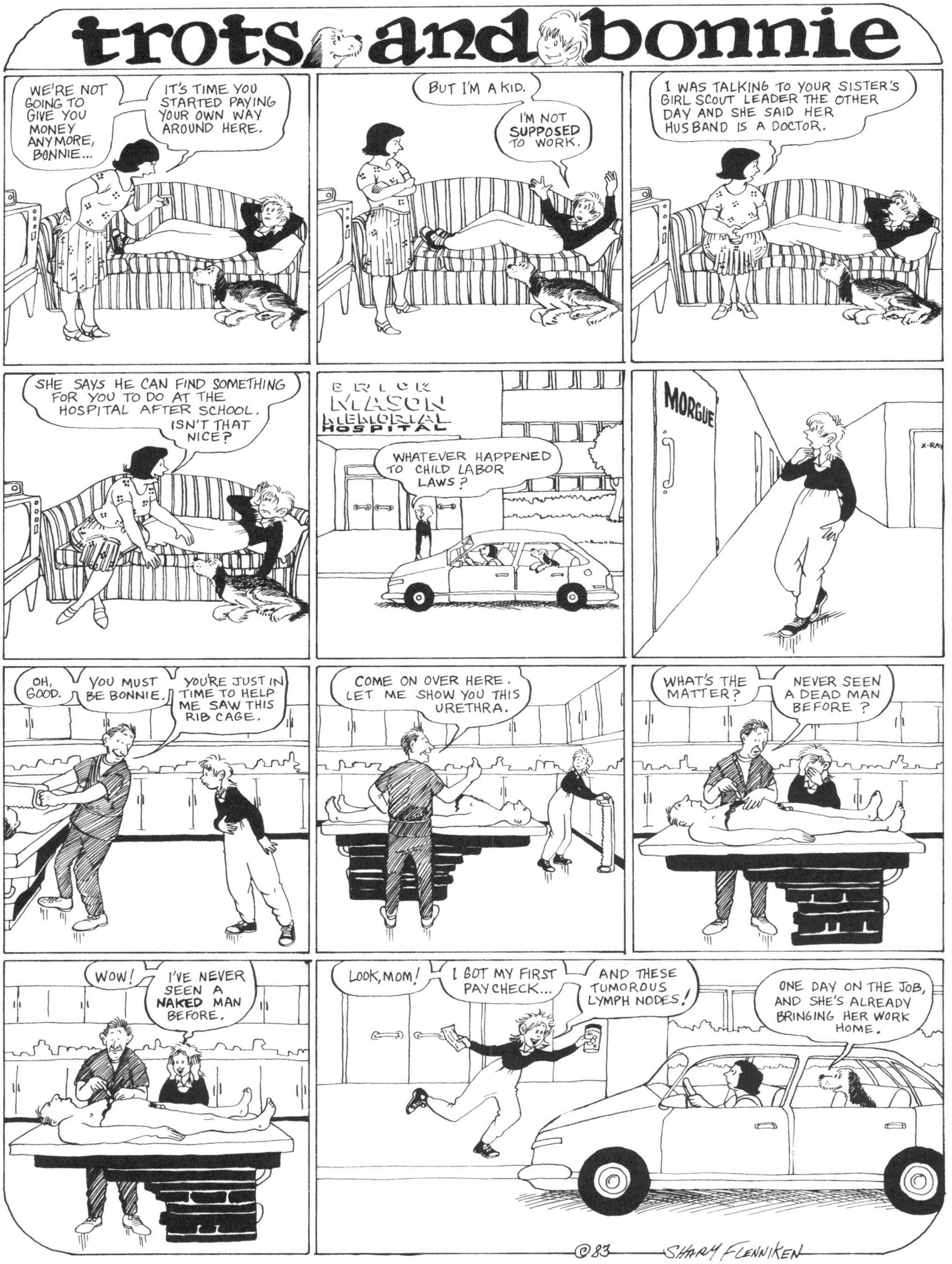
trots and bonnie
WE'RE NOT GOING TO GIVE YOU MONEY ANYMORE, BONNIE...
IT'S TIME YOU STARTED PAYING YOUR OWN WAY AROUND HERE.
BUT I'M A KID.
I'M NOT SUPPOSED TO WORK.
I WAS TALKING TO YOUR SISTER'S GIRL SCOUT LEADER THE OTHER DAY AND SHE SAID HER HUSBAND IS A DOCTOR.
SHE SAYS HE CAN FIND SOMETHING FOR YOU TO DO AT THE HOSPITAL AFTER SCHOOL.
ISN'T THAT NICE?
ERICK MASON MEMORIAL HOSPITAL
WHATEVER HAPPENED TO CHILD LABOR LAWS?
MORGUE
X-RAY
OH, GOOD.
YOU MUST BE BONNIE.
YOU'RE JUST IN TIME TO HELP ME SAW THIS RIB CAGE.
COME ON OVER HERE. LET ME SHOW YOU THIS URETHRA.
WHAT'S THE MATTER?
NEVER SEEN A DEAD MAN BEFORE?
WOW!
I'VE NEVER SEEN A NAKED MAN BEFORE.
LOOK, MOM!
I GOT MY FIRST PAYCHECK...
AND THESE TUMOROUS LYMPH NODES!
ONE DAY ON THE JOB, AND SHE'S ALREADY BRINGING HER WORK HOME.
©83 SHARY FLENNIKEN

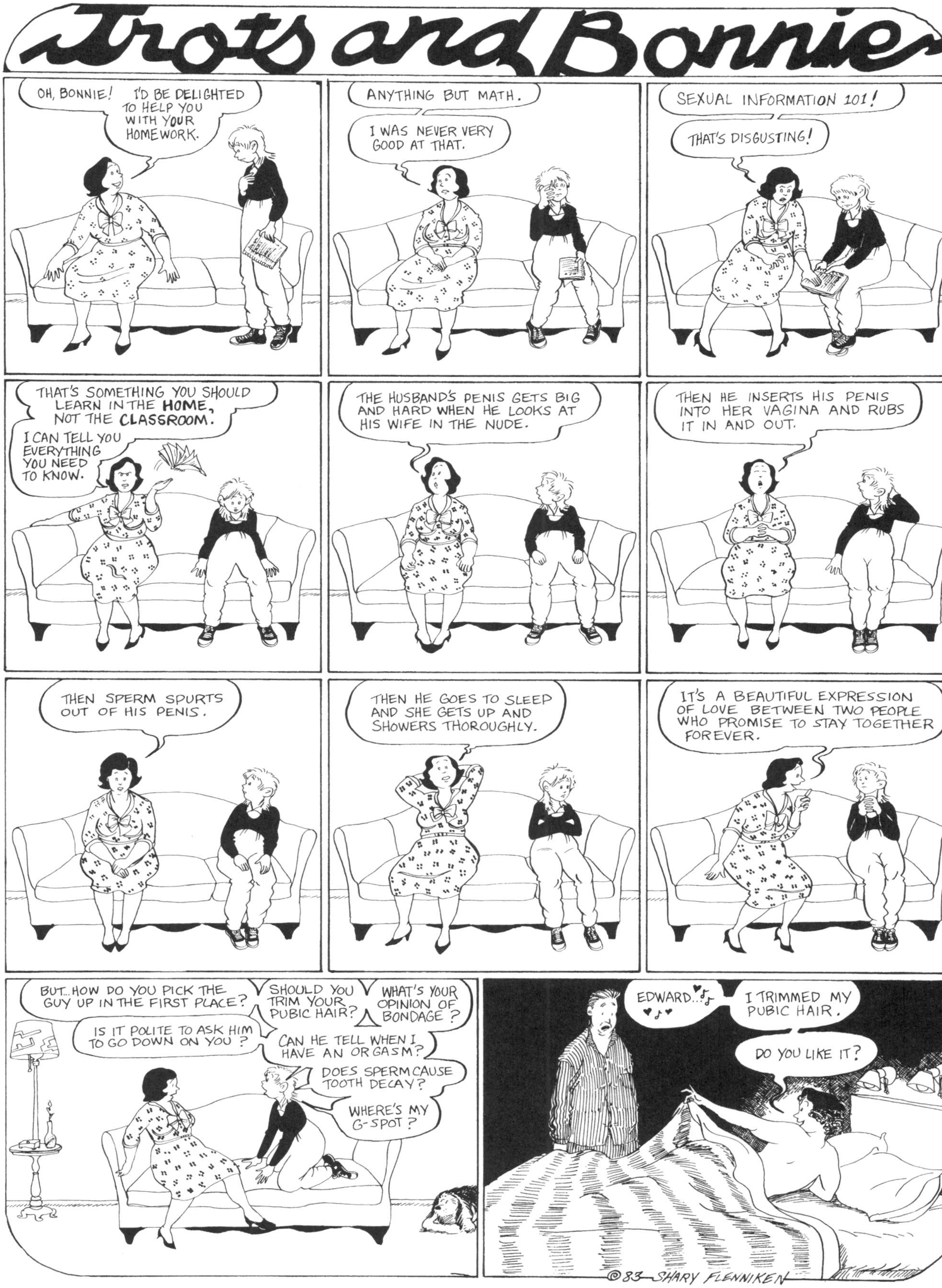
Trots and Bonnie
OH, BONNIE! I'D BE DELIGHTED TO HELP YOU WITH YOUR HOMEWORK.
ANYTHING BUT MATH.
I WAS NEVER VERY GOOD AT THAT.
SEXUAL INFORMATION 101!
THAT'S DISGUSTING!
THAT'S SOMETHING YOU SHOULD LEARN IN THE HOME, NOT THE CLASSROOM.
I CAN TELL YOU EVERYTHING YOU NEED TO KNOW.
THE HUSBAND'S PENIS GETS BIG AND HARD WHEN HE LOOKS AT HIS WIFE IN THE NUDE.
THEN HE INSERTS HIS PENIS INTO HER VAGINA AND RUBS IT IN AND OUT.
THEN SPERM SPURTS OUT OF HIS PENIS.
THEN HE GOES TO SLEEP AND SHE GETS UP AND SHOWERS THOROUGHLY.
IT'S A BEAUTIFUL EXPRESSION OF LOVE BETWEEN TWO PEOPLE WHO PROMISE TO STAY TOGETHER FOREVER.
BUT...HOW DO YOU PICK THE GUY UP IN THE FIRST PLACE?
SHOULD YOU TRIM YOUR PUBIC HAIR?
WHAT'S YOUR OPINION OF BONDAGE?
IS IT POLITE TO ASK HIM TO GO DOWN ON YOU?
CAN HE TELL WHEN I HAVE AN ORGASM?
DOES SPERM CAUSE TOOTH DECAY?
WHERE'S MY G-SPOT?
EDWARD...
I TRIMMED MY PUBIC HAIR.
DO YOU LIKE IT?
©83 SHARY FLENNIKEN

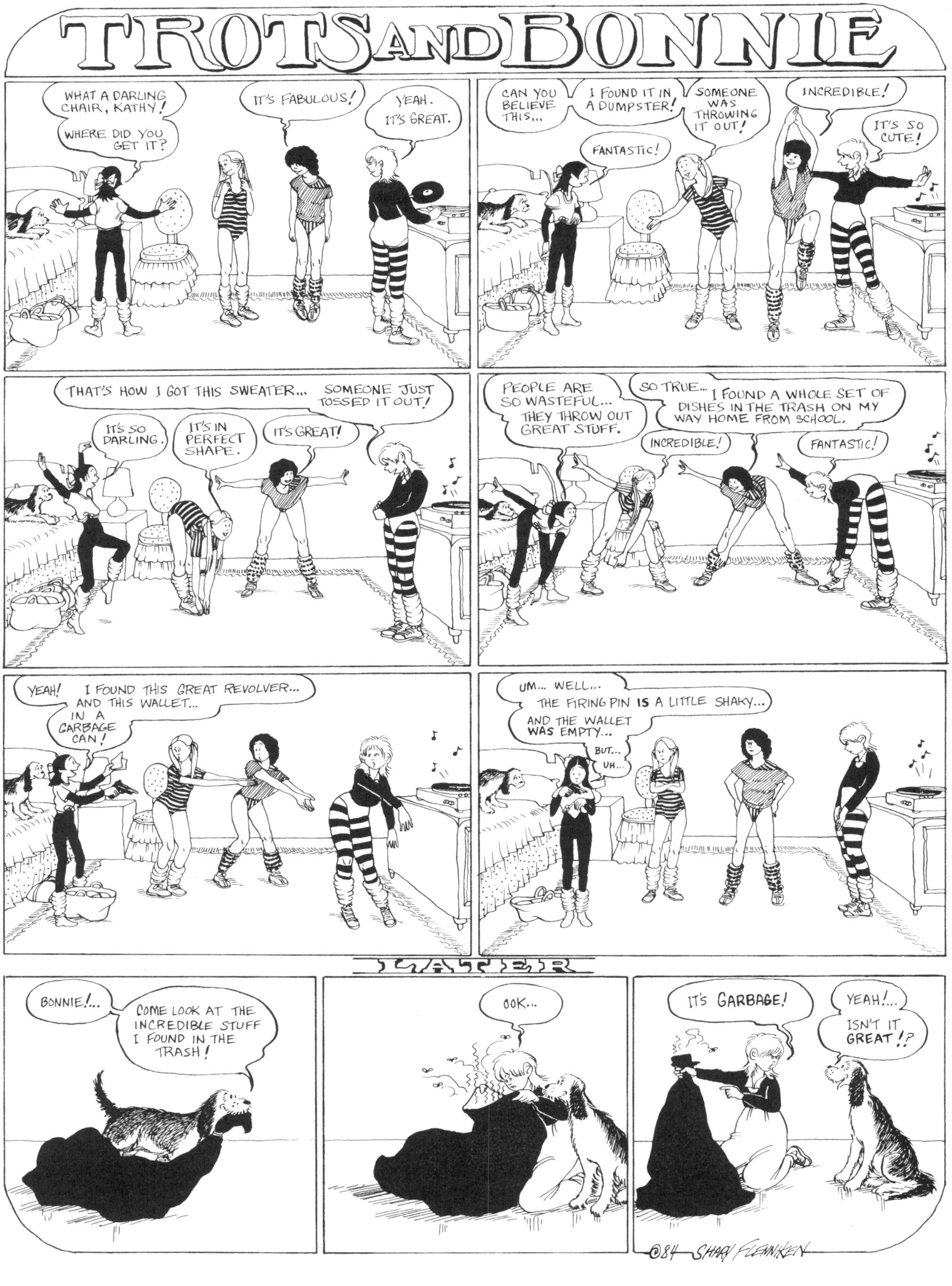
TROTS AND BONNIE
WHAT A DARLING CHAIR, KATHY!
WHERE DID YOU GET IT?
IT'S FABULOUS!
YEAH. IT'S GREAT.
CAN YOU BELIEVE THIS...
I FOUND IT IN A DUMPSTER!
SOMEONE WAS THROWING IT OUT!
INCREDIBLE!
FANTASTIC!
IT'S SO CUTE!
THAT'S HOW I GOT THIS SWEATER... SOMEONE JUST TOSSED IT OUT!
IT'S SO DARLING.
IT'S IN PERFECT SHAPE.
IT'S GREAT!
PEOPLE ARE SO WASTEFUL... THEY THROW OUT GREAT STUFF.
SO TRUE... I FOUND A WHOLE SET OF DISHES IN THE TRASH ON MY WAY HOME FROM SCHOOL.
INCREDIBLE!
FANTASTIC!
YEAH! I FOUND THIS GREAT REVOLVER... AND THIS WALLET... IN A GARBAGE CAN!
UM... WELL...
THE FIRING PIN IS A LITTLE SHAKY...
AND THE WALLET WAS EMPTY...
BUT... UH...
LATER
BONNIE!...
COME LOOK AT THE INCREDIBLE STUFF I FOUND IN THE TRASH!
OOK...
IT'S GARBAGE!
YEAH!... ISN'T IT GREAT!?
©84 SHARY FLENNIKEN

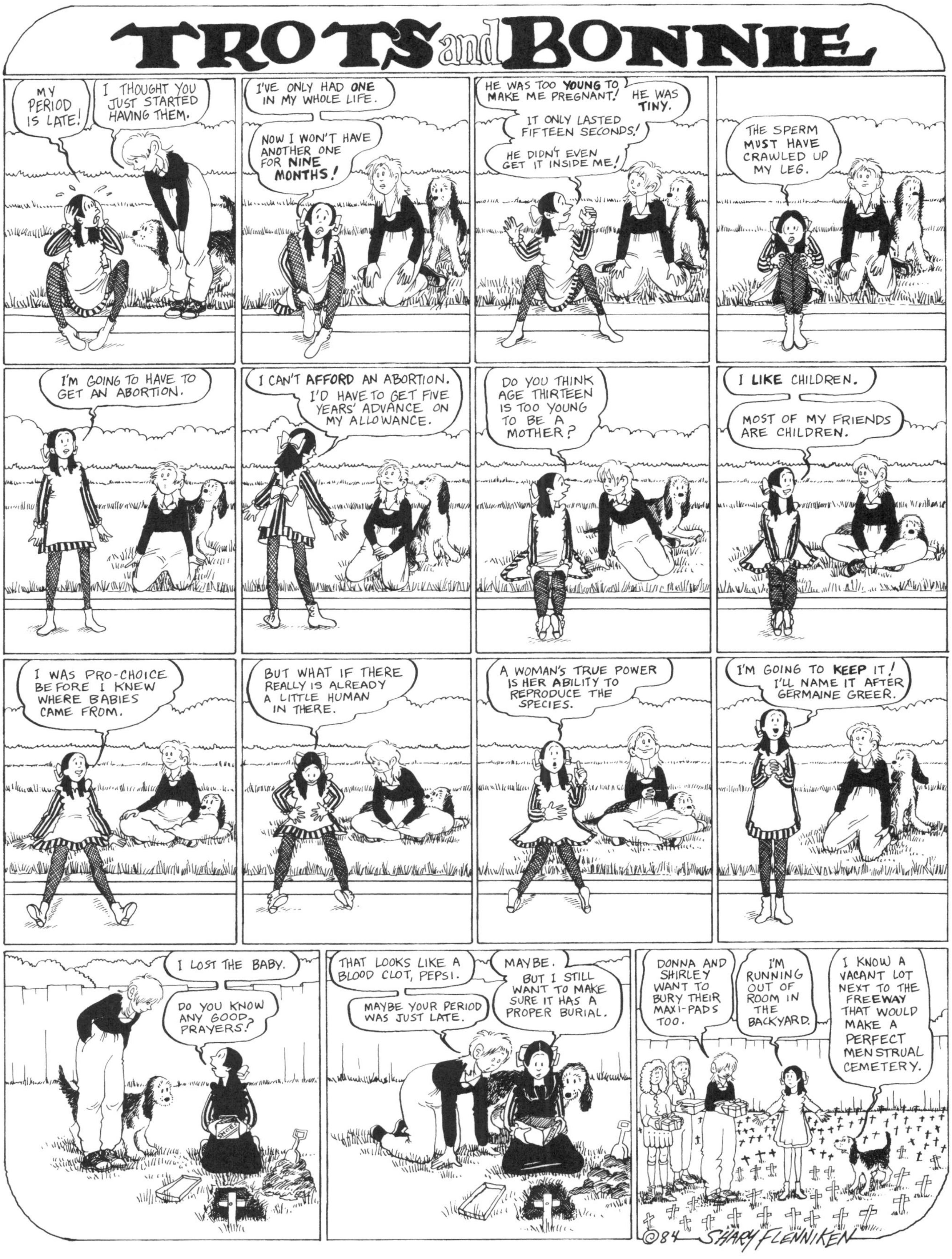
TROTS and BONNIE
MY PERIOD IS LATE!
I THOUGHT YOU JUST STARTED HAVING THEM.
I'VE ONLY HAD ONE IN MY WHOLE LIFE.
NOW I WON'T HAVE ANOTHER ONE FOR NINE MONTHS!
HE WAS TOO YOUNG TO MAKE ME PREGNANT!
HE WAS TINY.
IT ONLY LASTED FIFTEEN SECONDS!
HE DIDN'T EVEN GET IT INSIDE ME!
THE SPERM MUST HAVE CRAWLED UP MY LEG.
I'M GOING TO HAVE TO GET AN ABORTION.
I CAN'T AFFORD AN ABORTION. I'D HAVE TO GET FIVE YEARS' ADVANCE ON MY ALLOWANCE.
DO YOU THINK AGE THIRTEEN IS TOO YOUNG TO BE A MOTHER?
I LIKE CHILDREN.
MOST OF MY FRIENDS ARE CHILDREN.
I WAS PRO-CHOICE BEFORE I KNEW WHERE BABIES CAME FROM.
BUT WHAT IF THERE REALLY IS ALREADY A LITTLE HUMAN IN THERE.
A WOMAN'S TRUE POWER IS HER ABILITY TO REPRODUCE THE SPECIES.
I'M GOING TO KEEP IT! I'LL NAME IT AFTER GERMAINE GREER.
I LOST THE BABY.
DO YOU KNOW ANY GOOD PRAYERS?
THAT LOOKS LIKE A BLOOD CLOT, PEPSI.
MAYBE YOUR PERIOD WAS JUST LATE.
MAYBE.
BUT I STILL WANT TO MAKE SURE IT HAS A PROPER BURIAL.
DONNA AND SHIRLEY WANT TO BURY THEIR MAXI-PADS TOO.
I'M RUNNING OUT OF ROOM IN THE BACKYARD.
I KNOW A VACANT LOT NEXT TO THE FREEWAY THAT WOULD MAKE A PERFECT MENSTRUAL CEMETERY.
©84 SHARY FLENNIKEN

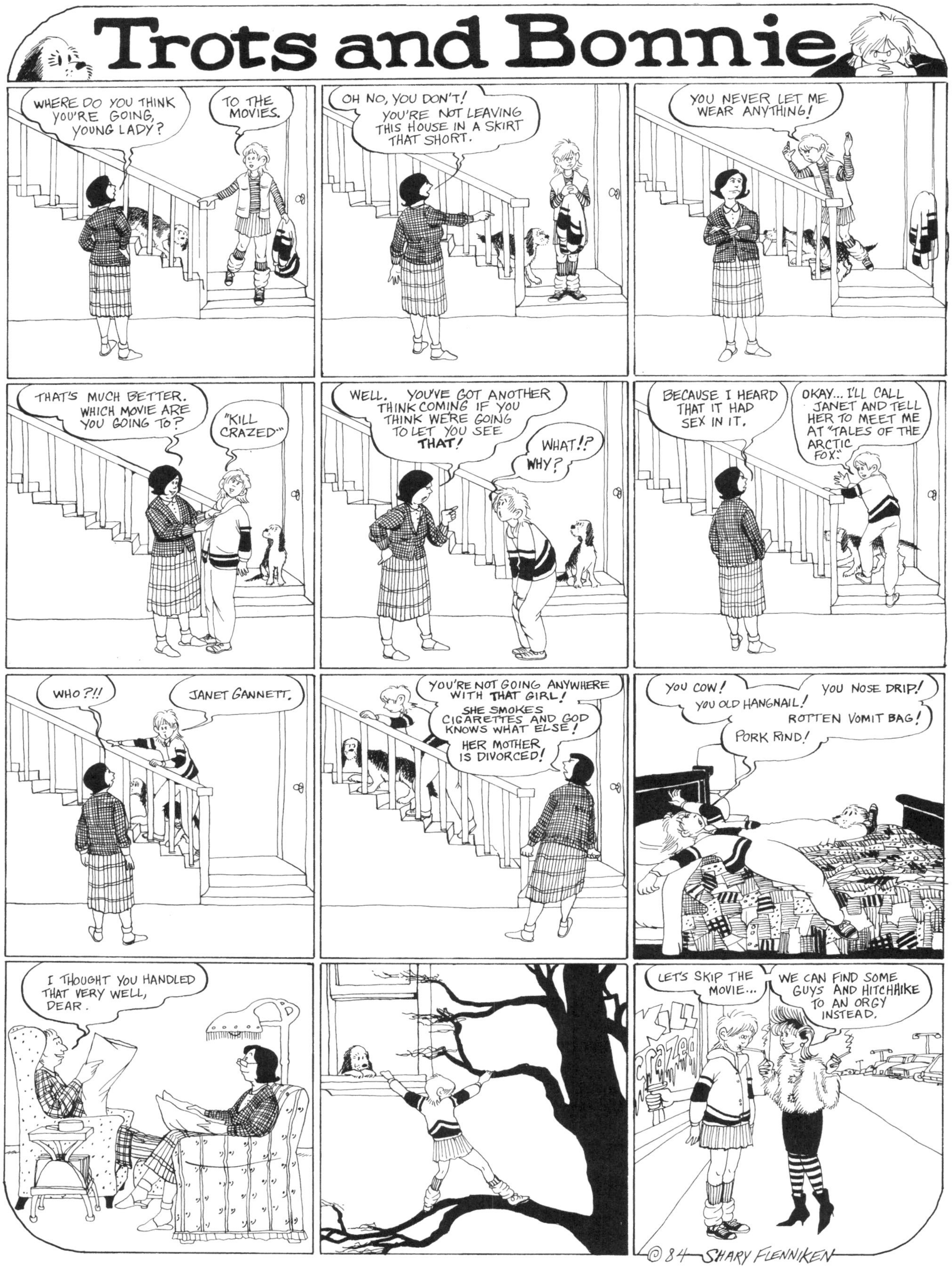
Trots and Bonnie
WHERE DO YOU THINK YOU'RE GOING, YOUNG LADY?
TO THE MOVIES.
OH NO, YOU DON'T! YOU'RE NOT LEAVING THIS HOUSE IN A SKIRT THAT SHORT.
YOU NEVER LET ME WEAR ANYTHING!
THAT'S MUCH BETTER. WHICH MOVIE ARE YOU GOING TO?
"KILL CRAZED."
WELL, YOU'VE GOT ANOTHER THINK COMING IF YOU THINK WE'RE GOING TO LET YOU SEE THAT!
WHAT!? WHY?
BECAUSE I HEARD THAT IT HAD SEX IN IT.
OKAY... I'LL CALL JANET AND TELL HER TO MEET ME AT "TALES OF THE ARCTIC FOX."
WHO?!!
JANET GANNETT.
YOU'RE NOT GOING ANYWHERE WITH THAT GIRL! SHE SMOKES CIGARETTES AND GOD KNOWS WHAT ELSE! HER MOTHER IS DIVORCED!
YOU COW! YOU OLD HANGNAIL! YOU NOSE DRIP! ROTTEN VOMIT BAG! PORK RIND!
I THOUGHT YOU HANDLED THAT VERY WELL, DEAR.
LET'S SKIP THE MOVIE...
WE CAN FIND SOME GUYS AND HITCHHIKE TO AN ORGY INSTEAD.
KILL CRAZED
© 84 SHARY FLENNIKEN

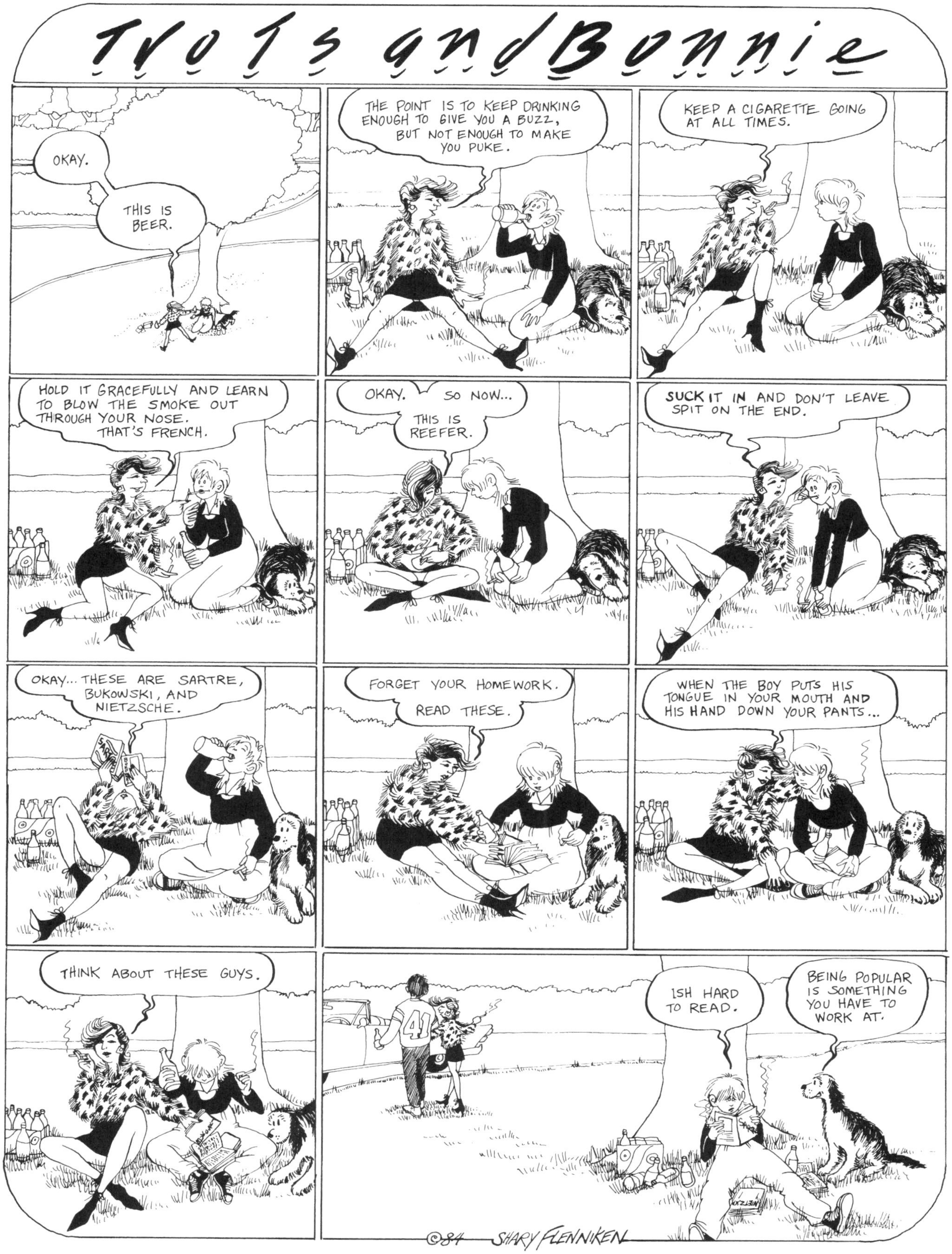
Trots and Bonnie
OKAY.
THIS IS BEER.
THE POINT IS TO KEEP DRINKING ENOUGH TO GIVE YOU A BUZZ, BUT NOT ENOUGH TO MAKE YOU PUKE.
KEEP A CIGARETTE GOING AT ALL TIMES.
HOLD IT GRACEFULLY AND LEARN TO BLOW THE SMOKE OUT THROUGH YOUR NOSE. THAT'S FRENCH.
OKAY. SO NOW...
THIS IS REEFER.
SUCK IT IN AND DON'T LEAVE SPIT ON THE END.
OKAY... THESE ARE SARTRE, BUKOWSKI, AND NIETZSCHE.
FORGET YOUR HOMEWORK.
READ THESE.
WHEN THE BOY PUTS HIS TONGUE IN YOUR MOUTH AND HIS HAND DOWN YOUR PANTS...
THINK ABOUT THESE GUYS.
ISH HARD TO READ.
BEING POPULAR IS SOMETHING YOU HAVE TO WORK AT.
©84 SHARY FLENNIKEN

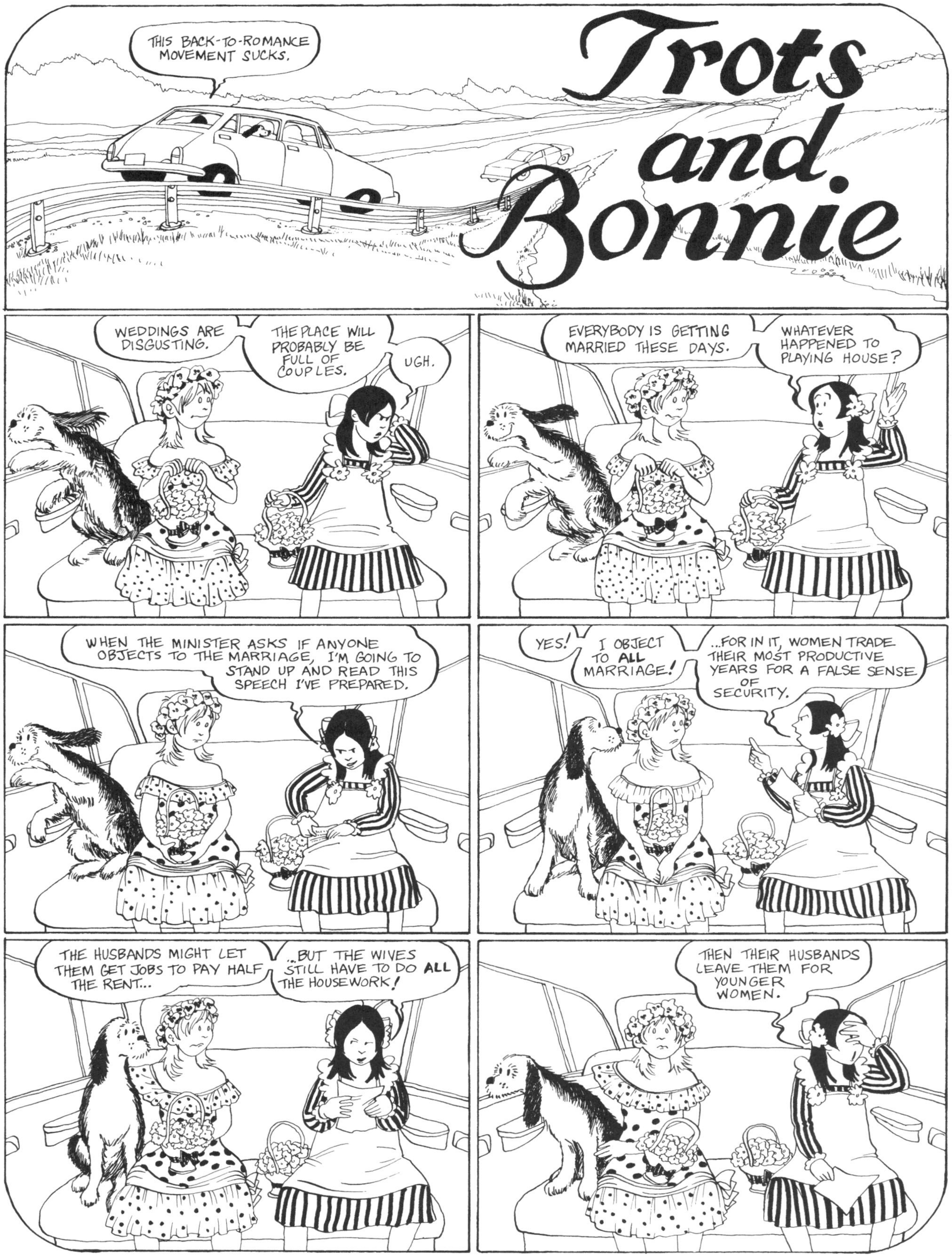
Trots and Bonnie
THIS BACK-TO-ROMANCE MOVEMENT SUCKS.
WEDDINGS ARE DISGUSTING.
THE PLACE WILL PROBABLY BE FULL OF COUPLES.
UGH.
EVERYBODY IS GETTING MARRIED THESE DAYS.
WHATEVER HAPPENED TO PLAYING HOUSE?
WHEN THE MINISTER ASKS IF ANYONE OBJECTS TO THE MARRIAGE, I'M GOING TO STAND UP AND READ THIS SPEECH I'VE PREPARED.
YES!
I OBJECT TO **ALL** MARRIAGE!
...FOR IN IT, WOMEN TRADE THEIR MOST PRODUCTIVE YEARS FOR A FALSE SENSE OF SECURITY.
THE HUSBANDS MIGHT LET THEM GET JOBS TO PAY HALF THE RENT...
...BUT THE WIVES STILL HAVE TO DO **ALL** THE HOUSEWORK!
THEN THEIR HUSBANDS LEAVE THEM FOR YOUNGER WOMEN.

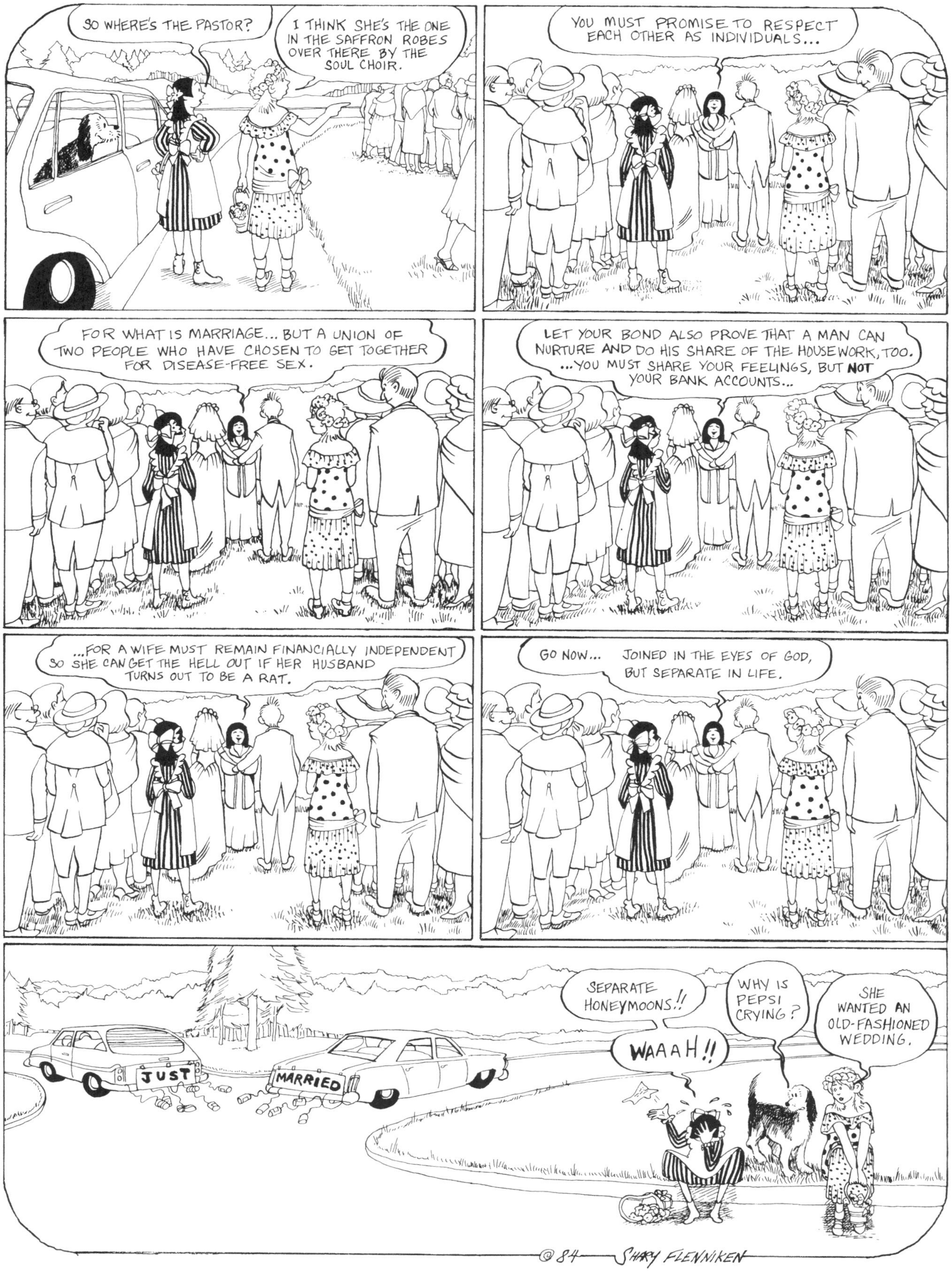
SO WHERE'S THE PASTOR?
I THINK SHE'S THE ONE IN THE SAFFRON ROBES OVER THERE BY THE SOUL CHOIR.
YOU MUST PROMISE TO RESPECT EACH OTHER AS INDIVIDUALS...
FOR WHAT IS MARRIAGE... BUT A UNION OF TWO PEOPLE WHO HAVE CHOSEN TO GET TOGETHER FOR DISEASE-FREE SEX.
LET YOUR BOND ALSO PROVE THAT A MAN CAN NURTURE AND DO HIS SHARE OF THE HOUSEWORK, TOO. ...YOU MUST SHARE YOUR FEELINGS, BUT NOT YOUR BANK ACCOUNTS...
...FOR A WIFE MUST REMAIN FINANCIALLY INDEPENDENT SO SHE CAN GET THE HELL OUT IF HER HUSBAND TURNS OUT TO BE A RAT.
GO NOW... JOINED IN THE EYES OF GOD, BUT SEPARATE IN LIFE.
JUST
MARRIED
SEPARATE HONEYMOONS!!
WAAAH!!
WHY IS PEPSI CRYING?
SHE WANTED AN OLD-FASHIONED WEDDING.
©84 SHARY FLENNIKEN

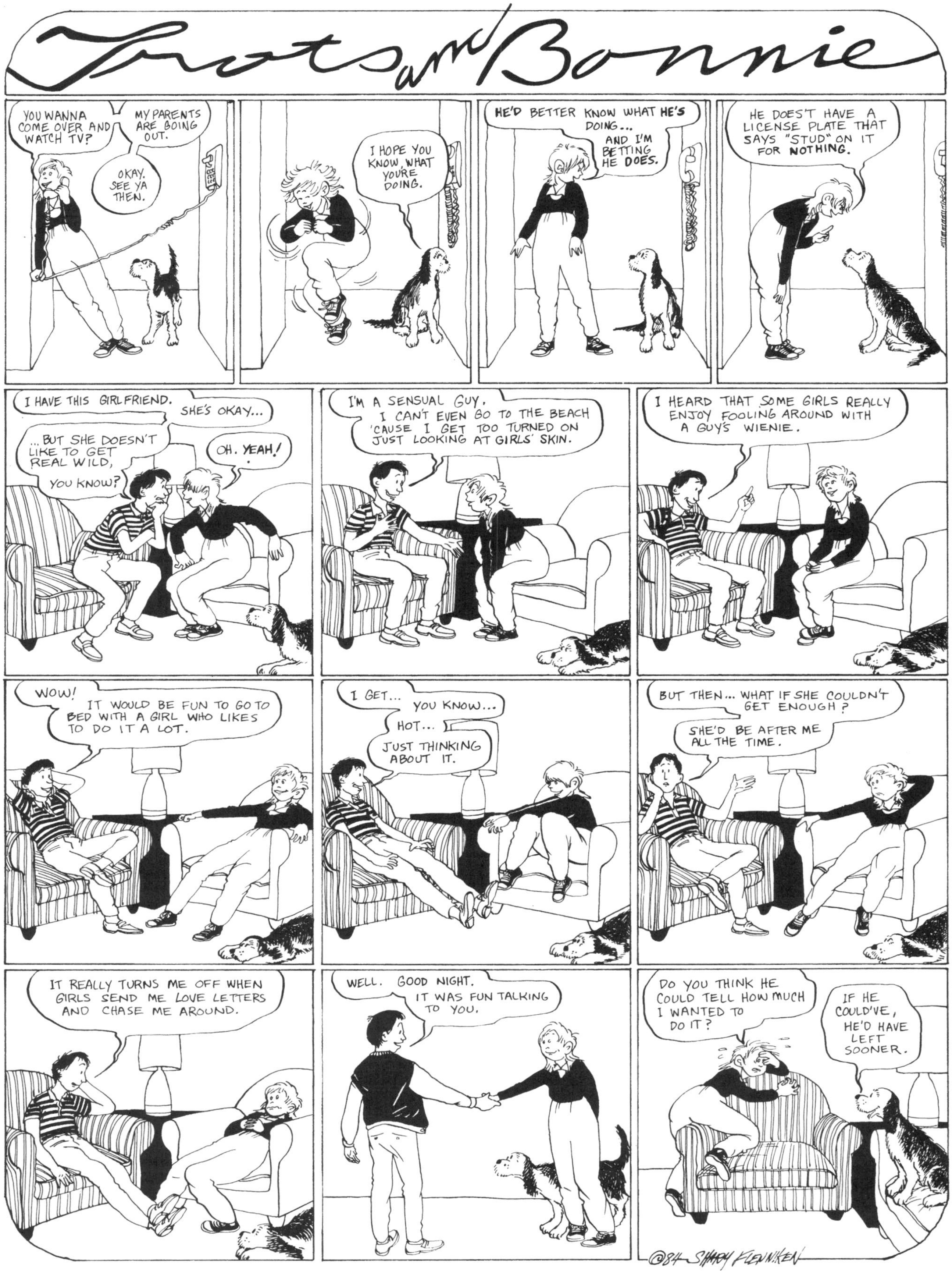
Trots and Bonnie
YOU WANNA COME OVER AND WATCH TV?
MY PARENTS ARE GOING OUT.
OKAY. SEE YA THEN.
I HOPE YOU KNOW WHAT YOU'RE DOING.
HE'D BETTER KNOW WHAT HE'S DOING...
AND I'M BETTING HE DOES.
HE DOES'T HAVE A LICENSE PLATE THAT SAYS "STUD" ON IT FOR NOTHING.
I HAVE THIS GIRLFRIEND.
SHE'S OKAY...
...BUT SHE DOESN'T LIKE TO GET REAL WILD,
YOU KNOW?
OH. YEAH!
I'M A SENSUAL GUY.
I CAN'T EVEN GO TO THE BEACH 'CAUSE I GET TOO TURNED ON JUST LOOKING AT GIRLS' SKIN.
I HEARD THAT SOME GIRLS REALLY ENJOY FOOLING AROUND WITH A GUY'S WIENIE.
WOW!
IT WOULD BE FUN TO GO TO BED WITH A GIRL WHO LIKES TO DO IT A LOT.
I GET...
YOU KNOW...
HOT...
JUST THINKING ABOUT IT.
BUT THEN... WHAT IF SHE COULDN'T GET ENOUGH?
SHE'D BE AFTER ME ALL THE TIME.
IT REALLY TURNS ME OFF WHEN GIRLS SEND ME LOVE LETTERS AND CHASE ME AROUND.
WELL. GOOD NIGHT.
IT WAS FUN TALKING TO YOU.
DO YOU THINK HE COULD TELL HOW MUCH I WANTED TO DO IT?
IF HE COULD'VE, HE'D HAVE LEFT SOONER.
©84 SHARY FLENNIKEN

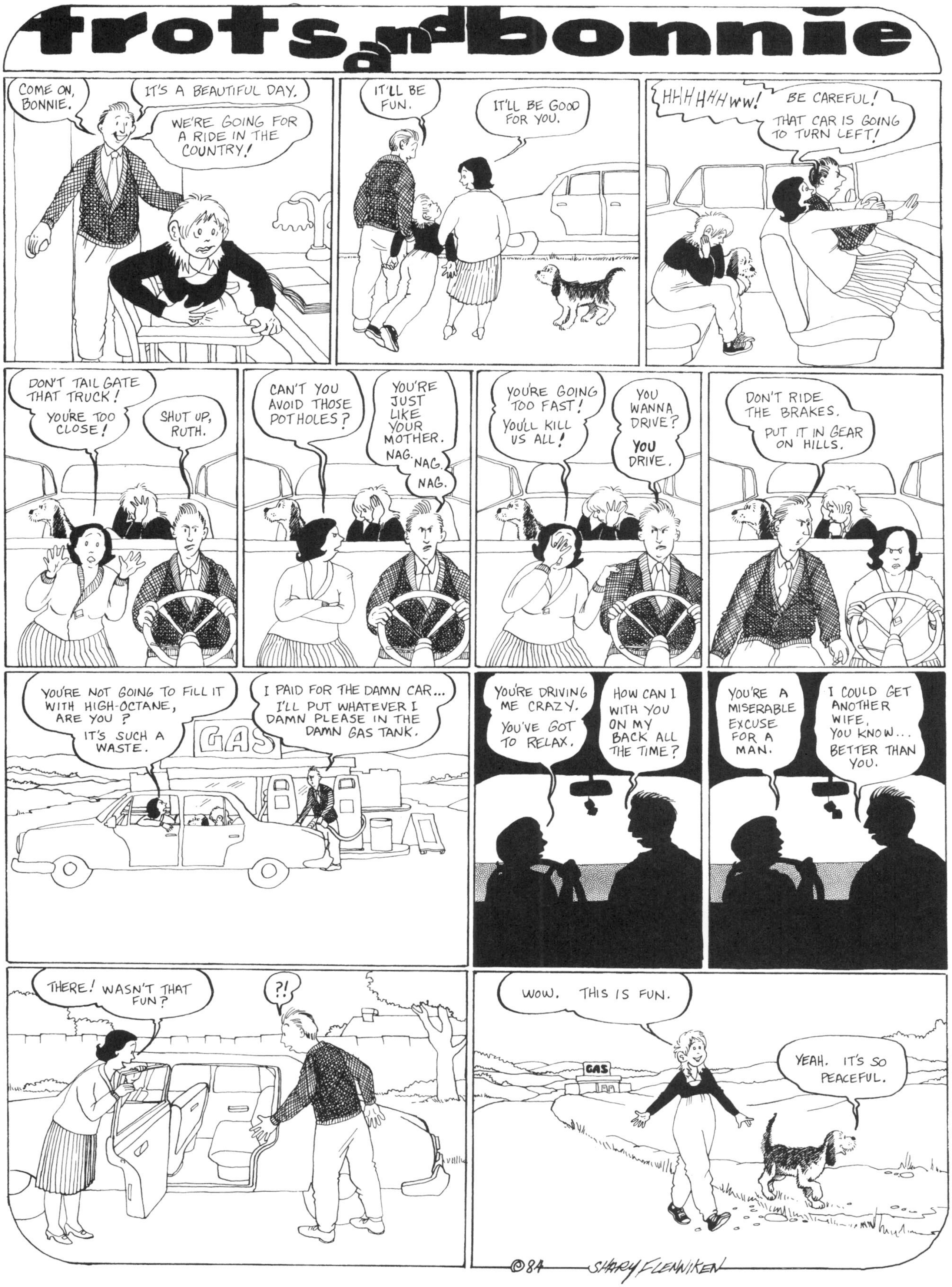
trots and bonnie
COME ON, BONNIE.
IT'S A BEAUTIFUL DAY.
WE'RE GOING FOR A RIDE IN THE COUNTRY!
IT'LL BE FUN.
IT'LL BE GOOD FOR YOU.
HHHHHHWW!
BE CAREFUL!
THAT CAR IS GOING TO TURN LEFT!
DON'T TAIL GATE THAT TRUCK!
YOU'RE TOO CLOSE!
SHUT UP, RUTH.
CAN'T YOU AVOID THOSE POTHOLES?
YOU'RE JUST LIKE YOUR MOTHER.
NAG. NAG. NAG.
YOU'RE GOING TOO FAST!
YOU'LL KILL US ALL!
YOU WANNA DRIVE?
YOU DRIVE.
DON'T RIDE THE BRAKES.
PUT IT IN GEAR ON HILLS.
YOU'RE NOT GOING TO FILL IT WITH HIGH-OCTANE, ARE YOU?
IT'S SUCH A WASTE.
GAS
I PAID FOR THE DAMN CAR... I'LL PUT WHATEVER I DAMN PLEASE IN THE DAMN GAS TANK.
YOU'RE DRIVING ME CRAZY.
YOU'VE GOT TO RELAX.
HOW CAN I WITH YOU ON MY BACK ALL THE TIME?
YOU'RE A MISERABLE EXCUSE FOR A MAN.
I COULD GET ANOTHER WIFE, YOU KNOW... BETTER THAN YOU.
THERE! WASN'T THAT FUN?
?!
WOW. THIS IS FUN.
GAS
YEAH. IT'S SO PEACEFUL.
©84 SHARY FLENNIKEN

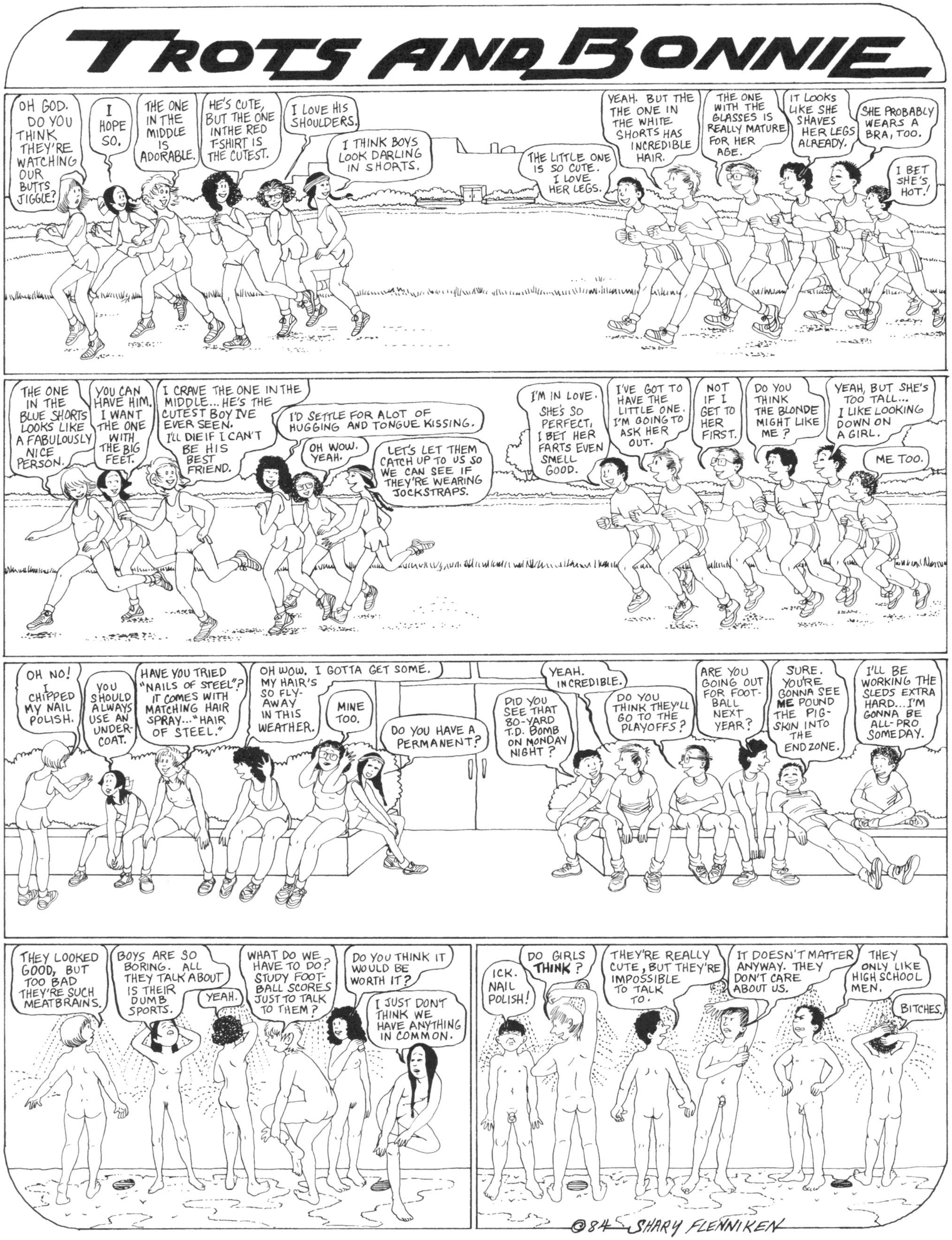
TROTS AND BONNIE
OH GOD. DO YOU THINK THEY'RE WATCHING OUR BUTTS JIGGLE?
I HOPE SO.
THE ONE IN THE MIDDLE IS ADORABLE.
HE'S CUTE, BUT THE ONE IN THE RED T-SHIRT IS THE CUTEST.
I LOVE HIS SHOULDERS.
I THINK BOYS LOOK DARLING IN SHORTS.
THE LITTLE ONE IS SO CUTE. I LOVE HER LEGS.
YEAH. BUT THE THE ONE IN THE WHITE SHORTS HAS INCREDIBLE HAIR.
THE ONE WITH THE GLASSES IS REALLY MATURE FOR HER AGE.
IT LOOKS LIKE SHE SHAVES HER LEGS ALREADY.
SHE PROBABLY WEARS A BRA, TOO.
I BET SHE'S HOT!
THE ONE IN THE BLUE SHORTS LOOKS LIKE A FABULOUSLY NICE PERSON.
YOU CAN HAVE HIM. I WANT THE ONE WITH THE BIG FEET.
I CRAVE THE ONE IN THE MIDDLE... HE'S THE CUTEST BOY I'VE EVER SEEN. I'LL DIE IF I CAN'T BE HIS BEST FRIEND.
I'D SETTLE FOR ALOT OF HUGGING AND TONGUE KISSING.
OH WOW. YEAH.
LET'S LET THEM CATCH UP TO US SO WE CAN SEE IF THEY'RE WEARING JOCKSTRAPS.
I'M IN LOVE. SHE'S SO PERFECT, I BET HER FARTS EVEN SMELL GOOD.
I'VE GOT TO HAVE THE LITTLE ONE. I'M GOING TO ASK HER OUT.
NOT IF I GET TO HER FIRST.
DO YOU THINK THE BLONDE MIGHT LIKE ME?
YEAH, BUT SHE'S TOO TALL... I LIKE LOOKING DOWN ON A GIRL.
ME TOO.
OH NO! I CHIPPED MY NAIL POLISH.
YOU SHOULD ALWAYS USE AN UNDER-COAT.
HAVE YOU TRIED "NAILS OF STEEL"? IT COMES WITH MATCHING HAIR SPRAY... "HAIR OF STEEL."
OH WOW. I GOTTA GET SOME. MY HAIR'S SO FLY-AWAY IN THIS WEATHER.
MINE TOO.
DO YOU HAVE A PERMANENT?
DID YOU SEE THAT 80-YARD T.D. BOMB ON MONDAY NIGHT?
YEAH. INCREDIBLE.
DO YOU THINK THEY'LL GO TO THE PLAYOFFS?
ARE YOU GOING OUT FOR FOOT-BALL NEXT YEAR?
SURE. YOU'RE GONNA SEE ME POUND THE PIG-SKIN INTO THE END ZONE.
I'LL BE WORKING THE SLEDS EXTRA HARD... I'M GONNA BE ALL-PRO SOMEDAY.
THEY LOOKED GOOD, BUT TOO BAD THEY'RE SUCH MEATBRAINS.
BOYS ARE SO BORING. ALL THEY TALK ABOUT IS THEIR DUMB SPORTS.
YEAH.
WHAT DO WE HAVE TO DO? STUDY FOOT-BALL SCORES JUST TO TALK TO THEM?
DO YOU THINK IT WOULD BE WORTH IT?
I JUST DON'T THINK WE HAVE ANYTHING IN COMMON.
ICK. NAIL POLISH!
DO GIRLS THINK?
THEY'RE REALLY CUTE, BUT THEY'RE IMPOSSIBLE TO TALK TO.
IT DOESN'T MATTER ANYWAY. THEY DON'T CARE ABOUT US.
THEY ONLY LIKE HIGH SCHOOL MEN.
BITCHES.
©84 SHARY FLENNIKEN

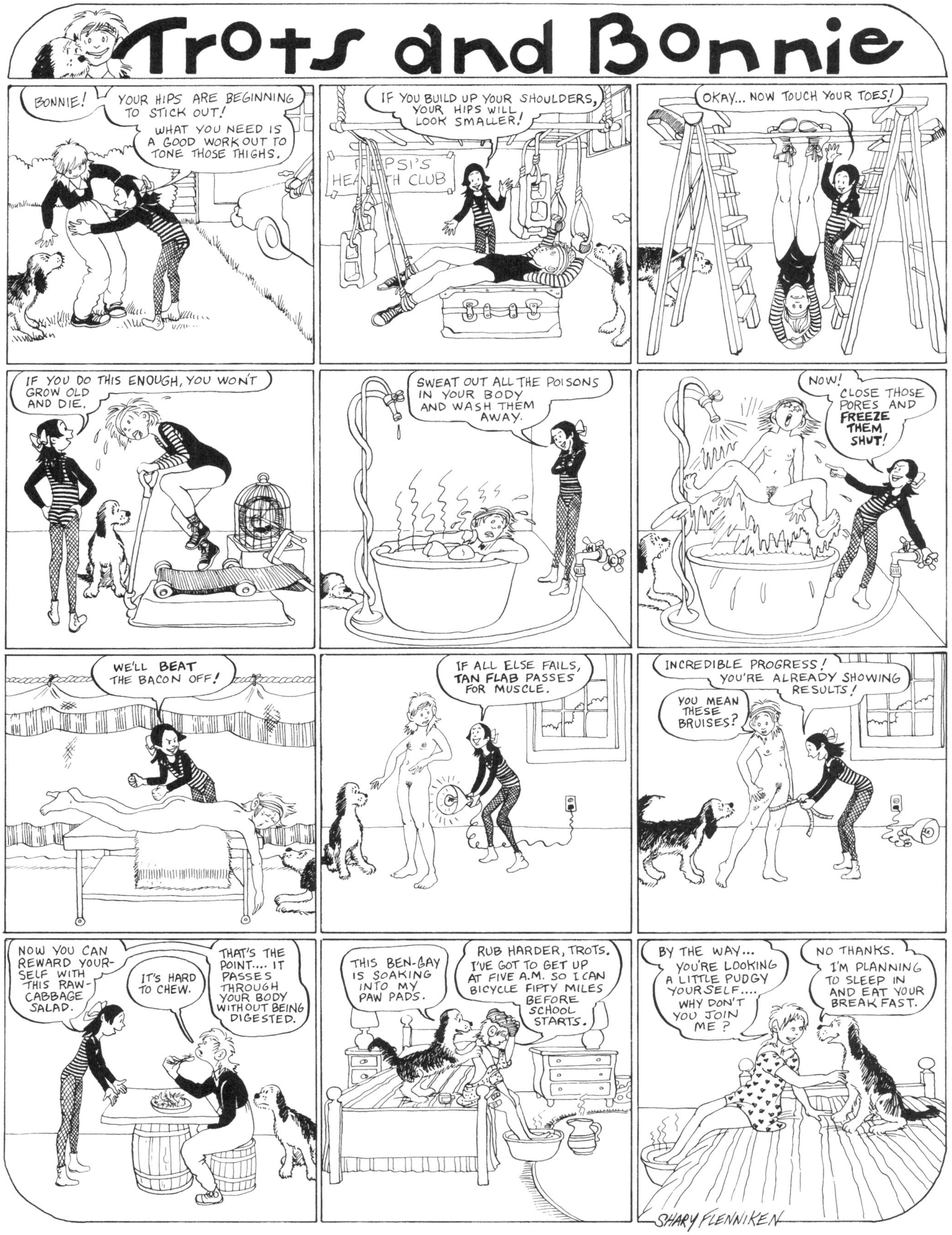
Trots and Bonnie
BONNIE!
YOUR HIPS ARE BEGINNING TO STICK OUT!
WHAT YOU NEED IS A GOOD WORK OUT TO TONE THOSE THIGHS.
IF YOU BUILD UP YOUR SHOULDERS, YOUR HIPS WILL LOOK SMALLER!
PEPSI'S HEALTH CLUB
OKAY... NOW TOUCH YOUR TOES!
IF YOU DO THIS ENOUGH, YOU WON'T GROW OLD AND DIE.
SWEAT OUT ALL THE POISONS IN YOUR BODY AND WASH THEM AWAY.
NOW!
CLOSE THOSE PORES AND FREEZE THEM SHUT!
WE'LL BEAT THE BACON OFF!
IF ALL ELSE FAILS, TAN FLAB PASSES FOR MUSCLE.
INCREDIBLE PROGRESS! YOU'RE ALREADY SHOWING RESULTS!
YOU MEAN THESE BRUISES?
NOW YOU CAN REWARD YOURSELF WITH THIS RAW-CABBAGE SALAD.
IT'S HARD TO CHEW.
THAT'S THE POINT.... IT PASSES THROUGH YOUR BODY WITHOUT BEING DIGESTED.
THIS BEN-GAY IS SOAKING INTO MY PAW PADS.
RUB HARDER, TROTS. I'VE GOT TO GET UP AT FIVE A.M. SO I CAN BICYCLE FIFTY MILES BEFORE SCHOOL STARTS.
BY THE WAY... YOU'RE LOOKING A LITTLE PUDGY YOURSELF.... WHY DON'T YOU JOIN ME?
NO THANKS. I'M PLANNING TO SLEEP IN AND EAT YOUR BREAKFAST.
SHARY FLENNIKEN

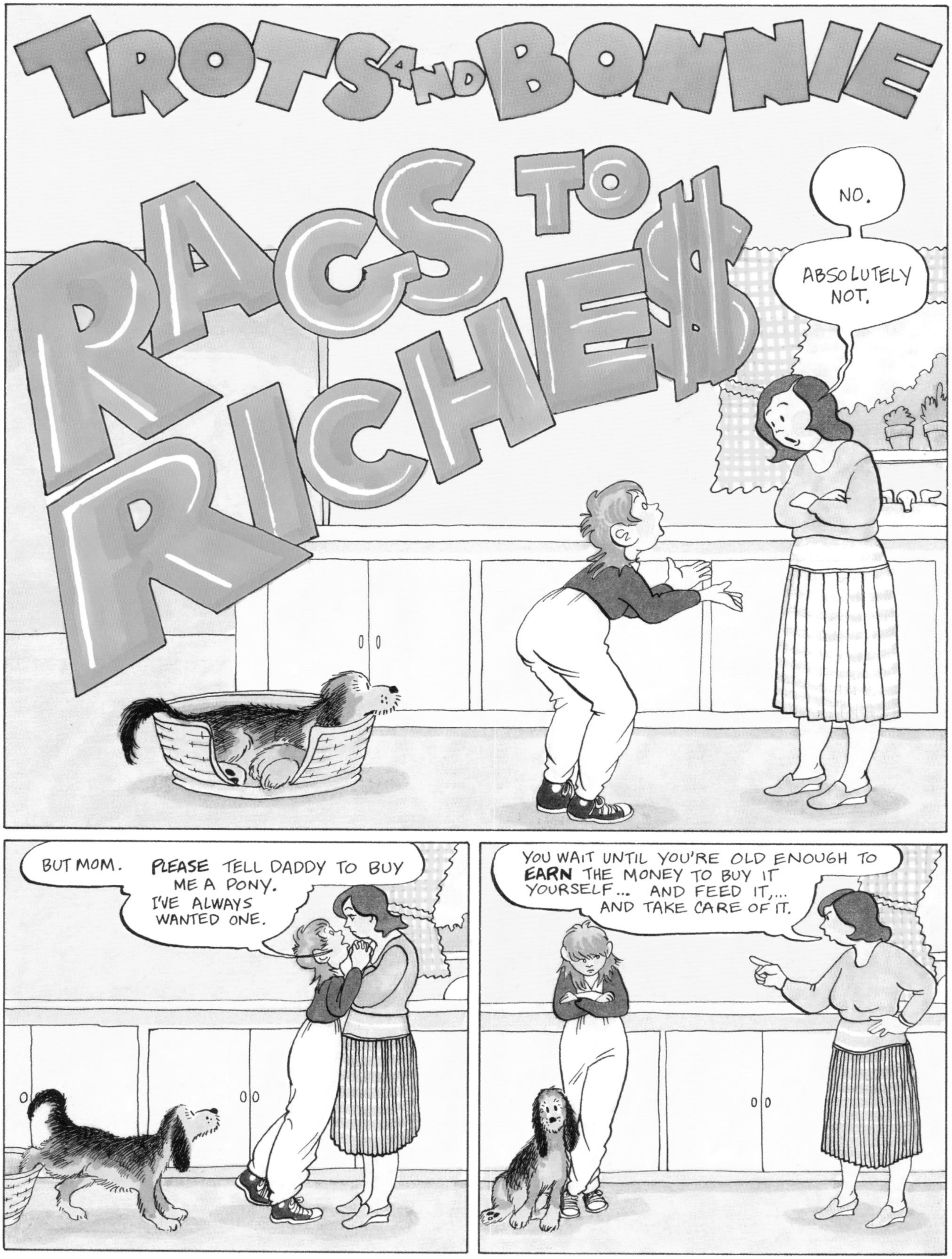
TROTS AND BONNIE
RAGS TO RICHE$
NO.
ABSOLUTELY NOT.
BUT MOM. PLEASE TELL DADDY TO BUY ME A PONY. I'VE ALWAYS WANTED ONE.
YOU WAIT UNTIL YOU'RE OLD ENOUGH TO EARN THE MONEY TO BUY IT YOURSELF... AND FEED IT,... AND TAKE CARE OF IT.

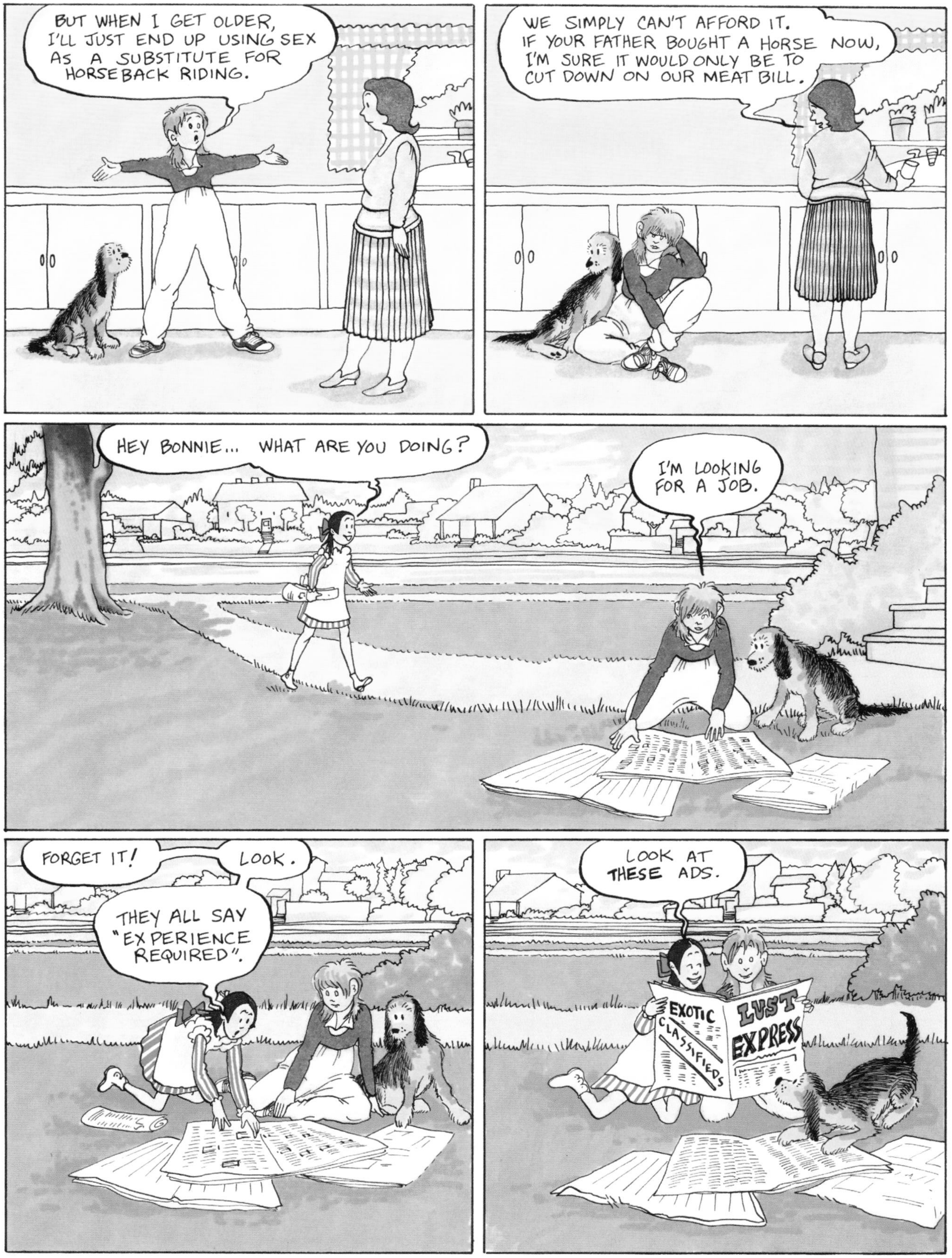
BUT WHEN I GET OLDER, I'LL JUST END UP USING SEX AS A SUBSTITUTE FOR HORSEBACK RIDING.
WE SIMPLY CAN'T AFFORD IT. IF YOUR FATHER BOUGHT A HORSE NOW, I'M SURE IT WOULD ONLY BE TO CUT DOWN ON OUR MEAT BILL.
HEY BONNIE... WHAT ARE YOU DOING?
I'M LOOKING FOR A JOB.
FORGET IT!
THEY ALL SAY "EXPERIENCE REQUIRED".
LOOK.
LOOK AT THESE ADS.
EXOTIC CLASSIFIEDS
LUST EXPRESS

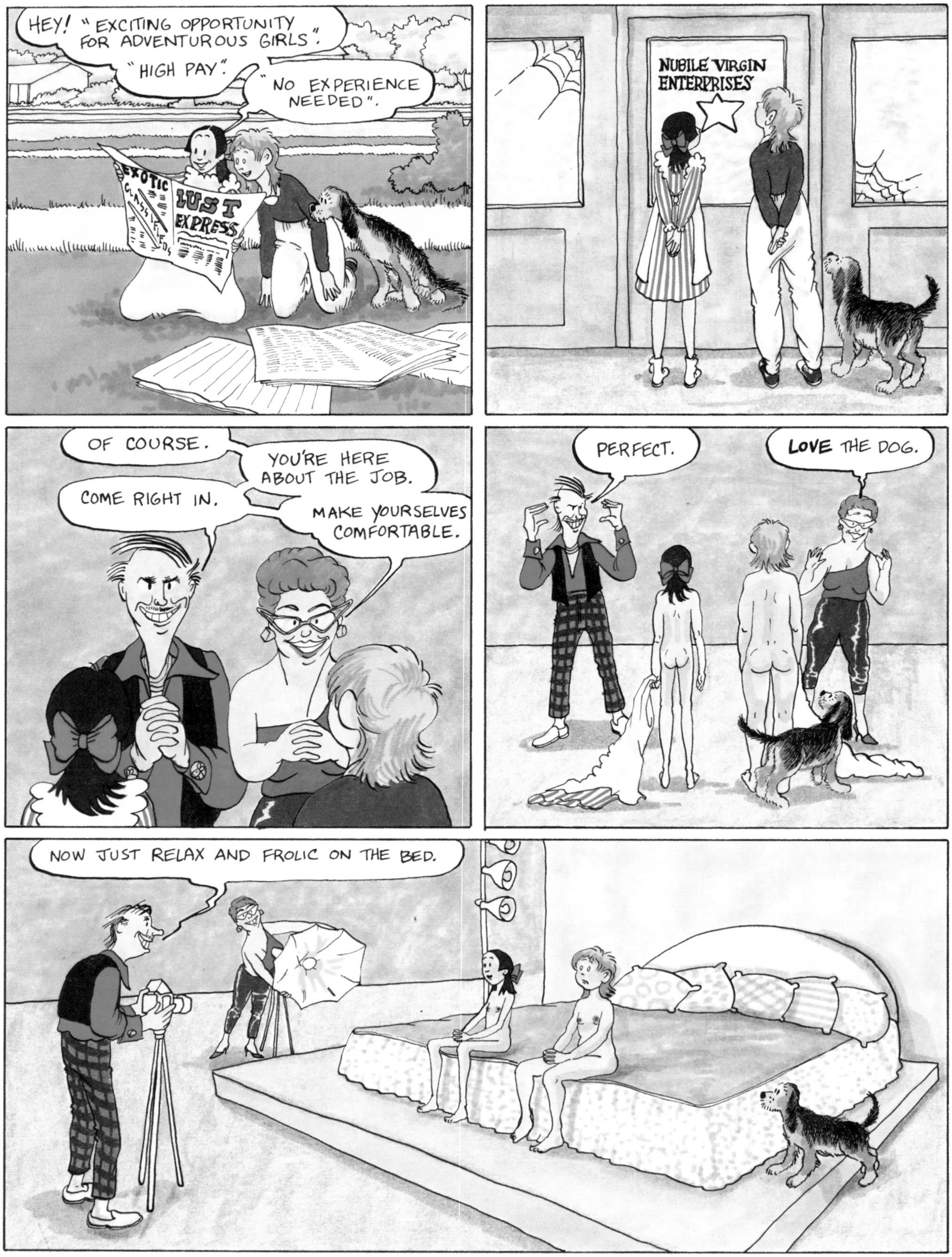
HEY! "EXCITING OPPORTUNITY FOR ADVENTUROUS GIRLS".
"HIGH PAY".
"NO EXPERIENCE NEEDED".
EXOTIC
LUST EXPRESS
NUBILE VIRGIN ENTERPRISES
OF COURSE.
YOU'RE HERE ABOUT THE JOB.
COME RIGHT IN.
MAKE YOURSELVES COMFORTABLE.
PERFECT.
LOVE THE DOG.
NOW JUST RELAX AND FROLIC ON THE BED.

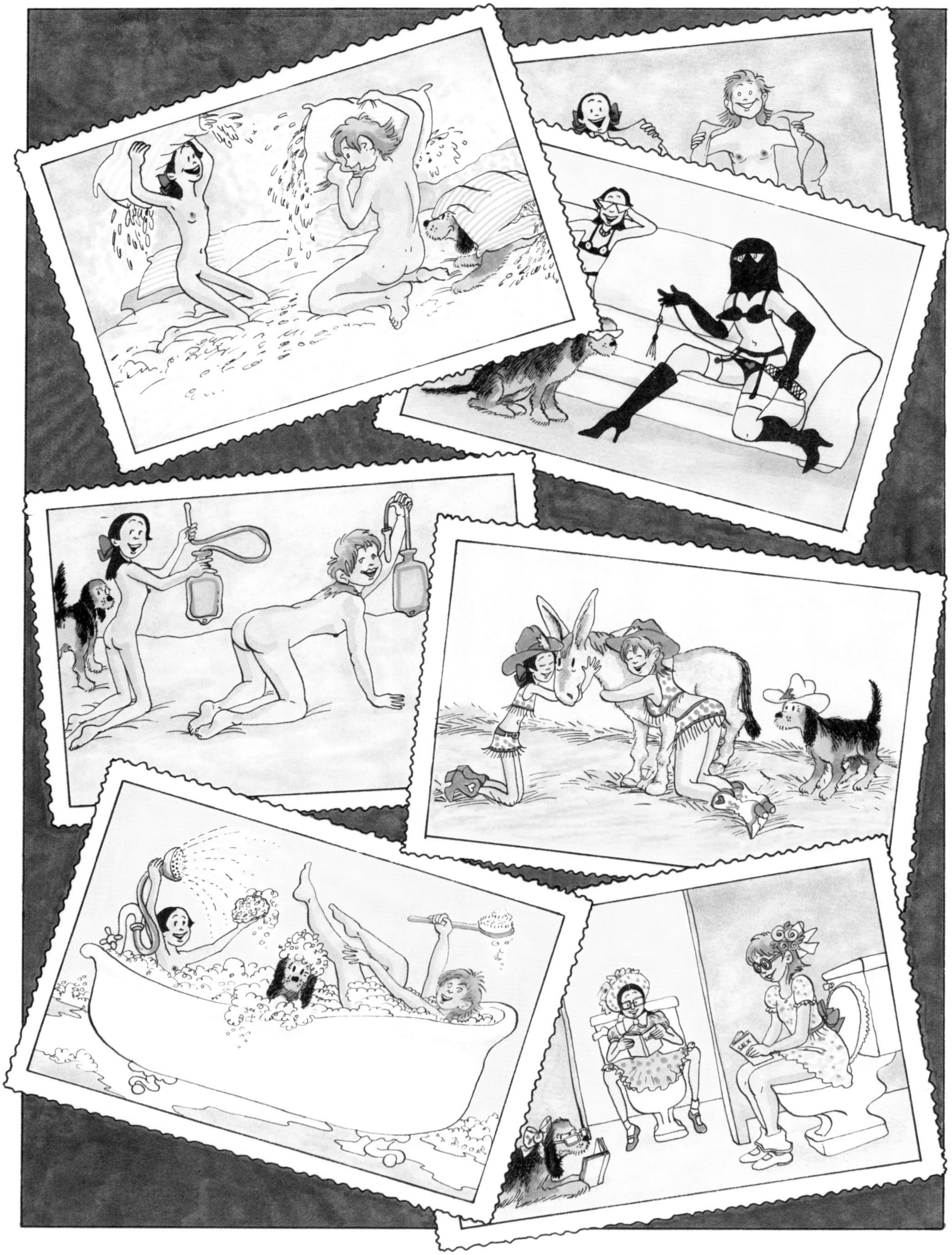
SEX

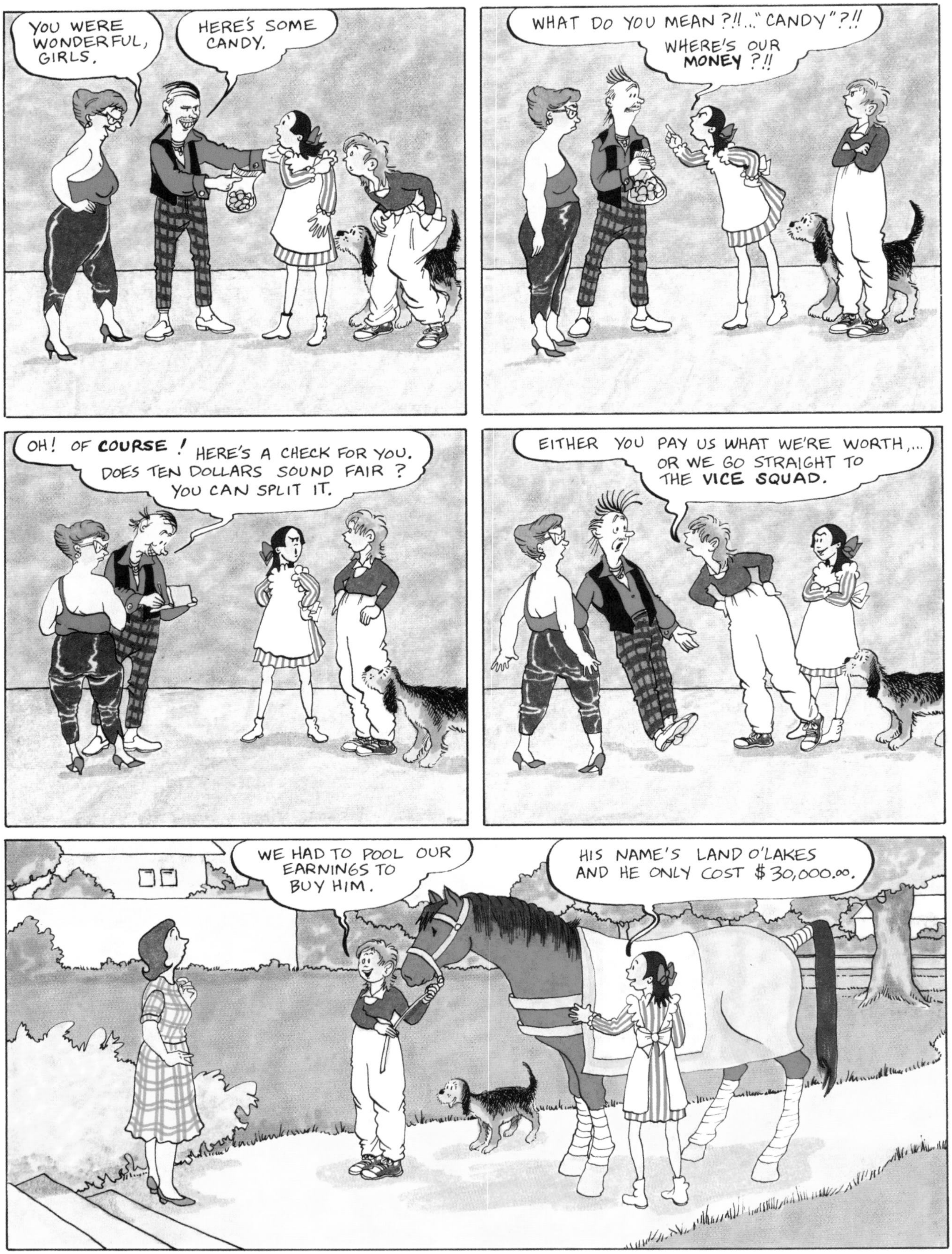

YOU WERE WONDERFUL, GIRLS.
HERE'S SOME CANDY.
WHAT DO YOU MEAN ?!! ... "CANDY" ?!!
WHERE'S OUR MONEY ?!!
OH! OF COURSE ! HERE'S A CHECK FOR YOU. DOES TEN DOLLARS SOUND FAIR ? YOU CAN SPLIT IT.
EITHER YOU PAY US WHAT WE'RE WORTH,... OR WE GO STRAIGHT TO THE VICE SQUAD.
WE HAD TO POOL OUR EARNINGS TO BUY HIM.
HIS NAME'S LAND O'LAKES AND HE ONLY COST $30,000.00.

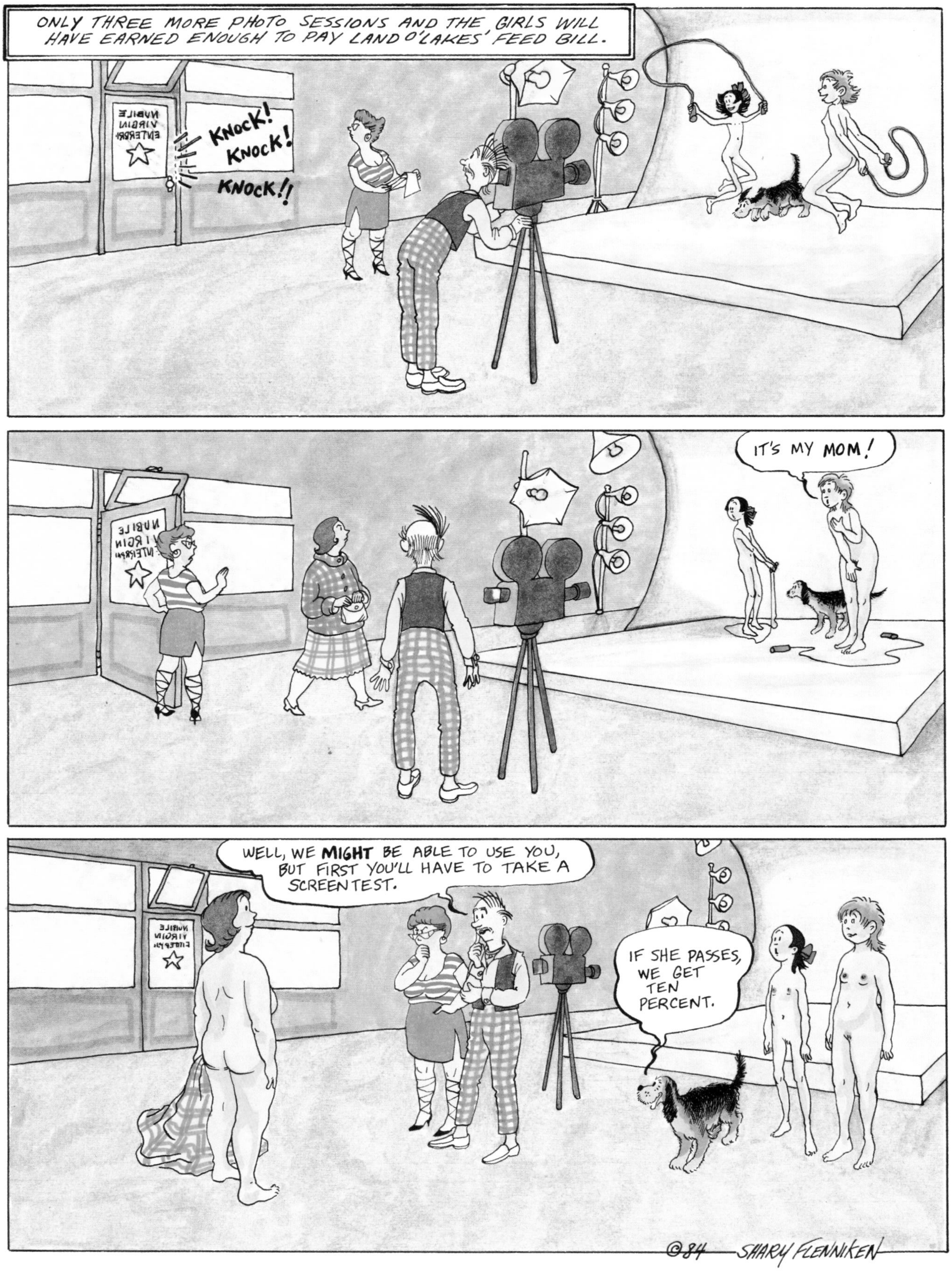
ONLY THREE MORE PHOTO SESSIONS AND THE GIRLS WILL HAVE EARNED ENOUGH TO PAY LAND O'LAKES' FEED BILL.
KNOCK!
KNOCK!
KNOCK!!
IT'S MY MOM!
WELL, WE MIGHT BE ABLE TO USE YOU, BUT FIRST YOU'LL HAVE TO TAKE A SCREENTEST.
IF SHE PASSES, WE GET TEN PERCENT.
©84 SHARY FLENNIKEN

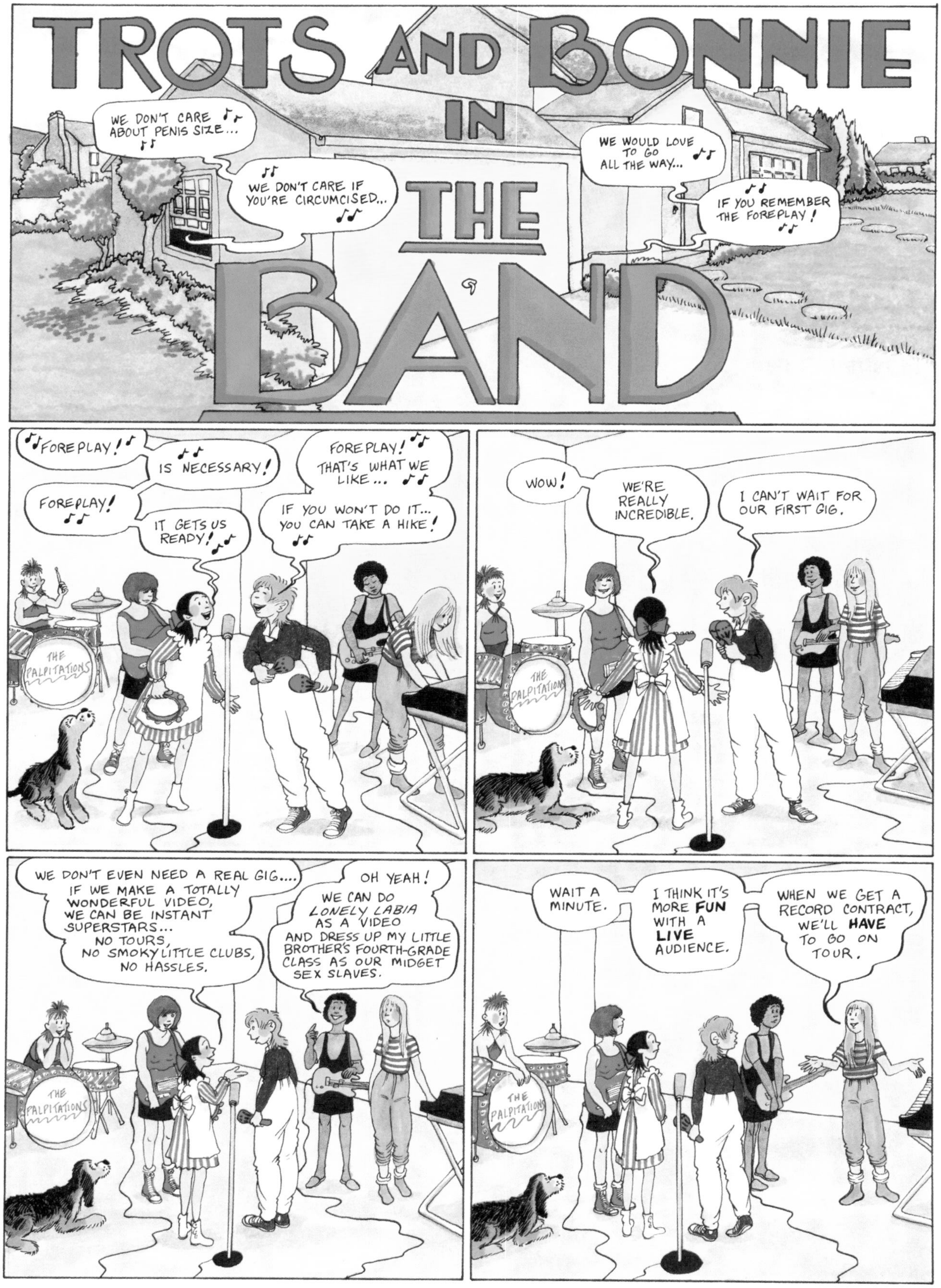
TROTS AND BONNIE IN THE BAND
WE DON'T CARE ABOUT PENIS SIZE...
WE DON'T CARE IF YOU'RE CIRCUMCISED...
WE WOULD LOVE TO GO ALL THE WAY...
IF YOU REMEMBER THE FOREPLAY!
FOREPLAY!
IS NECESSARY!
FOREPLAY!
IT GETS US READY!
FOREPLAY! THAT'S WHAT WE LIKE...
IF YOU WON'T DO IT... YOU CAN TAKE A HIKE!
THE PALPITATIONS
WOW!
WE'RE REALLY INCREDIBLE.
I CAN'T WAIT FOR OUR FIRST GIG.
THE PALPITATIONS
WE DON'T EVEN NEED A REAL GIG.... IF WE MAKE A TOTALLY WONDERFUL VIDEO, WE CAN BE INSTANT SUPERSTARS... NO TOURS, NO SMOKY LITTLE CLUBS, NO HASSLES.
OH YEAH!
WE CAN DO LONELY LABIA AS A VIDEO AND DRESS UP MY LITTLE BROTHER'S FOURTH-GRADE CLASS AS OUR MIDGET SEX SLAVES.
THE PALPITATIONS
WAIT A MINUTE.
I THINK IT'S MORE FUN WITH A LIVE AUDIENCE.
WHEN WE GET A RECORD CONTRACT, WE'LL HAVE TO GO ON TOUR.
THE PALPITATIONS

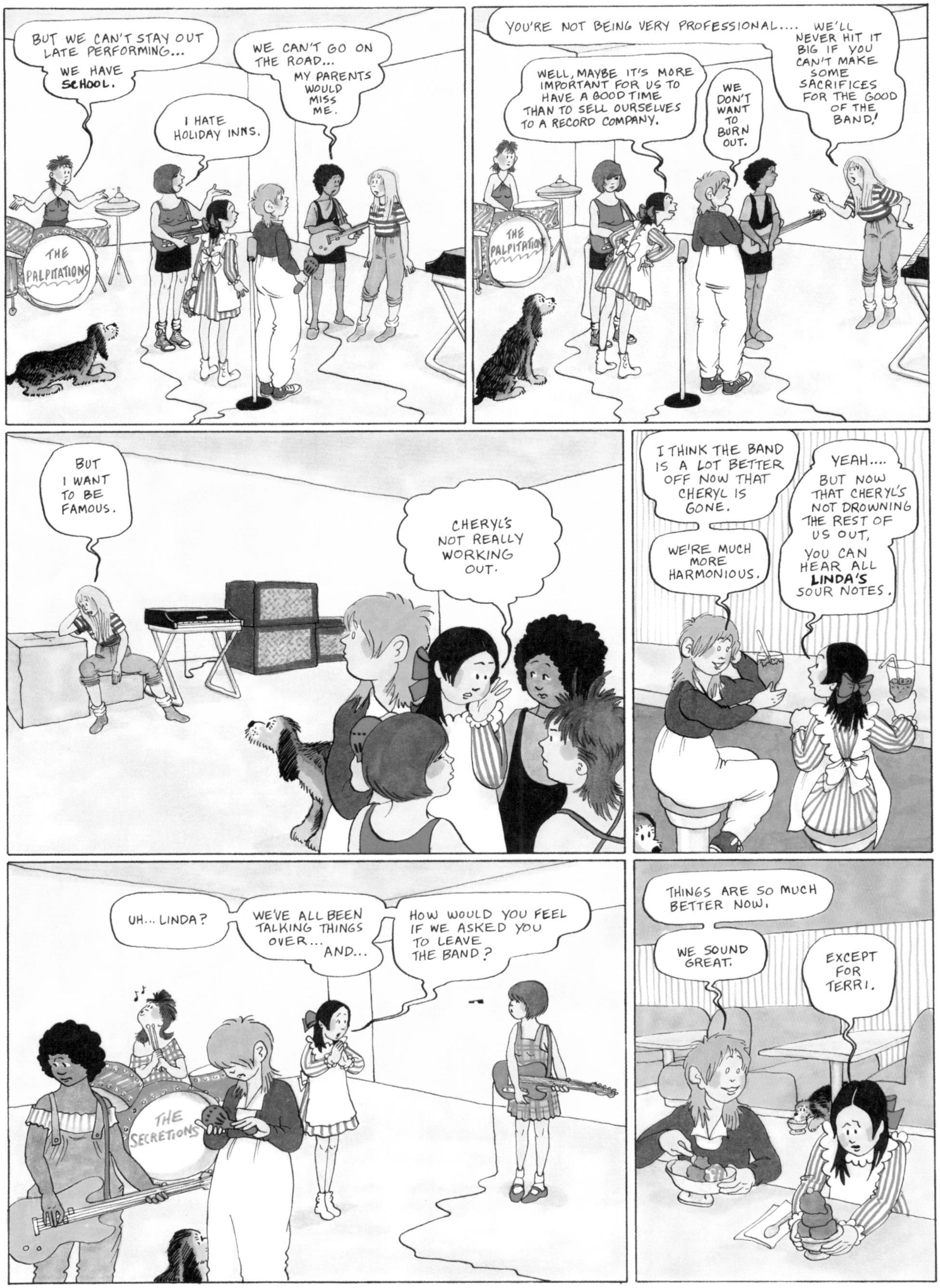
BUT WE CAN'T STAY OUT LATE PERFORMING...
WE HAVE SCHOOL.
I HATE HOLIDAY INNS.
WE CAN'T GO ON THE ROAD...
MY PARENTS WOULD MISS ME.
YOU'RE NOT BEING VERY PROFESSIONAL....
WE'LL NEVER HIT IT BIG IF YOU CAN'T MAKE SOME SACRIFICES FOR THE GOOD OF THE BAND!
WELL, MAYBE IT'S MORE IMPORTANT FOR US TO HAVE A GOOD TIME THAN TO SELL OURSELVES TO A RECORD COMPANY.
WE DON'T WANT TO BURN OUT.
BUT I WANT TO BE FAMOUS.
CHERYL'S NOT REALLY WORKING OUT.
I THINK THE BAND IS A LOT BETTER OFF NOW THAT CHERYL IS GONE.
WE'RE MUCH MORE HARMONIOUS.
YEAH....
BUT NOW THAT CHERYL'S NOT DROWNING THE REST OF US OUT,
YOU CAN HEAR ALL LINDA'S SOUR NOTES.
UH... LINDA?
WE'VE ALL BEEN TALKING THINGS OVER...
AND...
HOW WOULD YOU FEEL IF WE ASKED YOU TO LEAVE THE BAND?
THINGS ARE SO MUCH BETTER NOW.
WE SOUND GREAT.
EXCEPT FOR TERRI.
THE PALPITATIONS
THE SECRETIONS

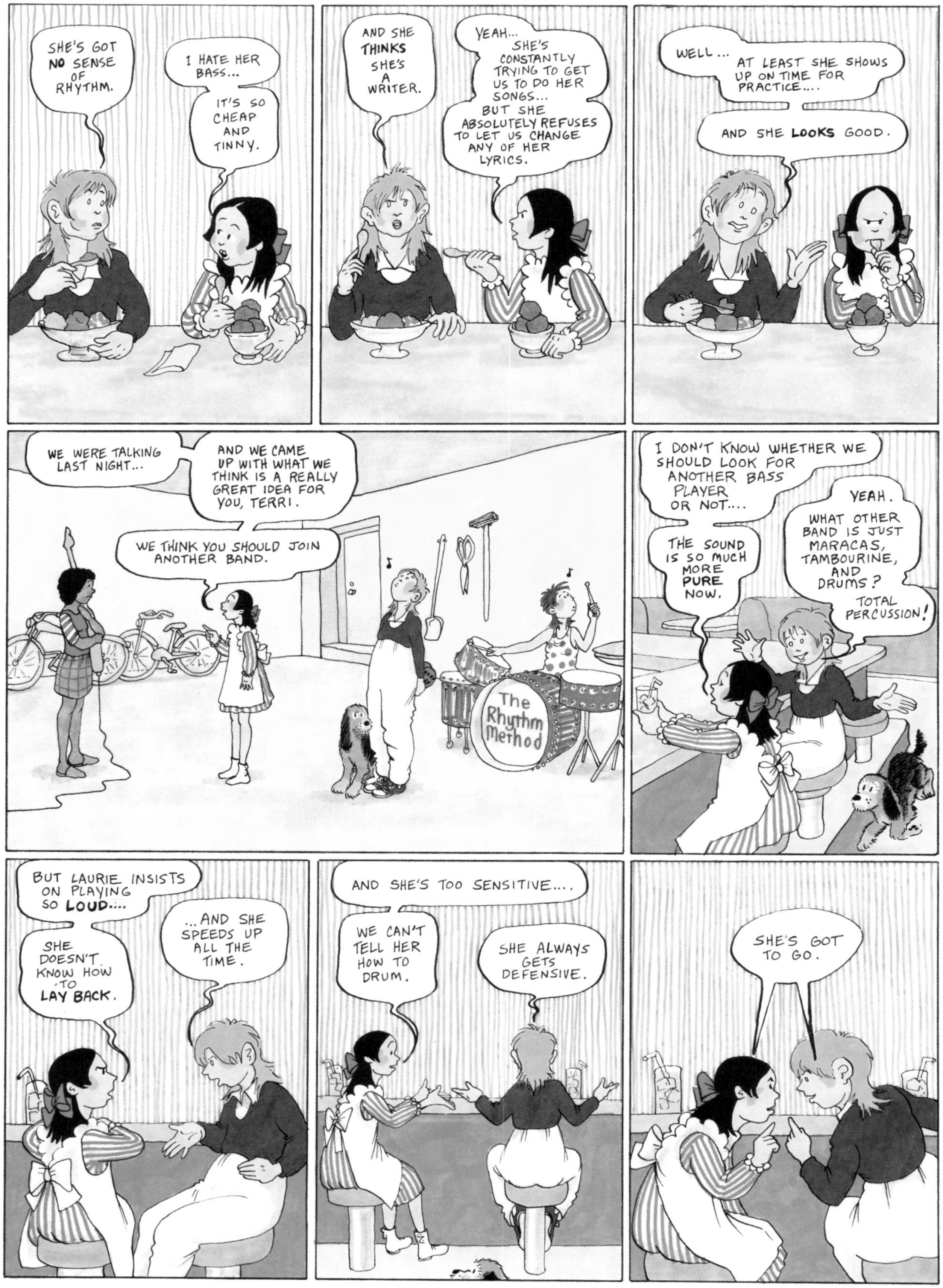
SHE'S GOT NO SENSE OF RHYTHM.
I HATE HER BASS...
IT'S SO CHEAP AND TINNY.
AND SHE THINKS SHE'S A WRITER.
YEAH... SHE'S CONSTANTLY TRYING TO GET US TO DO HER SONGS... BUT SHE ABSOLUTELY REFUSES TO LET US CHANGE ANY OF HER LYRICS.
WELL... AT LEAST SHE SHOWS UP ON TIME FOR PRACTICE....
AND SHE LOOKS GOOD.
WE WERE TALKING LAST NIGHT...
AND WE CAME UP WITH WHAT WE THINK IS A REALLY GREAT IDEA FOR YOU, TERRI.
WE THINK YOU SHOULD JOIN ANOTHER BAND.
The Rhythm Method
I DON'T KNOW WHETHER WE SHOULD LOOK FOR ANOTHER BASS PLAYER OR NOT....
THE SOUND IS SO MUCH MORE PURE NOW.
YEAH. WHAT OTHER BAND IS JUST MARACAS, TAMBOURINE, AND DRUMS?
TOTAL PERCUSSION!
BUT LAURIE INSISTS ON PLAYING SO LOUD....
SHE DOESN'T KNOW HOW TO LAY BACK.
...AND SHE SPEEDS UP ALL THE TIME.
AND SHE'S TOO SENSITIVE....
WE CAN'T TELL HER HOW TO DRUM.
SHE ALWAYS GETS DEFENSIVE.
SHE'S GOT TO GO.

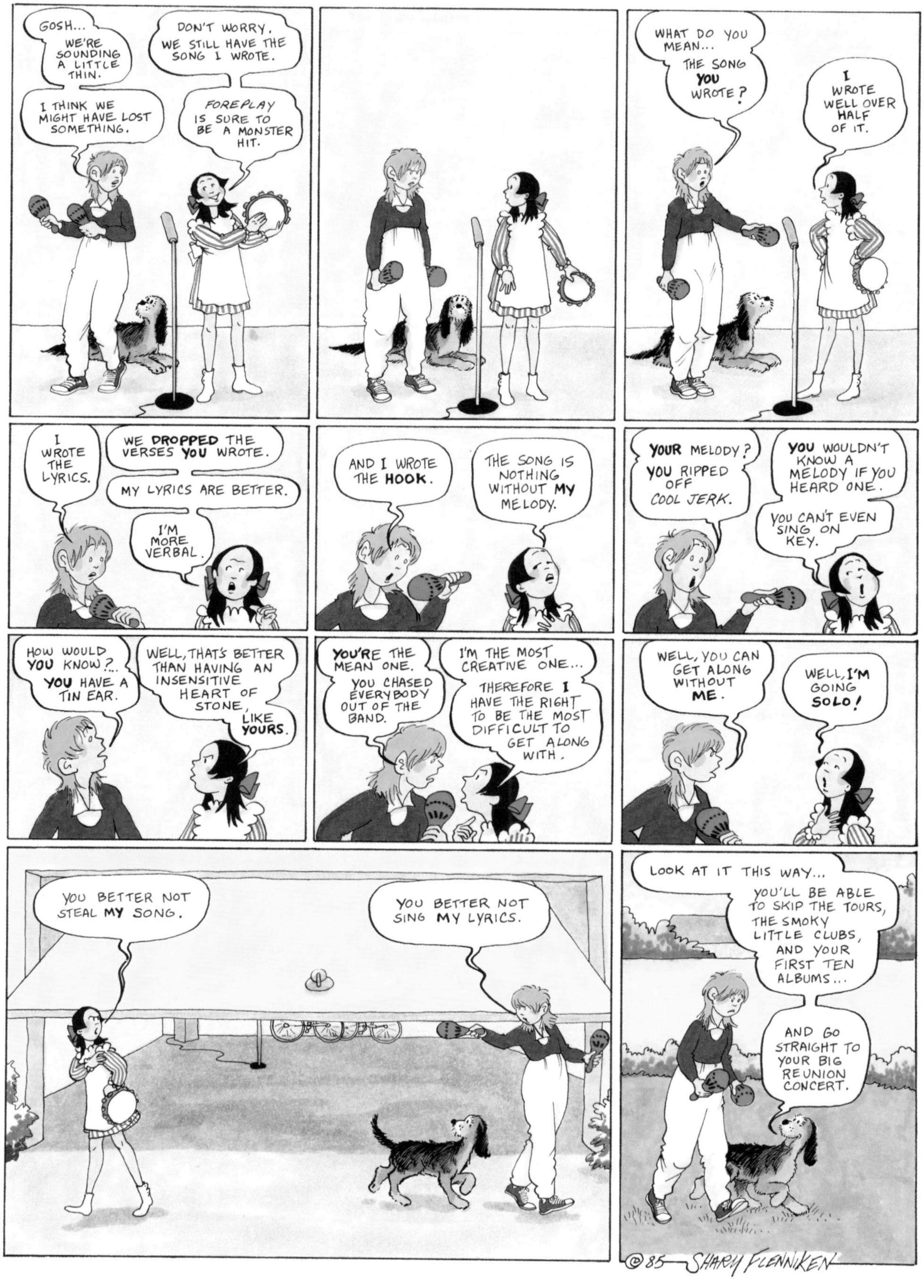
GOSH... WE'RE SOUNDING A LITTLE THIN.
I THINK WE MIGHT HAVE LOST SOMETHING.
DON'T WORRY. WE STILL HAVE THE SONG I WROTE.
FOREPLAY IS SURE TO BE A MONSTER HIT.
WHAT DO YOU MEAN...
THE SONG YOU WROTE?
I WROTE WELL OVER HALF OF IT.
I WROTE THE LYRICS.
WE DROPPED THE VERSES YOU WROTE.
MY LYRICS ARE BETTER.
I'M MORE VERBAL.
AND I WROTE THE HOOK.
THE SONG IS NOTHING WITHOUT MY MELODY.
YOUR MELODY?
YOU RIPPED OFF COOL JERK.
YOU WOULDN'T KNOW A MELODY IF YOU HEARD ONE.
YOU CAN'T EVEN SING ON KEY.
HOW WOULD YOU KNOW?... YOU HAVE A TIN EAR.
WELL, THAT'S BETTER THAN HAVING AN INSENSITIVE HEART OF STONE, LIKE YOURS.
YOU'RE THE MEAN ONE.
YOU CHASED EVERYBODY OUT OF THE BAND.
I'M THE MOST CREATIVE ONE...
THEREFORE I HAVE THE RIGHT TO BE THE MOST DIFFICULT TO GET ALONG WITH.
WELL, YOU CAN GET ALONG WITHOUT ME.
WELL, I'M GOING SOLO!
YOU BETTER NOT STEAL MY SONG.
YOU BETTER NOT SING MY LYRICS.
LOOK AT IT THIS WAY...
YOU'LL BE ABLE TO SKIP THE TOURS, THE SMOKY LITTLE CLUBS, AND YOUR FIRST TEN ALBUMS...
AND GO STRAIGHT TO YOUR BIG REUNION CONCERT.
©85 SHARY FLENNIKEN

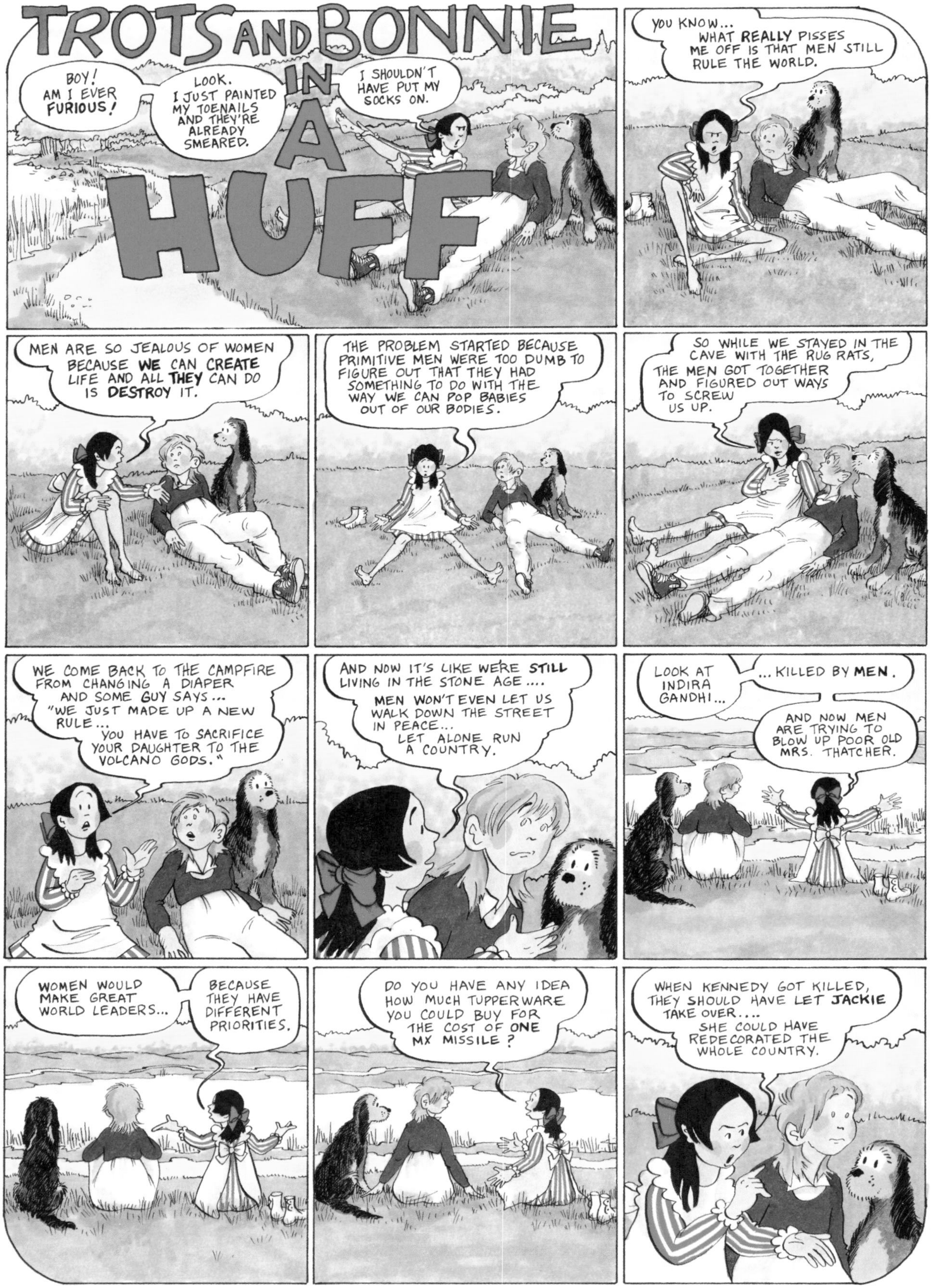
TROTS AND BONNIE IN A HUFF
BOY! AM I EVER FURIOUS!
LOOK. I JUST PAINTED MY TOENAILS AND THEY'RE ALREADY SMEARED.
I SHOULDN'T HAVE PUT MY SOCKS ON.
YOU KNOW... WHAT REALLY PISSES ME OFF IS THAT MEN STILL RULE THE WORLD.
MEN ARE SO JEALOUS OF WOMEN BECAUSE WE CAN CREATE LIFE AND ALL THEY CAN DO IS DESTROY IT.
THE PROBLEM STARTED BECAUSE PRIMITIVE MEN WERE TOO DUMB TO FIGURE OUT THAT THEY HAD SOMETHING TO DO WITH THE WAY WE CAN POP BABIES OUT OF OUR BODIES.
SO WHILE WE STAYED IN THE CAVE WITH THE RUG RATS, THE MEN GOT TOGETHER AND FIGURED OUT WAYS TO SCREW US UP.
WE COME BACK TO THE CAMPFIRE FROM CHANGING A DIAPER AND SOME GUY SAYS... "WE JUST MADE UP A NEW RULE... YOU HAVE TO SACRIFICE YOUR DAUGHTER TO THE VOLCANO GODS."
AND NOW IT'S LIKE WE'RE STILL LIVING IN THE STONE AGE.... MEN WON'T EVEN LET US WALK DOWN THE STREET IN PEACE... LET ALONE RUN A COUNTRY.
LOOK AT INDIRA GANDHI...
...KILLED BY MEN.
AND NOW MEN ARE TRYING TO BLOW UP POOR OLD MRS. THATCHER.
WOMEN WOULD MAKE GREAT WORLD LEADERS...
BECAUSE THEY HAVE DIFFERENT PRIORITIES.
DO YOU HAVE ANY IDEA HOW MUCH TUPPERWARE YOU COULD BUY FOR THE COST OF ONE MX MISSILE?
WHEN KENNEDY GOT KILLED, THEY SHOULD HAVE LET JACKIE TAKE OVER.... SHE COULD HAVE REDECORATED THE WHOLE COUNTRY.

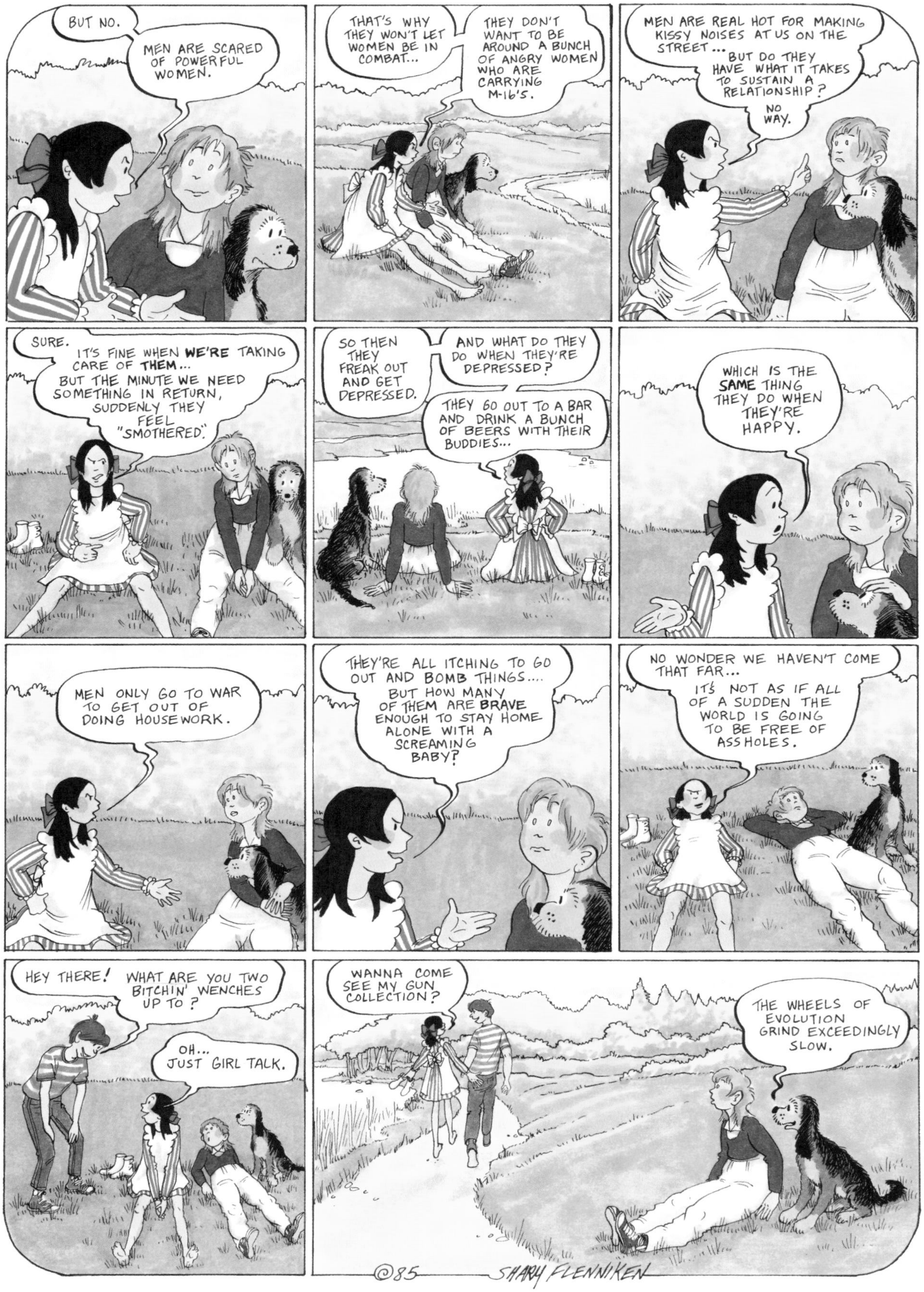
BUT NO.
MEN ARE SCARED OF POWERFUL WOMEN.
THAT'S WHY THEY WON'T LET WOMEN BE IN COMBAT...
THEY DON'T WANT TO BE AROUND A BUNCH OF ANGRY WOMEN WHO ARE CARRYING M-16'S.
MEN ARE REAL HOT FOR MAKING KISSY NOISES AT US ON THE STREET... BUT DO THEY HAVE WHAT IT TAKES TO SUSTAIN A RELATIONSHIP?
NO WAY.
SURE. IT'S FINE WHEN WE'RE TAKING CARE OF THEM... BUT THE MINUTE WE NEED SOMETHING IN RETURN, SUDDENLY THEY FEEL "SMOTHERED."
SO THEN THEY FREAK OUT AND GET DEPRESSED.
AND WHAT DO THEY DO WHEN THEY'RE DEPRESSED?
THEY GO OUT TO A BAR AND DRINK A BUNCH OF BEERS WITH THEIR BUDDIES...
WHICH IS THE SAME THING THEY DO WHEN THEY'RE HAPPY.
MEN ONLY GO TO WAR TO GET OUT OF DOING HOUSEWORK.
THEY'RE ALL ITCHING TO GO OUT AND BOMB THINGS.... BUT HOW MANY OF THEM ARE BRAVE ENOUGH TO STAY HOME ALONE WITH A SCREAMING BABY?
NO WONDER WE HAVEN'T COME THAT FAR...
IT'S NOT AS IF ALL OF A SUDDEN THE WORLD IS GOING TO BE FREE OF ASSHOLES.
HEY THERE! WHAT ARE YOU TWO BITCHIN' WENCHES UP TO?
OH... JUST GIRL TALK.
WANNA COME SEE MY GUN COLLECTION?
THE WHEELS OF EVOLUTION GRIND EXCEEDINGLY SLOW.
©85 SHARY FLENNIKEN

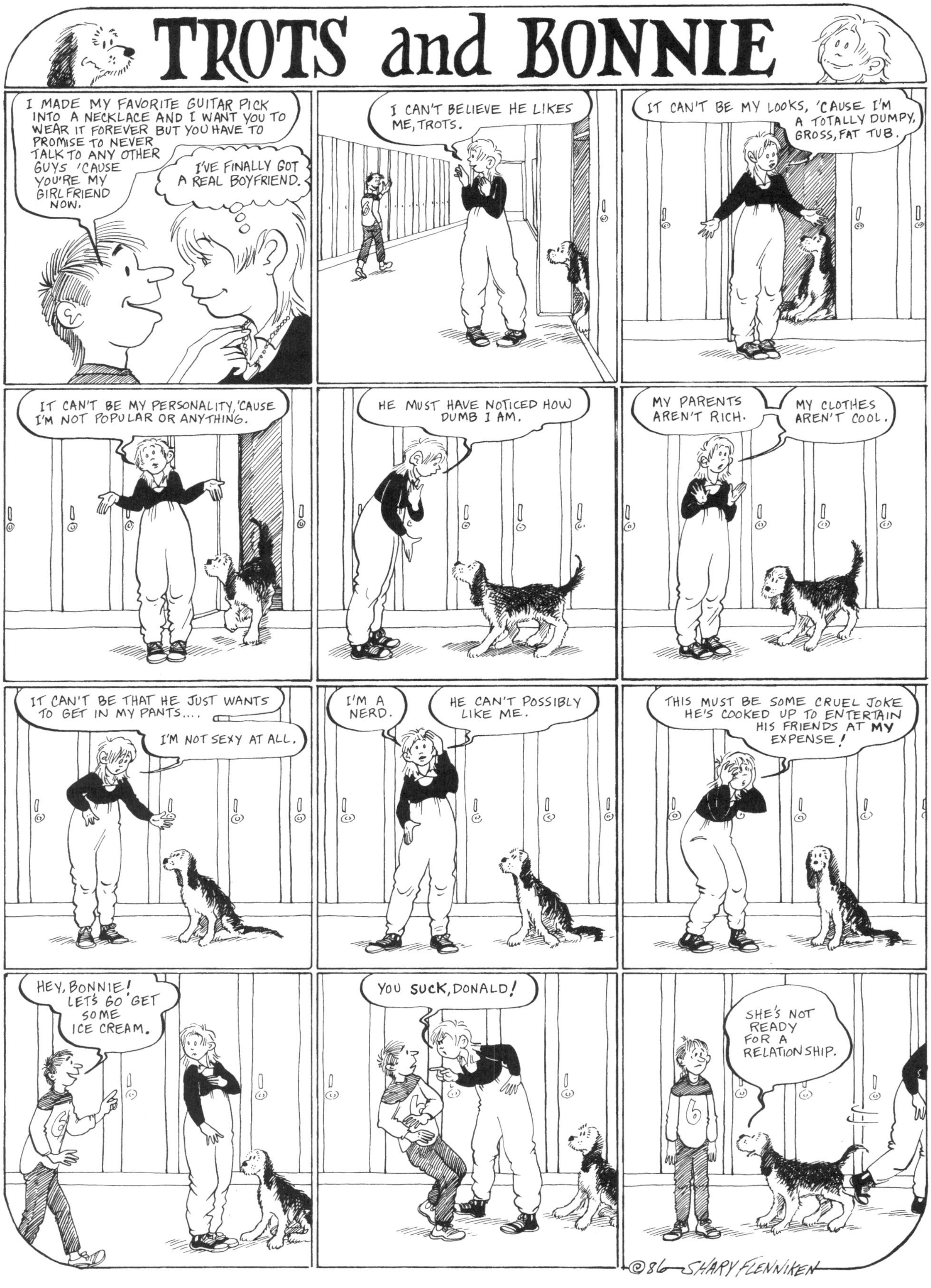
TROTS and BONNIE
I MADE MY FAVORITE GUITAR PICK INTO A NECKLACE AND I WANT YOU TO WEAR IT FOREVER BUT YOU HAVE TO PROMISE TO NEVER TALK TO ANY OTHER GUYS 'CAUSE YOU'RE MY GIRLFRIEND NOW.
I'VE FINALLY GOT A REAL BOYFRIEND.
I CAN'T BELIEVE HE LIKES ME, TROTS.
IT CAN'T BE MY LOOKS, 'CAUSE I'M A TOTALLY DUMPY, GROSS, FAT TUB.
IT CAN'T BE MY PERSONALITY, 'CAUSE I'M NOT POPULAR OR ANYTHING.
HE MUST HAVE NOTICED HOW DUMB I AM.
MY PARENTS AREN'T RICH.
MY CLOTHES AREN'T COOL.
IT CAN'T BE THAT HE JUST WANTS TO GET IN MY PANTS....
I'M NOT SEXY AT ALL.
I'M A NERD.
HE CAN'T POSSIBLY LIKE ME.
THIS MUST BE SOME CRUEL JOKE HE'S COOKED UP TO ENTERTAIN HIS FRIENDS AT MY EXPENSE!
HEY, BONNIE! LET'S GO GET SOME ICE CREAM.
YOU SUCK, DONALD!
SHE'S NOT READY FOR A RELATIONSHIP.
©86 SHARY FLENNIKEN

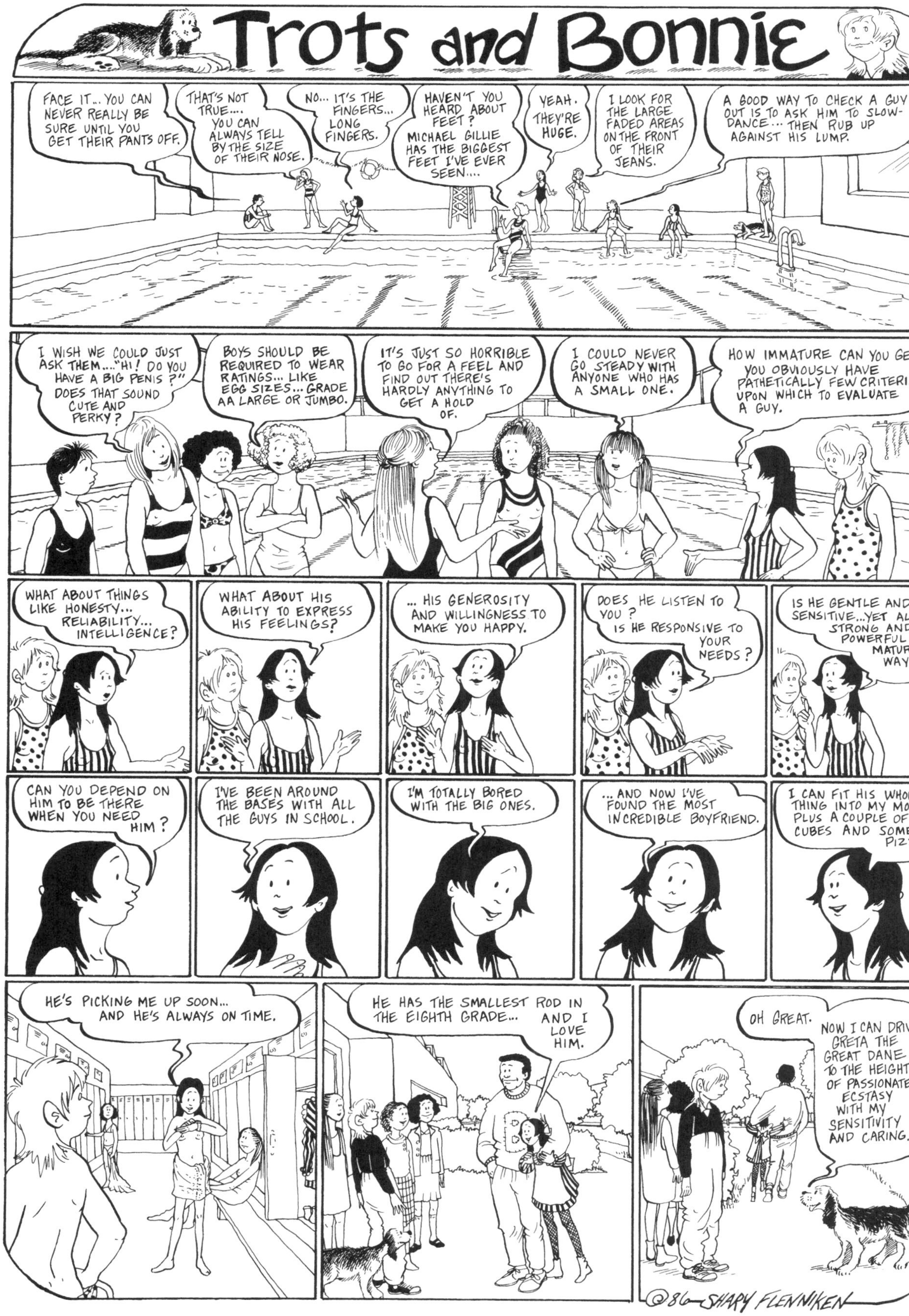
Trots and Bonnie
FACE IT... YOU CAN NEVER REALLY BE SURE UNTIL YOU GET THEIR PANTS OFF.
THAT'S NOT TRUE.... YOU CAN ALWAYS TELL BY THE SIZE OF THEIR NOSE.
NO... IT'S THE FINGERS... LONG FINGERS.
HAVEN'T YOU HEARD ABOUT FEET? MICHAEL GILLIE HAS THE BIGGEST FEET I'VE EVER SEEN....
YEAH. THEY'RE HUGE.
I LOOK FOR THE LARGE FADED AREAS ON THE FRONT OF THEIR JEANS.
A GOOD WAY TO CHECK A GUY OUT IS TO ASK HIM TO SLOW-DANCE... THEN RUB UP AGAINST HIS LUMP.
I WISH WE COULD JUST ASK THEM...."HI! DO YOU HAVE A BIG PENIS?" DOES THAT SOUND CUTE AND PERKY?
BOYS SHOULD BE REQUIRED TO WEAR RATINGS... LIKE EGG SIZES... GRADE AA LARGE OR JUMBO.
IT'S JUST SO HORRIBLE TO GO FOR A FEEL AND FIND OUT THERE'S HARDLY ANYTHING TO GET A HOLD OF.
I COULD NEVER GO STEADY WITH ANYONE WHO HAS A SMALL ONE.
HOW IMMATURE CAN YOU GET?! YOU OBVIOUSLY HAVE PATHETICALLY FEW CRITERIA UPON WHICH TO EVALUATE A GUY.
WHAT ABOUT THINGS LIKE HONESTY... RELIABILITY... INTELLIGENCE?
WHAT ABOUT HIS ABILITY TO EXPRESS HIS FEELINGS?
... HIS GENEROSITY AND WILLINGNESS TO MAKE YOU HAPPY.
DOES HE LISTEN TO YOU? IS HE RESPONSIVE TO YOUR NEEDS?
IS HE GENTLE AND SENSITIVE...YET ALSO STRONG AND POWERFUL IN A MATURE WAY?
CAN YOU DEPEND ON HIM TO BE THERE WHEN YOU NEED HIM?
I'VE BEEN AROUND THE BASES WITH ALL THE GUYS IN SCHOOL.
I'M TOTALLY BORED WITH THE BIG ONES.
... AND NOW I'VE FOUND THE MOST INCREDIBLE BOYFRIEND.
I CAN FIT HIS WHOLE THING INTO MY MOUTH PLUS A COUPLE OF ICE CUBES AND SOME PIZZA.
HE'S PICKING ME UP SOON... AND HE'S ALWAYS ON TIME.
HE HAS THE SMALLEST ROD IN THE EIGHTH GRADE... AND I LOVE HIM.
OH GREAT.
NOW I CAN DRIVE GRETA THE GREAT DANE TO THE HEIGHTS OF PASSIONATE ECSTASY WITH MY SENSITIVITY AND CARING.
©86 SHARY FLENNIKEN

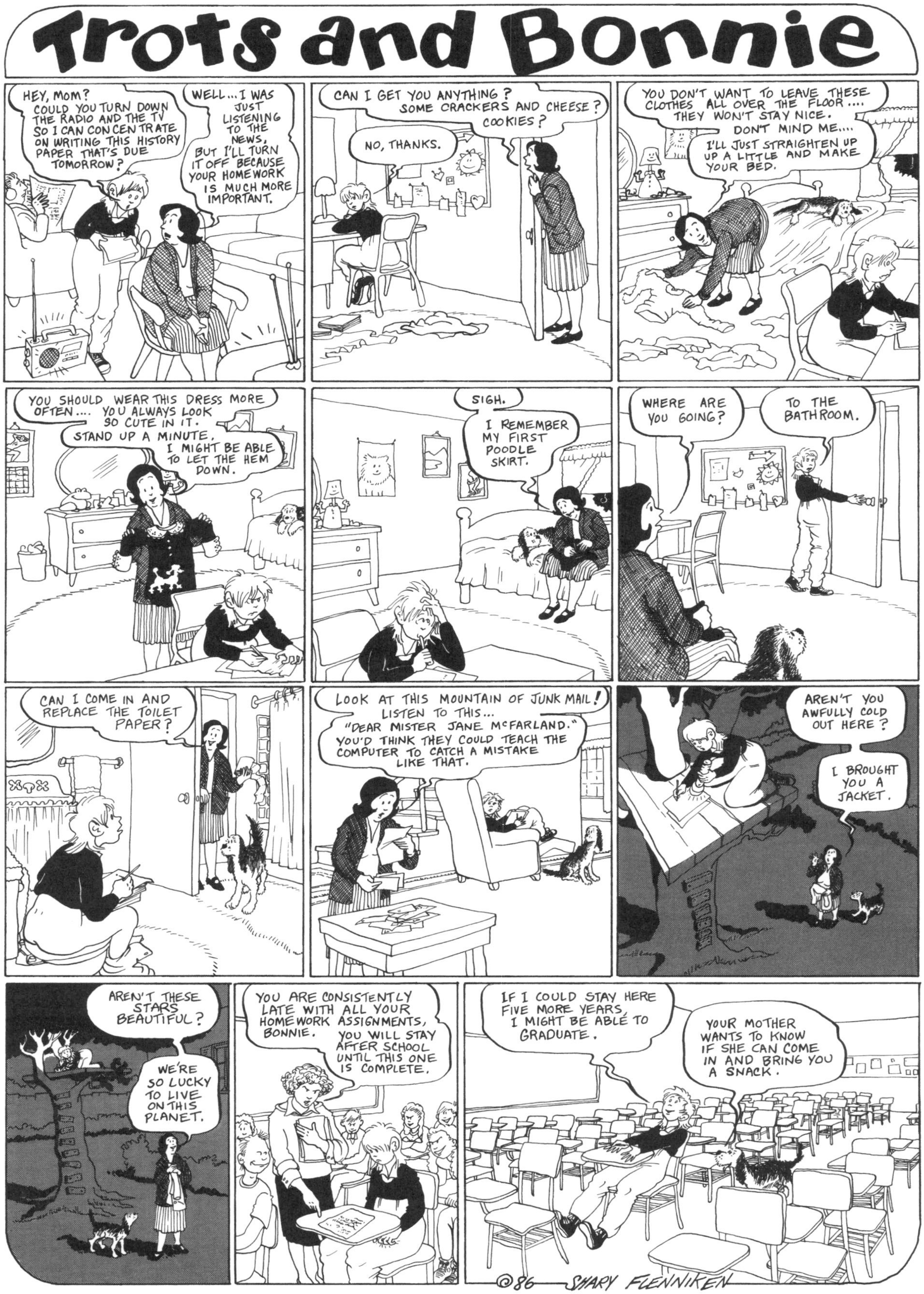
Trots and Bonnie
HEY, MOM? COULD YOU TURN DOWN THE RADIO AND THE TV SO I CAN CONCENTRATE ON WRITING THIS HISTORY PAPER THAT'S DUE TOMORROW?
WELL... I WAS JUST LISTENING TO THE NEWS, BUT I'LL TURN IT OFF BECAUSE YOUR HOMEWORK IS MUCH MORE IMPORTANT.
CAN I GET YOU ANYTHING? SOME CRACKERS AND CHEESE? COOKIES?
NO, THANKS.
YOU DON'T WANT TO LEAVE THESE CLOTHES ALL OVER THE FLOOR.... THEY WON'T STAY NICE.
DON'T MIND ME.... I'LL JUST STRAIGHTEN UP UP A LITTLE AND MAKE YOUR BED.
YOU SHOULD WEAR THIS DRESS MORE OFTEN.... YOU ALWAYS LOOK SO CUTE IN IT.
STAND UP A MINUTE, I MIGHT BE ABLE TO LET THE HEM DOWN.
SIGH.
I REMEMBER MY FIRST POODLE SKIRT.
WHERE ARE YOU GOING?
TO THE BATHROOM.
CAN I COME IN AND REPLACE THE TOILET PAPER?
LOOK AT THIS MOUNTAIN OF JUNK MAIL! LISTEN TO THIS... "DEAR MISTER JANE McFARLAND." YOU'D THINK THEY COULD TEACH THE COMPUTER TO CATCH A MISTAKE LIKE THAT.
AREN'T YOU AWFULLY COLD OUT HERE?
I BROUGHT YOU A JACKET.
AREN'T THESE STARS BEAUTIFUL?
WE'RE SO LUCKY TO LIVE ON THIS PLANET.
YOU ARE CONSISTENTLY LATE WITH ALL YOUR HOMEWORK ASSIGNMENTS, BONNIE. YOU WILL STAY AFTER SCHOOL UNTIL THIS ONE IS COMPLETE.
IF I COULD STAY HERE FIVE MORE YEARS, I MIGHT BE ABLE TO GRADUATE.
YOUR MOTHER WANTS TO KNOW IF SHE CAN COME IN AND BRING YOU A SNACK.
©86 SHARY FLENNIKEN

TROTS AND BONNIE
IT'S THE EIGHTIES.... CASUAL SEX IS OUT.
I'VE STOPPED SLEEPING AROUND AND SO HAVE ALL MY FRIENDS.
MARY SHULTZ BIGGEST BREASTS IN THE 7TH GRADE SEE them Now $1.00 FEEL them $2.00 other requests considered $3.75 SEASON TICKETS watch them grow! $50.00
THESE GUYS ARE PROBABLY GOING TO HAVE TO WAIT UNTIL THEY'RE TWENTY OR THIRTY AND MARRIED BEFORE THEY GET TO GO TO BED WITH A GIRL.
NOBODY'S ACTUALLY HAVING SEX ANYMORE, SO THERE'S GOING TO BE A BIG BOOM IN SECONDARY SEXUAL EXPERIENCES.
MARY AND I ARE GOING TO RIDE THE CREST OF THE TREND AND CASH IN.
WE'RE GOING TO START A MAGAZINE AND GET INTO VIDEO.
I'M HER MANAGER AND SHE CUTS ME IN ON A SHARE OF THE PROFITS.
WE'RE GOING TO INCORPORATE, THEN INVESTIGATE A MERGER WITH THE NINTH-GRADERS.
THEN WE'LL RAISE OUR PRICES.
BUT PEPSI... I THOUGHT YOU WERE A FEMINIST.... ISN'T THIS EXPLOITING?
IT'S THE EIGHTIES! FEMINISM IS OUT.
BIG BUCKS ARE IN.
HOW CAN PEOPLE JUST LOSE THEIR SCRUPLES?...
WHATEVER HAPPENED TO IDEALISM?...
AT FOUR DOLLARS AN HOUR, HOW MUCH CAN I MAKE HERE A WEEK?
WHEN THEY GO PUBLIC, I'M GOING TO BUY STOCK.
TITS TICKETS PAY HERE
©86 SHARY FLENNIKEN

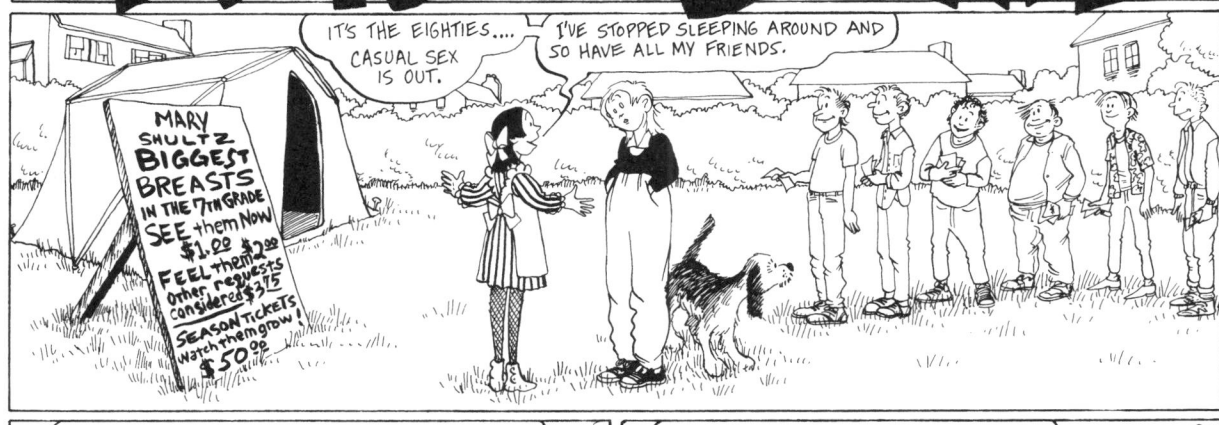

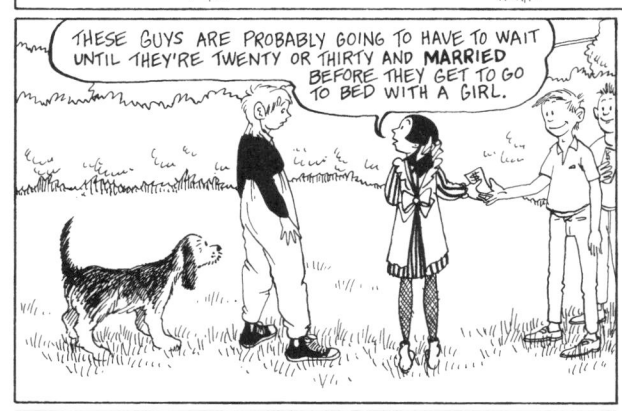

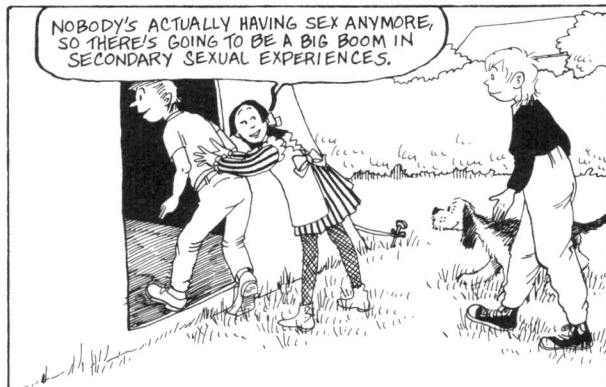

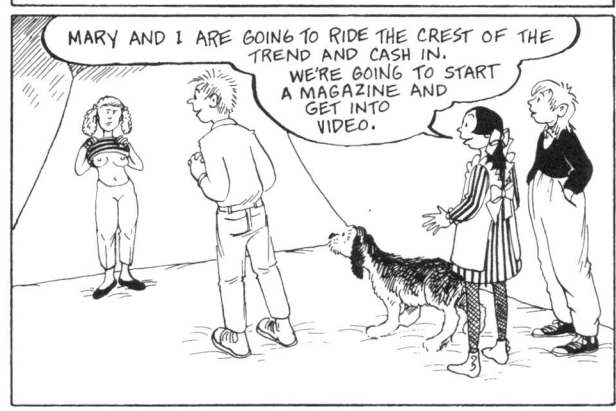

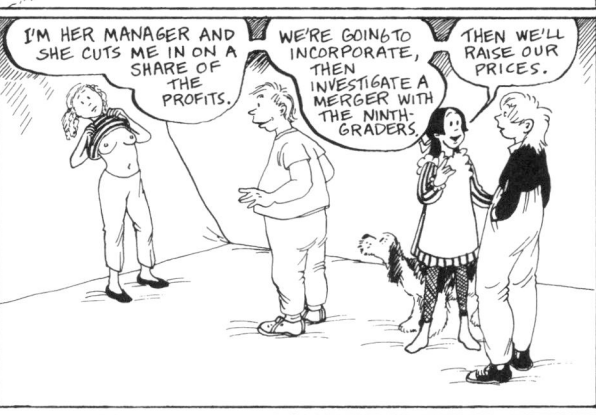

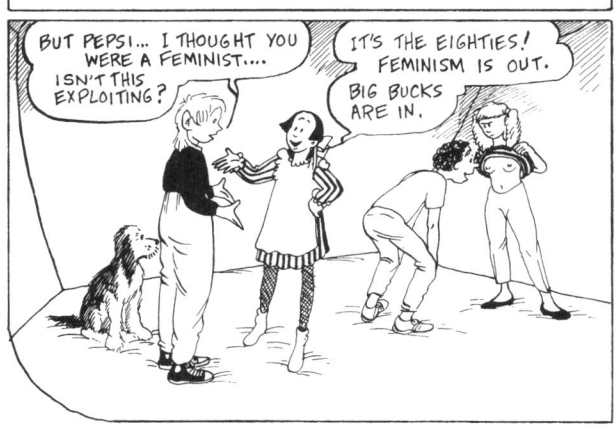

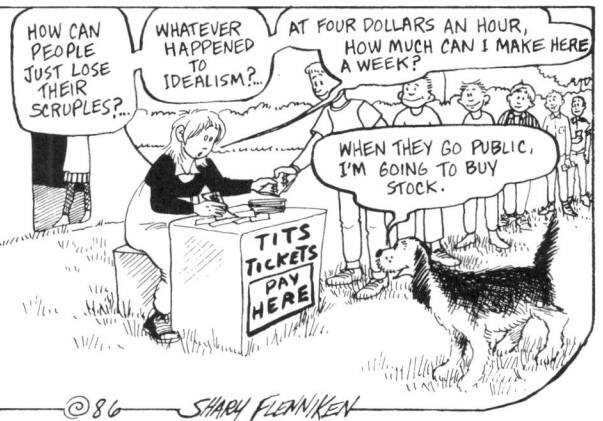

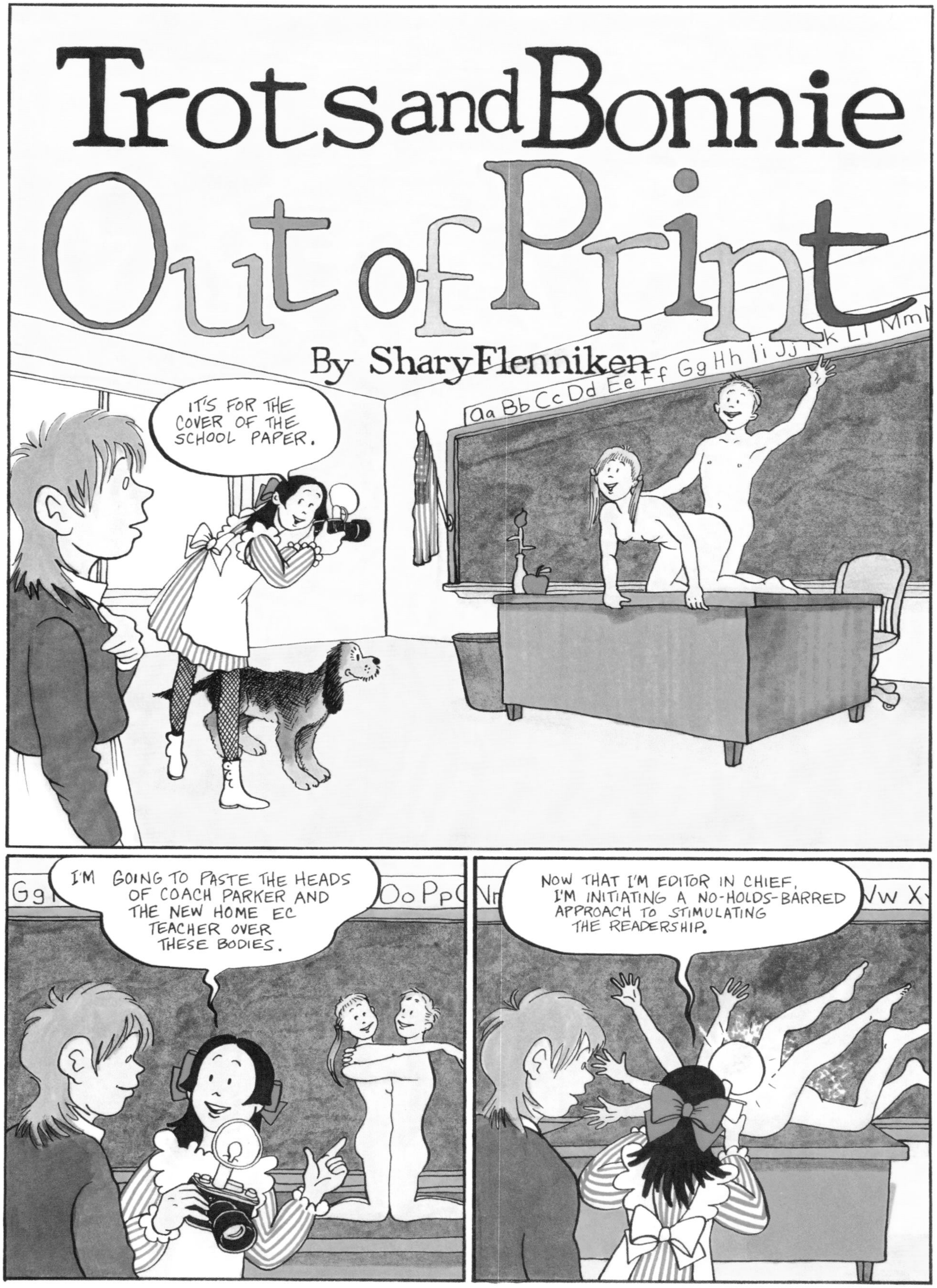
Trots and Bonnie
Out of Print
By Shary Flenniken
IT'S FOR THE COVER OF THE SCHOOL PAPER.
I'M GOING TO PASTE THE HEADS OF COACH PARKER AND THE NEW HOME EC TEACHER OVER THESE BODIES.
NOW THAT I'M EDITOR IN CHIEF, I'M INITIATING A NO-HOLDS-BARRED APPROACH TO STIMULATING THE READERSHIP.

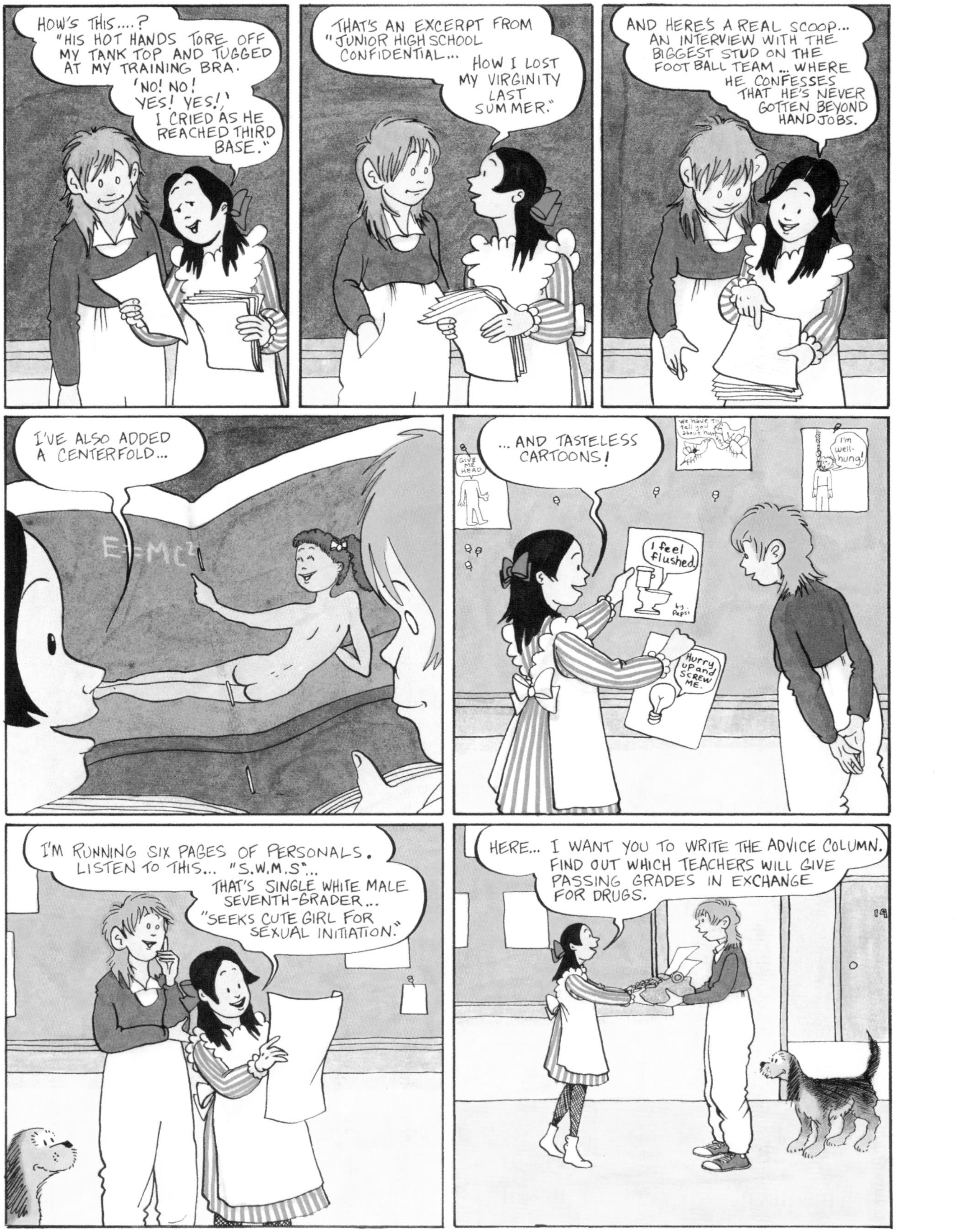
HOW'S THIS....? "HIS HOT HANDS TORE OFF MY TANK TOP AND TUGGED AT MY TRAINING BRA. 'NO! NO! YES! YES!,' I CRIED AS HE REACHED THIRD BASE."
THAT'S AN EXCERPT FROM "JUNIOR HIGH SCHOOL CONFIDENTIAL... HOW I LOST MY VIRGINITY LAST SUMMER."
AND HERE'S A REAL SCOOP... AN INTERVIEW WITH THE BIGGEST STUD ON THE FOOTBALL TEAM... WHERE HE CONFESSES THAT HE'S NEVER GOTTEN BEYOND HANDJOBS.
I'VE ALSO ADDED A CENTERFOLD...
E=MC²
...AND TASTELESS CARTOONS!
GIVE ME HEAD
I'm well-hung!
I feel flushed
Hurry up and SCREW ME.
I'M RUNNING SIX PAGES OF PERSONALS. LISTEN TO THIS... "S.W.M.S"... THAT'S SINGLE WHITE MALE SEVENTH-GRADER... "SEEKS CUTE GIRL FOR SEXUAL INITIATION."
HERE... I WANT YOU TO WRITE THE ADVICE COLUMN. FIND OUT WHICH TEACHERS WILL GIVE PASSING GRADES IN EXCHANGE FOR DRUGS.

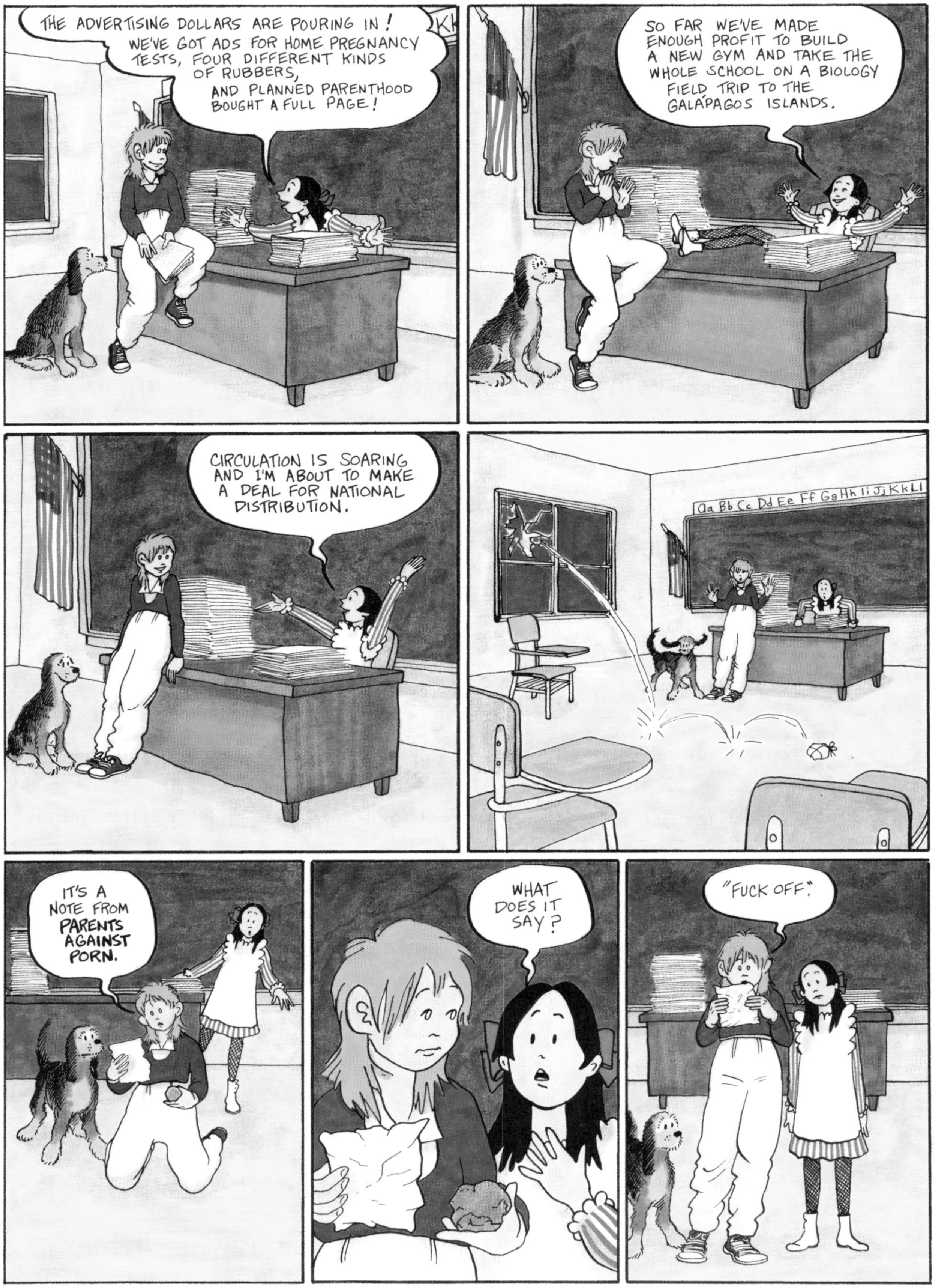
THE ADVERTISING DOLLARS ARE POURING IN! WE'VE GOT ADS FOR HOME PREGNANCY TESTS, FOUR DIFFERENT KINDS OF RUBBERS, AND PLANNED PARENTHOOD BOUGHT A FULL PAGE!
SO FAR WE'VE MADE ENOUGH PROFIT TO BUILD A NEW GYM AND TAKE THE WHOLE SCHOOL ON A BIOLOGY FIELD TRIP TO THE GALÁPAGOS ISLANDS.
CIRCULATION IS SOARING AND I'M ABOUT TO MAKE A DEAL FOR NATIONAL DISTRIBUTION.
Aa Bb Cc Dd Ee Ff Gg Hh Ii Jj Kk Ll
IT'S A NOTE FROM **PARENTS AGAINST PORN.**
WHAT DOES IT SAY?
"FUCK OFF."

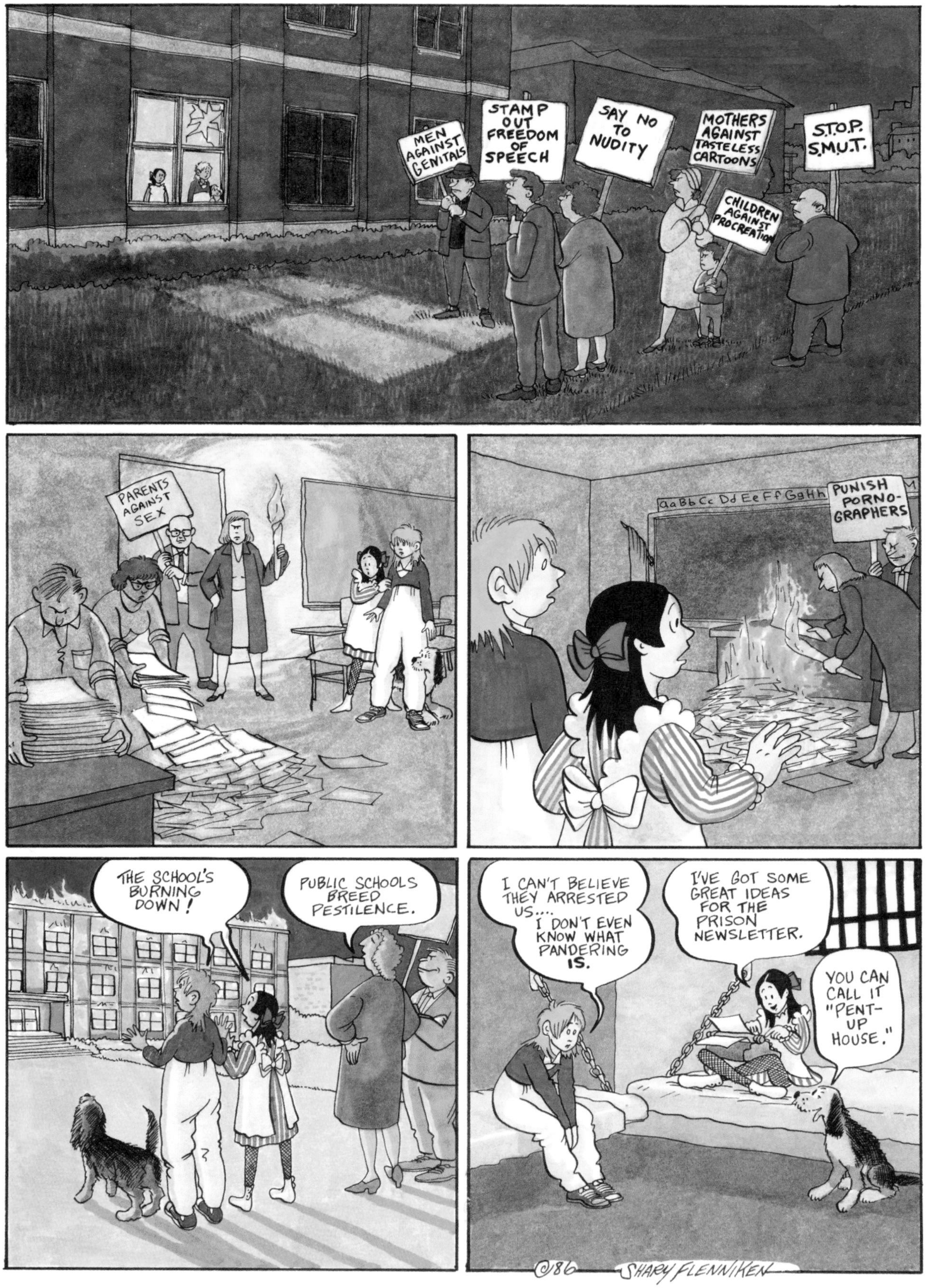
MEN AGAINST GENITALS
STAMP OUT FREEDOM OF SPEECH
SAY NO TO NUDITY
MOTHERS AGAINST TASTELESS CARTOONS
S.T.O.P. S.M.U.T.
CHILDREN AGAINST PROCREATION
PARENTS AGAINST SEX
PUNISH PORNOGRAPHERS
THE SCHOOL'S BURNING DOWN!
PUBLIC SCHOOLS BREED PESTILENCE.
I CAN'T BELIEVE THEY ARRESTED US.... I DON'T EVEN KNOW WHAT PANDERING IS.
I'VE GOT SOME GREAT IDEAS FOR THE PRISON NEWSLETTER.
YOU CAN CALL IT "PENT-UP HOUSE."
©86 SHARY FLENNIKEN

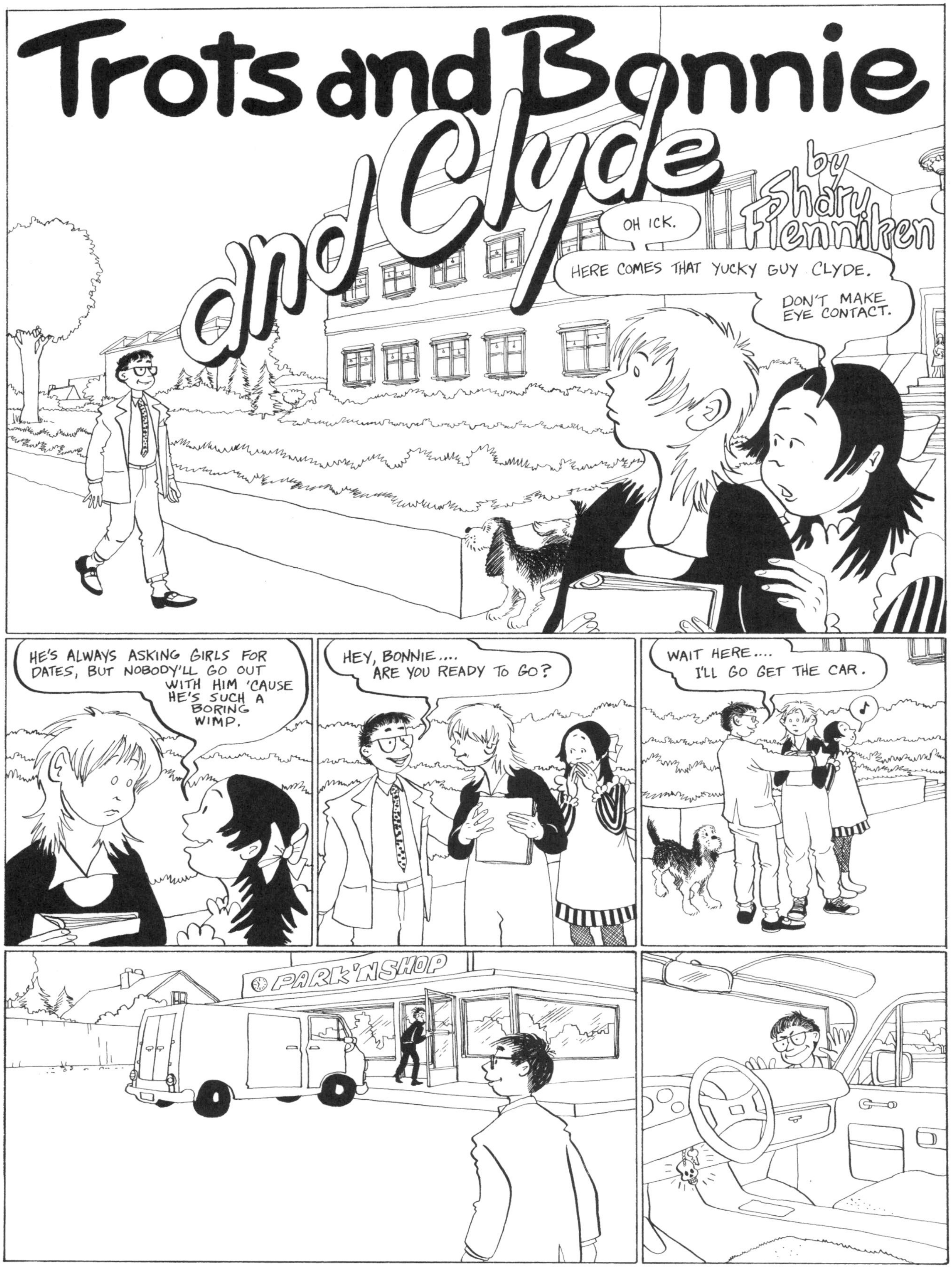
Trots and Bonnie and Clyde
by Shary Flenniken
OH ICK.
HERE COMES THAT YUCKY GUY CLYDE.
DON'T MAKE EYE CONTACT.
HE'S ALWAYS ASKING GIRLS FOR DATES, BUT NOBODY'LL GO OUT WITH HIM 'CAUSE HE'S SUCH A BORING WIMP.
HEY, BONNIE.... ARE YOU READY TO GO?
WAIT HERE.... I'LL GO GET THE CAR.
PARK'N SHOP

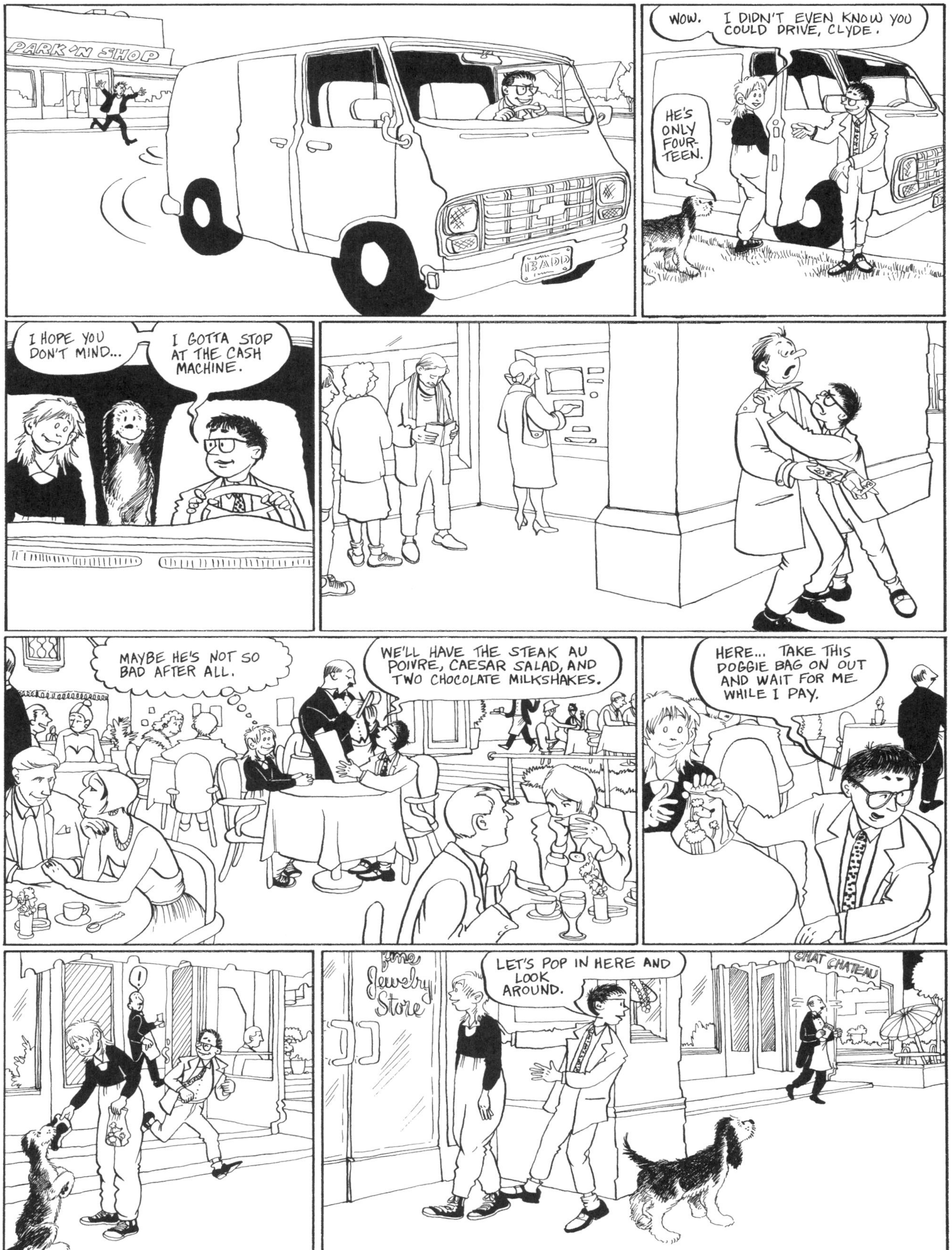
PARK 'N SHOP
BADD
WOW. I DIDN'T EVEN KNOW YOU COULD DRIVE, CLYDE.
HE'S ONLY FOUR-TEEN.
I HOPE YOU DON'T MIND...
I GOTTA STOP AT THE CASH MACHINE.
MAYBE HE'S NOT SO BAD AFTER ALL.
WE'LL HAVE THE STEAK AU POIVRE, CAESAR SALAD, AND TWO CHOCOLATE MILKSHAKES.
HERE... TAKE THIS DOGGIE BAG ON OUT AND WAIT FOR ME WHILE I PAY.
!
Fine Jewelry Store
LET'S POP IN HERE AND LOOK AROUND.
CHAT CHATEAU

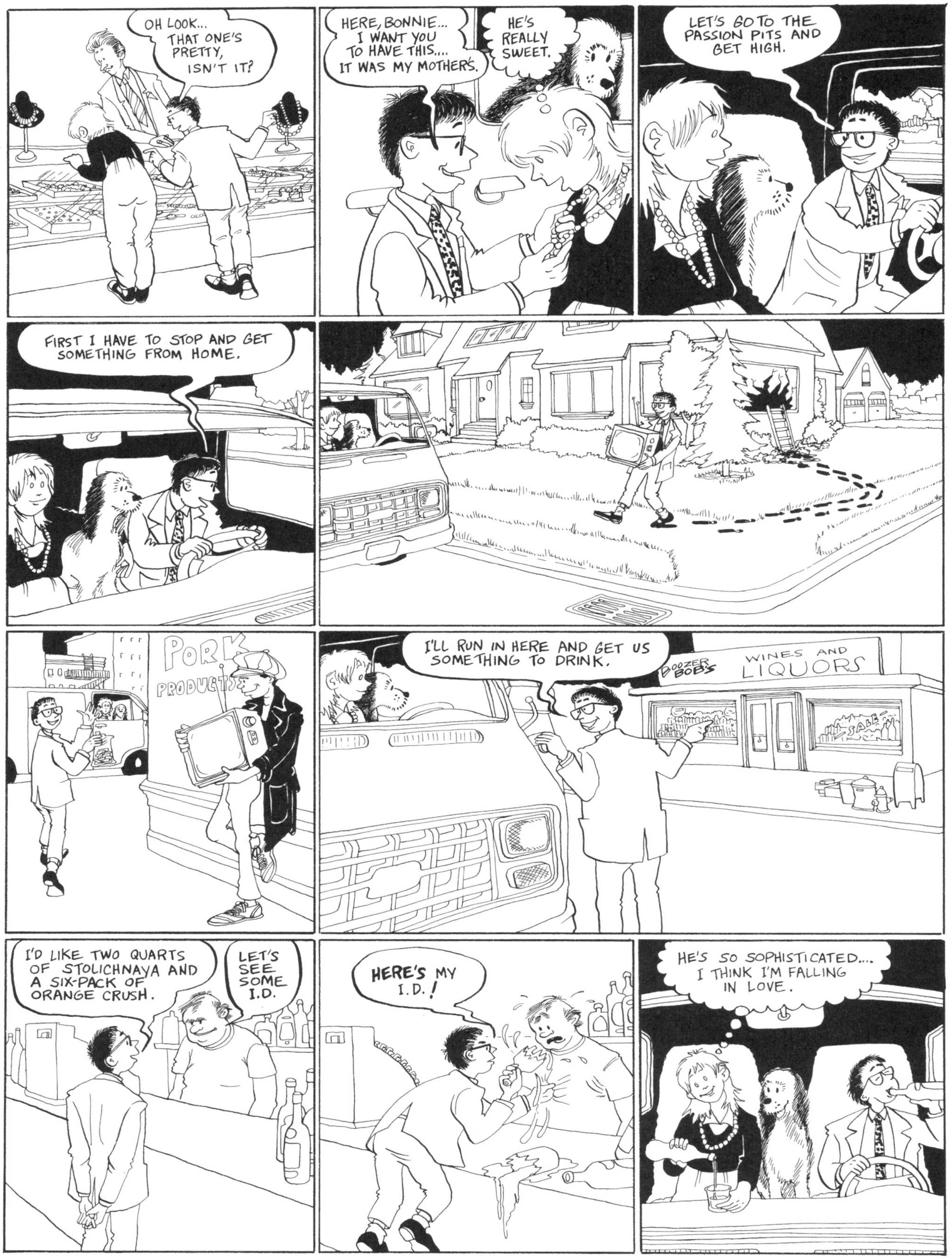
OH LOOK... THAT ONE'S PRETTY, ISN'T IT?
HERE, BONNIE... I WANT YOU TO HAVE THIS.... IT WAS MY MOTHER'S.
HE'S REALLY SWEET.
LET'S GO TO THE PASSION PITS AND GET HIGH.
FIRST I HAVE TO STOP AND GET SOMETHING FROM HOME.
PORK PRODUCTS
I'LL RUN IN HERE AND GET US SOMETHING TO DRINK.
BOOZER BOBS
WINES AND LIQUORS
SALE
I'D LIKE TWO QUARTS OF STOLICHNAYA AND A SIX-PACK OF ORANGE CRUSH.
LET'S SEE SOME I.D.
HERE'S MY I.D.!
HE'S SO SOPHISTICATED.... I THINK I'M FALLING IN LOVE.

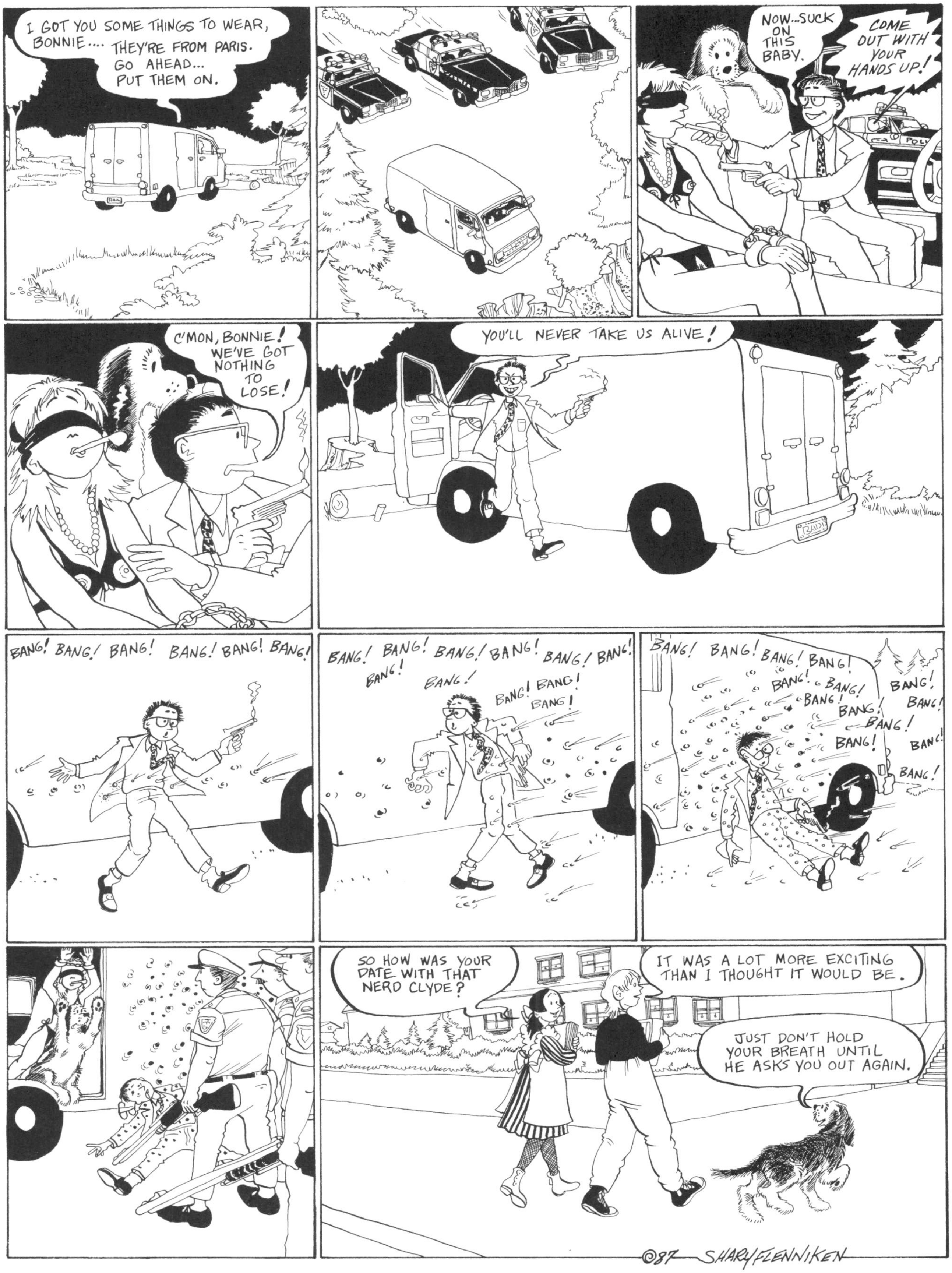
I GOT YOU SOME THINGS TO WEAR, BONNIE.... THEY'RE FROM PARIS. GO AHEAD... PUT THEM ON.
NOW...SUCK ON THIS BABY.
COME OUT WITH YOUR HANDS UP!
C'MON, BONNIE! WE'VE GOT NOTHING TO LOSE!
YOU'LL NEVER TAKE US ALIVE!
BANG! BANG! BANG! BANG! BANG! BANG!
BANG! BANG! BANG! BANG! BANG! BANG! BANG! BANG! BANG! BANG! BANG!
BANG! BANG! BANG! BANG! BANG! BANG! BANG! BANG! BANG! BANG! BANG! BANG! BANG! BANG!
SO HOW WAS YOUR DATE WITH THAT NERD CLYDE?
IT WAS A LOT MORE EXCITING THAN I THOUGHT IT WOULD BE.
JUST DON'T HOLD YOUR BREATH UNTIL HE ASKS YOU OUT AGAIN.
©87 SHARY FLENNIKEN

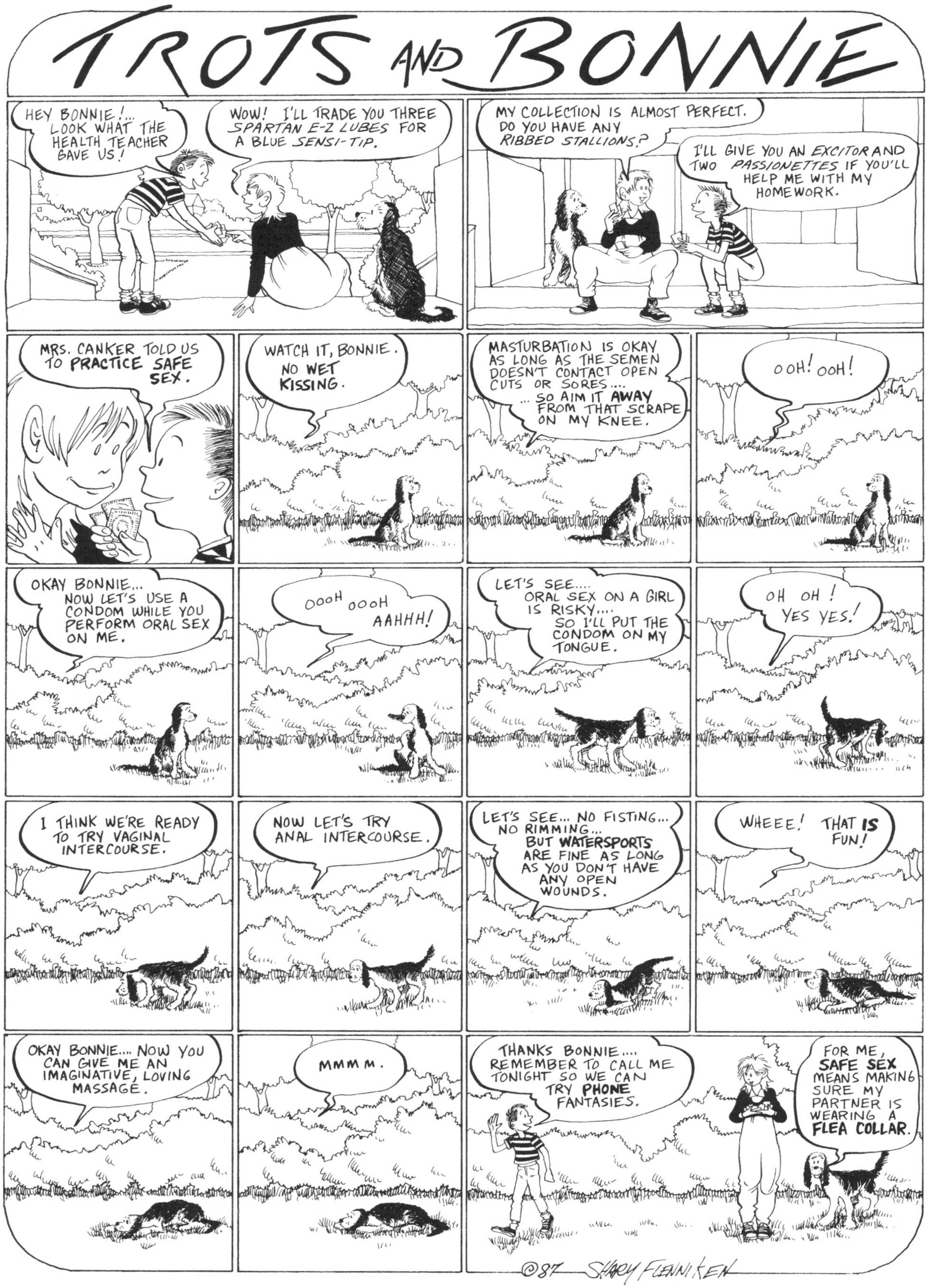
TROTS AND BONNIE
HEY BONNIE!... LOOK WHAT THE HEALTH TEACHER GAVE US!
WOW! I'LL TRADE YOU THREE SPARTAN E-Z LUBES FOR A BLUE SENSI-TIP.
MY COLLECTION IS ALMOST PERFECT. DO YOU HAVE ANY RIBBED STALLIONS?
I'LL GIVE YOU AN EXCITOR AND TWO PASSIONETTES IF YOU'LL HELP ME WITH MY HOMEWORK.
MRS. CANKER TOLD US TO PRACTICE SAFE SEX.
WATCH IT, BONNIE. NO WET KISSING.
MASTURBATION IS OKAY AS LONG AS THE SEMEN DOESN'T CONTACT OPEN CUTS OR SORES.... ...SO AIM IT AWAY FROM THAT SCRAPE ON MY KNEE.
OOH! OOH!
OKAY BONNIE... NOW LET'S USE A CONDOM WHILE YOU PERFORM ORAL SEX ON ME.
OOOH OOOH AAHHH!
LET'S SEE.... ORAL SEX ON A GIRL IS RISKY.... SO I'LL PUT THE CONDOM ON MY TONGUE.
OH OH! YES YES!
I THINK WE'RE READY TO TRY VAGINAL INTERCOURSE.
NOW LET'S TRY ANAL INTERCOURSE.
LET'S SEE... NO FISTING... NO RIMMING... BUT WATERSPORTS ARE FINE AS LONG AS YOU DON'T HAVE ANY OPEN WOUNDS.
WHEEE! THAT IS FUN!
OKAY BONNIE.... NOW YOU CAN GIVE ME AN IMAGINATIVE, LOVING MASSAGE.
MMMM.
THANKS BONNIE.... REMEMBER TO CALL ME TONIGHT SO WE CAN TRY PHONE FANTASIES.
FOR ME, SAFE SEX MEANS MAKING SURE MY PARTNER IS WEARING A FLEA COLLAR.
©87 SHARY FLENNIKEN

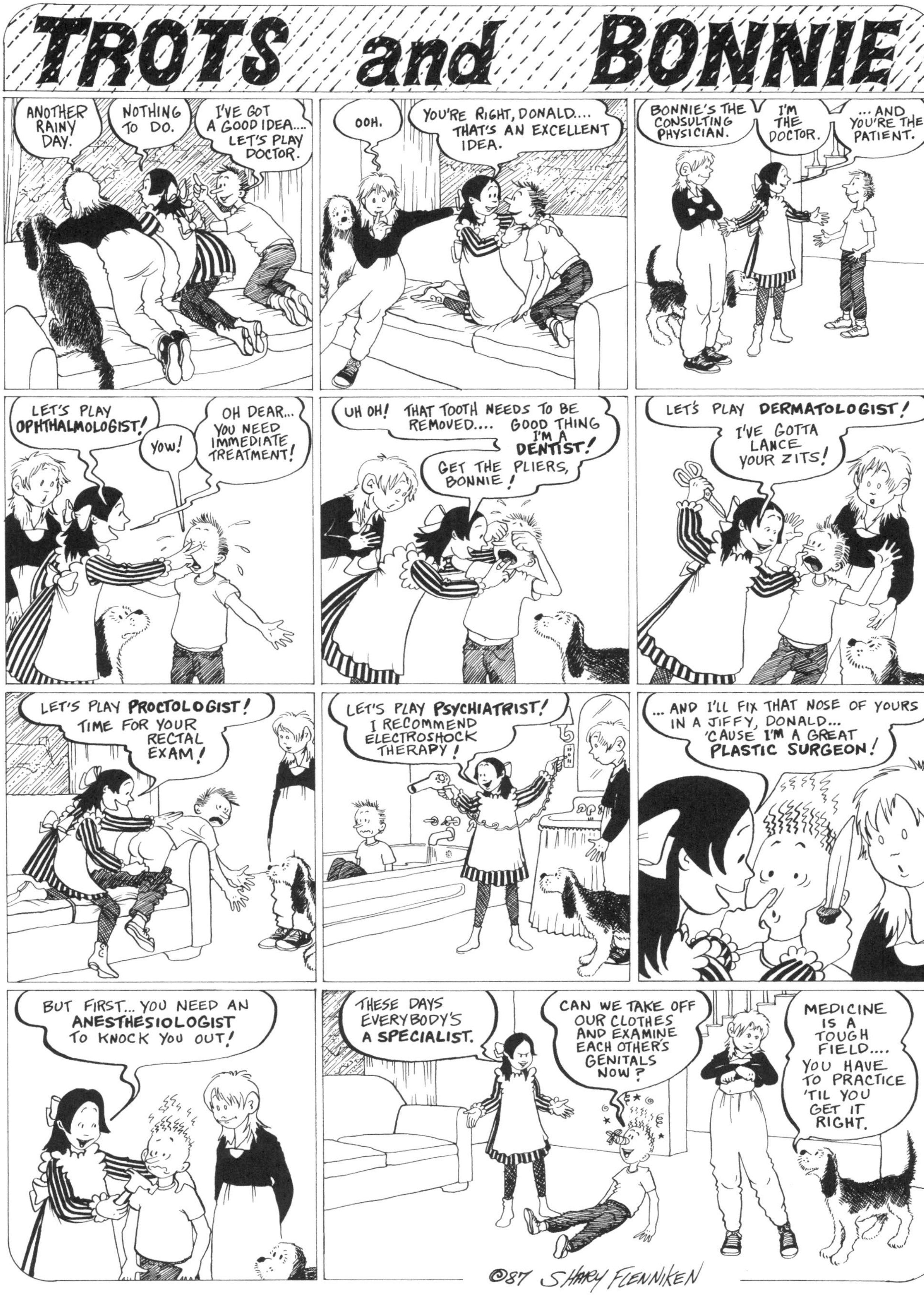
TROTS and BONNIE
ANOTHER RAINY DAY.
NOTHING TO DO.
I'VE GOT A GOOD IDEA.... LET'S PLAY DOCTOR.
OOH.
YOU'RE RIGHT, DONALD.... THAT'S AN EXCELLENT IDEA.
BONNIE'S THE CONSULTING PHYSICIAN.
I'M THE DOCTOR.
... AND YOU'RE THE PATIENT.
LET'S PLAY OPHTHALMOLOGIST!
YOW!
OH DEAR... YOU NEED IMMEDIATE TREATMENT!
UH OH! THAT TOOTH NEEDS TO BE REMOVED.... GOOD THING I'M A DENTIST!
GET THE PLIERS, BONNIE!
LET'S PLAY DERMATOLOGIST!
I'VE GOTTA LANCE YOUR ZITS!
LET'S PLAY PROCTOLOGIST! TIME FOR YOUR RECTAL EXAM!
LET'S PLAY PSYCHIATRIST! I RECOMMEND ELECTROSHOCK THERAPY!
... AND I'LL FIX THAT NOSE OF YOURS IN A JIFFY, DONALD... 'CAUSE I'M A GREAT PLASTIC SURGEON!
BUT FIRST... YOU NEED AN ANESTHESIOLOGIST TO KNOCK YOU OUT!
THESE DAYS EVERYBODY'S A SPECIALIST.
CAN WE TAKE OFF OUR CLOTHES AND EXAMINE EACH OTHER'S GENITALS NOW?
MEDICINE IS A TOUGH FIELD.... YOU HAVE TO PRACTICE 'TIL YOU GET IT RIGHT.
©87 SHARY FLENNIKEN

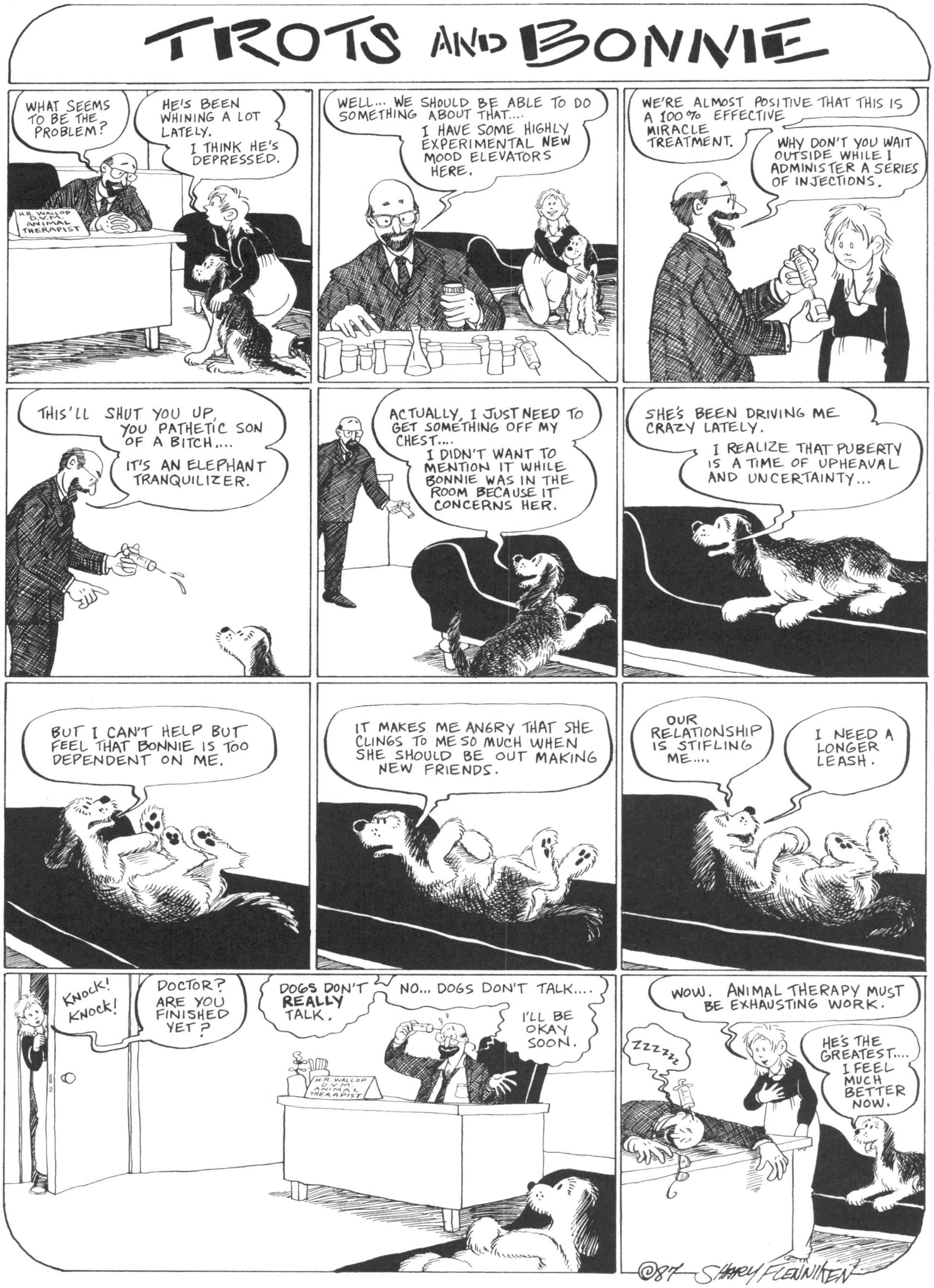
TROTS AND BONNIE
WHAT SEEMS TO BE THE PROBLEM?
HE'S BEEN WHINING A LOT LATELY.
I THINK HE'S DEPRESSED.
H.R. WALLOP D.V.M. ANIMAL THERAPIST
WELL... WE SHOULD BE ABLE TO DO SOMETHING ABOUT THAT....
I HAVE SOME HIGHLY EXPERIMENTAL NEW MOOD ELEVATORS HERE.
WE'RE ALMOST POSITIVE THAT THIS IS A 100% EFFECTIVE MIRACLE TREATMENT.
WHY DON'T YOU WAIT OUTSIDE WHILE I ADMINISTER A SERIES OF INJECTIONS.
THIS'LL SHUT YOU UP, YOU PATHETIC SON OF A BITCH....
IT'S AN ELEPHANT TRANQUILIZER.
ACTUALLY, I JUST NEED TO GET SOMETHING OFF MY CHEST....
I DIDN'T WANT TO MENTION IT WHILE BONNIE WAS IN THE ROOM BECAUSE IT CONCERNS HER.
SHE'S BEEN DRIVING ME CRAZY LATELY.
I REALIZE THAT PUBERTY IS A TIME OF UPHEAVAL AND UNCERTAINTY...
BUT I CAN'T HELP BUT FEEL THAT BONNIE IS TOO DEPENDENT ON ME.
IT MAKES ME ANGRY THAT SHE CLINGS TO ME SO MUCH WHEN SHE SHOULD BE OUT MAKING NEW FRIENDS.
OUR RELATIONSHIP IS STIFLING ME....
I NEED A LONGER LEASH.
KNOCK! KNOCK!
DOCTOR? ARE YOU FINISHED YET?
DOGS DON'T REALLY TALK.
NO... DOGS DON'T TALK....
I'LL BE OKAY SOON.
H.R. WALLOP D.V.M. ANIMAL THERAPIST
WOW. ANIMAL THERAPY MUST BE EXHAUSTING WORK.
ZZZZZZ
HE'S THE GREATEST.... I FEEL MUCH BETTER NOW.
©87 SHARY FLENNIKEN

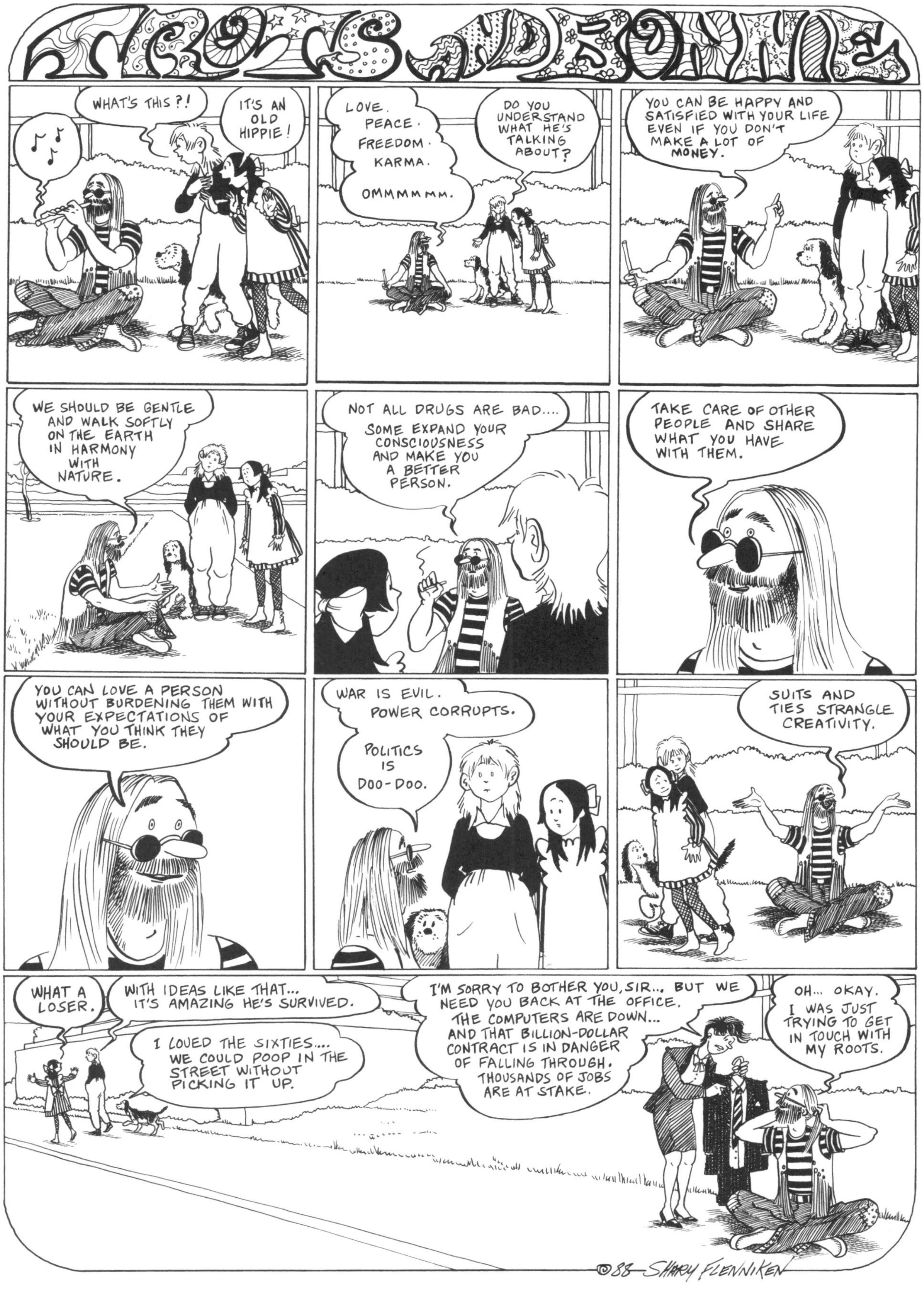
TROTS AND BONNIE
WHAT'S THIS ?!
IT'S AN OLD HIPPIE!
LOVE. PEACE. FREEDOM. KARMA. OMMMMMM.
DO YOU UNDERSTAND WHAT HE'S TALKING ABOUT?
YOU CAN BE HAPPY AND SATISFIED WITH YOUR LIFE EVEN IF YOU DON'T MAKE A LOT OF MONEY.
WE SHOULD BE GENTLE AND WALK SOFTLY ON THE EARTH IN HARMONY WITH NATURE.
NOT ALL DRUGS ARE BAD.... SOME EXPAND YOUR CONSCIOUSNESS AND MAKE YOU A BETTER PERSON.
TAKE CARE OF OTHER PEOPLE AND SHARE WHAT YOU HAVE WITH THEM.
YOU CAN LOVE A PERSON WITHOUT BURDENING THEM WITH YOUR EXPECTATIONS OF WHAT YOU THINK THEY SHOULD BE.
WAR IS EVIL. POWER CORRUPTS.
POLITICS IS DOO-DOO.
SUITS AND TIES STRANGLE CREATIVITY.
WHAT A LOSER.
WITH IDEAS LIKE THAT... IT'S AMAZING HE'S SURVIVED.
I LOVED THE SIXTIES.... WE COULD POOP IN THE STREET WITHOUT PICKING IT UP.
I'M SORRY TO BOTHER YOU, SIR... BUT WE NEED YOU BACK AT THE OFFICE. THE COMPUTERS ARE DOWN... AND THAT BILLION-DOLLAR CONTRACT IS IN DANGER OF FALLING THROUGH. THOUSANDS OF JOBS ARE AT STAKE.
OH... OKAY. I WAS JUST TRYING TO GET IN TOUCH WITH MY ROOTS.
©88 SHARY FLENNIKEN

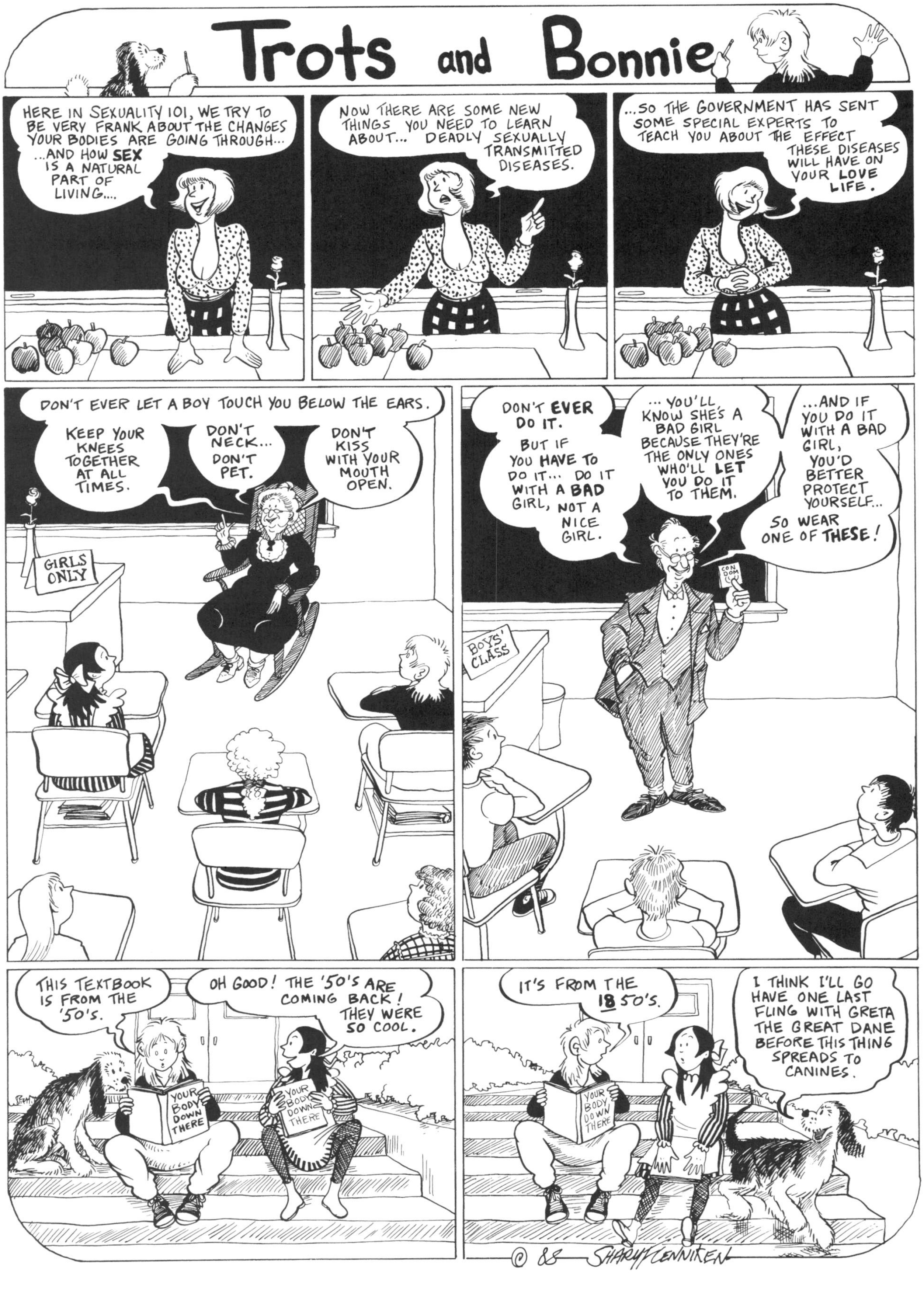
Trots and Bonnie
HERE IN SEXUALITY 101, WE TRY TO BE VERY FRANK ABOUT THE CHANGES YOUR BODIES ARE GOING THROUGH... ...AND HOW SEX IS A NATURAL PART OF LIVING....
NOW THERE ARE SOME NEW THINGS YOU NEED TO LEARN ABOUT... DEADLY SEXUALLY TRANSMITTED DISEASES.
...SO THE GOVERNMENT HAS SENT SOME SPECIAL EXPERTS TO TEACH YOU ABOUT THE EFFECT THESE DISEASES WILL HAVE ON YOUR LOVE LIFE.
DON'T EVER LET A BOY TOUCH YOU BELOW THE EARS.
KEEP YOUR KNEES TOGETHER AT ALL TIMES.
DON'T NECK... DON'T PET.
DON'T KISS WITH YOUR MOUTH OPEN.
GIRLS ONLY
DON'T EVER DO IT. BUT IF YOU HAVE TO DO IT... DO IT WITH A BAD GIRL, NOT A NICE GIRL.
... YOU'LL KNOW SHE'S A BAD GIRL BECAUSE THEY'RE THE ONLY ONES WHO'LL LET YOU DO IT TO THEM.
...AND IF YOU DO IT WITH A BAD GIRL, YOU'D BETTER PROTECT YOURSELF... SO WEAR ONE OF THESE!
CON DOM
BOYS' CLASS
THIS TEXTBOOK IS FROM THE '50'S.
OH GOOD! THE '50'S ARE COMING BACK! THEY WERE SO COOL.
YOUR BODY DOWN THERE
YOUR BODY DOWN THERE
IT'S FROM THE 1850'S.
I THINK I'LL GO HAVE ONE LAST FLING WITH GRETA THE GREAT DANE BEFORE THIS THING SPREADS TO CANINES.
YOUR BODY DOWN THERE
© 88 SHARY FLENNIKEN

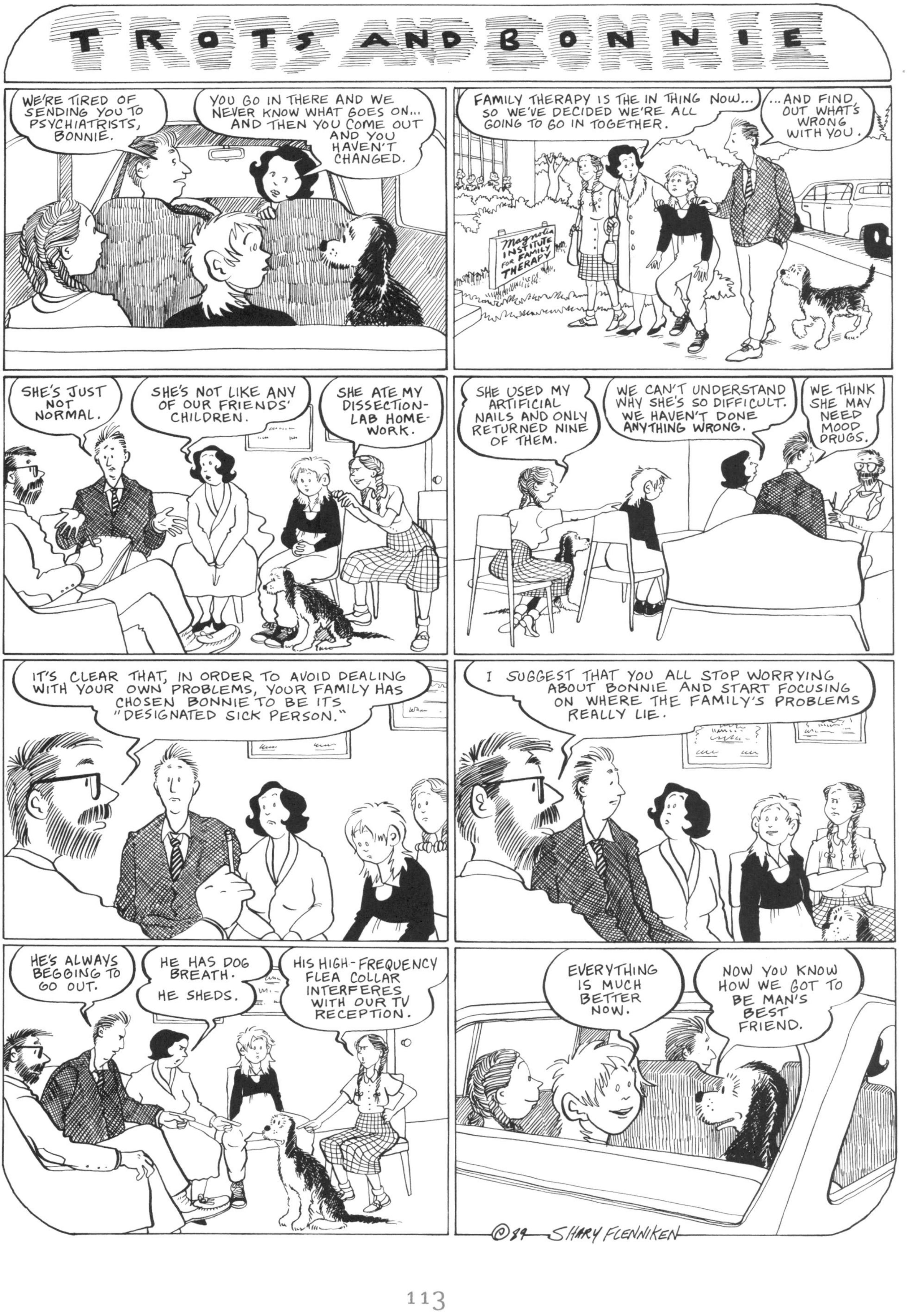

TROTS AND BONNIE
WE'RE TIRED OF SENDING YOU TO PSYCHIATRISTS, BONNIE.
YOU GO IN THERE AND WE NEVER KNOW WHAT GOES ON... AND THEN YOU COME OUT AND YOU HAVEN'T CHANGED.
FAMILY THERAPY IS THE IN THING NOW... SO WE'VE DECIDED WE'RE ALL GOING TO GO IN TOGETHER.
...AND FIND OUT WHAT'S WRONG WITH YOU.
Magnolia INSTITUTE FOR FAMILY THERAPY
SHE'S JUST NOT NORMAL.
SHE'S NOT LIKE ANY OF OUR FRIENDS' CHILDREN.
SHE ATE MY DISSECTION-LAB HOMEWORK.
SHE USED MY ARTIFICIAL NAILS AND ONLY RETURNED NINE OF THEM.
WE CAN'T UNDERSTAND WHY SHE'S SO DIFFICULT. WE HAVEN'T DONE ANYTHING WRONG.
WE THINK SHE MAY NEED MOOD DRUGS.
IT'S CLEAR THAT, IN ORDER TO AVOID DEALING WITH YOUR OWN PROBLEMS, YOUR FAMILY HAS CHOSEN BONNIE TO BE ITS "DESIGNATED SICK PERSON."
I SUGGEST THAT YOU ALL STOP WORRYING ABOUT BONNIE AND START FOCUSING ON WHERE THE FAMILY'S PROBLEMS REALLY LIE.
HE'S ALWAYS BEGGING TO GO OUT.
HE HAS DOG BREATH.
HE SHEDS.
HIS HIGH-FREQUENCY FLEA COLLAR INTERFERES WITH OUR TV RECEPTION.
EVERYTHING IS MUCH BETTER NOW.
NOW YOU KNOW HOW WE GOT TO BE MAN'S BEST FRIEND.
©84 SHARY FLENNIKEN

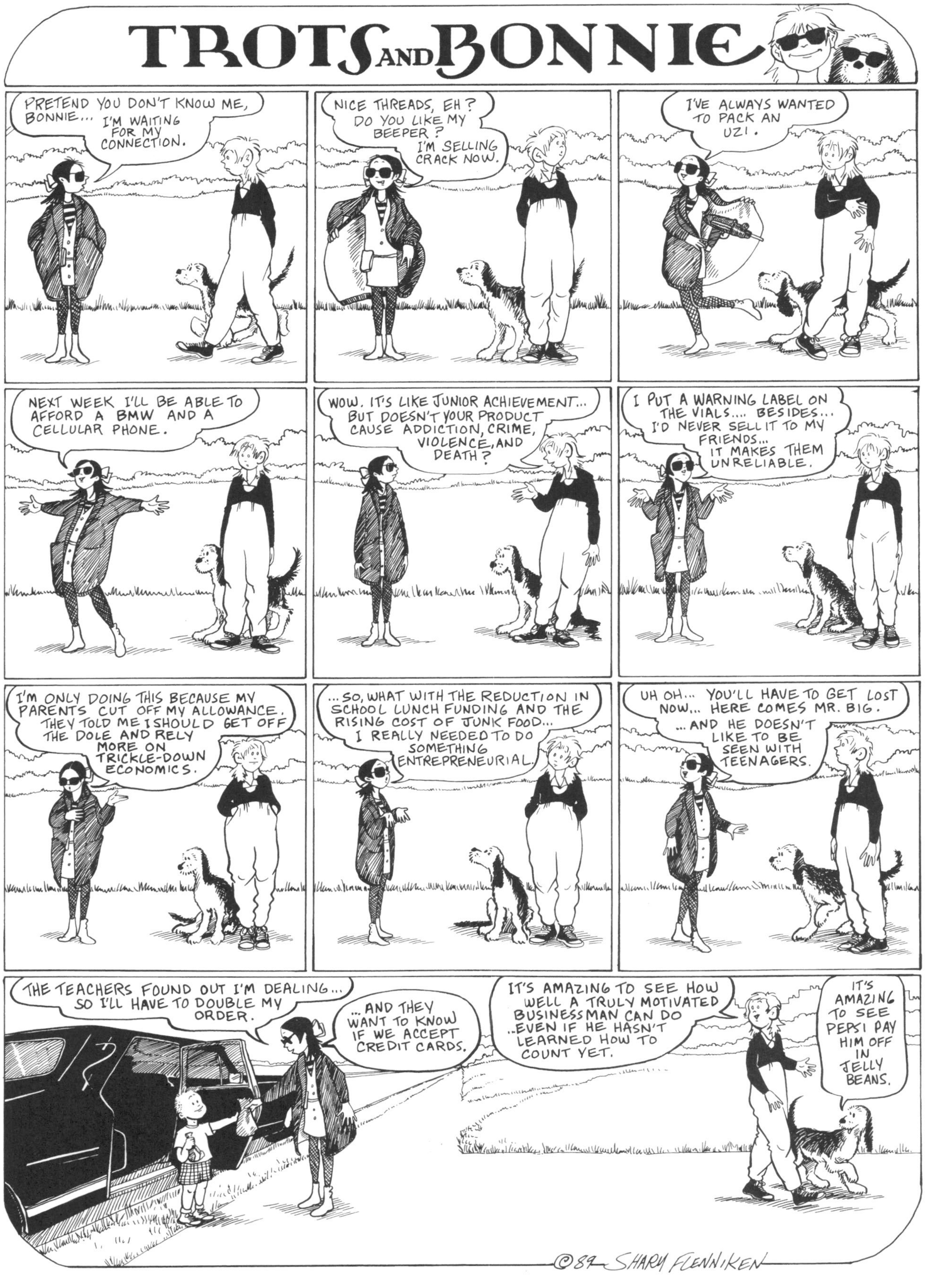
TROTS AND BONNIE
PRETEND YOU DON'T KNOW ME, BONNIE... I'M WAITING FOR MY CONNECTION.
NICE THREADS, EH? DO YOU LIKE MY BEEPER? I'M SELLING CRACK NOW.
I'VE ALWAYS WANTED TO PACK AN UZI.
NEXT WEEK I'LL BE ABLE TO AFFORD A BMW AND A CELLULAR PHONE.
WOW. IT'S LIKE JUNIOR ACHIEVEMENT... BUT DOESN'T YOUR PRODUCT CAUSE ADDICTION, CRIME, VIOLENCE, AND DEATH?
I PUT A WARNING LABEL ON THE VIALS.... BESIDES... I'D NEVER SELL IT TO MY FRIENDS... IT MAKES THEM UNRELIABLE.
I'M ONLY DOING THIS BECAUSE MY PARENTS CUT OFF MY ALLOWANCE. THEY TOLD ME I SHOULD GET OFF THE DOLE AND RELY MORE ON TRICKLE-DOWN ECONOMICS.
...SO, WHAT WITH THE REDUCTION IN SCHOOL LUNCH FUNDING AND THE RISING COST OF JUNK FOOD... I REALLY NEEDED TO DO SOMETHING ENTREPRENEURIAL.
UH OH... YOU'LL HAVE TO GET LOST NOW... HERE COMES MR. BIG.
...AND HE DOESN'T LIKE TO BE SEEN WITH TEENAGERS.
THE TEACHERS FOUND OUT I'M DEALING... SO I'LL HAVE TO DOUBLE MY ORDER.
...AND THEY WANT TO KNOW IF WE ACCEPT CREDIT CARDS.
IT'S AMAZING TO SEE HOW WELL A TRULY MOTIVATED BUSINESSMAN CAN DO ..EVEN IF HE HASN'T LEARNED HOW TO COUNT YET.
IT'S AMAZING TO SEE PEPSI PAY HIM OFF IN JELLY BEANS.
©87 SHARY FLENNIKEN

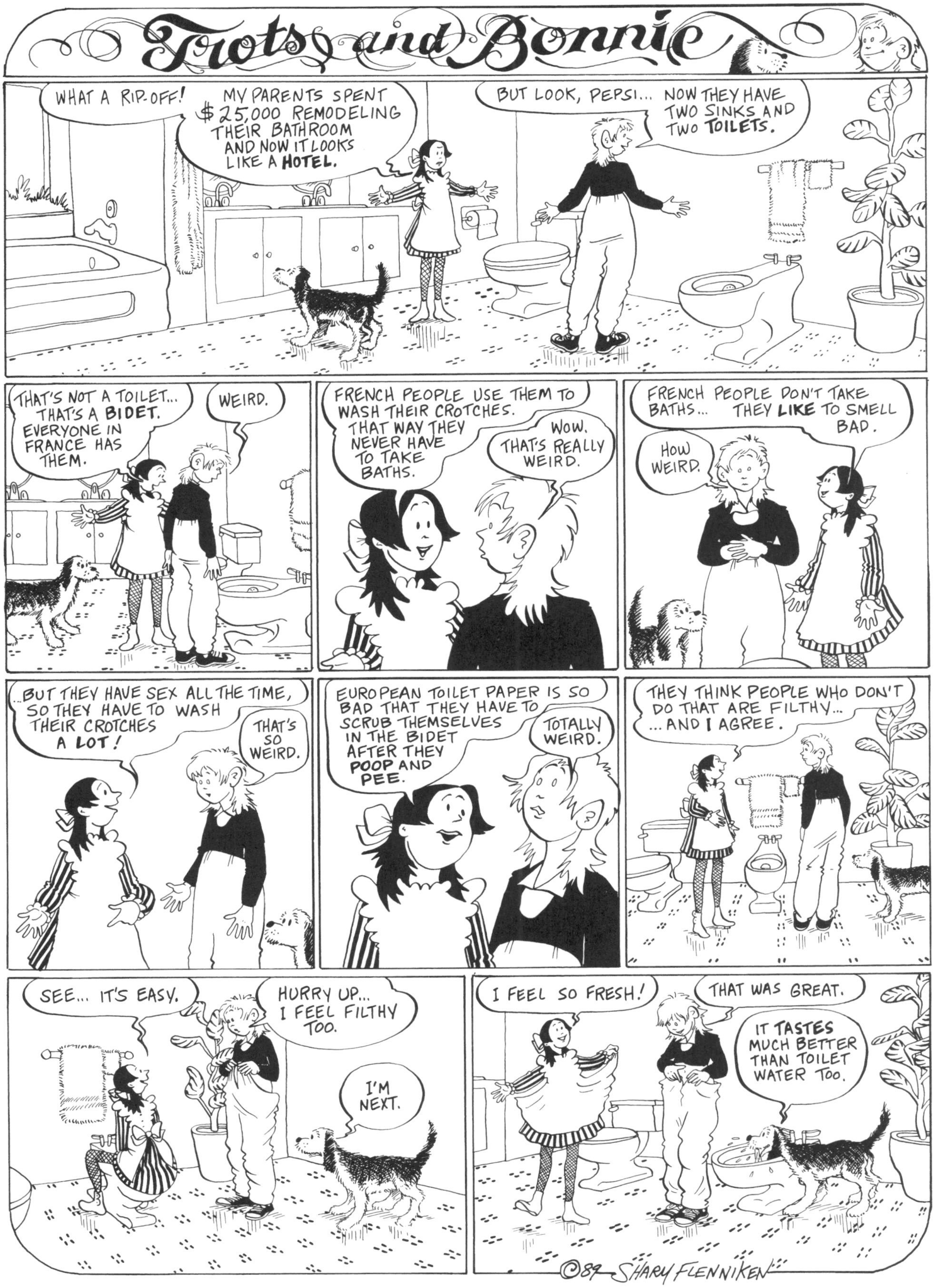
Trots and Bonnie
WHAT A RIP-OFF!
MY PARENTS SPENT $25,000 REMODELING THEIR BATHROOM AND NOW IT LOOKS LIKE A HOTEL.
BUT LOOK, PEPSI... NOW THEY HAVE TWO SINKS AND TWO TOILETS.
THAT'S NOT A TOILET... THAT'S A BIDET. EVERYONE IN FRANCE HAS THEM.
WEIRD.
FRENCH PEOPLE USE THEM TO WASH THEIR CROTCHES. THAT WAY THEY NEVER HAVE TO TAKE BATHS.
WOW. THAT'S REALLY WEIRD.
FRENCH PEOPLE DON'T TAKE BATHS... THEY LIKE TO SMELL BAD.
HOW WEIRD.
...BUT THEY HAVE SEX ALL THE TIME, SO THEY HAVE TO WASH THEIR CROTCHES A LOT!
THAT'S SO WEIRD.
EUROPEAN TOILET PAPER IS SO BAD THAT THEY HAVE TO SCRUB THEMSELVES IN THE BIDET AFTER THEY POOP AND PEE.
TOTALLY WEIRD.
THEY THINK PEOPLE WHO DON'T DO THAT ARE FILTHY... ...AND I AGREE.
SEE... IT'S EASY.
HURRY UP... I FEEL FILTHY TOO.
I'M NEXT.
I FEEL SO FRESH!
THAT WAS GREAT.
IT TASTES MUCH BETTER THAN TOILET WATER TOO.
©89 SHARY FLENNIKEN

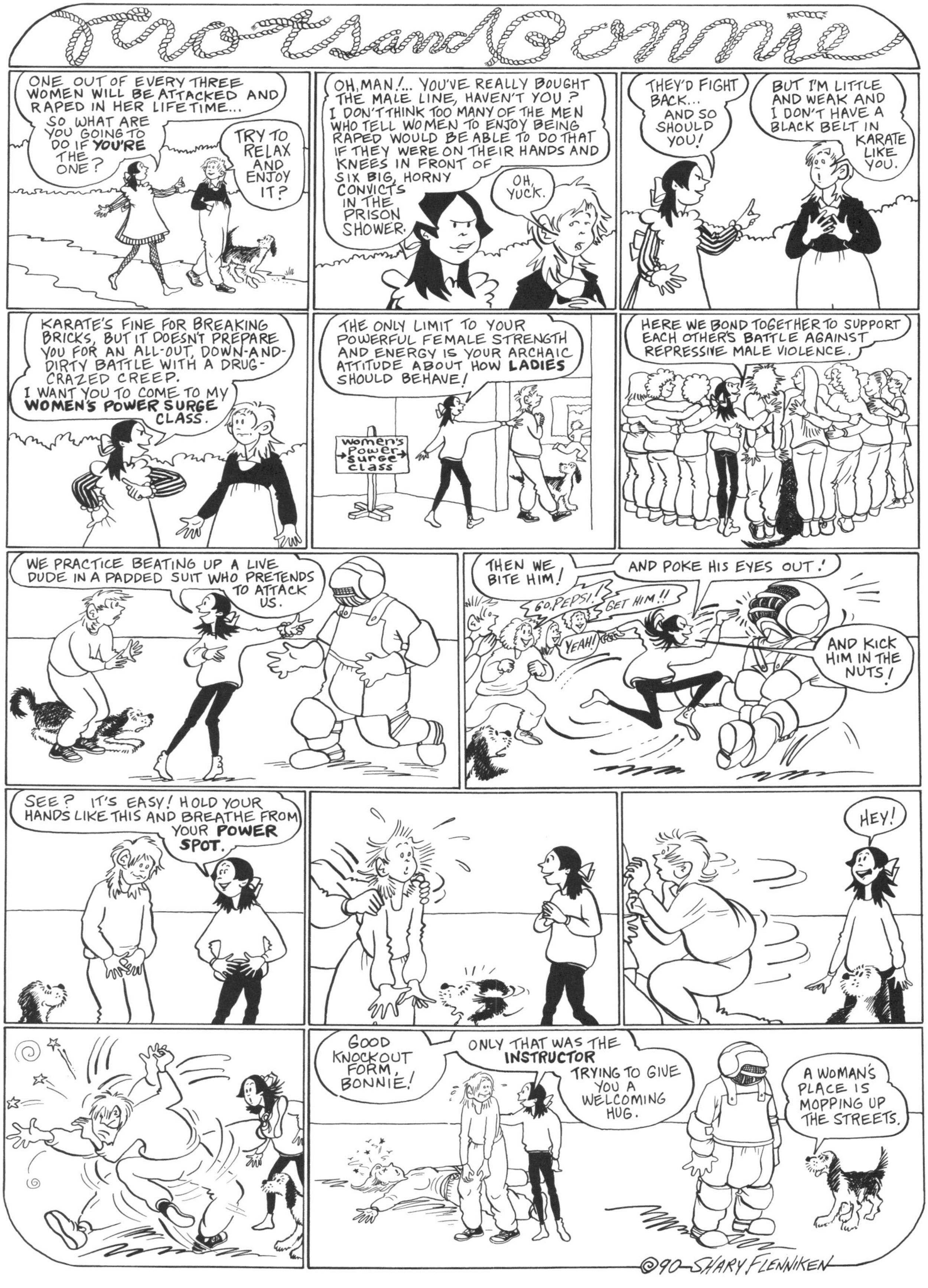
Trots and Bonnie
ONE OUT OF EVERY THREE WOMEN WILL BE ATTACKED AND RAPED IN HER LIFETIME... SO WHAT ARE YOU GOING TO DO IF YOU'RE THE ONE?
TRY TO RELAX AND ENJOY IT?
OH, MAN!... YOU'VE REALLY BOUGHT THE MALE LINE, HAVEN'T YOU? I DON'T THINK TOO MANY OF THE MEN WHO TELL WOMEN TO ENJOY BEING RAPED WOULD BE ABLE TO DO THAT IF THEY WERE ON THEIR HANDS AND KNEES IN FRONT OF SIX BIG, HORNY CONVICTS IN THE PRISON SHOWER.
OH, YUCK.
THEY'D FIGHT BACK... AND SO SHOULD YOU!
BUT I'M LITTLE AND WEAK AND I DON'T HAVE A BLACK BELT IN KARATE LIKE YOU.
KARATE'S FINE FOR BREAKING BRICKS, BUT IT DOESN'T PREPARE YOU FOR AN ALL-OUT, DOWN-AND-DIRTY BATTLE WITH A DRUG-CRAZED CREEP. I WANT YOU TO COME TO MY WOMEN'S POWER SURGE CLASS.
THE ONLY LIMIT TO YOUR POWERFUL FEMALE STRENGTH AND ENERGY IS YOUR ARCHAIC ATTITUDE ABOUT HOW LADIES SHOULD BEHAVE!
Women's Power Surge Class
HERE WE BOND TOGETHER TO SUPPORT EACH OTHER'S BATTLE AGAINST REPRESSIVE MALE VIOLENCE.
WE PRACTICE BEATING UP A LIVE DUDE IN A PADDED SUIT WHO PRETENDS TO ATTACK US.
THEN WE BITE HIM!
AND POKE HIS EYES OUT!
GO, PEPSI!
GET HIM!!
YEAH!
AND KICK HIM IN THE NUTS!
SEE? IT'S EASY! HOLD YOUR HANDS LIKE THIS AND BREATHE FROM YOUR POWER SPOT.
HEY!
GOOD KNOCKOUT FORM, BONNIE!
ONLY THAT WAS THE INSTRUCTOR TRYING TO GIVE YOU A WELCOMING HUG.
A WOMAN'S PLACE IS MOPPING UP THE STREETS.
©90 SHARY FLENNIKEN

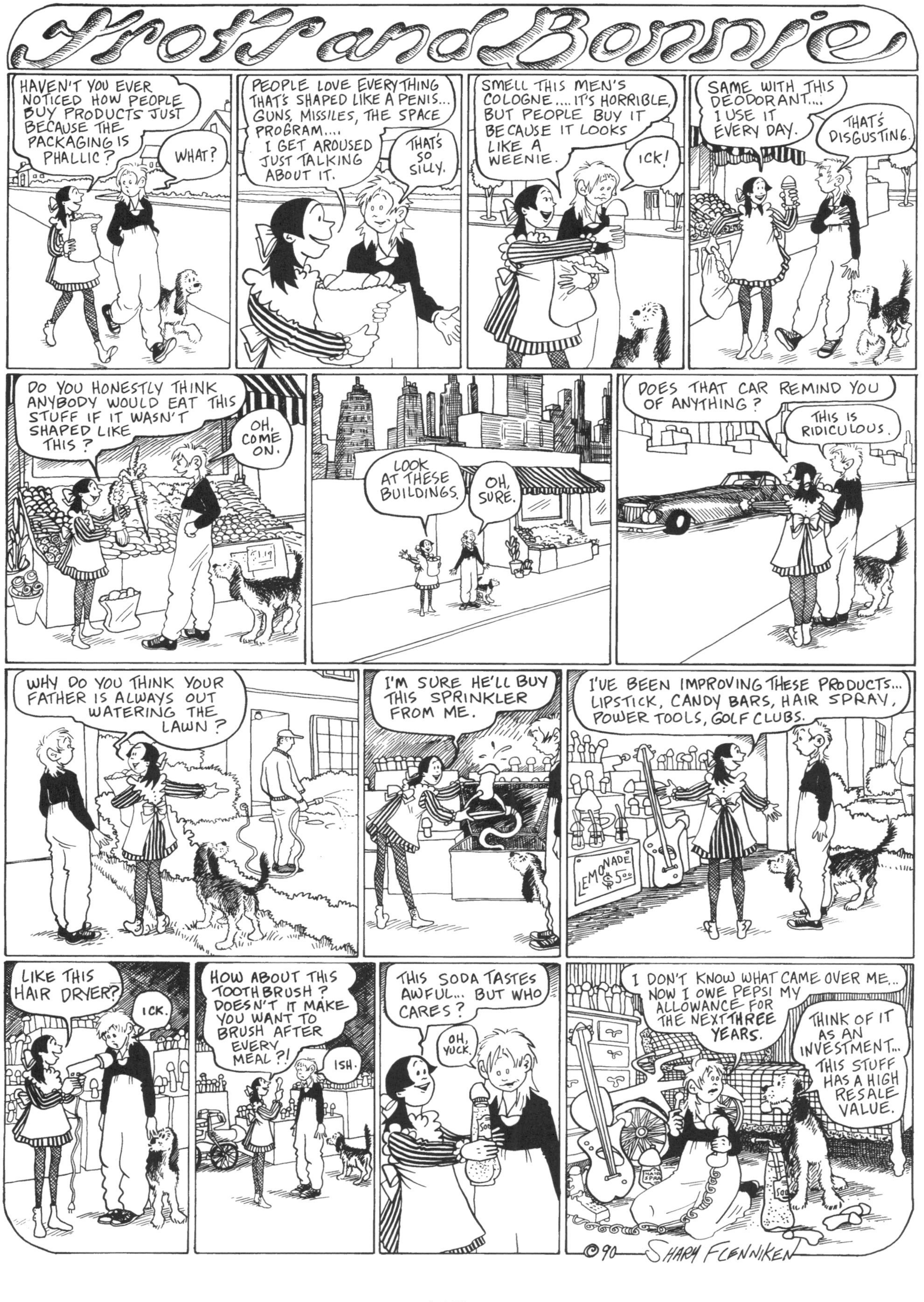
Trots and Bonnie
HAVEN'T YOU EVER NOTICED HOW PEOPLE BUY PRODUCTS JUST BECAUSE THE PACKAGING IS PHALLIC?
WHAT?
PEOPLE LOVE EVERYTHING THAT'S SHAPED LIKE A PENIS... GUNS, MISSILES, THE SPACE PROGRAM.... I GET AROUSED JUST TALKING ABOUT IT.
THAT'S SO SILLY.
SMELL THIS MEN'S COLOGNE.... IT'S HORRIBLE, BUT PEOPLE BUY IT BECAUSE IT LOOKS LIKE A WEENIE.
ICK!
SAME WITH THIS DEODORANT.... I USE IT EVERY DAY.
THAT'S DISGUSTING.
DO YOU HONESTLY THINK ANYBODY WOULD EAT THIS STUFF IF IT WASN'T SHAPED LIKE THIS?
OH, COME ON.
LOOK AT THESE BUILDINGS.
OH, SURE.
DOES THAT CAR REMIND YOU OF ANYTHING?
THIS IS RIDICULOUS.
WHY DO YOU THINK YOUR FATHER IS ALWAYS OUT WATERING THE LAWN?
I'M SURE HE'LL BUY THIS SPRINKLER FROM ME.
I'VE BEEN IMPROVING THESE PRODUCTS... LIPSTICK, CANDY BARS, HAIR SPRAY, POWER TOOLS, GOLF CLUBS.
LEMONADE $5.00
LIKE THIS HAIR DRYER?
ICK.
HOW ABOUT THIS TOOTHBRUSH? DOESN'T IT MAKE YOU WANT TO BRUSH AFTER EVERY MEAL?!
ISH.
THIS SODA TASTES AWFUL... BUT WHO CARES?
OH, YUCK.
I DON'T KNOW WHAT CAME OVER ME... NOW I OWE PEPSI MY ALLOWANCE FOR THE NEXT THREE YEARS.
THINK OF IT AS AN INVESTMENT... THIS STUFF HAS A HIGH RESALE VALUE.
©90 SHARY FLENNIKEN

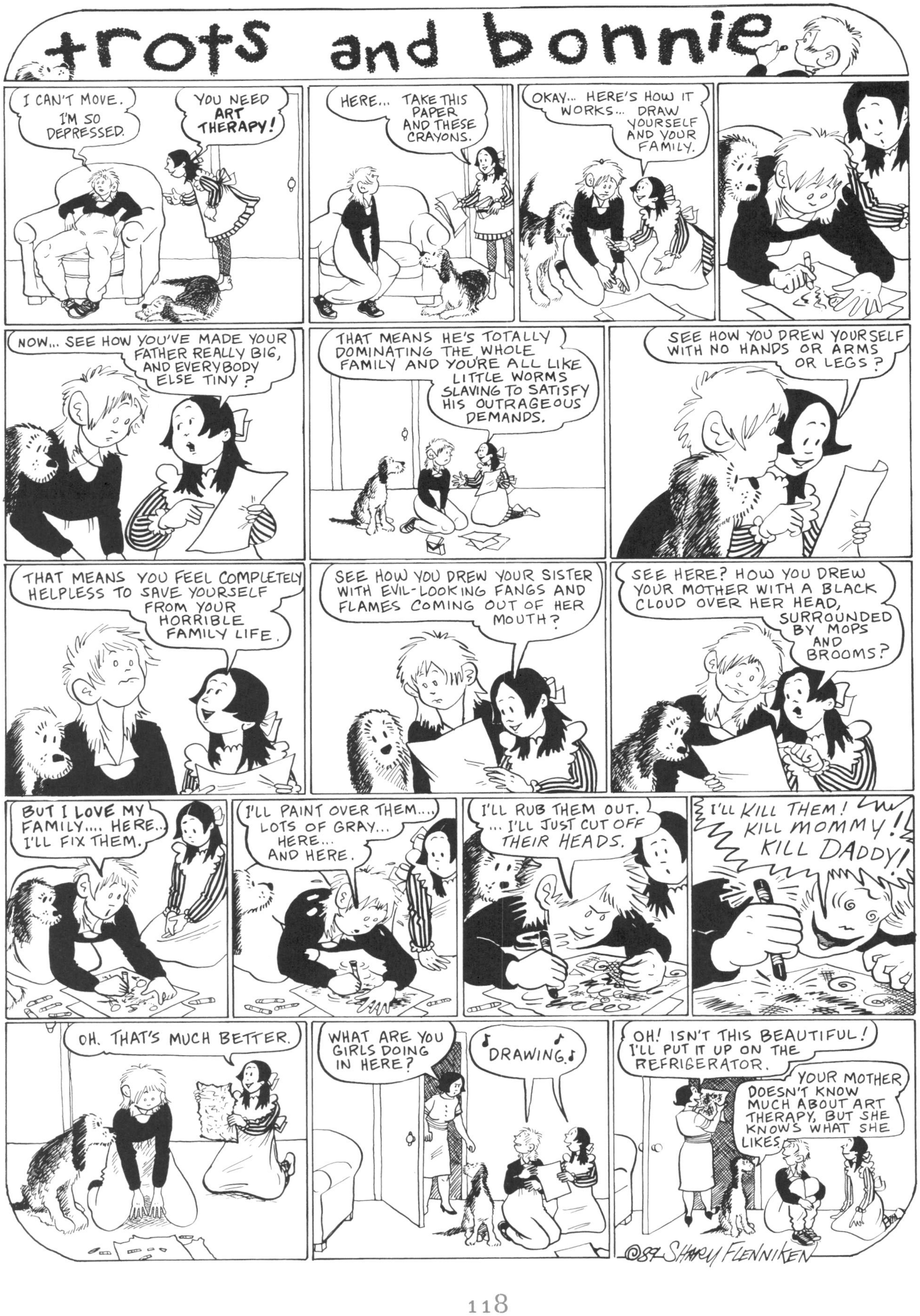
trots and bonnie
I CAN'T MOVE. I'M SO DEPRESSED.
YOU NEED ART THERAPY!
HERE... TAKE THIS PAPER AND THESE CRAYONS.
OKAY... HERE'S HOW IT WORKS... DRAW YOURSELF AND YOUR FAMILY.
NOW... SEE HOW YOU'VE MADE YOUR FATHER REALLY BIG, AND EVERYBODY ELSE TINY?
THAT MEANS HE'S TOTALLY DOMINATING THE WHOLE FAMILY AND YOU'RE ALL LIKE LITTLE WORMS SLAVING TO SATISFY HIS OUTRAGEOUS DEMANDS.
SEE HOW YOU DREW YOURSELF WITH NO HANDS OR ARMS OR LEGS?
THAT MEANS YOU FEEL COMPLETELY HELPLESS TO SAVE YOURSELF FROM YOUR HORRIBLE FAMILY LIFE.
SEE HOW YOU DREW YOUR SISTER WITH EVIL-LOOKING FANGS AND FLAMES COMING OUT OF HER MOUTH?
SEE HERE? HOW YOU DREW YOUR MOTHER WITH A BLACK CLOUD OVER HER HEAD, SURROUNDED BY MOPS AND BROOMS?
BUT I LOVE MY FAMILY.... HERE... I'LL FIX THEM.
I'LL PAINT OVER THEM.... LOTS OF GRAY... HERE... AND HERE.
I'LL RUB THEM OUT. ... I'LL JUST CUT OFF THEIR HEADS.
I'LL KILL THEM! KILL MOMMY! KILL DADDY!
OH. THAT'S MUCH BETTER.
WHAT ARE YOU GIRLS DOING IN HERE?
DRAWING.
OH! ISN'T THIS BEAUTIFUL! I'LL PUT IT UP ON THE REFRIGERATOR.
YOUR MOTHER DOESN'T KNOW MUCH ABOUT ART THERAPY, BUT SHE KNOWS WHAT SHE LIKES.
©87 SHARY FLENNIKEN

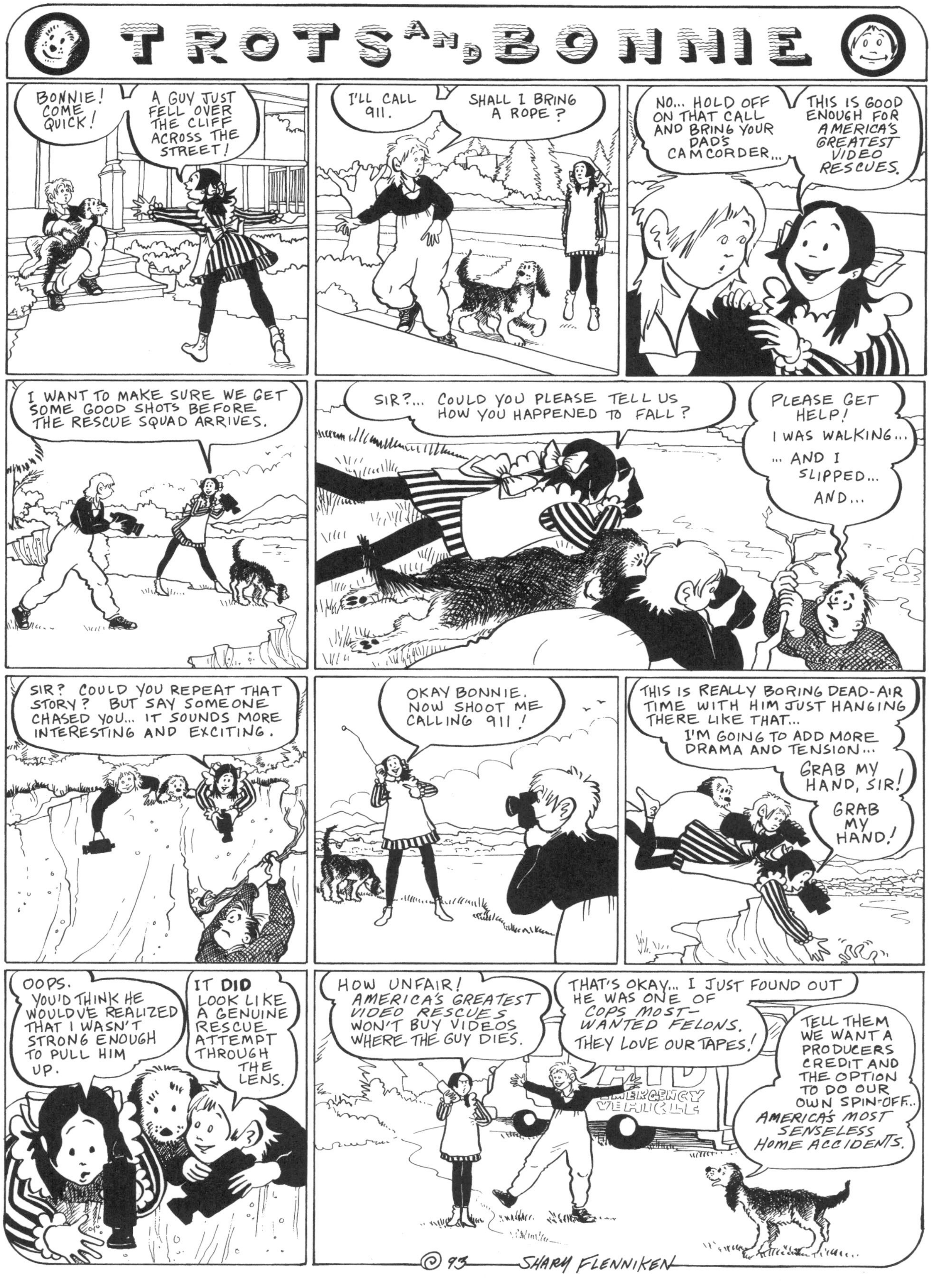
TROTS AND BONNIE
BONNIE! COME QUICK!
A GUY JUST FELL OVER THE CLIFF ACROSS THE STREET!
I'LL CALL 911.
SHALL I BRING A ROPE?
NO... HOLD OFF ON THAT CALL AND BRING YOUR DAD'S CAMCORDER...
THIS IS GOOD ENOUGH FOR AMERICA'S GREATEST VIDEO RESCUES.
I WANT TO MAKE SURE WE GET SOME GOOD SHOTS BEFORE THE RESCUE SQUAD ARRIVES.
SIR?... COULD YOU PLEASE TELL US HOW YOU HAPPENED TO FALL?
PLEASE GET HELP! I WAS WALKING... ...AND I SLIPPED... AND...
SIR? COULD YOU REPEAT THAT STORY? BUT SAY SOMEONE CHASED YOU... IT SOUNDS MORE INTERESTING AND EXCITING.
OKAY BONNIE. NOW SHOOT ME CALLING 911!
THIS IS REALLY BORING DEAD-AIR TIME WITH HIM JUST HANGING THERE LIKE THAT...
I'M GOING TO ADD MORE DRAMA AND TENSION...
GRAB MY HAND, SIR!
GRAB MY HAND!
OOPS. YOU'D THINK HE WOULD'VE REALIZED THAT I WASN'T STRONG ENOUGH TO PULL HIM UP.
IT DID LOOK LIKE A GENUINE RESCUE ATTEMPT THROUGH THE LENS.
HOW UNFAIR! AMERICA'S GREATEST VIDEO RESCUES WON'T BUY VIDEOS WHERE THE GUY DIES.
THAT'S OKAY... I JUST FOUND OUT HE WAS ONE OF COPS MOST-WANTED FELONS. THEY LOVE OUR TAPES!
TELL THEM WE WANT A PRODUCERS CREDIT AND THE OPTION TO DO OUR OWN SPIN-OFF.. AMERICA'S MOST SENSELESS HOME ACCIDENTS.
EMERGENCY VEHICLE
©93 SHARY FLENNIKEN

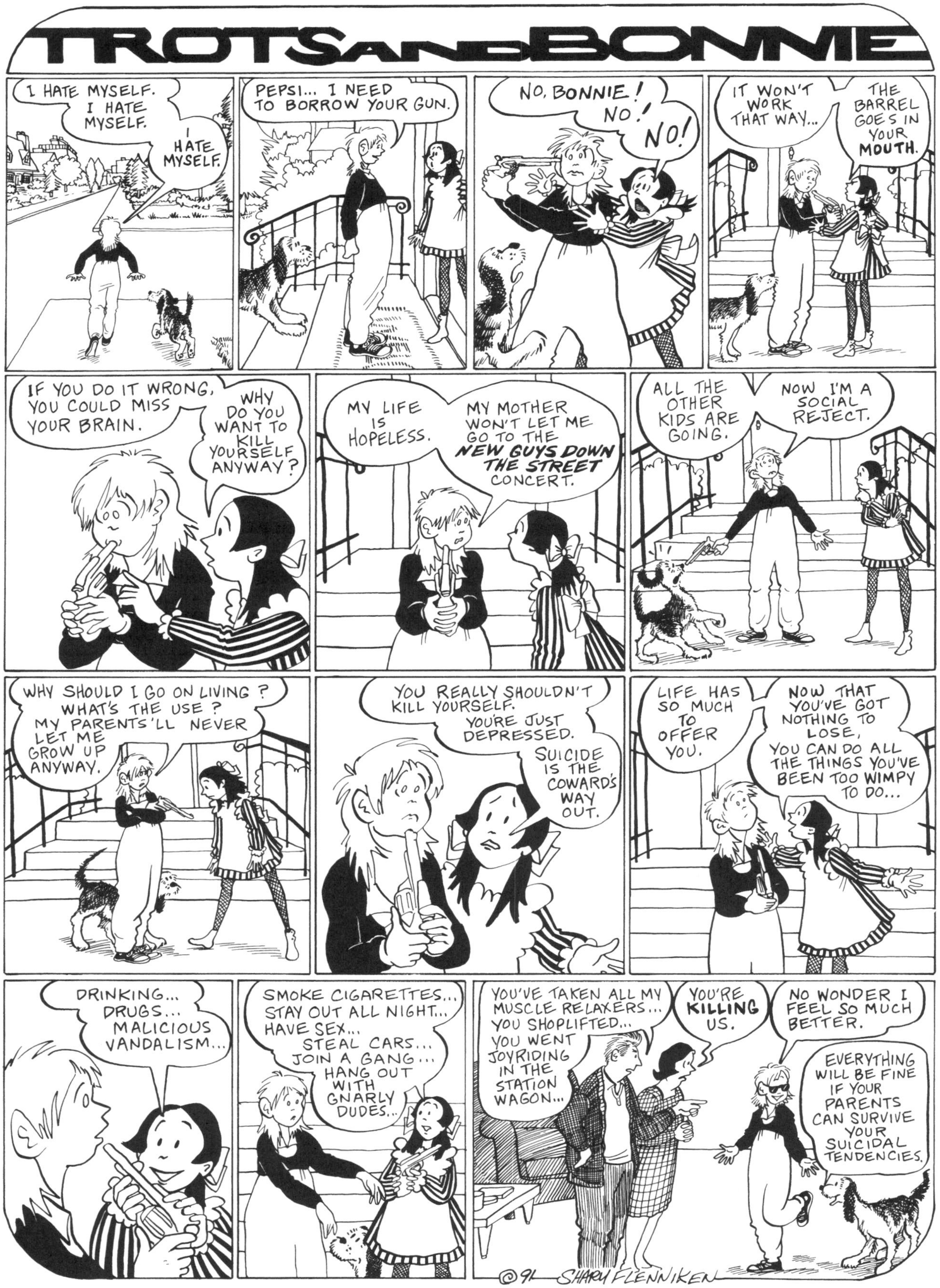
TROTS AND BONNIE
I HATE MYSELF. I HATE MYSELF.
I HATE MYSELF.
PEPSI... I NEED TO BORROW YOUR GUN.
NO, BONNIE! NO! NO!
IT WON'T WORK THAT WAY...
THE BARREL GOES IN YOUR MOUTH.
IF YOU DO IT WRONG, YOU COULD MISS YOUR BRAIN.
WHY DO YOU WANT TO KILL YOURSELF ANYWAY?
MY LIFE IS HOPELESS.
MY MOTHER WON'T LET ME GO TO THE NEW GUYS DOWN THE STREET CONCERT.
ALL THE OTHER KIDS ARE GOING.
NOW I'M A SOCIAL REJECT.
WHY SHOULD I GO ON LIVING? WHAT'S THE USE? MY PARENTS'LL NEVER LET ME GROW UP ANYWAY.
YOU REALLY SHOULDN'T KILL YOURSELF. YOU'RE JUST DEPRESSED.
SUICIDE IS THE COWARD'S WAY OUT.
LIFE HAS SO MUCH TO OFFER YOU.
NOW THAT YOU'VE GOT NOTHING TO LOSE, YOU CAN DO ALL THE THINGS YOU'VE BEEN TOO WIMPY TO DO...
DRINKING... DRUGS... MALICIOUS VANDALISM...
SMOKE CIGARETTES... STAY OUT ALL NIGHT... HAVE SEX... STEAL CARS... JOIN A GANG... HANG OUT WITH GNARLY DUDES...
YOU'VE TAKEN ALL MY MUSCLE RELAXERS... YOU SHOPLIFTED... YOU WENT JOYRIDING IN THE STATION WAGON...
YOU'RE KILLING US.
NO WONDER I FEEL SO MUCH BETTER.
EVERYTHING WILL BE FINE IF YOUR PARENTS CAN SURVIVE YOUR SUICIDAL TENDENCIES.
©91 SHARY FLENNIKEN

Author's Note

I waited several decades before putting these *Trots and Bonnie* pages together into a book in America. I agreed to do so for a few reasons. Most important was that I was tired of telling people I'd get around to it eventually, or that they could pick up the French version on eBay. Then, my good friend Norman Hathaway told me he would design the book. Soon after, when New York Review Comics offered to publish it, that really woke me up.

You may have noticed that a few of the *Trots and Bonnie* strips from *National Lampoon*'s Funny Pages section are not included in the book. I decided that some were outdated or just not that funny.

I agonized over including the strip that Emily Flake mentions in her introduction, where Bonnie is "rubbing off" while Trots reads a romantic novel out loud (possibly one he wrote). In a world where male masturbation has become a cliché and a long list of metaphors, the mechanics of the female version is still mysterious to some people. The boundless freedom of the *Lampoon* Funny Pages allowed me to address that situation. However, jerking off is also something that is inappropriate in public. Just as I eliminated a few strips that I felt might be construed as insulting or hurtful, I decided to leave that one out.

The nature of a book is different from that of the periodicals I have been working in most of my life. Even though the *Lampoon*'s publishing schedule was three months after the finished comic page was delivered, the subject matter could be fairly timely. I could explore my own questions and theories in relation to what life was like at the time.

During much of that time though, a magazine or comic was not a collector's item. I never expected my work to be relevant or even around decades later. I thought we would all be better by now.

—Shary Flenniken

Trots and Bonnie
The stories behind the strips

Page 5

The First *Trots and Bonnie* Page

Merton of the Movement 1972

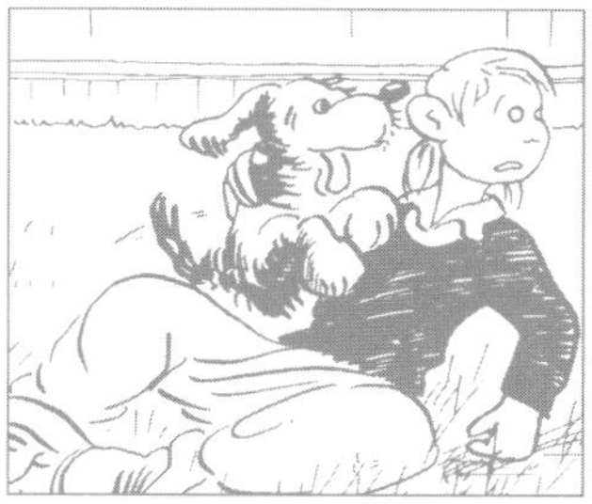

This is the birth of Bonnie McFarland. When I was Bonnie's age, 13, pantyhose had not been invented. I wore a girdle with garters that held my nylon stockings up on my skinny legs. Girls were not allowed to wear pants to junior high. That is why God invented feminism.

When this comic page appeared in Bobby London's *Merton of the Movement* in 1972, shedding underwear was a big deal. Not wearing a bra was a revolutionary act. And being revolutionary could result in being kicked out of your house.

That's why I was living in a warehouse loft in San Francisco with four guys who called themselves the Air Pirates. They were plotting to take down an evil corporate giant by drawing comics. It made sense at the time. The Air Pirates taught me how to create a comic. We used tools like special paper, rulers, and a quill pen that dribbled ink. We copied great cartoonists who had come long enough before us that most people would not know we were copying them. You have probably noticed that good comics and stories are character-driven. Creating that character is the most important first step.

Bonnie was the name of my Shetland Sheepdog. McFarland is our clan. Trots named himself in a dream I had after eating a hash brownie. Frustration, anger, and resentment were my muses.

—

Page 6

The General's Daughter

Dopin' Dan 1972

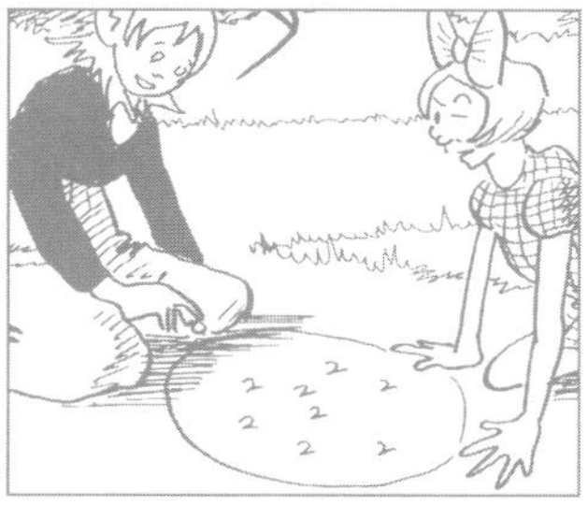

Ted Richards invited me to create a story for his *Dopin' Dan* comic. Our military was then still in Vietnam and a few other places they were not supposed to be like Laos and Cambodia. The CIA had already murdered Che Guevara in Bolivia.

I was feeling dirty because my father was a career naval officer and a war hero. Ted called me "the general's daughter," because I was spoiled and bossy. I immortalized that persona in the form of a girl who lived on our Magnolia neighborhood's "rich hill" and really did have a glass eye that fascinated me. Our house was full of daddy's war booty. During the Korean War, he found an enemy skull on one of the Aleutian Islands. We really can't help who our parents are, can we?

—

Page 9

Pepsi's First Appearance

Merton of the Movement 1972

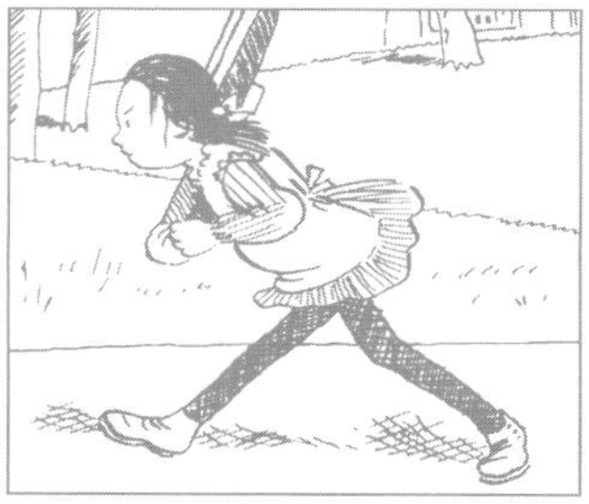

Do you know who Hugh Hefner was? He was a cartoonist who realized early on that cartooning wouldn't make him a millionaire, so he created *Playboy* magazine, which exploited beautiful but totally oppressed naked sex slaves. See how the way we look at things has changed? Millionaires are small change. Now, everybody has to be a billionaire. Bonnie's friend Pepsi has an attitude and the gun to prove it. She is every friend I have ever had who knew right from wrong immediately and never had to figure anything out. If you are like Bonnie and me, then you know what it's like to have to do a bunch of pondering, then get some help from your dog in order to conjure up an opinion.

—

Page 10

On the Defensive

Left Field Funnies 1972

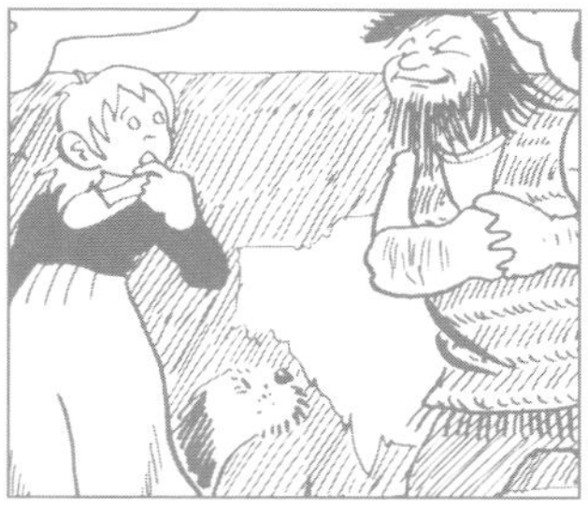

You can see that I was still learning to write and draw when this four-page comic appeared in Bobby London's *Left Field Funnies* in 1972. But lack of skill couldn't stop me. I had a lot of complaining to do. Not only was I dissatisfied with the inability of martial arts to adequately protect women from street harassment, but I also thought that a certain comic book publisher deserved to be the model for this lecherous harasser.

—

Page 14

Free Clinic Pelvic Exam

Facts o' Life Sex Education Funnies 1972

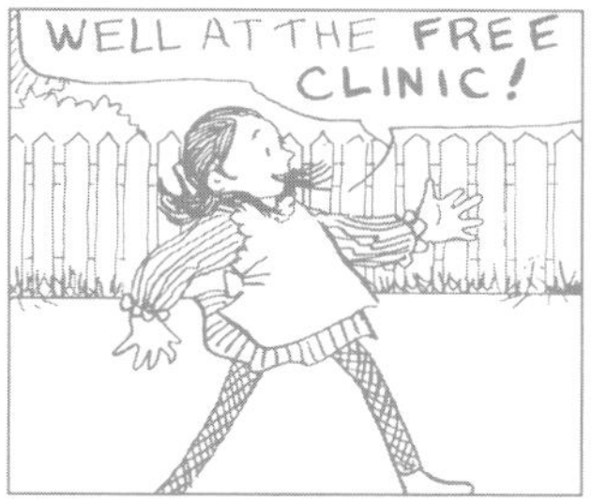
WELL AT THE FREE CLINIC!

Lora Fountain asked me to be in her medically themed *Facts o' Life Sex Education Funnies*. It was one of the first underground comics to equally employ women cartoonists. Men and women alike had a lot of genitally-oriented problems back then, but nothing compared to what you can catch these days. If you had never been to the free clinic in 1972, you were not having a social life.

—

Page 18

Trots, the Wonder Dog

National Lampoon 1972

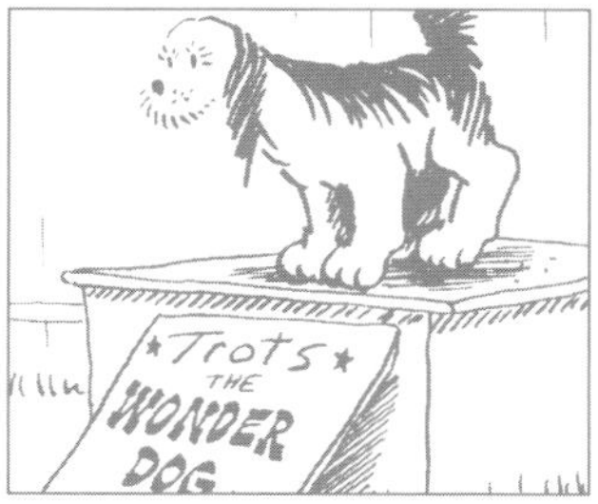
Trots
THE
WONDER
DOG

When you debut a comic strip, you need to introduce your characters. In this case, you learn that the dog can talk, but only on his own terms. "The Eggplant That Ate Chicago" is a real song.

Here also, I wanted to address a controversy that was raging among the San Francisco underground cartoonist crowd — the idea that to work in any commercial venue publication would be "selling out" to commercialism. Although several prominent artists had secret side gigs with companies such as Topps bubble gum or got their start working for Hallmark, to appear in *National Lampoon* was to risk ostracism from underground purists. One of my Air Pirates buddies had already torn up and trashed my early copies of *Lampoon* as contraband.

While many of the male cartoonists argued among themselves about commercialism-free purity, I just wanted to make a living.

—

Page 19

Pawns of Male Dominance

National Lampoon 1972

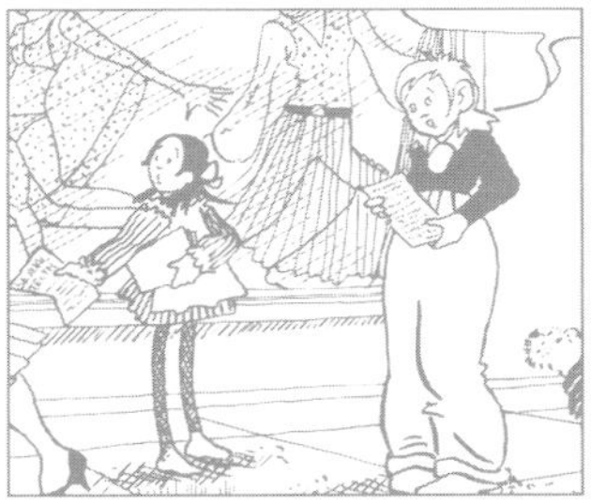

Feminism became an anathema in the 1980s, when a lot of women began referring to it as "I'm not a feminist." I've always preferred "women's liberation," which seems like it is much more about freedom than equal employment.
I ended up at the *Ms.* magazine office not long after the first issue came out in 1972. My dream was to graduate immediately from an 18-to-24-year-old boy demographic to a classy, slick, smart, intellectual, and ideologically perfect women's magazine.
Gloria Steinem was there, sitting on a desk and flirting with some guy who looked like a salesman.
I got the key to the lady's room out in the hall and all of a sudden Gloria was standing next to me, waiting for me to unlock the door, which I could not do because my hands had begun to shake. I handed her the key and she unlocked the door for us.
This was my big opportunity to tell her about the feminist battles women in San Francisco were fighting by drawing underground comics. I choke out one sentence while we pee. She says, "Yeah. I really love Wonder Woman." A strip created by a man, I thought. So much for ideological purity. As I remember, neither one of us stopped to wash our hands.
This strip expresses what my gut was telling me though: change happens in spite of our ambivalence.

Page 20

Bonnie's Book Report

National Lampoon 1973

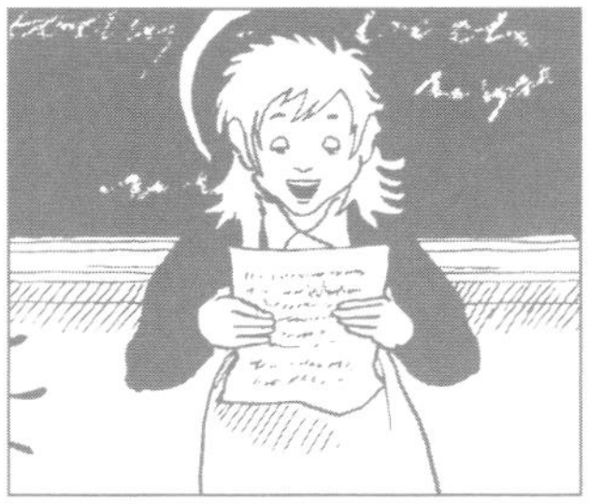

Being inappropriate is one of my major life themes. Didn't you ever want to give a report on the books you found in your parents' underwear drawer?

Page 21

Bad Dogs

National Lampoon 1973

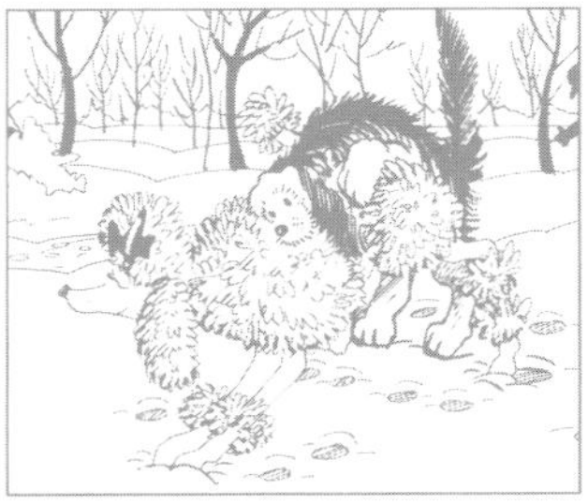

The way dogs mate is one of the scariest things I've ever seen. Who knew it could be so romantic?

Page 22

Sex Symbols

National Lampoon 1973

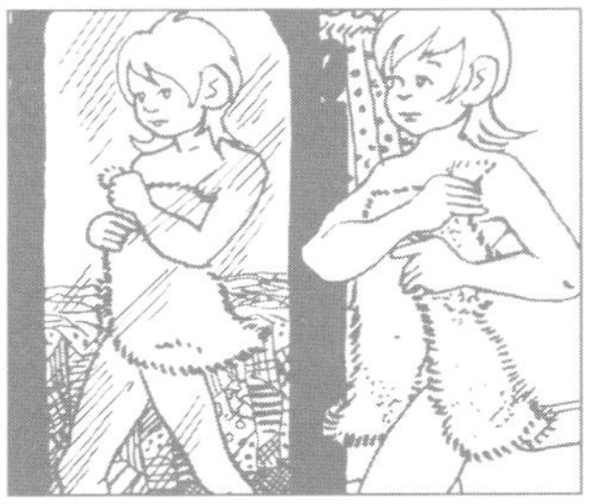

I was really pissed off when I wrote this strip. *National Lampoon* had rejected my strip about hairspray destroying the earth's ozone layer. The art director followed up by advising me to focus on "sex, sex, and more sex." That made me feel like a whore. Cute little child star Shirley Temple, who even had an alcohol-free cocktail named after her, had grown up and become a Republican. She had just been in the news because she had announced that she had breast cancer and had a breast removed, which in those days was something that no one talked about in public. Now that Angelina Jolie has had her boobs removed, it's like, yeah, I might have mine done too.

Page 23

He's So Cute!

National Lampoon 1973

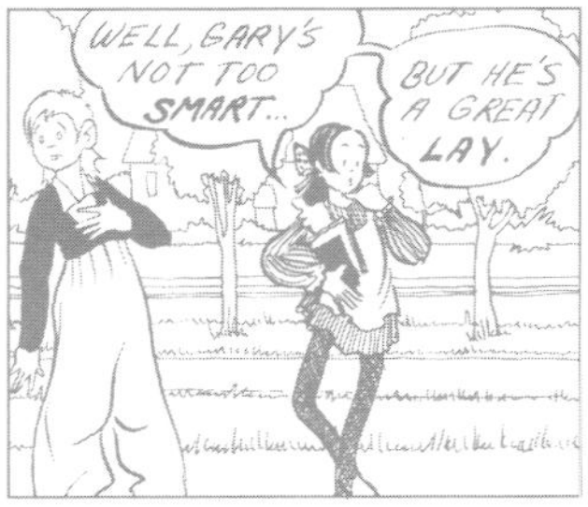
WELL, GARY'S NOT TOO SMART...
BUT HE'S A GREAT LAY.

I was madly in love with this guy — a very talented cartoonist who loved drugs. He was a very bad boy, but very fun.

Page 24

Nude Beach

National Lampoon 1973

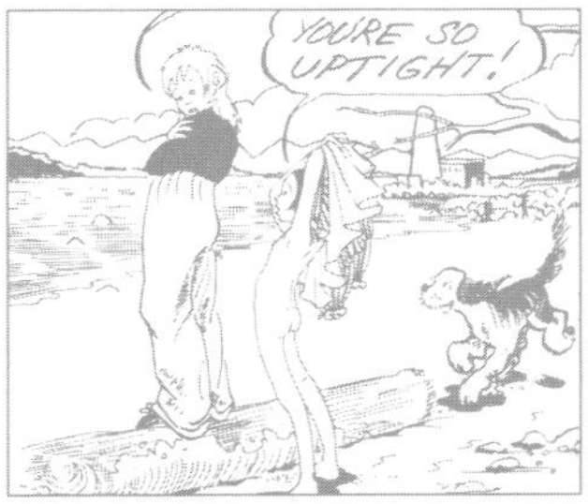
YOU'RE SO UPTIGHT!

I convinced him that I needed him to take his clothes off and pose for me. It was wonderful.

Page 25

Fried Placenta

National Lampoon 1973

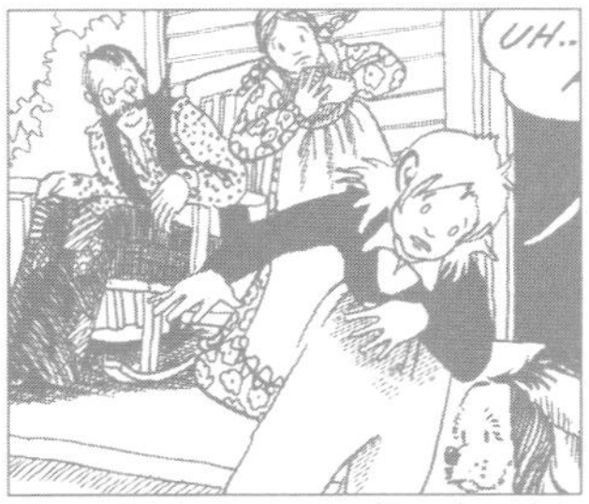
UH..

Eating afterbirth was not the only weird or gross thing that hippies did. My Marin County cousin's girlfriend breast-fed their five-year-old son at the dinner table.

Page 26

Perverts in the Park

National Lampoon 1973

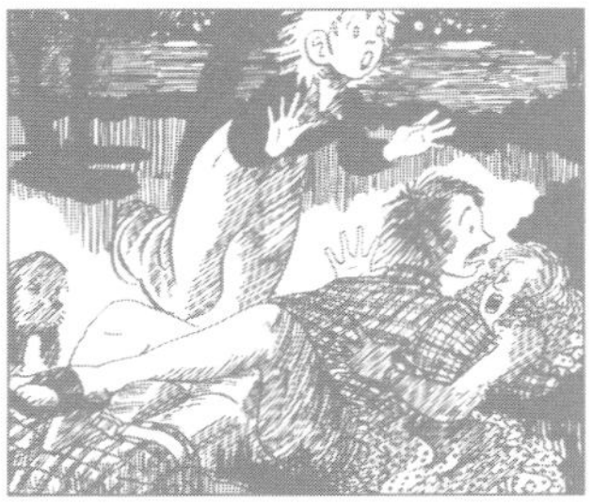

Having a paying gig drawing for a national magazine set my husband and me apart from the San Francisco cartoonist scene. Some people were judgmental. Some were jealous.
So, we bought a Volkswagen bus and drove to Seattle where we moved in with my parents who lived two blocks from this park. Seattle was a backwater town in 1973. New Yorkers told me they thought we still had dirt streets and rode horses. This park looks the same now. When I was 13, a flasher there had caught my attention. I was mortified, and I still think about it when I am there.

Page 27

The Passion Pits

National Lampoon 1974

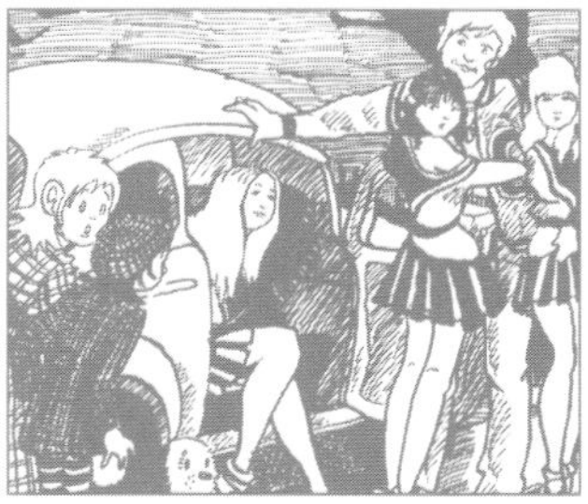

The Passion Pits is a parking lot at a beautiful scenic viewpoint in my neighborhood overlooking Elliott Bay. It was a romantic place to park at night and get laid with most of your clothes still on. What does it say about life that it's only a place for drug deals now?

—

Page 28

Dr. Pepsi's Vasectomy Clinic

National Lampoon 1974

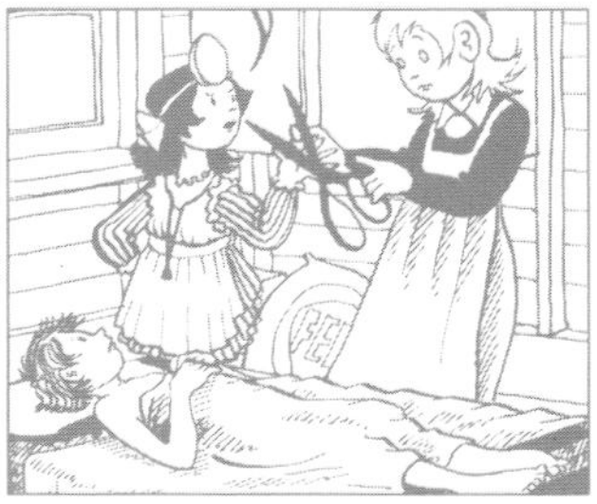

Everybody knows that we only play doctor in order to get our friends to take off their clothes, right? Pepsi frequently plays doctor. However, she is seriously on a mission to make the world a better place.

—

Page 29

Bonnie's First Period

National Lampoon 1974

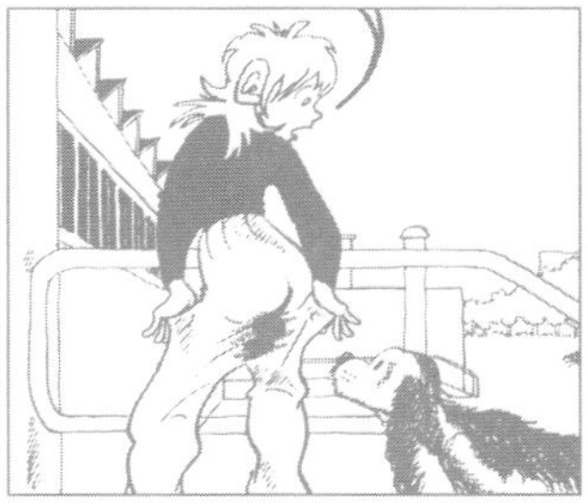

Bloodstains on your butt. I'm going to take a leap and say this is arguably every woman's nightmare. For boys, the closest experience may be that hard-on you get in class. You figure out how to walk with a book in front of your crotch, and then you grow up and for some reason, you don't have to worry about that anymore — which is unfair, because women have to worry about the bloodstains until menopause.

I think Bonnie takes it pretty well in this strip even though she is totally blindsided. Wait until she finds out it's going to happen every month.

—

Page 30

Kidnapping Elrod

National Lampoon 1974

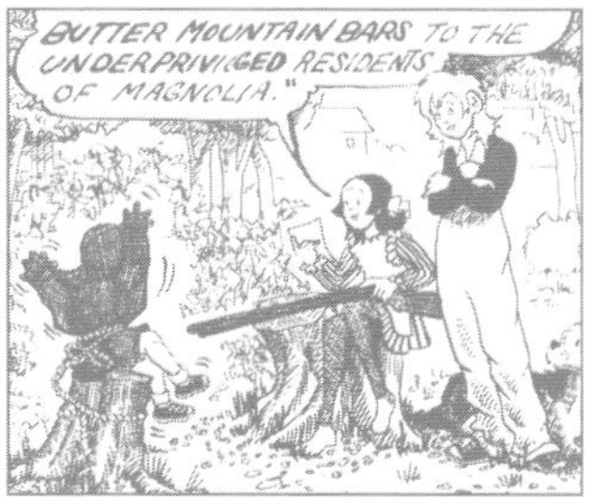
BUTTER MOUNTAIN BARS TO THE UNDERPRIVILGED RESIDENTS OF MAGNOLIA."

Did you notice that Pepsi has already neutered Elrod Stelmack while playing doctor in the garage? Some people are born to be victims. I wrote this strip in the middle of the Patty Hearst kidnapping odyssey. It was before the bank robbery and the final shoot-out. She was probably still trapped in the closet by the Symbionese Army.

I had been hanging out with all kinds of gun-toting radicals. They put a lot of thought into picking their targets. What seemed so wrong in the case of Patty Hearst was that they chose to kidnap a woman. Aren't women victimized enough as it is? That was my message to the Symbionese Army — that they were ridiculous.

—

Page 31

Rape Survivor

National Lampoon 1974

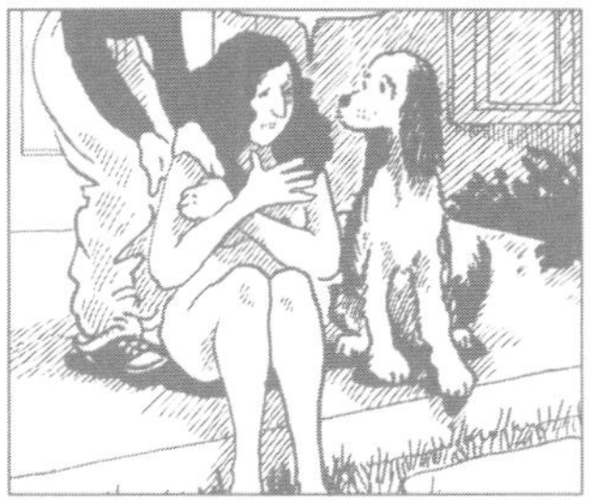

You might say I was taking the subject lightly here, but at least I was introducing this to an audience that wasn't going to see anything like this anywhere else. Hey, *National Lampoon* 18-to-24-year-old male demographic.

Let's talk about rape!

—

Page 32

Sylvia Sasquatch

National Lampoon 1974

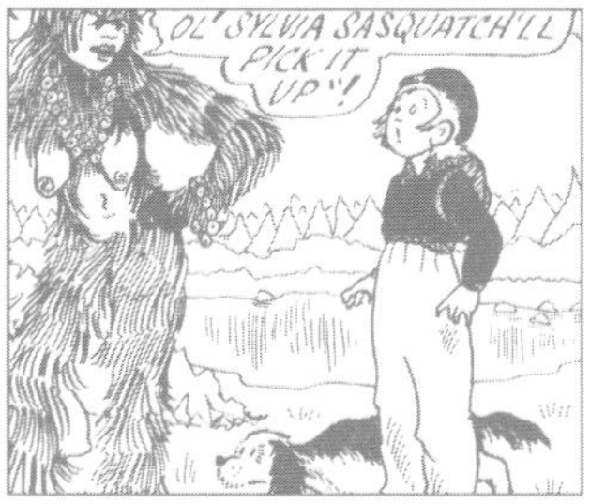
OL' SYLVIA SASQUATCH'LL PICK IT UP"!

I grew up in the Pacific Northwest, home of Bigfoot. This one is even more rare... an equal-opportunity *female* Sasquatch.

—

Page 33

A Simple Menorah

National Lampoon 1974

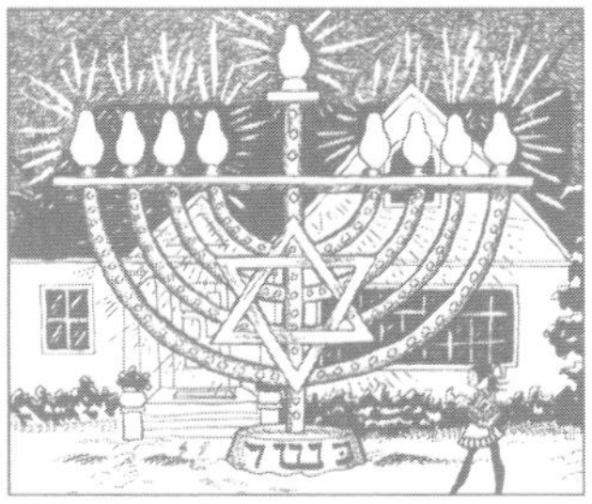

I was raised in the navy, so we had no particular religion beyond "God Bless America." But I have been a shiksa goddess to two Jewish husbands. So it was that my first husband and I spent Christmas 1973 in Queens, NY, which is a suburb very much like my Magnolia neighborhood in Seattle. Except there was not one Christmas tree for miles. The house where Trots is playing the part of baby Jesus is the home I live in now.

—

Page 34

Long Fingers

National Lampoon 1975

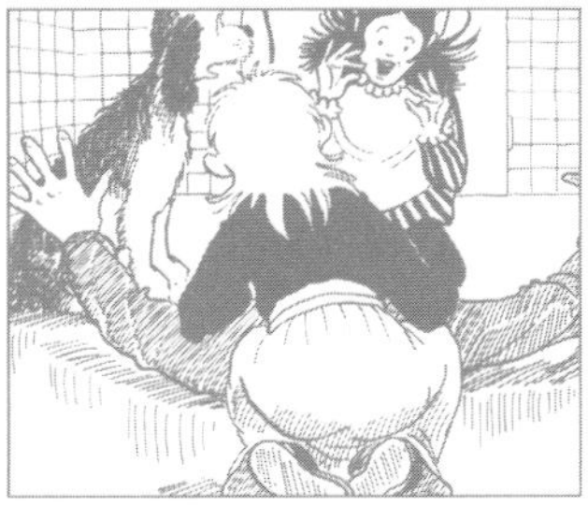

Have you noticed that there is some role reversal going on in these stories? You tell me, are men concerned about the size of their schlongs? Do they worry about whether they are large enough? I sure hope so. I have been doing my part to make men as nervous about their primary and secondary sex characteristics as I am about mine.

—

Page 35

Robot Dog

National Lampoon 1975

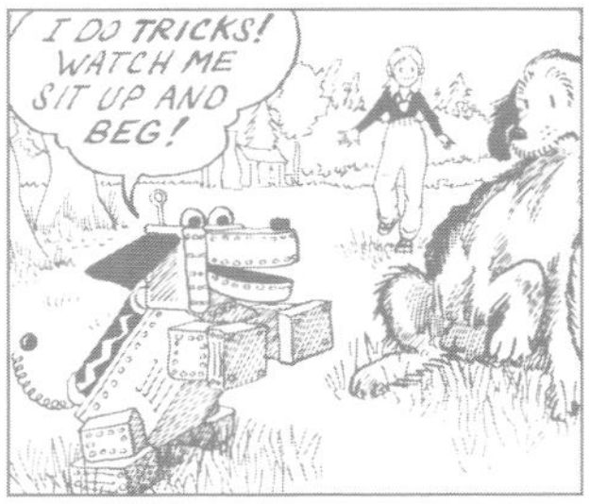
I DO TRICKS! WATCH ME SIT UP AND BEG!

Look! It's an incredibly prescient comic strip about the future of robotics and the hazards of uncontrolled AI! Or it might just be wishful thinking that my toy wind-up dog could talk. No, it's definitely about a dangerous robot, because I had been reading Isaac Asimov's robot stories since I was twelve.

Page 36

Lincoln Dickwielder

National Lampoon 1975

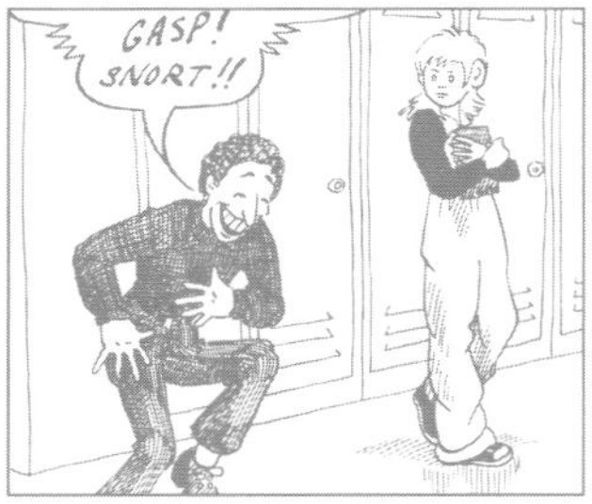
GASP! SNORT!!

Telling true stories about the trauma and harassment I endured in junior high school was cathartic. I had never heard about harassment or PTSD when I wrote this strip in 1975. It was unnerving to run into the real Lincoln Dickwielder at a high school reunion and find out how honored he was to have been portrayed in a national magazine.

Page 37

Drowning Elrod

National Lampoon 1975

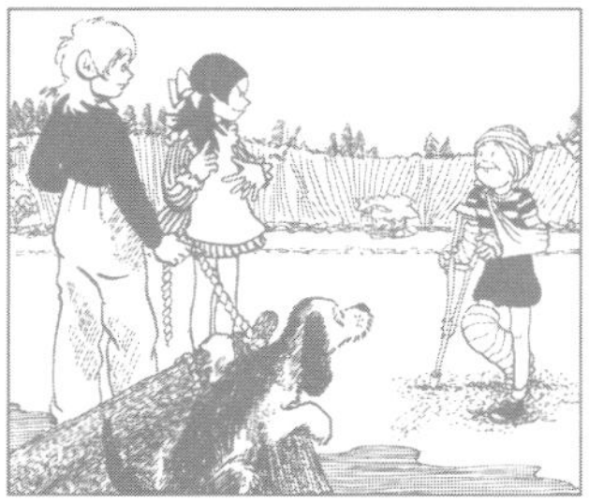

Hmmm... I haven't victimized Elrod for a while. What can I do to him this month?

Page 38

Women's Erotic Art Gallery

National Lampoon 1975

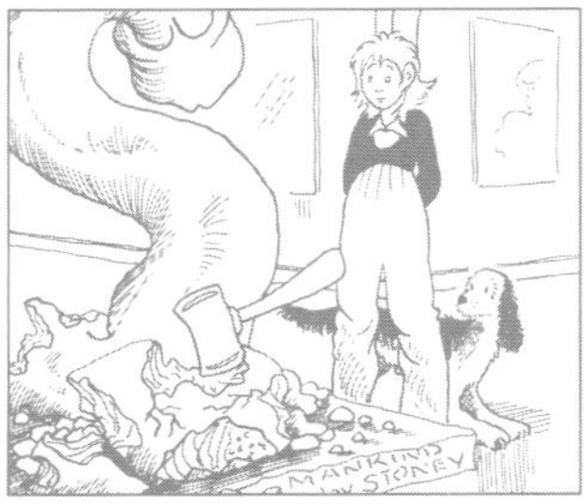

Due to the hard work of intellectual Pulitzer Prize–winning cartoonists, comics are now considered legitimate art. This was not always the case. I carried a large chip on my shoulder about how easy it seemed to be for capital-A Artists who did not have to learn the intense craft and repetitive drawing skills that cartooning involves. Eventually I learned that A-Art has its own struggles that we should appreciate. It's A-Apples and oranges—although I still think the oranges should be better paid. Then there is Women's Art. Am I mistaken or is it always about sex, even when it's about horses?

Page 39

Elrod's Death Sentence

National Lampoon 1975

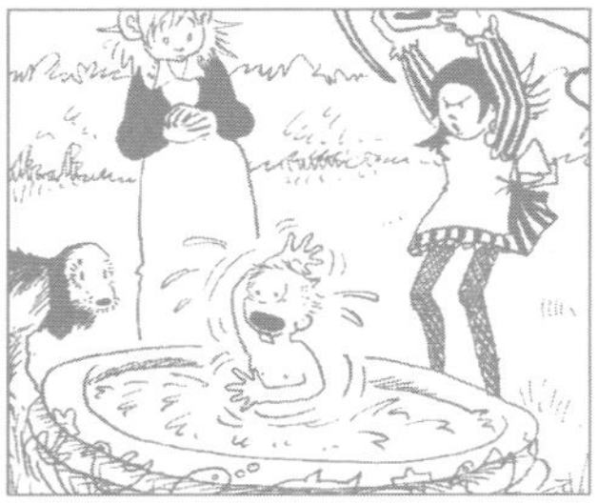

What better way to portray the illogical use of capital punishment than to execute Elrod Stelmack?
Elrod has become an icon of irrational victimization. Possibly eligible for sainthood after a few more resurrections.

Page 40

Soft Core

National Lampoon 1976

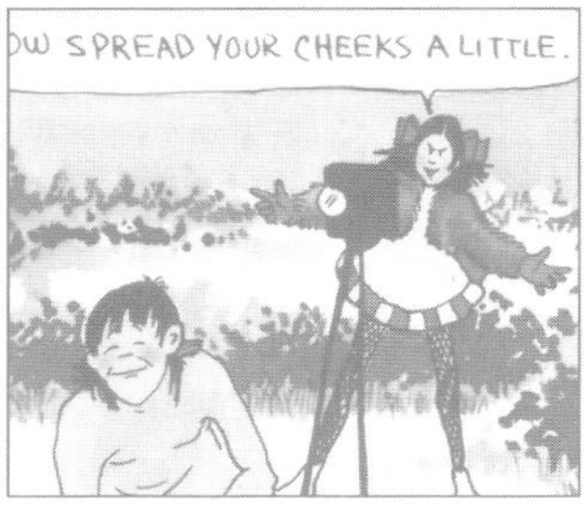
SPREAD YOUR CHEEKS A LITTLE.

This pretty story may make you wonder why Pepsi is always so competitive and career-minded. You might notice that what is going on fairly accurately portrays a typical X-rated photo or film shoot. It's really all about the camera angles and messy details. How did I know that back in 1976, you ask? When I first started drawing comics in the San Francisco underground scene, I hung out in a famous porn theater with my Air Pirates cohort. It was all business there, just managing the lighting and the actors, which made a potentially revolting situation tolerable. Just as this comic does.

Page 42

Science Fair

National Lampoon 1977

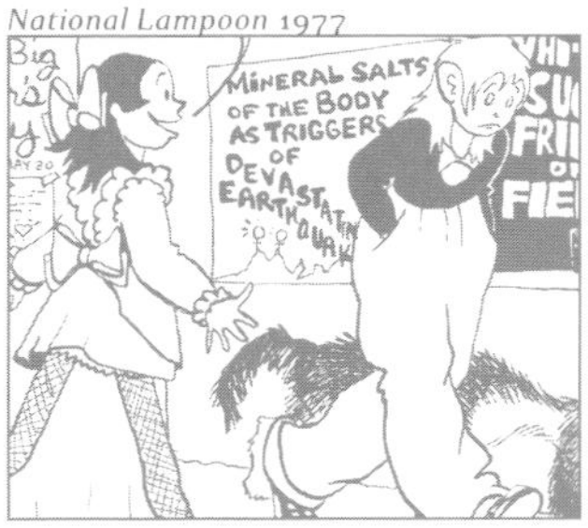
MINERAL SALTS OF THE BODY AS TRIGGERS OF

True story. I was going to build a scale model of the ocean as a science fair project. It seemed feasible at the time. Until I tried to figure out how to do it. In the end, Bonnie learns how to deal with personal failure.

Page 44

Christmas Shopping

National Lampoon 1977

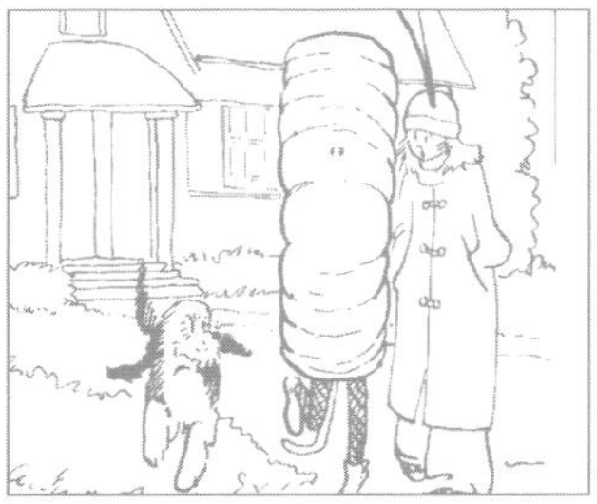

There is a big part of me that cannot figure out what would be illegal about wearing a giant tampon suit in a department store. That's the power of cartooning ... you can act out your fantasies on paper. The shoplifting part though — that was solely Pepsi's idea. I was shocked.

Page 46

Pepsi's Birth Control

National Lampoon 1977

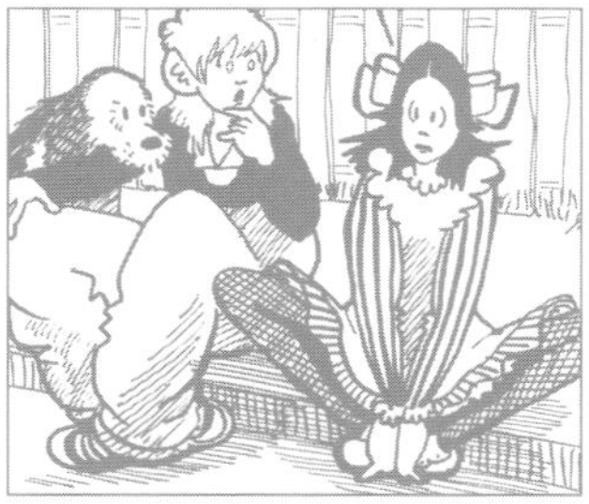

Bonnie's friend Pepsi knows that birth control is the best thing that ever happened to women. And men. Birth control let us sleep with anyone we wanted to.

A girl's first birth control is a big moment in her life. I got my first birth control pill prescription by sneaking out to a doctor's office far from my home, when I was not sure it was actually legal. Only eight years before, it was not. I would have fainted if my mom found my pills.

A lot of my comic strips are written to portray our lives in a way that I would have preferred them to be. In this case, Pepsi views her mom through the lens of sisterhood and wants her to have all the advantages that birth control grants women.

—

Page 47

Writing on the Wall

National Lampoon 1978

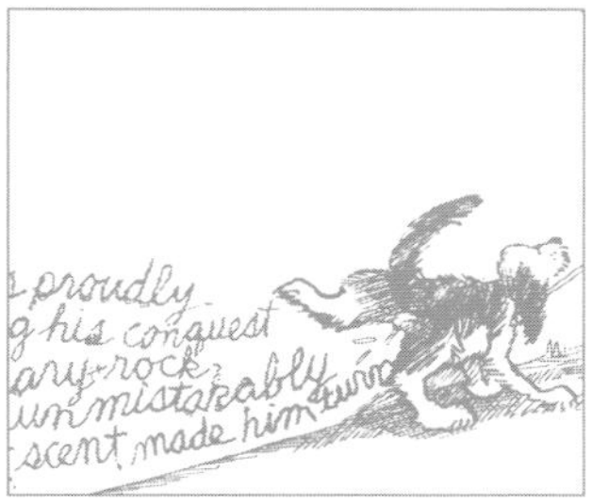
proudly
his conquest
unmistakably
scent made him

Trots is not only an intelligent dog, he is a talented writer. I suspect your dog is too. They love to read each other's writing, don't they? We know women had been writing important things for a long time, right? Or there would be no *Frankenstein*. But in 1977 when I wrote this comic, women's ability to create good comic strips was still questioned by many men.

—

Page 48

Bonnie Shops for Makeup

National Lampoon 1978

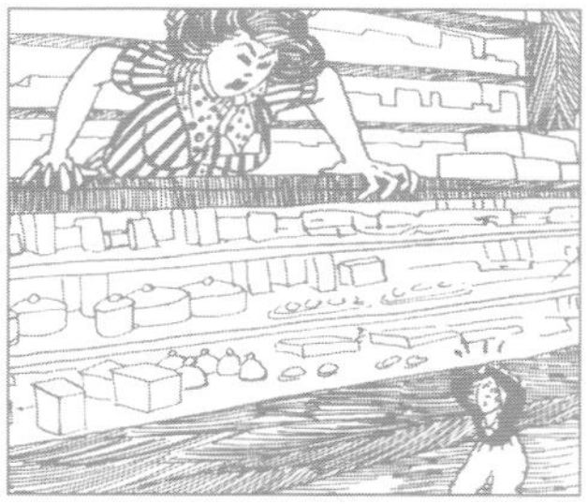

True story. Women who sell cosmetics in department stores are so intimidating. They are even scarier than shrinks because before you can even speak, they are absolutely sure that you are a massively flawed human being and only their products can save you.

—

Page 49

Bonnie Goes Out to Dinner

National Lampoon 1978

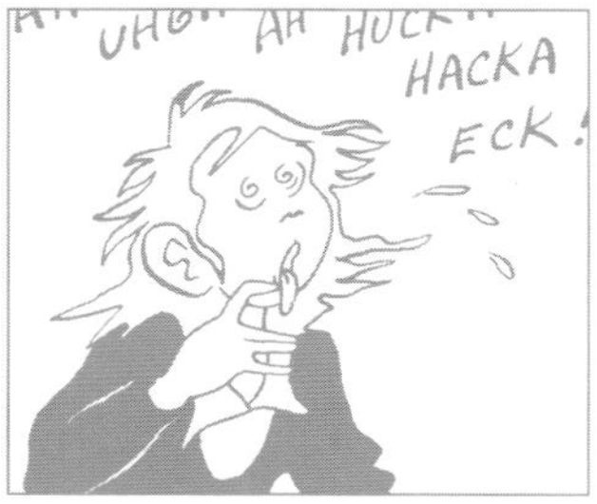
AH
HACKA
ECK!

Bonnie's parents made their first appearance here. I saw my family as a team of incompetent assholes whose goal in life was to break me like a rodeo pony. This comic was total wish fulfillment fantasy. My real battles did not turn out so well.

—

Page 50

Strange Noises in the Night

National Lampoon 1978

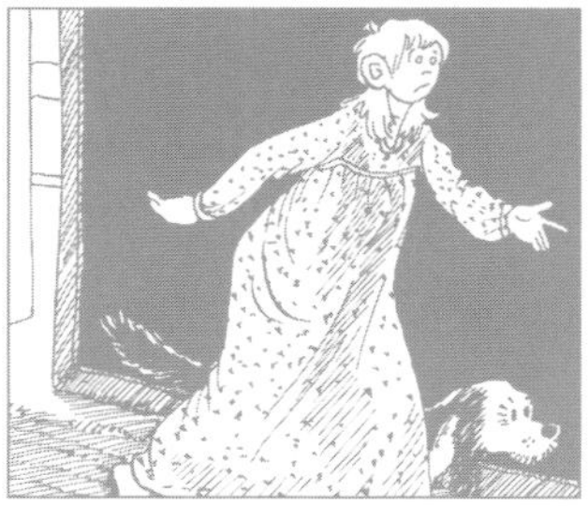

I used to sit at the top of the stairs in our house and listen to my parents yell at each other. Never in a million years would I have ever realized that was foreplay.

—

Page 51

Pet Abortion Clinic

National Lampoon 1978

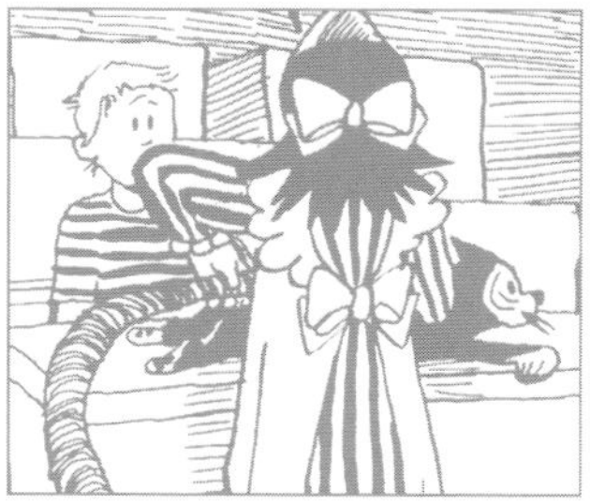

There is a message here, and it is not just for your pets. Just in case I have not been clear … effective birth control dramatically reduces the need for abortions. And if an abortion is needed, you definitely don't want to have it done in a garage by a teenager.

—

Page 52

Football Fans

National Lampoon 1978

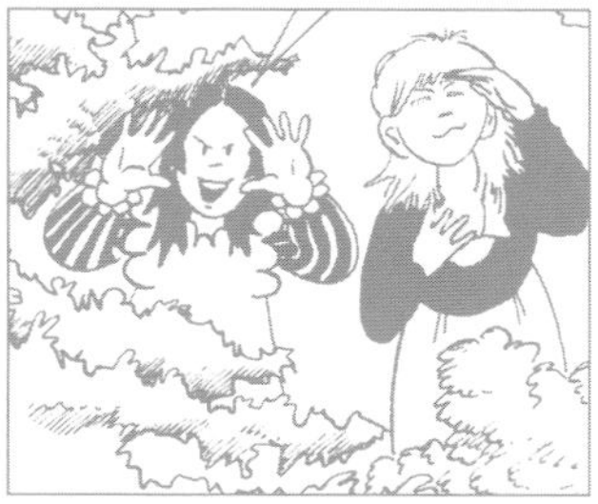

This is the only way I can enjoy men's sports of any kind.

—

Page 53

Cornucopia of Condoms

National Lampoon 1978

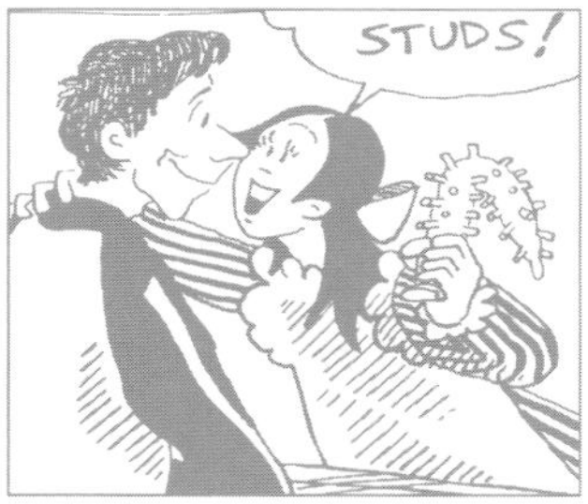
STUDS!

The message here is that if you have a lot of knowledge, good things are likely to happen for you.

Sex is just one of Pepsi's specialties.

—

Page 54

Bomb Jokes

National Lampoon 1978

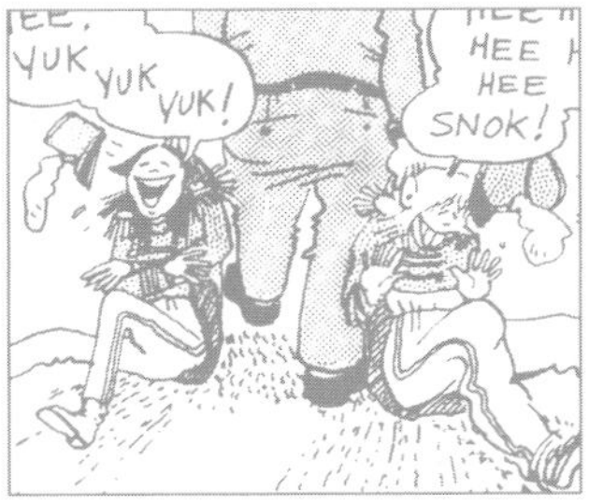
YUK YUK YUK!
HEE HEE SNOK!

Oh yeah... I wrote this while waiting for a flight. There really was a sign. Hard to control cosmic levity when it hits you. This could have happened.

—

Page 55

Girl Scout Cookies

National Lampoon 1978

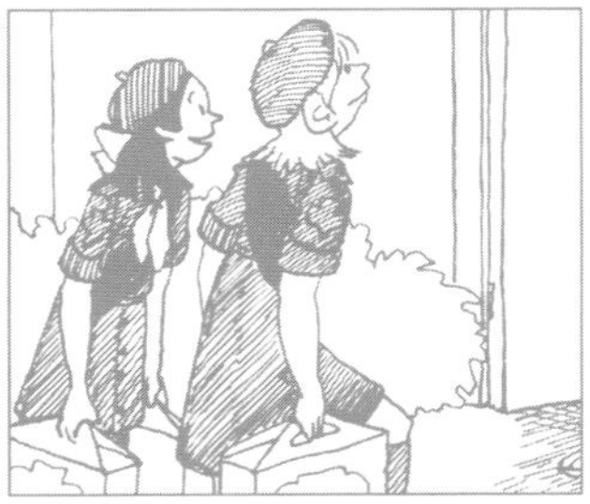

The *Lampoon* received an angry letter from the Girl Scouts about this comic. However, I did sell a buttload of Girl Scout cookies door to door when I was Bonnie's age. Our scout leaders told us it was dangerous to go into houses. Nowadays, your parents have to accompany you everywhere. I am sure that is because of this comic page.

—

Page 56

Celebration of Life

National Lampoon 1978

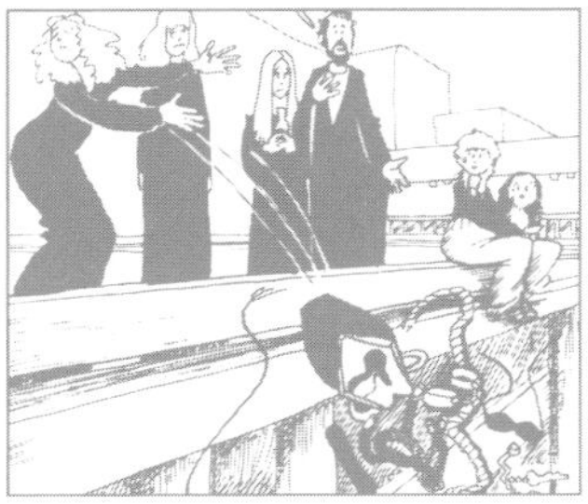

In my twenties, I thought death was pretty funny. Now, after losing two husbands and a bunch of friends, I still do.

—

Page 57

Bonnie and Bubble Butt Go to the Movies

National Lampoon 1979

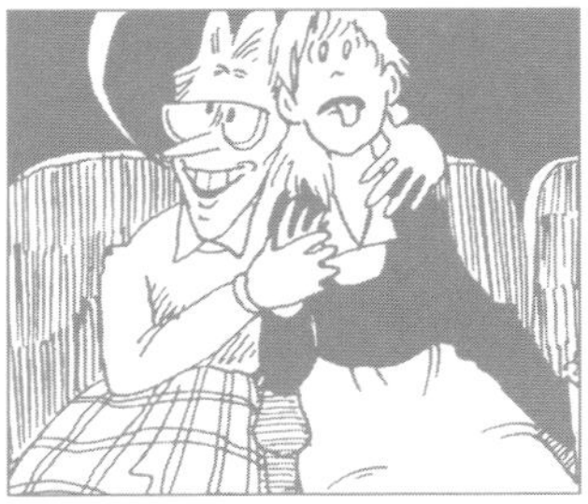

Oh guys. You all are so cool. We girls are desperate to date you, sleep with you, and then marry you as soon as possible after that. Bubble Butt is a dreamboat, just like you.

Of course, I'm kidding. You are as nerdy and offensive as Bubble Butt. Girls are just too nice to tell you that.

—

Page 58

Bonnie Visits the Shrink

National Lampoon 1979

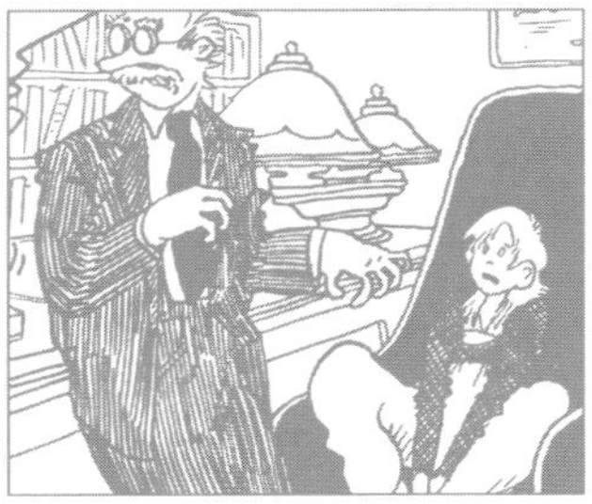

I'm remembering the first time my mother sent me to a shrink. I sat in a big wing chair like that, and the psychiatrist looked like this guy only fatter. I was petrified that he would tell me to give up smoking and make me go on a diet.

I thought the only things that were wrong with me were that I was fat and smoked too much. I still don't know why I was there, but I do know shrinks are scary. They really can read your thoughts, right?

—

Page 59

Pepsi's Performance Art

National Lampoon 1979

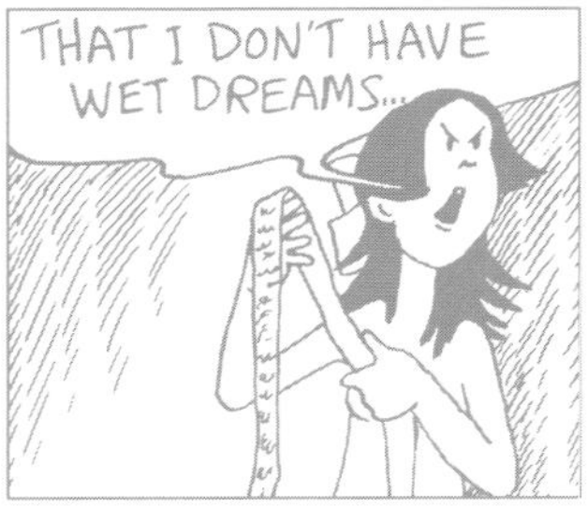
THAT I DON'T HAVE WET DREAMS...

Pepsi is a poet and a performance artist. She leads a lofty, purpose-driven life. If you google "yams in her ass," the performance artist Karen Finley comes up. In NYC, several years after this strip appeared, I saw Finley live, doing that thing with the yams. I am sure that Finley got the idea from Pepsi and, like Pepsi, that Finley is a devout feminist too.

—

Page 60

All You Can Eat

National Lampoon 1979

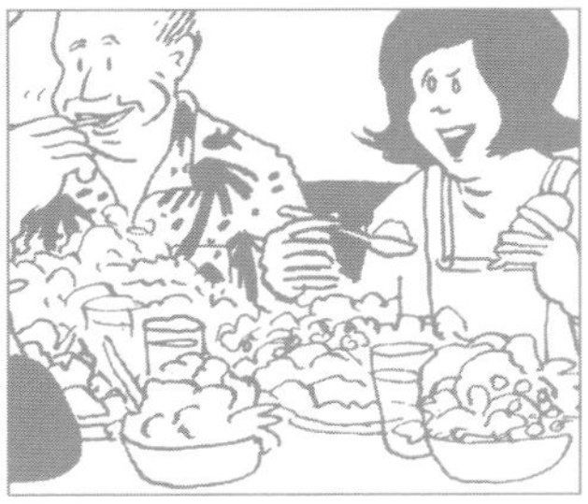

I love all-you-can-eat restaurants and so did my parents. Massive buffets symbolize the abundance and diversity of our country, while at the same time revealing our selfish gluttony. Like the sign says, put the food on your plate, don't just fill up the tray.

—

Page 61

Mom's Period Talk

National Lampoon 1979

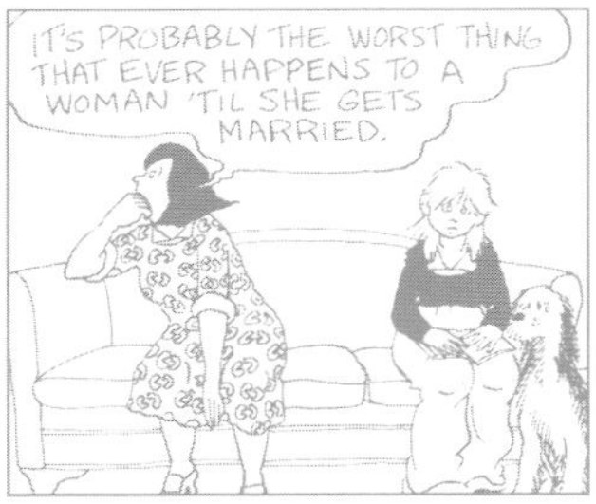
IT'S PROBABLY THE WORST THING THAT EVER HAPPENS TO A WOMAN 'TIL SHE GETS MARRIED.

That was my mom, verbatim. She knew it was bad news, really bad news. She was not good at happy talk. In 1963, otherwise known as the dark ages, pads were not designed to stick to your underpants. Mini pads would not be invented for over a decade. We had to tie (giant, thick) pads onto an apparatus similar to but more uncomfortable than a jockstrap, and wear that around for almost a week. If tampons had been invented, I did not know, because they were only for nonvirgins. Not only did that make swimming implausible, but they also said swimming at "that time of the month," when you "have your friend, the curse," was for some reason dangerous.

—

Page 62

Bonnie's Porn Collection

National Lampoon 1979

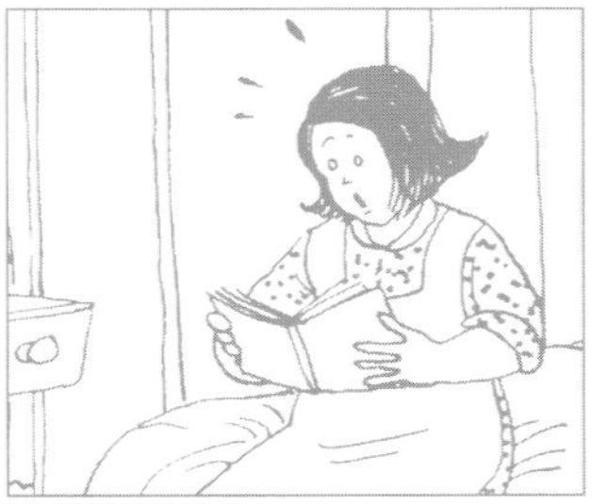

I am partial to gay male porn. And so is Bonnie's mom now. If you can't figure out why, you don't need to know.

Page 63

Trots Trapped in Hot Car

National Lampoon 1979

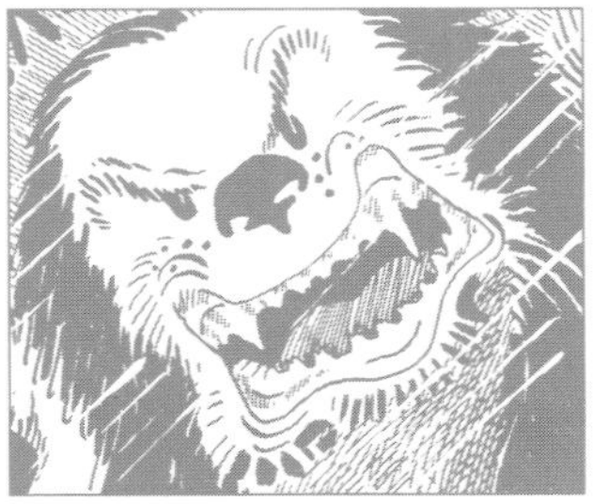

Unfortunately, this comic is wishful thinking. Too many pets have not survived this situation. So, remember this... don't leave pets or children in a hot car, and comics can be very deadly serious.

Page 64

In the Therapy Pool

National Lampoon June 1980

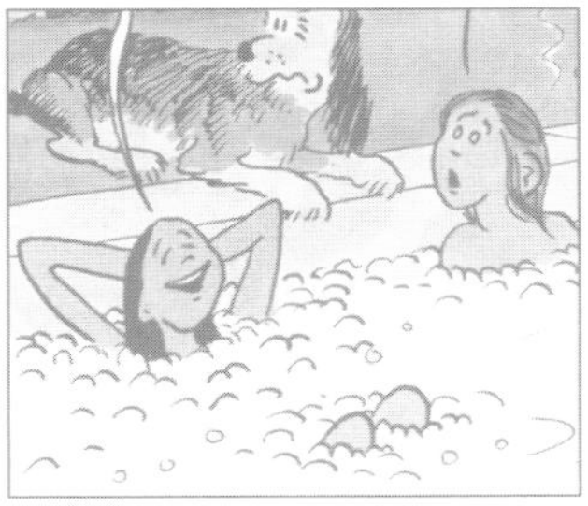

I wanted to retire in Florida, in a giant condo with multiple swimming pools and hot tubs. And a live-in doctor.

Page 67

Developing a Personality

National Lampoon 1983

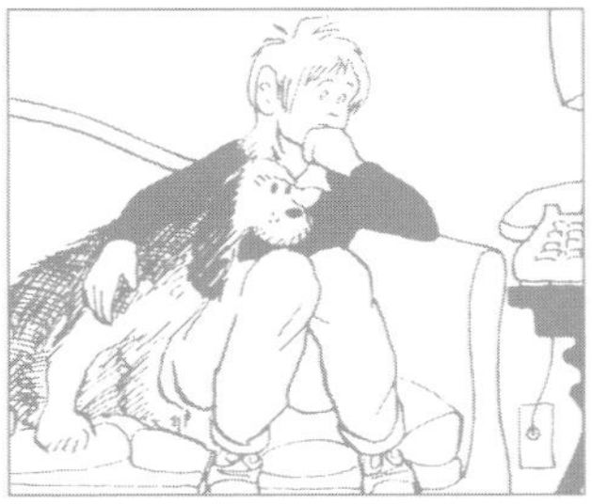

It's embarrassing, but most of these *Trots and Bonnie* pages reveal how flawed my reasoning is. When I was that young, like anywhere between birth and fifty-something, I thought I would be happier and much more self-confident if I were very beautiful with a perfect body, just like Bonnie says.

The idea of developing a personality started when I was Bonnie's age and read a book about Mata Hari, the infamous, exotic spy from the First World War. They said she was not beautiful but could enchant men with her attractive personality. Whatever that was, I wanted it. You know what it was don't you? Power. Who doesn't want that when you are dating? BTW, they executed Mata Hari.

Page 68

Romantic Couples

National Lampoon 1983

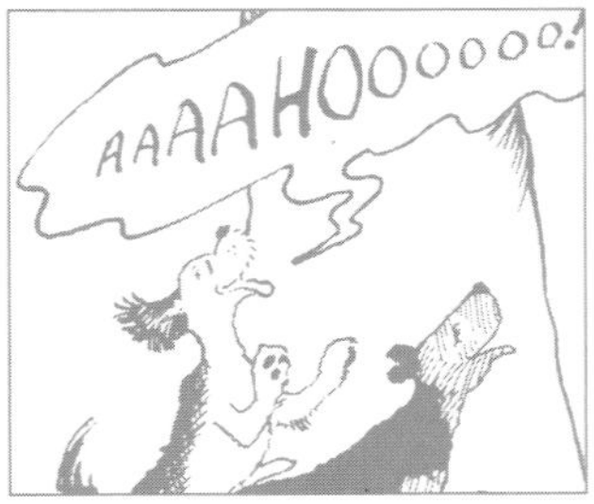
AAAAHOOOOOOO!

Here... I will interpret this comic strip for you hopeless romantics. Sex is the glue that binds love relationships together. Hot sex is like hot glue. Having said that, I recommend you research the longevity of various adhesives.

Page 69

Bonnie's Bad Dream

National Lampoon 1983

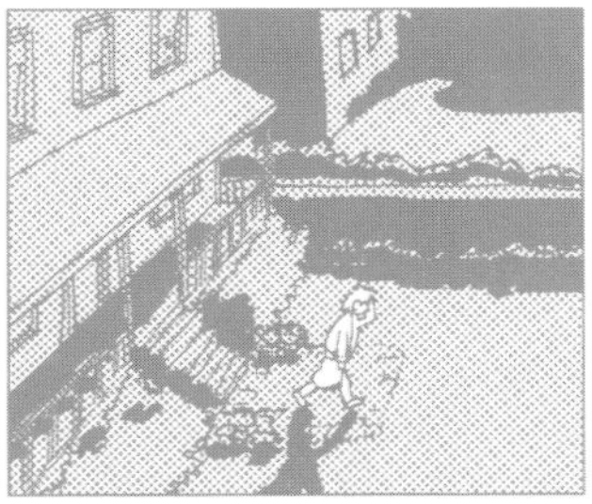

My favorite thing about Stephen King's stories is that the worst horror in them is the bullying and violence that is perpetrated by seemingly normal family members in seemingly normal places. The scary thing is that it's true.

Page 70

Party Guy Scores

National Lampoon 1983

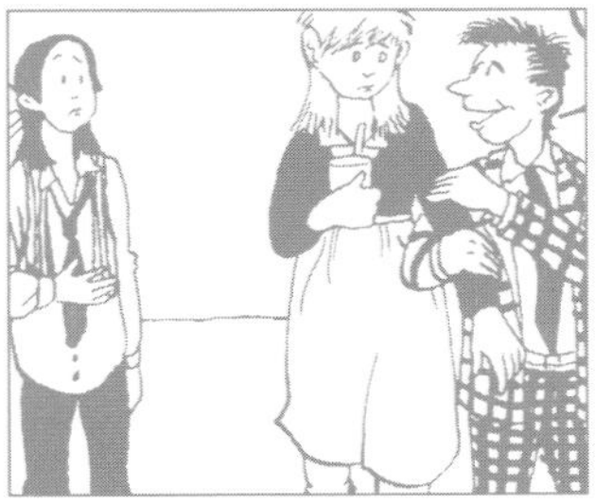

I like men. I really do. Sorry, I'm just still angry about what happened at this party that I went to in 1963.

Page 71

Bonnie Gets Drunk

National Lampoon 1983

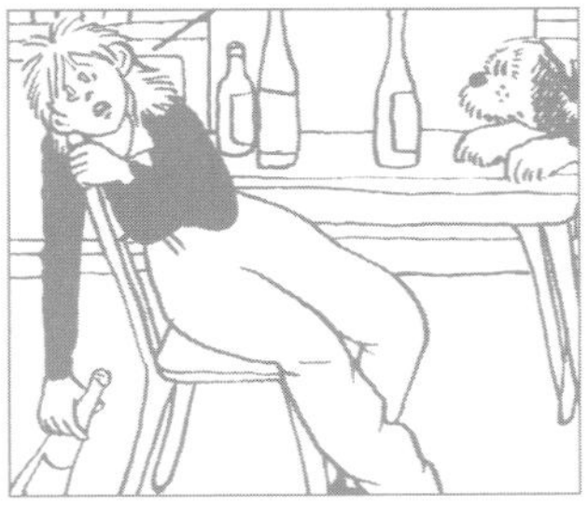

You know, I wrote and drew these comic strips once a month for years. I did not realize at the time how autobiographical a lot of them are. Starting when I was close to Bonnie's age, I have tried vodka and cheap wine a few times to kill the pain of both a toothache and a broken heart. Even heavily laced with 7-Up, liquor just made it worse. At least that confirms the theory that some people are genetically prone to alcohol addiction and some aren't.

Page 72

Bonnie's First Job

National Lampoon 1983

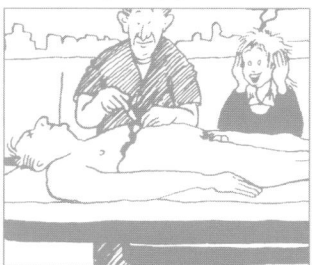

My boyfriend Brick Mason gave Bonnie the tumorous lymph nodes, so I named the hospital after him. Brick is a famous theatrical film storyboard artist.

—

Page 73

Bonnie's Mom's Sex Talk

National Lampoon 1983

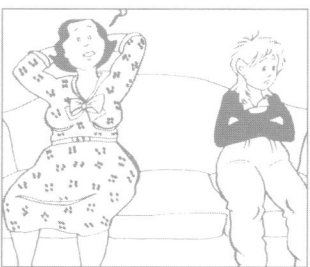

Darn. That was a total fantasy. I'm sure my parents never had sex, so mom didn't know any of that stuff and would not have wanted to. That is why sex belongs in the schools.

—

Page 74

Treasures in the Trash

National Lampoon 1984

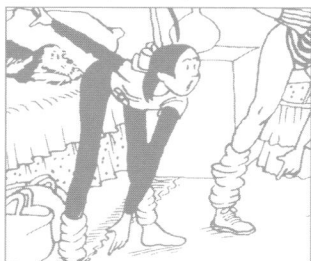

A couple of cultural trends are showing up on this page. Jane Fonda had recently popularized aerobic workouts, and Jennifer Beals in the film *Flashdance* made it fashionable to wear cut-up sweatshirts and leg warmers. I lived on an antique store block in the East Village that had amazing things (like my bright orange, super-long shag rug) left out in the trash every day.

—

Page 75

Pepsi's Menstrual Cemetery

National Lampoon 1984

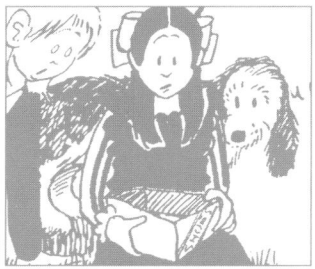

Roe v. Wade was just ten years old when I wrote this strip. That decision said simply that what happens in a woman's uterus is nobody else's business. When a Republican was elected president in 1980, I knew that women's autonomy was in for a rough ride. It seemed like a good time to remind any *Lampoon* readers who were on the fence about this issue that women need to make their own decisions.

—

Page 76

Bonnie's Bad Girlfriend

National Lampoon 1984

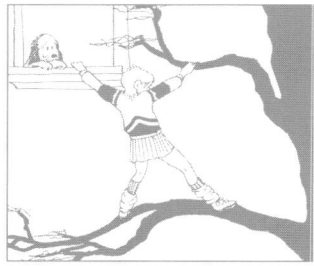

Will someone please tell me why we are supposed to like our parents? Does parenting not violate almost all of the Bill of Rights? Isn't a kid's mission in life to break out of her parents' prison?

Age 13 is when I moved my bed closer to the open window.

—

Page 77

How to Be a Bad Girl

National Lampoon 1984

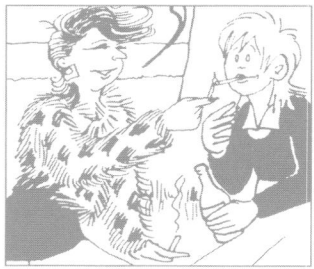

The truth is that in junior high school, we worshipped the bad girls. We talked about them all the time. They were sex symbols with mature bodies and raunchy taste in clothes. They may have screwed boys, but maybe not. We couldn't know for sure because we were too awestruck to ask.

I'm guessing now that the bad girls were probably pretty lonely and had a lot of time to study philosophy and play guitar. I was as nonjudgmental as Bonnie and cultivated several bad girlfriends who taught me that getting into trouble was fun and interesting.

—

Page 78

The Wedding

National Lampoon 1984

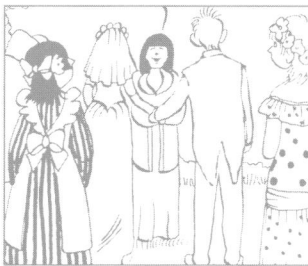

This strip was inspired by my boyfriend's female friend who disinvited me from her wedding because she thought that I didn't approve of weddings. Nothing could have been further from the truth. I love wedding cake and the cheap champagne they serve. This little story proves that all women have to do to have a happy marriage is to rewrite the contract.

—

Page 80

Bonnie Doesn't Get It

National Lampoon 1984

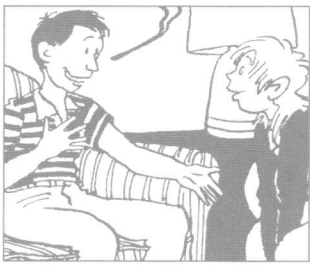

Men are so inscrutable. This happened to me when I was a horny adult woman in the 80s and it happened to my 65-year-old girlfriend last week. Decades after, I am still struggling to figure out what is going on here.

Any ideas?

—

Page 81

On the Road with Bonnie's Parents

National Lampoon 1984

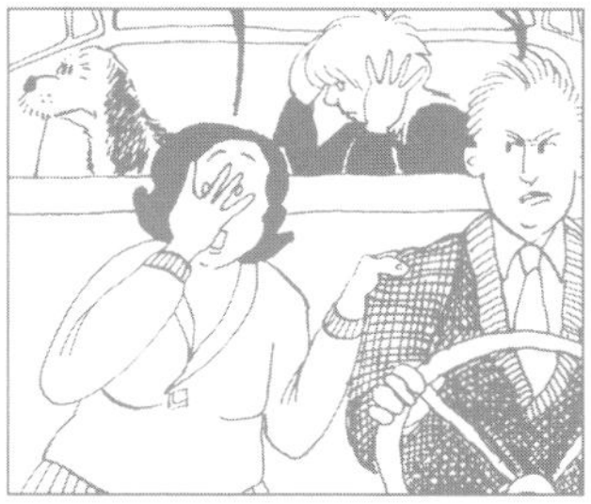

Ugh. My parents. So many road trips with the parents. I finally ran away from home to avoid even one more. If my dearly departed dead parents came back to life to take me on a road trip now, I would hide.

—

Page 82

Girls and Boys

National Lampoon 1984

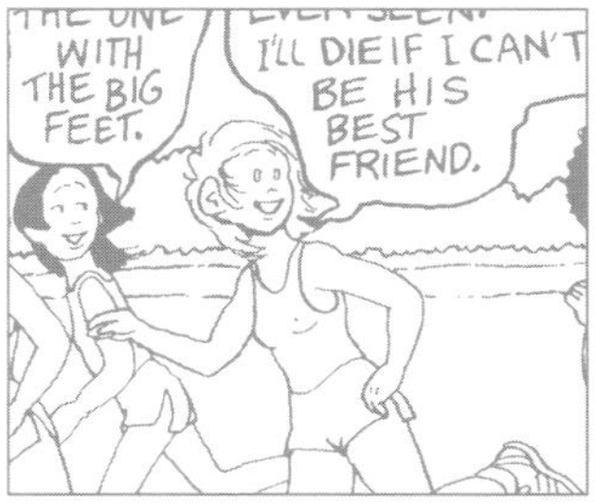
WITH THE BIG FEET.
I'LL DIE IF I CAN'T BE HIS BEST FRIEND.

You may not know this, but it was only after Title IX passed into law that public schools were forced to spend money on girls' sports. That caused a sea change in the way that women have come to approach life. Real athletics taught women how to compete with self-confidence while at the same time becoming reliable team players. So, just the fact that this comic shows women running on the same page with boys who are not chasing them is fairly novel. Their conversational progression is secondary here, but it does underscore that even though women and men may think alike, it is still difficult to get across the vast communication gap between them.

—

Page 83

Bonnie's Workout

National Lampoon 1984

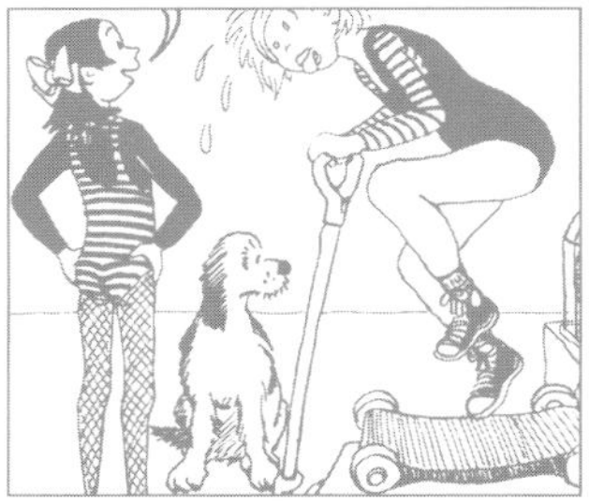

Every exercise class I have ever taken has given me a three-day backache. The merciless critiquing of women's bodies, coupled with the painful cruelty of workout routines, was the basis of this strip. I like to think of my intent as lofty, but really... I knew a lot of guys would just like to see Bonnie suffer (naked).

—

Page 84

Rags to Riches

National Lampoon 1985

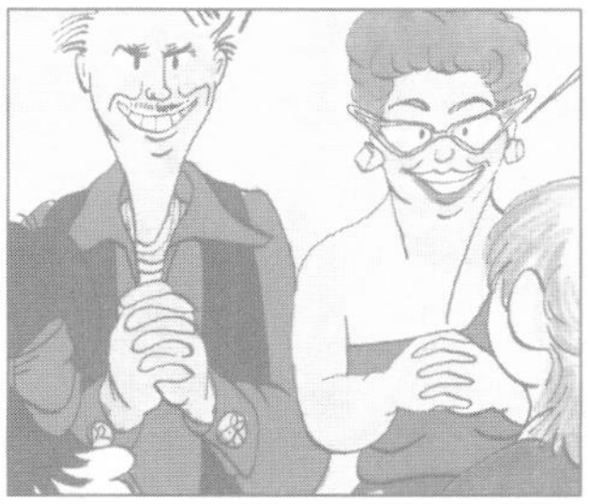

I really wanted a horse. I want one now. The desire for a horse will drive women crazy. I am fascinated by how easy it is for us to lose our moral compass.

—

Page 90

The Band

National Lampoon 1985

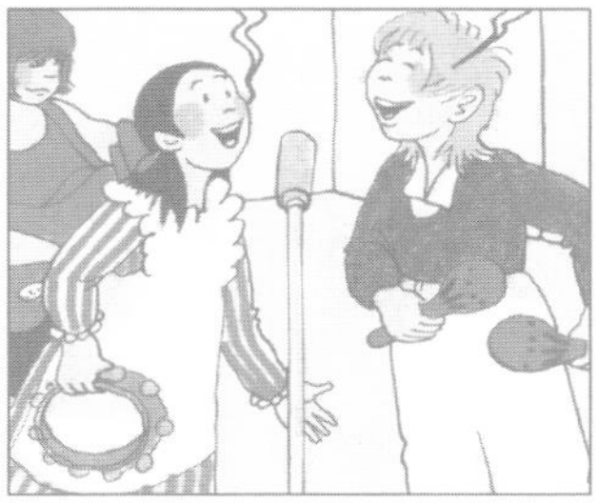

Thank you, *National Lampoon*, for giving me more than one page to tell a story with virtually no editing.
Most bands do not stay intact. This story is about a typical way that they break up, tearing themselves apart in pieces. I was pretty much reporting here what I was seeing with my local cartoonist band, but now it occurs to me that this is what makes some groups of any kind fail. They criticize the person closest to them and drive them away. Jeez. I am not funny at all. Sorry.

—

Page 94

In a Huff

National Lampoon 1985

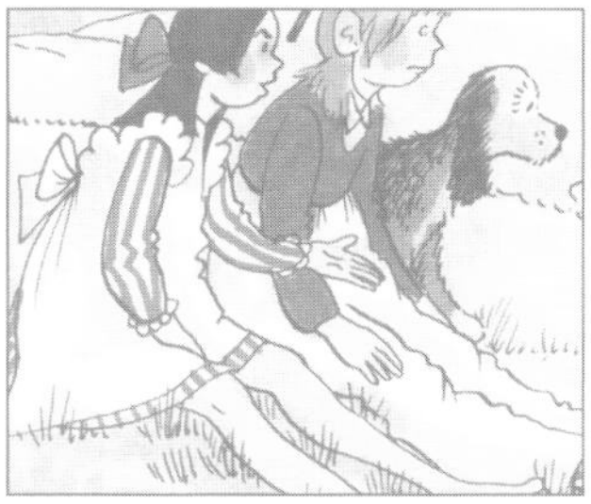

You can now imagine that you and I just woke up and are drinking our morning coffee. Pepsi's ranting in this comic is exactly what I would be saying, especially if fueled by recent news reports.
Like Pepsi, I am easily distracted and do not hold a grudge.
Many thanks to my good friend Jim Wilson for the punchline I never will forget.

—

Page 96

Not Ready for a Relationship

National Lampoon 1986

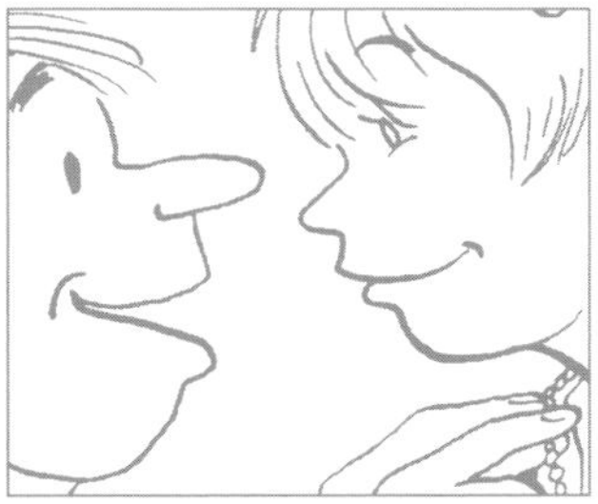

Well, a couple of years of intensive psychotherapy and this is what you get... It's hard to have good relationships if you don't have healthy self-esteem. Learning that cost me a lot of time and money. I think they are teaching it in public schools now, aren't they?

—

Page 97

Penis Size

National Lampoon 1986

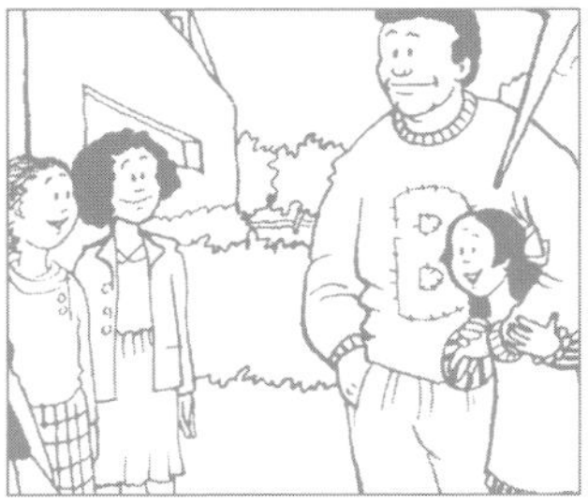

Here is the God's honest truth about the subject of this comic strip. If you can manage to be as wonderful as Pepsi's boyfriend, I know your dick is HUGE.

—

Page 98

Mothering Smothering

National Lampoon 1986

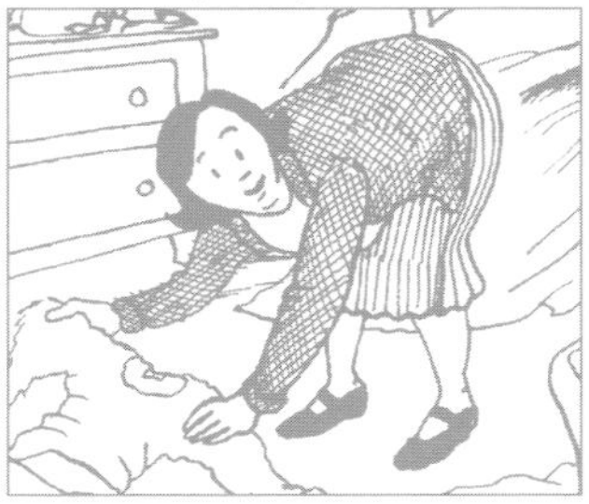

I had just had my heart broken by a famous author in Los Angeles. I went to stay with my mother in Seattle to lick my wounds and contemplate revenge. But my monthly *Trots and Bonnie* page was due, so I had to try really hard to come up with a clever idea. I couldn't do that because my mother followed me all over the house even as I tried to escape her. She was opening her mail, which was all junk mail, and reading the most tempting offers out loud to me. My other famous Hollywood writer friend, the good one, Mark Evanier, gave me Trots's punchline.

Page 99

Entrepreneurial Pepsi

National Lampoon 1986

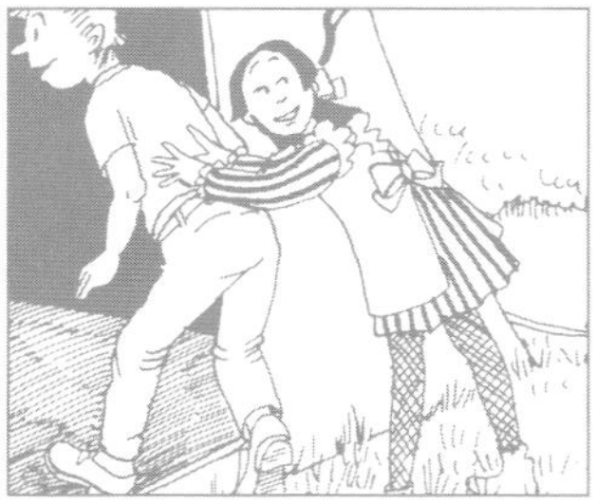

There you go. The AIDS epidemic and the economic boom — a brief history in one comic. My old boyfriend who used to be a drug dealer cut his hair, went back to college, and became a fiscal conservative yuppie. Trickle-down economics even trickled down to 13-year-olds.

Page 100

Out of Print

National Lampoon 1986

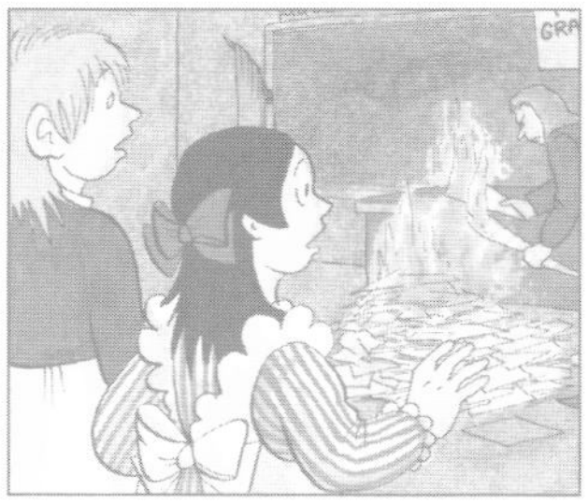

A comic strip can be much more complex than it seems at first look. This story is not just about a little girl publishing a bawdy school newspaper. Even though I did exactly that when I was 11 and still resent being forced to cease distribution. This strip is about Pepsi's right to practice free-market capitalism and be a libertarian goddess.

Page 104

Bonnie and Clyde

National Lampoon 1987

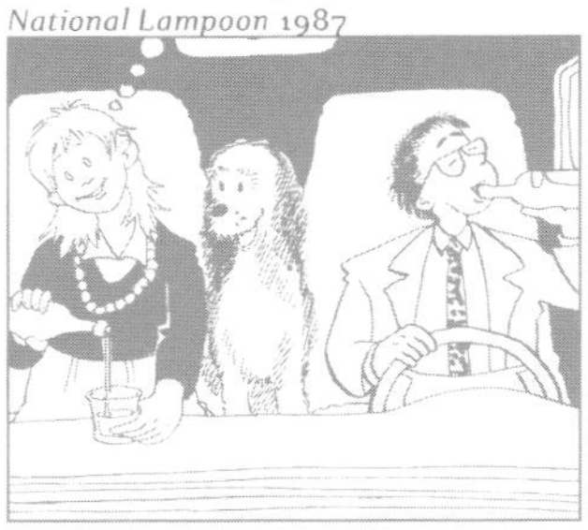

Thank you, Marty Simmons, fun-loving publisher of *National Lampoon* magazine, for suggesting the title of this story. Devising a story to fit the title was like playing a challenging improvisational theater game. I think the result is even better than the 1967 movie with Faye Dunaway and Warren Beatty, don't you?

Page 108

Safe Sex

National Lampoon 1987

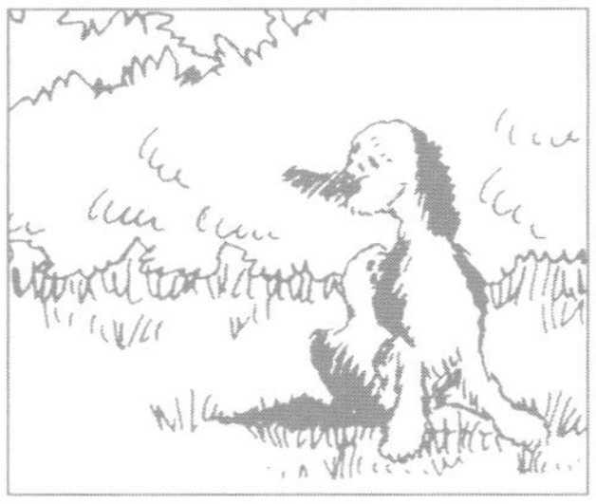

The AIDS epidemic had spread to every corner of the world. President Reagan had finally publicly recognized the then-incurable disease. Changing our sexual habits was the only way to stay safe. You might wonder why this was the only strip about sex that the magazine considered too hot to print? It was later published in a special collection.

Page 109

Doctor Pepsi Is a Specialist

National Lampoon 1987

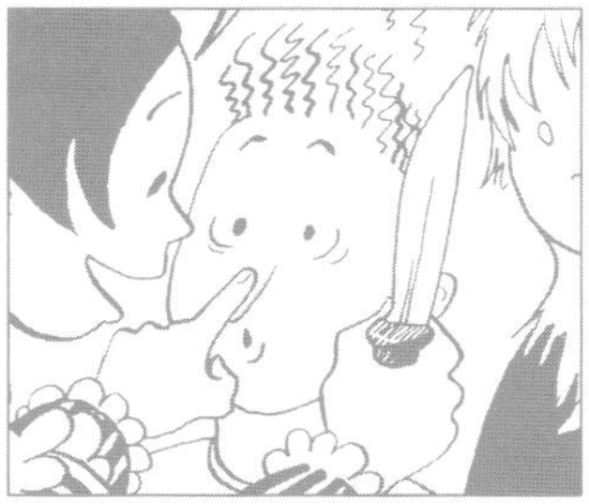

This one is for all you guys who think you can manipulate women into taking their panties off. Pepsi prefers men who take a more honest and direct approach.

Page 110

Trots in Therapy

National Lampoon 1987

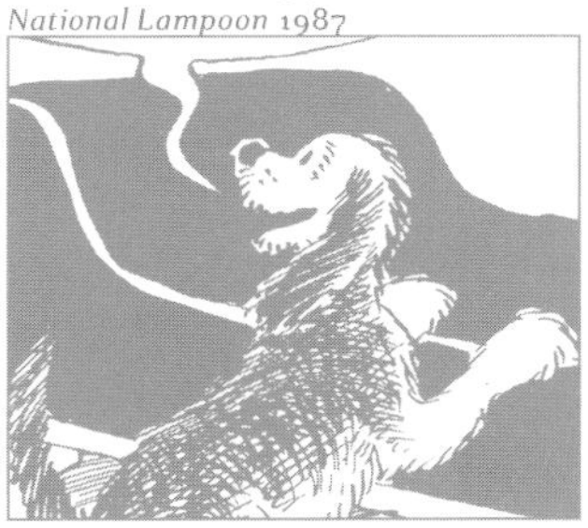

Western medicine wants there to be a pharmaceutical product that will instantly cure anything that is wrong with us. Trots is more into talk therapy and long walks. Too bad Bonnie didn't pick a dog therapist that was a better fit.

Page 111

The Old Hippie

National Lampoon 1988

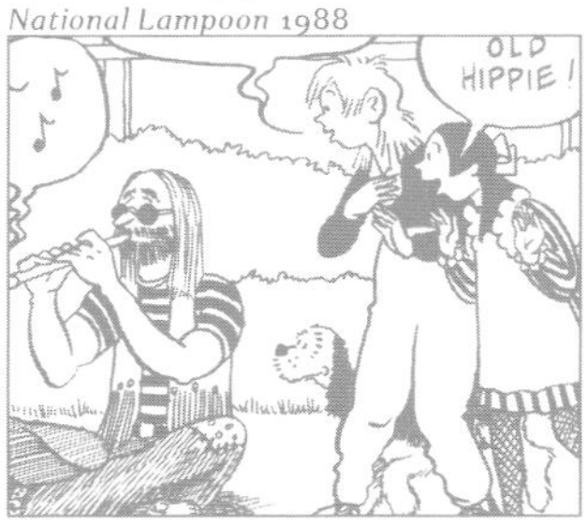
OLD HIPPIE!

1988… the world was taking a giant step into the era of technology. Bonnie and Pepsi have already rejected the ethics of the 1960s and 70s. Only Trots is reminiscing about how good it used to be. And he is usually the smartest one.

Page 112

Sex Education

National Lampoon 1988

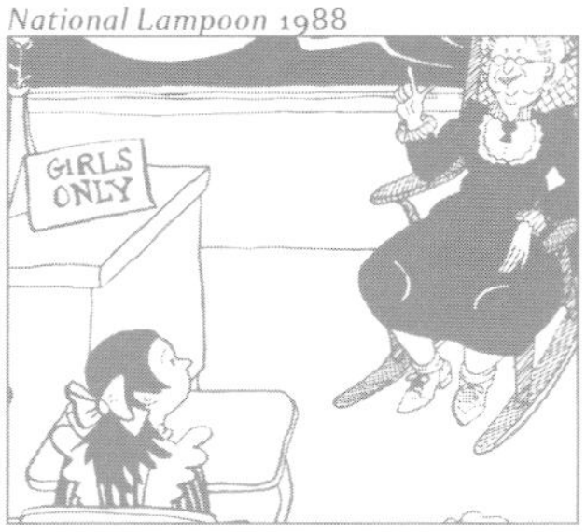
GIRLS ONLY

Republican administrations have never been very good for public education. My neighbor was an editor at a schoolbook publisher. I could hear her crying through the walls about how the Texas school board insisted on textbooks loaded with outdated information and outright lies.

Page 113

Family Therapy

National Lampoon 1989

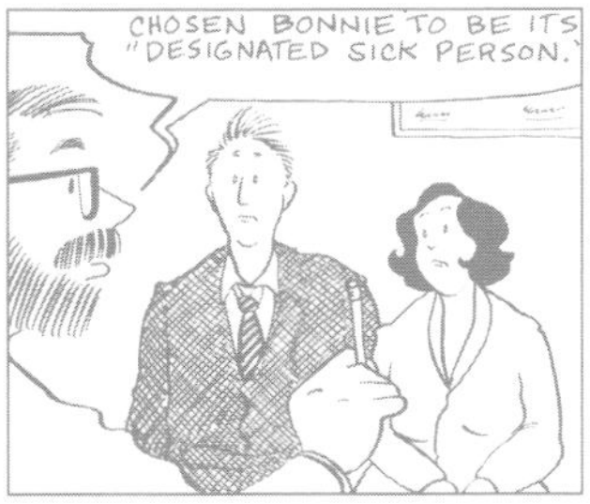
CHOSEN BONNIE TO BE ITS "DESIGNATED SICK PERSON."

I am a big fan of John Bradshaw, the self-help guru who wrote about how fucked-up families perpetuate themselves for generations. If your parents weren't perfect, at least you're not alone.

—

Page 114

Pepsi the Dealer

National Lampoon June 1989

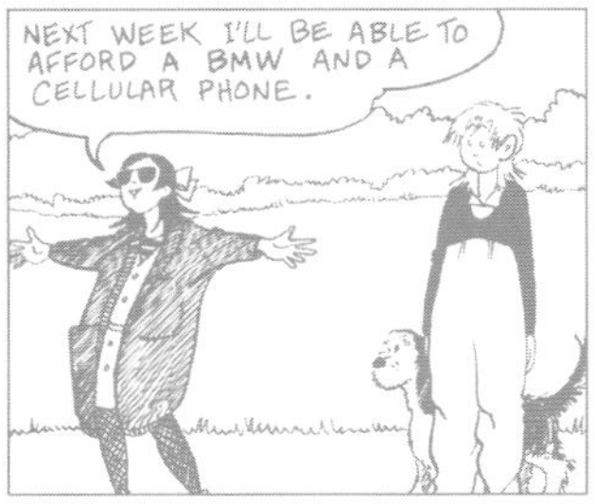
NEXT WEEK I'LL BE ABLE TO AFFORD A BMW AND A CELLULAR PHONE.

When I wrote this strip, I was hopelessly in love with and married to a highly intelligent and talented musician who was also a drug addict. We went to a White Castle at 2 AM one night. I was amazed that the place was full of very young teenage boys. My husband said they were all doing drug deals. Apparently, there can be a lot of that going on right in front of us, and if we aren't in the business, we don't see it.

—

Page 115

The Bidet

National Lampoon 1989

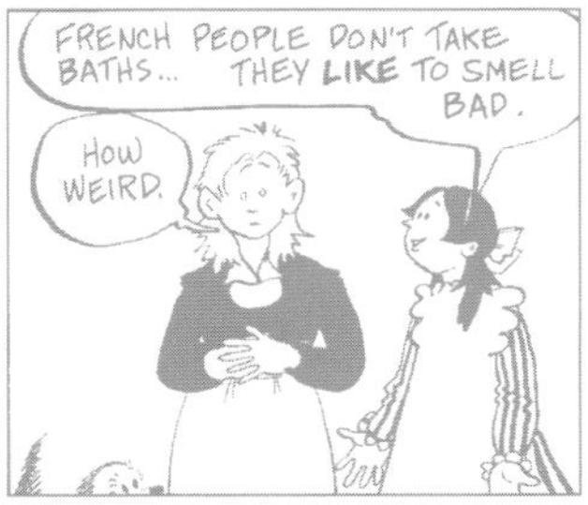
FRENCH PEOPLE DON'T TAKE BATHS... THEY LIKE TO SMELL BAD.
HOW WEIRD.

I once stayed at a house on Long Island where the homeowner showed me a bidet that had been used by the actress Kathleen Turner. He said there were fans who would have paid thousands of dollars to have that bidet.

Like Bonnie, I think bidets are weird. But maybe I need one.

—

Page 116

Self-Defense Dummy

National Lampoon 1990

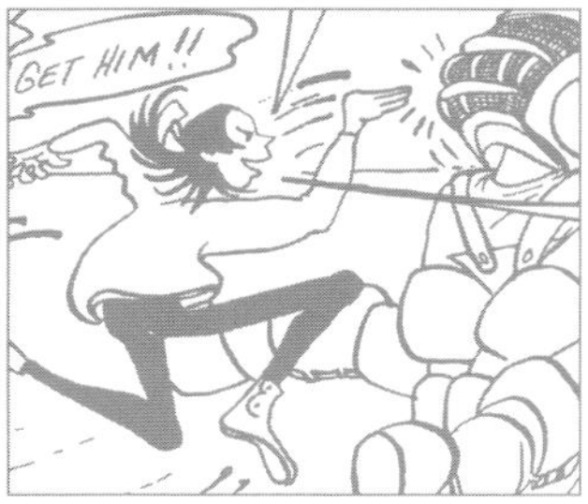
GET HIM!!

I took this Model Mugging course in Seattle. It was one of the most satisfying things I have ever done. A killer attitude makes all the difference. They teach you to yell so loud that any sane person will leave you alone. I've used that a lot.

—

Page 117

Phallic Packaging

National Lampoon 1990

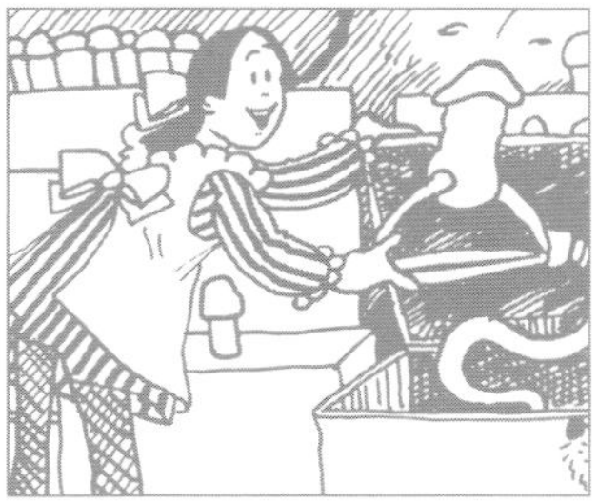

When I was in high school, my friends and I discovered *The Hidden Persuaders* by Vance Packard, a super sexy paperback about how every image in print advertising looks like a curvy woman's body with a big schlong pointing toward it. Seen through that lens, even *Good Housekeeping* magazine became a stroke book. It was a popular best seller. This strip was inspired by Norman Hathaway's wife, Jan, who did a flawless imitation of her father watering the lawn.

—

Page 118

Art Therapy

National Lampoon 1990

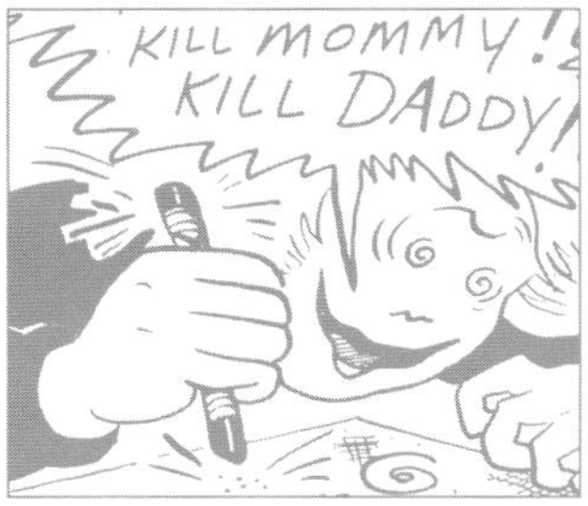
KILL MOMMY!!
KILL DADDY!

Bonnie has had a lot of therapy over the years. Art therapy may be the most successful.

—

Page 119

Reality TV Show

National Lampoon 1993

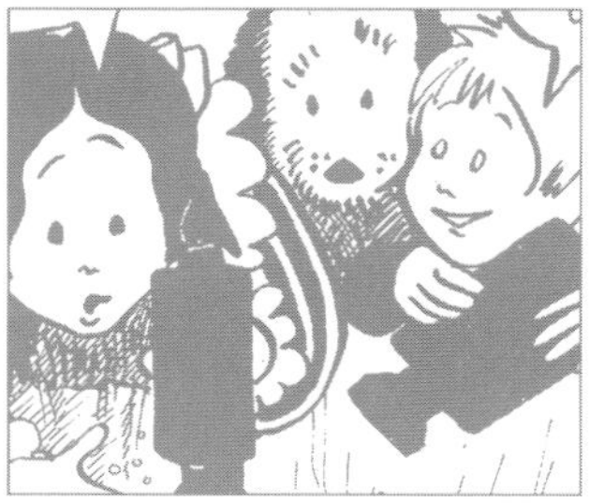

Before smart phones, before YouTube, before the Kardashians, there was *Cops*. And I had a video camera that recorded onto VHS tape. It was tethered to a VCR, which I wore in a shoulder bag. Despite that complicated apparatus, I had recorded vital parts of my family's history, and the last few years of my mother's life. Before that, all I had was a Polaroid camera to save images of people who I loved. It was an important technological advancement that I included in the *Trots and Bonnie* lexicon. Of course, being too young to collect even minimum wage, Bonnie and especially Pepsi were in it for the big bucks, and already seeing themselves as professional videographers.

—

Page 120

Bonnie Ends It All

National Lampoon 1991

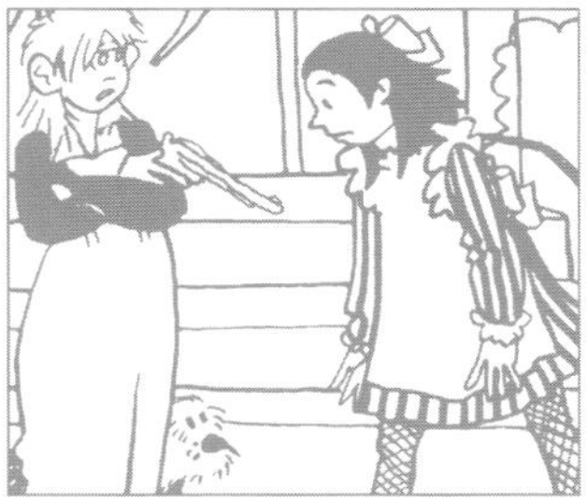

The thing with therapy is that you never really get better. You just get to appreciate the things that you used to think were wrong with you. Bonnie will never get over her low self-esteem, but like so many of us, she can use it as a good excuse for bad behavior.

—

When I was a teen in Seattle in the 1970s, a friend told me he had met Shary Flenniken and Bobby London the previous night. I was extremely skeptical. What would two of my favorite artists from the super-hip humor magazine *National Lampoon* be doing in humdrum Seattle? Baffling. Shary and Bobby had been underground cartoonists in San Francisco, but were now drawing monthly strips for the *Lampoon* that brilliantly melded antique drawing styles with contemporary satirical storytelling. I shook my friend down for their address and walked down to the quiet downtown waterfront warehouse where they worked. Their building seemed a perfect home for private detectives. I knocked, but no one was in. I lifted the mail slot to spy on their studio and was elated to see some of their work. I returned about a half dozen times with no better luck, so I decided to do a drawing with my number on it and leave it for them. A week later my mother casually told me Bobby London was on the phone for me. Somehow, I managed to form words and set a time to go and meet them.

When I walked in, Shary was on the phone. Bobby offered me a chair, but I declined as I was hell-bent on looking through their original art. I grabbed a pile from a drawer and reveled in their beauty. Bobby's effortless-seeming, gestural linework entranced me. Both his and Shary's drawings were surprisingly large, similar to a full Sunday comics newspaper page, which was unusual, as the printed version was letter-sized. Shary's originals fascinated me as her drawing wasn't classically "cartoony." I was impressed by the level of realism and amount of effort put in to convey actual environments. The drawings had two-point perspective guides penciled in to enable her to place her subjects in a believable world. Shary got off the phone, happy about the conversation she'd had with a client. She said perhaps I'd be interested in contributing some drawings to them too. This gesture of kindness to a stranger and level of excitement about her work were things I would come to love about her.

I had always thought cartooning was primarily about goofy drawings and really only focused on draftsmanship. But being able to hang out with both of them and witness the level of seriousness they took toward their work was compelling and changed my view. Shary would have a very rough idea for a story, then spend hours contemplating different approaches for telling it in the best way. Once this had been decided upon, she would write lines of dialogue in her notepad and refine these until she broke down the action visually. Then, she'd then pull out a giant sheet of drawing paper and begin the final artwork. As a beginner, I was astounded by how quickly and effortlessly she drew, lettered, and inked her pages. All the hard work was in the conceptual stage, and the drawing that followed seemed effortless by comparison.

Shary is the rare cartoonist who questions social issues while also being hilarious. She gleefully skewers the self-righteous and is one of the most entertaining soap-boxers out there. She's always been a very curious person and deeply fascinated by social mores. If she is ever confused by something, she has no embarrassment about her specific lack of knowledge. She'll ask keenly if you have the answer or, even better, want to know what your theory might be. Even though *Trots and Bonnie* has been out of the public eye for decades, fans continue to ask about Shary, and where they might view her work. I'm pleased for those fans, and the newcomers to her work, that after all this time they can now see her curiosity, humor, draftsmanship, and bravery for themselves.

–Norman Hathaway

134

Interview
Shary Flenniken
Conducted by Norman Hathaway

Shary and Webster
1978

Norman Hathaway   Where did you grow up?

Shary Flenniken   I was born in a navy town where my father was stationed, and he shipped out right away to the Aleutian Islands for the Korean War. My mother moved my sister and me out to California. We lived in Coronado, which is the rich people's island next to San Diego. When the Korean War was over, we moved to Kodiak Island, Alaska, which was heaven for us two little girls. Even at age four you can run wild in a place like that, since everybody's in the military. As far as I know, there were no bad guys on Kodiak.

We came down here to Seattle when I was four. We first stayed in navy housing and then my parents bought the house that I am living in now. My father was in military intelligence. Then, for some reason, he was given a government job that was not a navy job, port captain of the Panama Canal Zone. Everyone worked for the American government there and lived in these fairly swanky cement-block houses with beautiful yards and gardeners and maids. It was heavenly.

In 1959 we came back to Seattle and I had to go back to my stuffy classmates at the same school I had left. It was fourth grade, and from then on, school was hell. It never ceased. It just was no fun. The kids were assholes. Once you've been somewhere exotic and you come back to Seattle, it's like you're a different duckling.

NH *When you think back to that time, were you generally unhappy?*

SF I think childhood is complex. You know? There are sublime moments and then there are these moments that are just horrible. Even when we were still living in Kodiak, I was trying to run away from home. I did not do a good job of it. I thought if I went and lived in our car, that was good enough. I left home many times, like an Alzheimer's patient wandering away.

The Flenniken family home
Seattle 1969

Shary's sister, Judy
1963

NH *Adults, oppression, and psychotic parents play a role in some of your strips. How would you describe your parents' parenting style?*

SF Benign neglect, and not a capital "B" on that "benign"—let's just say capital "N" on "Neglect." When I was little, as soon as I could read, it was like, because I was so bored, I had to have something to read all the time. My sister was really helpful. She would play school and she taught me to read. So, my parents' parenting style? I remember it was a lot of, "We go to cocktail parties and you can play with the other kids who are also being ignored."

You're talking to somebody who spent ten years in therapy. Twice a week, delving through all my family of origin stuff. It really is so good and so bad, and the thing is, you don't remember how bad it was. You don't really think about it. I mean, I didn't. I didn't realize that my parents were bad parents for a long time. I didn't realize other people had different lives. But my parents laughed at me! I was like, the butt of their jokes. They thought I was useless. One time my mother hit me with coat hangers because I was swimming in a fountain down in Panama. I told her that policemen had

Shary with her
father and mother
1967

chased me out of the fountain, and she lost it. She just lost her temper and started hitting me. And my father— they both had this irrational anger thing, which just made me tolerant of irrational anger things. I still have a lot of tolerance for that.

They scare the hell out of you when they go ballistic, you know. You're a little kid and your parents are explosive, and there's something inside of you that knows that they could kill you. It's that frightening.

Daddy Flenniken's drawings
circa 1960s

NH   Were you always drawing as a kid, or did that come later?

SF   My dad was drawing cartoons when he was at the Naval Academy. They're in the 1932 Naval Academy yearbook. He had a regular character with jokes and stuff about his classmates. We would draw together. You learn how to draw in a lot of ways, mostly by copying other people, when you're a kid.

I was reading and I was writing. I was drawing like all kids draw; kids draw in school all the time. But I was into publishing. I published a fifth-grade gossip newsletter when I was eleven. I drew little Christmas cards and my dad took me around the neighborhood selling them for a nickel. He was with his daughter because he had no son, and I think he gave me a little business boost in that way.

Shary, thirteen years old
1963

NH   Were you cartooning at all as a kid?

SF   Actually, I was more interested in writing science fiction. I created a super-hero cartoon character called Rubber Ronald. I was drawing cartoons, but I didn't know how to draw comic pages with boxes, dialogue, and sequential action.

NH   Were you reading comics?

I read what I think is a lot of comics—*Superman* and *Aquaman* and J'onn J'onzz, "Manhunter from Mars," and the Disney things. I was into *Uncle Scrooge*. Carl Barks had these great stories where the ducks were going around the world and doing all kinds of things—going to Peru and stuff. All duck comics are great.

I grew up with a lot of big, hardcover collections of single-panel cartoons. *New Yorker* cartoons from the thirties and forties. They are what I have always loved, and

137

Art school student
1969

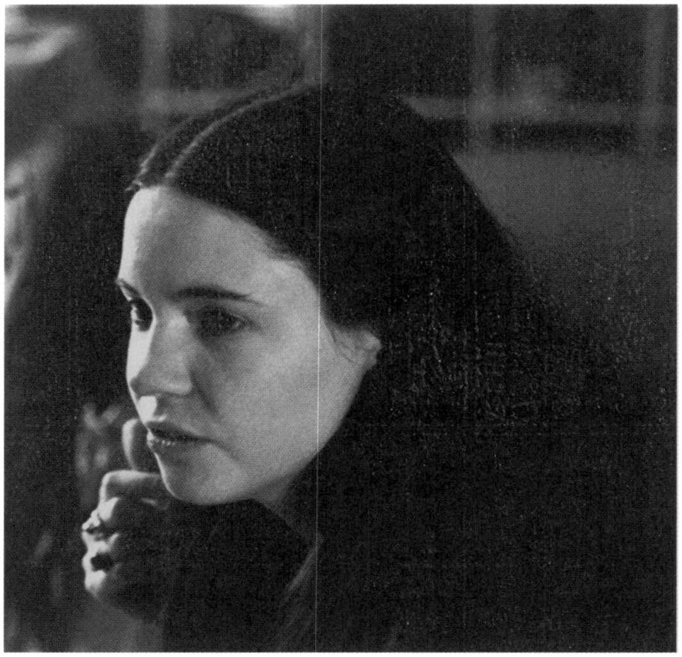

certainly that's what I was looking at. When I was reading comic books and the comics in the newspaper, I never associated them with a human being producing them. It just never occurred to me, because they looked so mechanical.

NH How did you get from reading and writing to going to art school?

SF My sister excelled in everything she did and had a lot of different majors in college, so that was not leaving very much for me to succeed at. I sold drawings at the Magnolia Village summer fair when I was fifteen. So, I like to say that there was really nothing left for me to do except to be an artist. That sort of explained how weird I was to my family. I wanted to be a lawyer. Even now I wish I had done something more useful with my life.

When I graduated from high school, I ran away from home and went across Canada in a Volkswagen bus. It was amazing. The people that I met and the things that we did really fed my head. It wasn't just camping out. We spent two or three weeks at Middlebury College in Vermont, then I stayed at a dorm at Harvard for a long time and went to Washington, D.C. Everything I did on that trip was enlightening. I got back to Seattle and went to art school, and art school was just really plebeian. They were training us to do layout and it wasn't very artsy. They didn't give you a very lofty goal.

NH I wouldn't consider the Magnolia neighborhood a hotbed of political radicals. How did your interest in politics come about?

SF My dad was a conservative, so I lived with political things. The thing that you need to remember is that Kennedy was shot when I was thirteen, and it was a big deal. I don't think my father was unhappy that Kennedy got shot, but we all watched the funeral for days.

When I was graduating from high school, that's when Martin Luther King Jr. and Bobby Kennedy got shot too, and the Vietnam War was going on at that time, so you knew something was happening. It's like that Buffalo Springfield lyric, "Something's happening here and it's not exactly clear." Life was a hotbed of politics by that time. I made a collage poster that juxtaposed the Kennedys playing football on their lawn with soldiers being killed. I got a vial of blood from a dentist and splattered the poster with it. I was trying to make a statement: "Wake up, you guys. There's something going on that's really important, and all you care about is your stupid football games and your pep rallies."

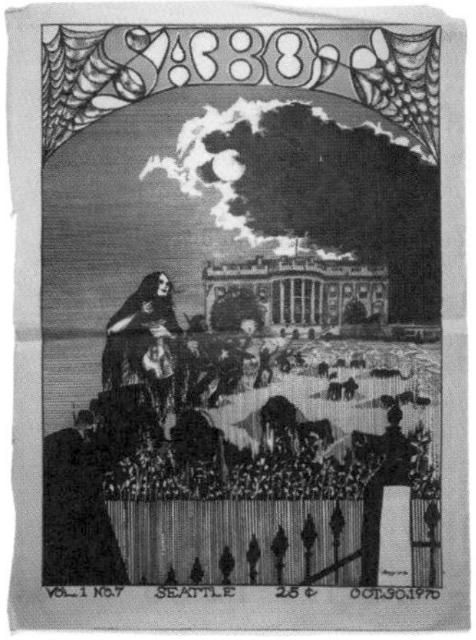
SABOT
VOL. 1 NO. 7 SEATTLE 25¢ OCT. 30. 1970

Shary's cover for *Sabot*
1967

While I was in art school, I started hanging out with people who were working on an underground newspaper, so that was my entrée to being considered a professional.

NH After art school, you kept working on the underground newspaper Sabot. *Then you met the Air Pirates gang—Ted Richards, Bobby London, Dan O'Neill, and Gary Hallgren—at Sky River Rock Festival. It must have been unusual to have people doing so much serious cartoon work who were also likeminded with you.*

SF By the time I got to Sky River, I was really starved for intellectual conversation and a goal. I wanted to find people who were doing things and believed in things. I was right at the age where people are doing that kind of searching, and that's what I was doing.

The four guys who soon became the Air Pirates were serious, working, bad-ass cartoonists. I learned a lot being with them, and I was intimidated by them. At the festival, we collaborated on *Sky River Funnies.* I went back to Seattle when that was over. My dad was dying of cancer, and it was really hard for me. That was always playing in the background. My mother kept sending me to psychiatrists because I was depressed or something—troubled is a better word for it. Angry is an even better word for it. Finally, a social worker made me feel okay about leaving home and moving to San Francisco. I planned on getting a job in Berkeley. But I went and hung out with the Air Pirates guys and that was all she wrote.

NH Tell me a bit about what the scene in San Francisco was like. Do you have any specific strong memories of people or their work that really struck you?

SF When I was in Seattle and probably still working on the paper, I went to a party, and they had a bunch of underground comics spread out on the dining room table. I spent the whole time at the party reading those comics, so I had an idea of what underground comics were just from that evening of reading.

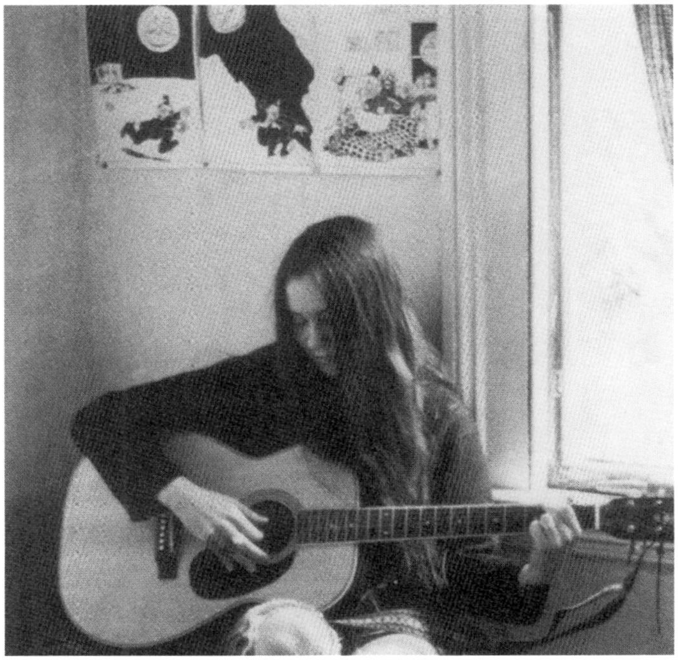

San Francisco, Air Pirates drawings on the wall
1971

The Air Pirates were a big influence on me, artistically and professionally. We were a really focused, tight crew—

at first, anyway. In the first warehouse, we were just kind of on our own mission. The guys were doing their Air Pirates books, planning to take over the world and destroy Disney. We were all nose to the drawing board, and there were people that came in and out who wanted to hang out with us. Some of them stayed and some of them didn't.

I remember feeling very critical of the kind of anti-woman stories that Crumb, S. Clay Wilson, and others were writing. Looking back, especially since I had come from an ideologically oriented, anti-war, underground newspaper, I saw being published as a kind of soapbox for social change. I suspect many of the guys in that scene saw it as building a career. When I started to be published by *Lampoon*, the way I felt was very much like it would feel these days if you discovered that your blog, YouTube channel, Facebook page, podcast, or whatever social media endeavor suddenly had half a million followers. Suddenly your voice is a lot louder.

NH It seems like there was a period when you were hanging out with those guys when you went through a little bit of an early-twentieth-century cartooning boot camp. Do I have that wrong?

SF No, that is true. Everybody was going through that. That was from Dan O'Neill's having hung out with improvisational theater people and bringing their exercises into our group.

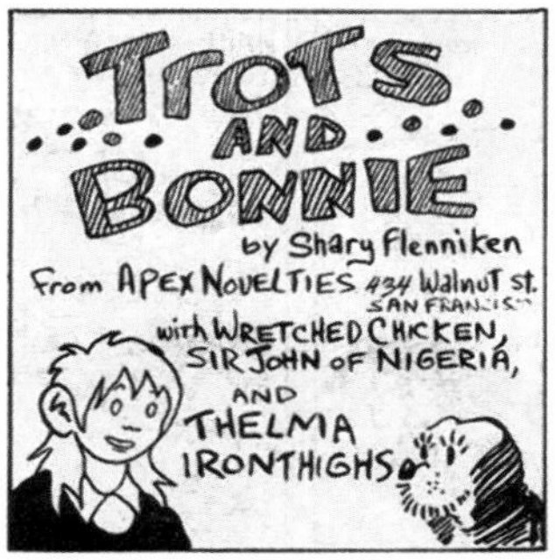
TROTS AND BONNIE
by Shary Flenniken
From APEX NOVELTIES 434 Walnut st.
with WRETCHED CHICKEN, SIR JOHN OF NIGERIA, AND THELMA IRONTHIGHS

Ad for unrealized comic book project
1972

Everybody was supposed to copy a classic cartoonist's art style. I don't know if any of the Air Pirates were really conscious of how distinctive that would make us. We did that partly so we could produce seamless art on improvisational comic pages. It was great. It was like being in school. Much better than the Burnley School of Professional Art.

NH Tell me a bit about the tools you used back then to create your strips.

SF When I was first with the Air Pirates, I was literally just drawing on paper bags because I didn't have good paper. They noticed what I was doing and let me have the good paper. We used Strathmore two-ply plate finish because when you use a dip pen, the India ink isn't absorbed into slick paper. We pinned the paper to lightweight balsa wood drawing boards and used T-squares to draw the panel outlines.

We used a type of blue pencil that was invisible to the camera when the printer photographed the pages. When I started doing the perspective layouts, I would do that in blue because you can't erase the blue. If I was drawing a figure, I might not always be sure where their feet were going to fall.

For lettering and panel borders, we used a Rapidograph. The Hunt #101 fleur-de-lys point is the only dip pen point I've ever used. We all did. It's the only one that holds ink long enough. It's a super-flexible point. It can give you a little teeny fine line or you can apply more pressure to stretch out the point and make a big swoop.

Play Doctor (detail)
National Lampoon, May 1977

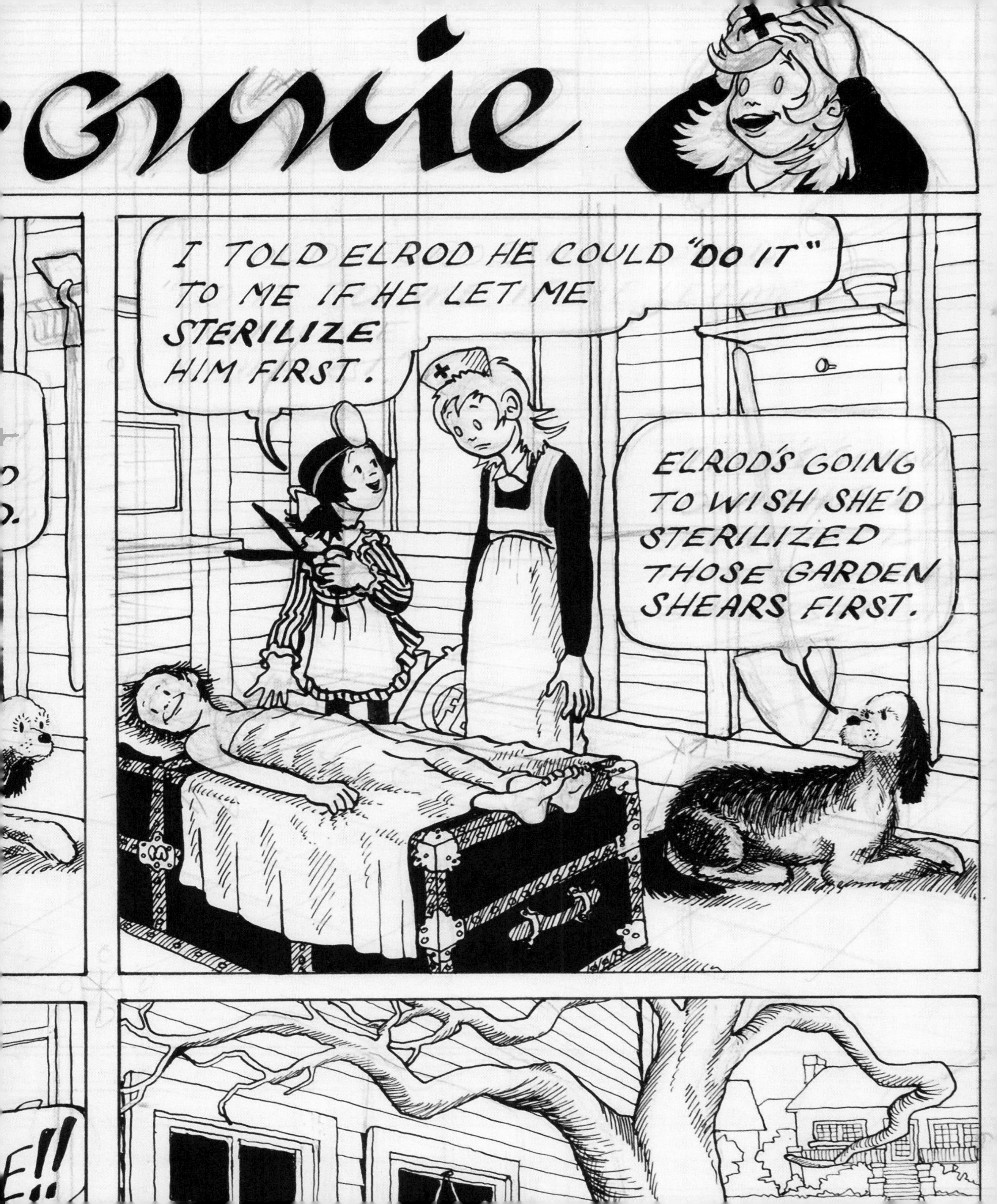
I TOLD ELROD HE COULD "DO IT" TO ME IF HE LET ME STERILIZE HIM FIRST.
ELROD'S GOING TO WISH SHE'D STERILIZED THOSE GARDEN SHEARS FIRST.

Flenniken painting her story "The Band" on her jury-rigged light table
1976

Later, when I started doing color strips, I had my black and white pages photographed and output onto clear film. I would tape the films to a piece of glass and lay a piece of watercolor paper on top. If you put a light behind the glass, it makes it easy to paint the colors in. When it was dry, I'd tape the black line art over the color. That way the printer could separate the black lines from the color and keep them nice and crisp.

NH   I've always admired your varied approaches to the title lettering. Can you tell me a little about your approach for those?

SF   I just decided to make the title a piece of the art. It's more interesting for the reader and it's more fun for me. The process of lettering the titles was like a doorway into the story. Deciding on the title lettering and adding it is one of the specific steps I take. I am very systematic. All the steps will come together. It's not overwhelming if you do that.

NH   Walk me through how it goes with the writing and roughing out the panels.

SF   I write a whole bunch. Sometimes I will write about what I want to do for days, because when you do that and open up that flow in your brain, it'll evolve. I will be able to pull out the storyline. Sometimes it won't evolve. Some things are dead ends.

TOO BAD YOU HAVE TOO PAY EXTRA FOR THE TARTAR SAUCE.
THIS FISH IS SO GOOD.
THEY PUT CORNSTARCH IN THE BATTER
P.
G G G
B T
THROWS WINE
B.T.
THROWS BAG
THROWS ASHES

Panel breakdown on a napkin and sketchbook dialogue breakdowns
1977

IT'S ALMOST TOO HORRIBLE FOR WORDS.
WHAT'S THE MATTER, PEPSIE?
MY MOTHER FOUND MY BIRTH CONTROL PILLS.
OH NO! HOW DID THAT HAPPEN?
I WAS AT MY RADICAL DETACHMENT OF WOMEN BALLET CLASS, AND SHE DECIDED TO CLEAN UP MY ROOM.
FIRST SHE FOUND MY DIAPHRAGM... THAT REALLY GOT HER GOING.
DID SHE FIND YOUR RUBBER COLLECTION?
YEAH... AND MY I.U.D. MOBILE.
AND MY PRE-LODED CONTRACEPTIVE CREAM INSERTER.
AND MY VAGINAL HEAT GAUGE.
DID SHE SPANK YOU.
WORSE.
ARE YOU ON RESTRICTION?
NO NO YOU CAN'T IMAGINE HOW BAD IT IS.
HOW BAD IS IT?
SHE DIDN'T KNOW WHAT THEY WERE FOR.
Bonnie: THAT'S NOT INCONCIEVABLE.
Treats: NEITHER IS PEPSI'S MOTHER.

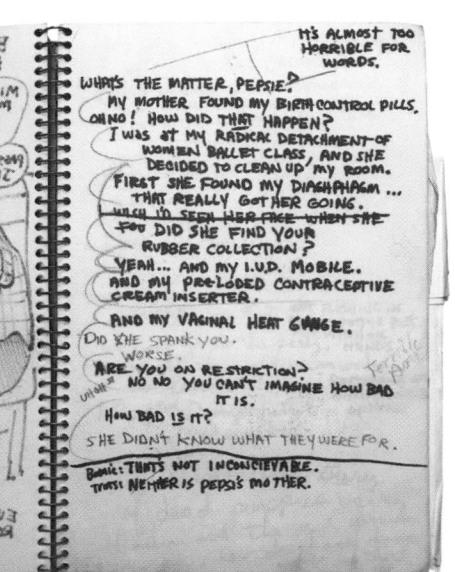

But with the *Lampoon*, I always knew what they wanted, so I had that extra slant, being outrageous.

NH *How would you then break down the storyline into panels?*

SF There might be dialogue, or there might be action, or there might be both. Maybe this issue's subject is cars, so I would think, "Bonnie's going to try to drive a car." So, I place Bonnie in the car in my mind and ask who's going to give her that lesson. Well, it might be Pepsi. I know if I put Pepsi in the car teaching Bonnie how to drive, that Pepsi's going to do what my first boyfriend did when he was teaching me to drive: he taught me fancy shifting and all these things that were illegal, like spinning donuts. Then I know most of the strip is going to be all the different dangerous things they do. I would write a strip like that and have no idea what the punchline was going to be. I'd be down to the wire on the deadline because I couldn't figure out how to end it. Something's going to happen, and then the dog's going to say something hopefully really funny or profound about it. You have a pattern that's easy to follow with that strip.

When I have the storyline written in my notebook, I draw lines where the panels break. Then I count the number of panels and design the page.

NH *It was a big leap jumping from underground comics to a national magazine. How did working for the* Lampoon *come about?*

SF Michel Choquette, who was an editor at *Lampoon*, wanted the Air Pirates to do something for his book project. Bobby London and I were married by then and staying with Bobby's parents in Queens. We went into Manhattan and hung out with Michel, who took us up to the *Lampoon* office where we met Michael Gross, who was the art director. He bought a couple of my single-panel cartoons, like the kind that I'd been doing for the *Good Times* and *Berkeley Barb* newspapers. Then Michael asked me to illustrate Ed Bluestone's "Telling a Kid His Parents Are Dead." After that, they asked Bobby and me to do half-page strips in the funny pages.

NH *The* Lampoon *seemed like a very prestigious publication to work for at the time. How did you feel about working for it?*

SF It's complex. When something like that happens, you don't know how long it's going to last. It's not like you go, "Oh, I'm going to have a venue to work in for the next twenty years." It doesn't happen like that. It's really moment to moment. I was very focused on each time I had to draw something. One important aspect of it was, you know, that my parents thought I was such a loser. They'd already gotten super mad at me about one of the naughty comic strips in Gary Hallgren's *Tortoise and the Hare* comic book. The whole family got on the phone and told me how sick and terrible I was. My parents thought I should be ashamed of myself. I think working for a national magazine was trying to overcome that shame.

NH *That's great.*

SF Knowing that somebody's buying your work and they're paying you and they're telling you to put more sex in it. They're going, like, "Forget that shame! Cast off your shame!"

NH Yeah. "Open up!"

SF That was *beautiful*. It was so welcoming.

NH Some Trots and Bonnie *stories are really outrageous in a way that I like. We omitted some problematic strips from this book, but I'm guessing some modern readers might still be horrified by others. What's your view on that?*

SF The things that I did that we omitted here in this book, I think we looked at those and went, "Oh, that might hurt somebody's feelings or something." That was me being naïve when I wrote those. A lot of times I was just exploring a subject rather than having a definitive stance. People are pretty darn outrageous today, more so than me. What has changed is what people think is offensive.

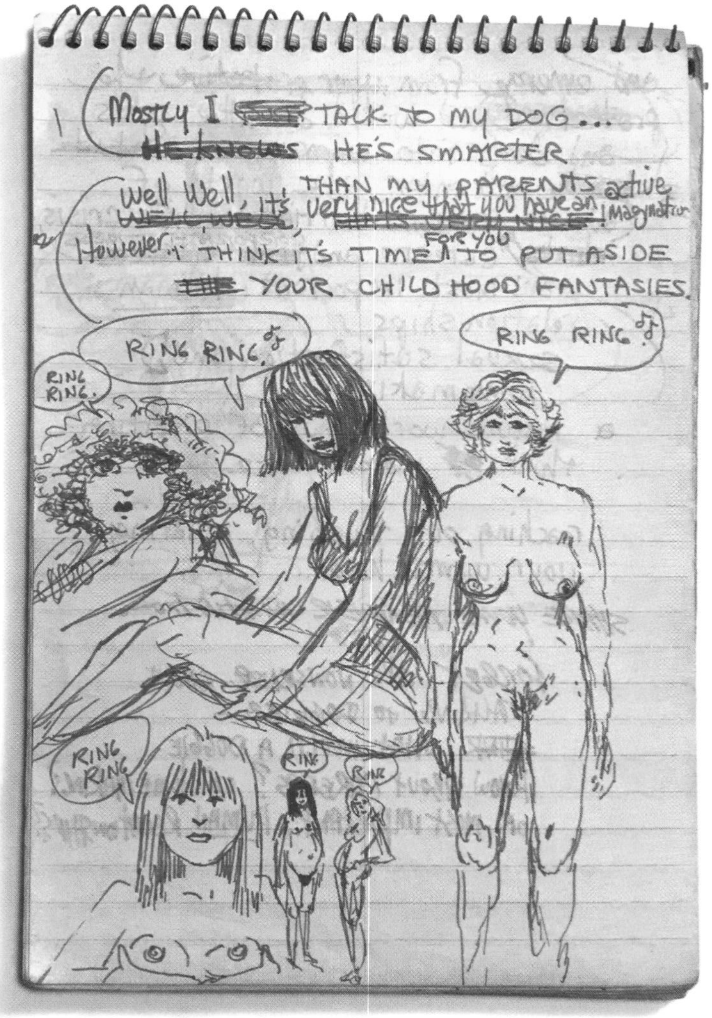

Mostly I TALK TO MY DOG...
HE'S SMARTER
THAN MY PARENTS
Well Well, it's very nice that you have an active imagination
However, I THINK IT'S TIME FOR YOU TO PUT ASIDE YOUR CHILDHOOD FANTASIES.
RING RING.
RING RING.
RING RING.
RING RING
RING

Sketchbook page
circa 1978

NH Sexuality is an important component of your work, and I'm interested to know whether the strip portrays your own mindset when you were younger. Does the duality of being young and fascinated with sex yet also afraid of it reflect you personally?

SF When I did the work, I was looking at what life was like for me when I was thirteen, but the strip isn't really about what was happening when I was thirteen. A lot of the strips are about what was happening in my twenties or thirties or forties when I was drawing them and then applying it back to this simpler world of children.

Having said that, when I was a kid, two neighbor boys said they were going to give me something if I pulled down my pants. So, I did. Then they went and told on me and got me in trouble. But the thing is, I still think, what was the whole deal with me pulling down my pants? They didn't know what to do with that. That's the stuff that's happening in my comics all the time.

NH   Did you experience any difficulties as a woman in the industry?

SF   It's funny that you ask that, because that's what everybody wants to know. I guess it's a legitimate question, but it always sounds like people want to hear sleazy stories about the cartoonist casting couch. I grew up on a block with five boys my age who I loved in spite of the way they terrorized me. That instilled in me a high tolerance for everything—much too high a tolerance for all kinds of behavior. When I worked in a hardware store, I told dirty jokes to the salesmen and I talked sports, which I don't know anything about, to the guys in the shipping room. You just go to their level. You go to whatever level you need to, or you keep your mouth shut if you need to keep your job.

High school portrait
1966

NH   Would it be fair to say that you had a drive or an underlying agenda to your work?

SF   Fuck yes! Are you kidding? I just spent half my session with my shrink talking about that. She tells me all the time that I can't save everybody. So, I would say one of my basic agendas in life and in my work is trying to save people from one thing or another.

NH   How?

SF   Well, sometimes it's just giving them information, and for me information equals love, so I'm big on information, the give and take of information. If you you look at my strips, there's almost always some underlying message.

For instance, I put a lot of naked boys in my comic strip. I knew the *Lampoon* demographic was eighteen-to-twenty-five-year-old men. I'm like, into equal opportunity nudity in the comics—but it's not simply equal opportunity objectification. I wanted men to feel what it's like to feel self-conscious about their bodies the way women do. Because it would be nice if men had more empathy, and it would make the world a better place, wouldn't it? I want to make the world a better place. I think that's a good goal.

Shary's gag from
Sky River Funnies
1970

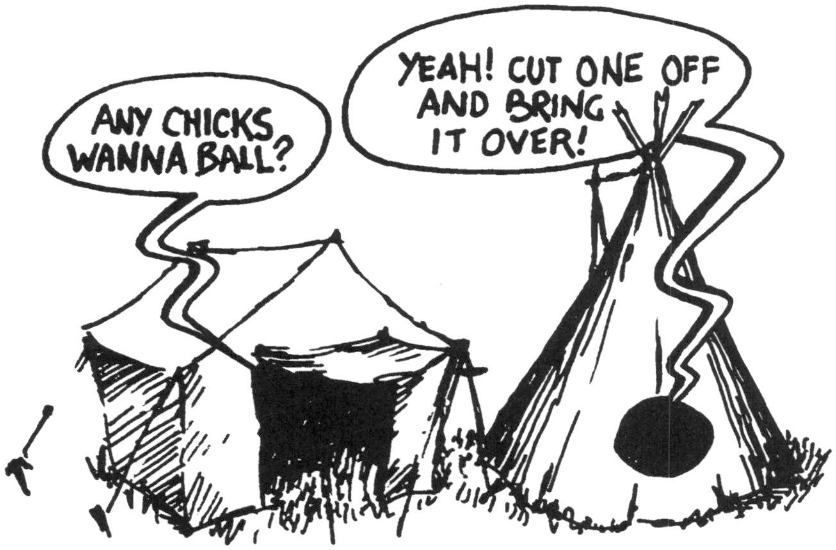
ANY CHICKS WANNA BALL?
YEAH! CUT ONE OFF AND BRING IT OVER!

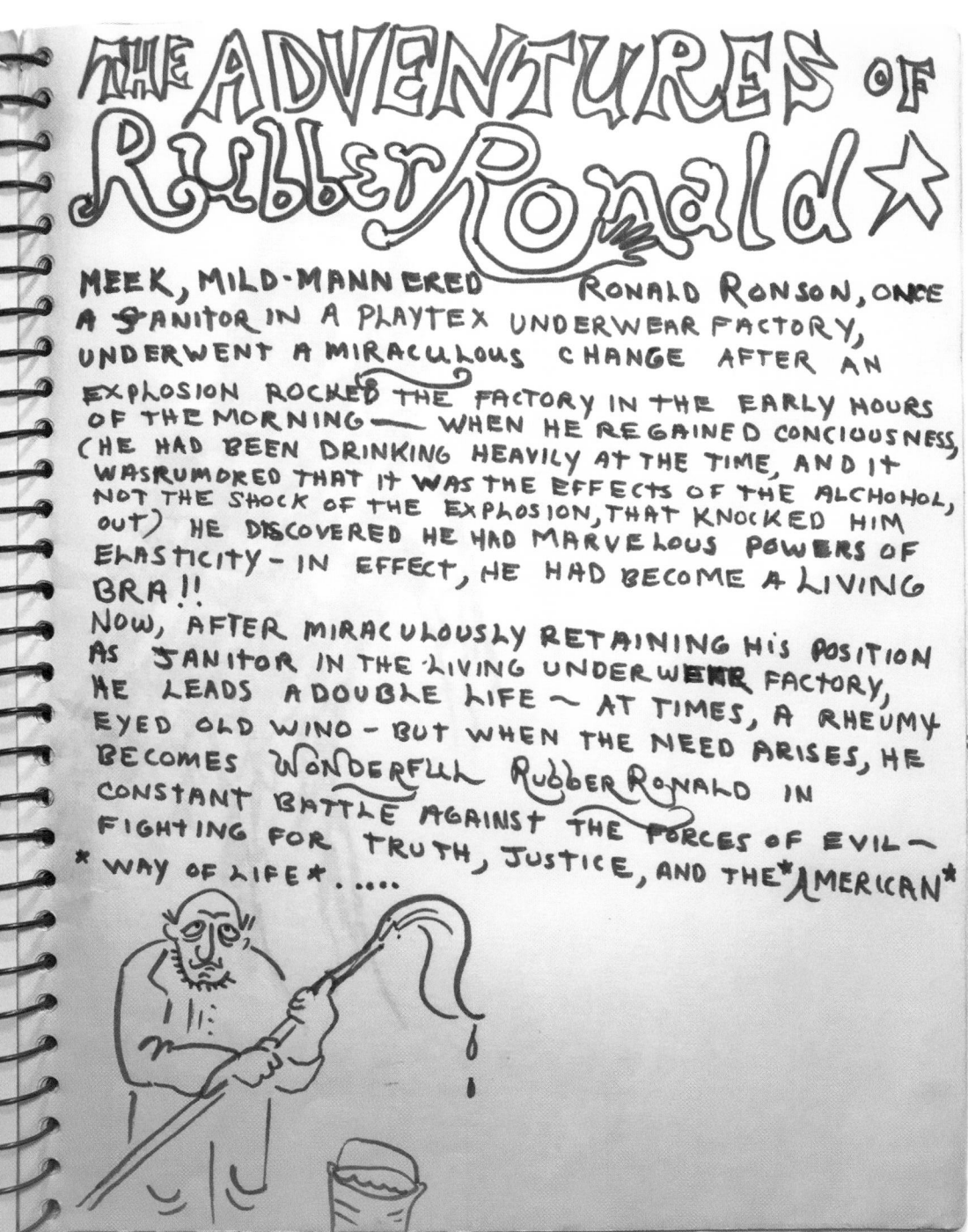

THE ADVENTURES OF Rubber Ronald ☆

MEEK, MILD-MANNERED RONALD RONSON, ONCE A JANITOR IN A PLAYTEX UNDERWEAR FACTORY, UNDERWENT A MIRACULOUS CHANGE AFTER AN EXPLOSION ROCKED THE FACTORY IN THE EARLY HOURS OF THE MORNING — WHEN HE REGAINED CONCIOUSNESS, (HE HAD BEEN DRINKING HEAVILY AT THE TIME, AND IT WAS RUMORED THAT IT WAS THE EFFECTS OF THE ALCHOHOL, NOT THE SHOCK OF THE EXPLOSION, THAT KNOCKED HIM OUT) HE DISCOVERED HE HAD MARVELOUS POWERS OF ELASTICITY — IN EFFECT, HE HAD BECOME A LIVING BRA !!
NOW, AFTER MIRACULOUSLY RETAINING HIS POSITION AS JANITOR IN THE LIVING UNDERWEAR FACTORY, HE LEADS A DOUBLE LIFE ~ AT TIMES, A RHEUMY EYED OLD WINO - BUT WHEN THE NEED ARISES, HE BECOMES WONDERFUL Rubber Ronald IN CONSTANT BATTLE AGAINST THE FORCES OF EVIL — FIGHTING FOR TRUTH, JUSTICE, AND THE *AMERICAN*
* WAY OF LIFE * . . . . .

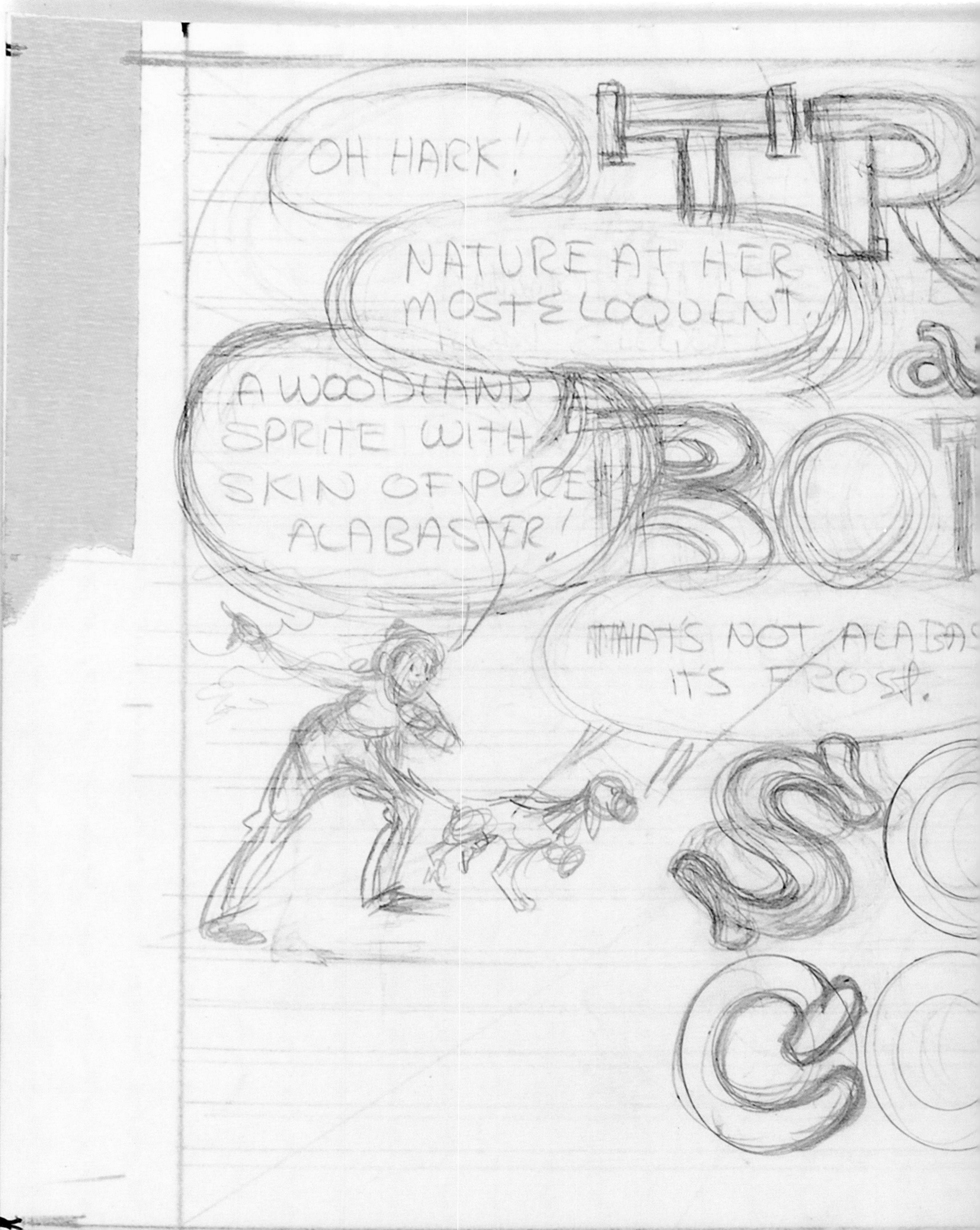
OH HARK!
NATURE AT HER MOST ELOQUENT.
A WOODLAND SPRITE WITH SKIN OF PURE ALABASTER!
THAT'S NOT ALABAS
IT'S FROST.

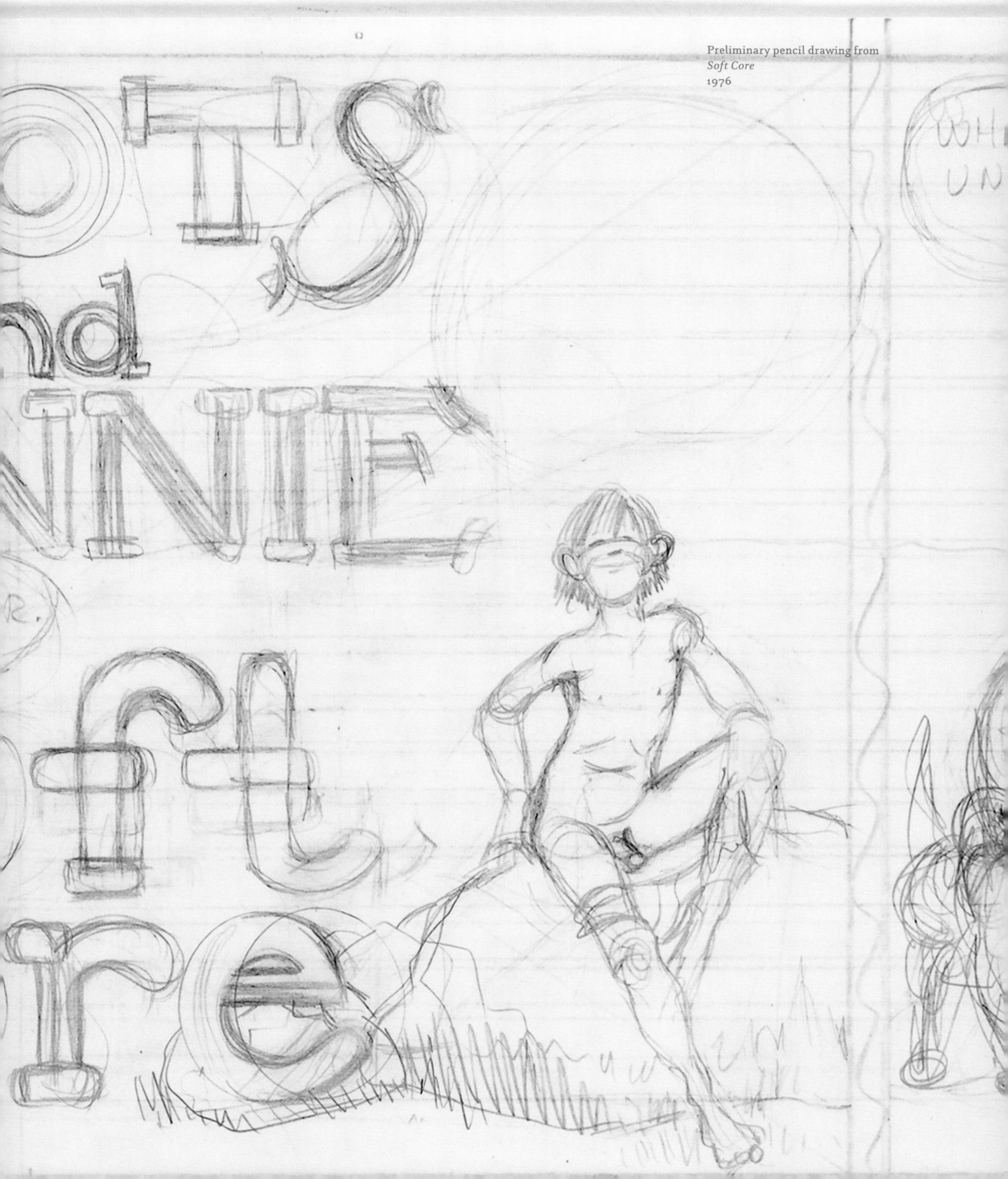

Preliminary pencil drawing from
Soft Core
1976

Mad magazine
At age eight, I began worshipping at the shrine
that Bill Gaines, Harvey Kurtzman, and their minions
built. Especially because my father found it
worth burning.

Lenny Bruce
Saint Lenny, who struggled and suffered to bring
us the free speech we have today — if we can keep it.

Joycelyn Elders
Who was fired as Surgeon General of the United
States in 1994 for advocating masturbation.

Margaret Sanger
Who devoted her life to fighting for birth control and
sex education.

Ruth Bader Ginsburg
Who was the most successful working woman in
every way.

Murdered abortion doctors and the countless clinic
workers and police officers
Who have been killed and wounded by "pro-life"
shooters and bombers.

The people of Vietnam and Cambodia
Who endured massive devastation and taught our
country a lesson in humility.

All American veterans against war
Ideally, everyone wants to live in peace, but these
people are the experts.

Doug Fast
Who was the coolest artist idol of my teenage years.
He inspired me to be like him. Still trying.

HT Webster & Clare Briggs
Turn of the century cartoonists whose styles
I emulate but will never surpass.

The Air Pirates: Dan O'Neill, Bobby London,
Ted Richards, and Gary Hallgren
Who taught me the illustrious history and power
of cartooning

Francis Ford Coppola and American Zoetrope
Who generously gave our group of revolutionary
cartoonists a home in the THX1138 warehouse.

Doug Kenney, PJ O'Rourke, Michael Gross, and all the
editors and staff at *National Lampoon*
By giving artists and writers unbounded creative
freedom, they shaped our careers and bent the humor
business for all time.

Matty, Michael, Julie, and Andy Simmons
They are like family to me. As complicated as that
may be, I will love them forever.

Douglas Tirola for *Drunk Stoned Brilliant Dead*
Ron Mann and Charley Lippincott for *Comic Book
Confidential*
Who must think I'm important or cute enough to be
in their feature films.

Michael Gerber
Auteur of *The American Bystander* magazine, who
has resuscitated the spirit and vitality of classic
humor publications.

Jeff Keibel
My loyal friend and webmaster of
sharyflenniken.com.

Gabriel Winslow-Yost and Lucas William Adams
Artists, visionaries, innovators, and the publishers of
this book. They are committed to truth and art in all
its iterations.

Will Simpson
Detail-oriented artist extraordinaire, who made
my comic pages look much better than they really are.

Norman Hathaway
Genius author, creative director, designer,
Renaissance man, royalty... I am proud to have known
His Majesty since he was 17. He was then every bit as
talented and fun as he is now.

Kristine Larsen
The talented art photographer who performed a
miracle by shooting all my comic pages in one day.

MacBird and Bonnie
Ted Richards' little spaniel mix MacBird, was smart
enough to sneak into restaurants and hide under our
table for his dinner. He was the original Trots. Bonnie
was our family's Shetland Sheepdog.

Jackie Zolshan
The original model for Pepsi, who carried a pistol in
her purse on peace marches.

Melody Anderson and Robin Gray
My beautiful therapists, who saved my life and
continue to keep my feet on the ground.

My friends, family, and fans
All brilliant and crazed in the best way.

Also Available
From New York Review Comics

YELLOW NEGROES AND OTHER IMAGINARY CREATURES
Yvan Alagbé

PIERO
Edmond Baudoin

ALMOST COMPLETELY BAXTER
Glen Baxter

AGONY
Mark Beyer

MITCHUM
Blutch

PEPLUM
Blutch

THE GREEN HAND AND OTHER STORIES
Nicole Claveloux

WHAT AM I DOING HERE?
Abner Dean

LETTER TO SURVIVORS
Gébé

PRETENDING IS LYING
Dominique Goblet

ALAY-OOP
William Gropper

SOFT CITY
Pushwagner

THE NEW WORLD
Chris Reynolds

PITTSBURGH
Frank Santoro

MACDOODLE ST.
Mark Alan Stamaty

SLUM WOLF
Tadao Tsuge

THE MAN WITHOUT TALENT
Yoshiharu Tsuge

RETURN TO ROMANCE
Ogden Whitney